Oxbridge Men

Oxbridge Men

BRITISH MASCULINITY
and the
UNDERGRADUATE
EXPERIENCE,
1850–1920

Paul R. Deslandes

INDIANA UNIVERSITY PRESS

BLOOMINGTON AND INDIANAPOLIS

This book is a publication of

Indiana University Press
Office of Scholarly Publishing
Herman B Wells Library 350
1320 East 10th Street
Bloomington, Indiana 47405 USA

iupress.indiana.edu

First paperback edition 2015
© 2005 by Paul R. Deslandes

MANUFACTURED IN THE UNITED STATES OF AMERICA

The Library of Congress has cataloged the original edition as follows:

Deslandes, Paul R., date
Oxbridge men : British masculinity and the undergraduate experience, 1850–1920 /
Paul R. Deslandes.
p.   cm.
Includes bibliographical references and index.
ISBN 0-253-34578-2 (cloth : alk. paper)
1. Male college students—England—History. 2. University of Oxford—
Students—History. 3. University of Cambridge—Students—History.
4. Masculinity—England—History. I. Title
LA637.7.D48 2005
378.1'981'0942—dc22   2004014525

ISBN 978-0-253-01783-3 (pbk : alk. paper)

2 3 4 5   20 19 18 17 16 15

For Andrew and Matthew

Contents

Preface

My first encounters with Oxford and Cambridge were through literature. In college, I read with great interest *Tom Brown's Schooldays* (1857) and *Tom Brown at Oxford* (1861) and devoured, for reasons that are only now apparent to me, E. M. Forster's *Maurice,* with its wonderful evocations of Cambridge society.[1] These books represented, to an undergraduate who had never been to Britain, let alone Oxford or Cambridge, a life that was distant and removed from my own, both literally and figuratively foreign. The sense of separation that I felt from this world was palpable. As I read further, poring over the pages of Evelyn Waugh's *Brideshead Revisited* (1945), Max Beerbohm's *Zulieka Dobson* (1911), and Dorothy Sayers's *Gaudy Night* (1935), the social and cultural spaces inhabited by Oxford and Cambridge undergraduates seemed almost unknowable: labyrinthine, mythological, and tradition-bound. In short, Oxford and Cambridge to me seemed to be worlds apart, distinct entities unknowable to the casual, but interested, interloper. Rather than explaining these institutional cultures to readers, the authors of university novels frequently demarcated and reinforced boundaries that separated insiders from outsiders, marked the universities off as special, privileged places, and emphasized an exclusivity that epitomized Britain's rigidly class-bound society.[2] In many ways, the study that follows functions as an attempt to "crack the code" that so perplexed me as I read these novels, by examining, in a detailed and systematic way, the myths, traditions, and rituals of these overwhelmingly masculine little worlds.

Most people, in both Britain and North America, experience Oxford and Cambridge for the first time in much the same way that I did. For these and many other reasons, certain aspects of life at these universities, collectively abbreviated throughout this book as Oxbridge, are probably familiar to many. Depictions of boat races and obsessed athletes, witty intellectual conversations in college rooms and debating societies, extravagant dinners, drunken parties, ceremonial caps and gowns, architectural splendor, royal patronage, and an intensely male atmosphere characterized by romantic attachments, seamless bonds of friendship, and misogyny represent, to those in both scholarly and popular reading audiences, the culture of these institutions.

Filmmakers, most notably the team of Ismail Merchant and James Ivory, who were especially active in the 1980s and early 1990s, have also tried to capture the beauty and allure of late Victorian and Edwardian Oxbridge in their celluloid evocations of a gloried and grand British past.[3] Similarly, movies like 1938's *A Yank at Oxford* and its quite dreadful 1984 remake *Oxford Blues* provided Americans with a vision of these institutions that both romanticized the peculiarities of an Oxbridge education and tapped into pronounced anglophilic tendencies. In recent years, the books and movies that have fueled the Harry Potter craze have provided readers and filmgoers with another view of the elite British educational institution by building on elements of that tradition drawn from both the public schools and the Oxbridge colleges. While occasionally satirical or sarcastic about, or downright critical of, undergraduate excesses and university traditions, these depictions all focus on the privileges, pleasures, and splendid isolation of university life.

The glimpses we get of the Oxbridge mystique from these popular representations are obviously limited, often focusing in highly stylized ways on very specific components of what is a remarkably complex set of traditions, myths, and cultural practices. Although they may be lambasted by insiders (especially intelligent undergraduates or recent B.A.s committed to proving that the Oxford of Waugh and Beerbohm no longer exists) as the product of film crews and mythologizers keen on making a quick buck (or pound, as the case may be), there is still something significant about these cultural images and perceptions.[4]

The emphasis on "uniqueness," which was consciously cultivated between the years 1850 and 1920 and perpetuated in subsequent decades by the likes of Waugh, Sayers, the producers of various cultural products like the *Inspector Morse* television series, and even the critics mentioned above, has assisted in carving out a place for Oxford and Cambridge in a broader national mythology that has emphasized tradition and continuity through the ages.[5] Furthermore, from the perspective of entrepreneurs in the late twentieth and early twenty-first centuries, it has provided a formidable position for these universities in the highly lucrative British tourist trade, at its high point in the summer when visitors from around the world flock to Oxford and Cambridge to participate in organized, open-air bus tours or incompetently negotiate a punt down the Cam or the Isis. Administrators and dons at both institutions have also recognized that these myths provide the universities with a special market niche that has drawn high-fee–paying and status-seeking international students, a lucrative conference trade, and substantial donations to these ancient foundations.

Most important of all, of course, has been the function these myths have served for those fortunate enough to reside among the dreaming spires of Oxford or walk along the Cambridge college "backs." The moniker of Oxford or Cambridge man or (in the years after 1920 at Oxford and 1948 at Cambridge) woman has provided students and former students alike with an identifiable and privileged cultural stamp that has served a vital role in demarcating and cementing their status in British society. Put quite simply, where you went to university counted and continues to count enormously, especially for the subjects of this book—those men of the late nineteenth and early twentieth centuries who attended these institutions and embraced a new professional vision of British masculinity as they sought to lead race, nation, and empire.

Naturally, changes since World War II have significantly broadened the class background of students attending these institutions. The Butler Education Act of 1944, which inaugurated a system of universal secondary education; the growth of public spending on universities; and significant changes to the class system brought about, in part, by the emergence of the welfare state have ensured the matriculation of more and more students from state-supported schools at Oxford and Cambridge colleges over the past fifty years. While the exclusively upper-class and male world of literary and filmic portrayals may no longer exist, the association of Oxford and Cambridge with masculine privilege, status, and power in British society persists. Critics of the system, as Joseph Soares notes in a recent study of postwar Oxford, knew that this represented a vulnerable sore point for the university in the 1950s, '60s, '70s, and '80s.[6] And, if we may judge by recent criticism by Gordon Brown, Labour Chancellor of the Exchequer, of Oxford's refusal to accept a young woman who had been educated at a state school and who was admitted to Harvard, and by the responses to his comments, attacks of this nature continue to sting.[7]

Critics and opponents notwithstanding, Oxbridge continues to be associated with masculine privilege, exclusivity, and male elitism, a fact reflected in the brief and somewhat limited revival of the 1920s "bright young thing" aesthetic that appeared at Oxford in the wake of the BBC's airing of *Brideshead Revisited* in the early 1980s.[8] While this revival clearly represented a tendency to romanticize a partially mythic past, it also reflected the endurance of these traditional associations. A more quantifiable indicator of the persistence of the notion that Oxford and Cambridge peculiarly fit Britons for positions of power continues to the present day in the form of the preferential hiring of Oxbridge graduates at the best law and investment firms in London and the desires (both stated and unstated) of socially ambitious parents. While they may be skewed reflections of post–World War II Oxbridge and broader British realities, it must be remembered that popular perceptions of the ancient universities as privileged bastions have served the needs of these institutions and their members particularly well in both historical and contemporary contexts.

Rather than debunking these myths about Oxbridge or even establishing the extent of their hold over these institutions in Tony Blair's "Cool Britannia," I examine their origins, noting the peculiar ways in which undergraduates themselves, not mythmaking novelists or filmmakers, created them during Oxford and Cambridge's golden years, a period during which these universities functioned, to quote the English writer Jan Morris, as "conscious instruments of . . . national greatness."[9] In particular, this study illustrates the ways in which these myths and traditions served, between the years 1850 and 1920, to reinforce male power (in an era when women were only provisional or marginalized students), solidify elite status, and formulate unique identities that reflected not only the certainties but also the anxieties associated with being both imperial leaders and "real" men in an era when British power was at its apex.

At its most basic level, this book provides some answers to a series of important questions that have frequently eluded institutional historians who, in detailing the development of the universities and their various colleges, in occasionally celebratory ways, have often neglected to systematically probe their distinctive cultural forms:[10] What did this particular form of education mean to those insiders for whom it was intended? From where did the traditions most often associated with Oxford and Cambridge life emerge? What were the preoccupations, concerns, anxieties, and fears of university students in a period of imperial hegemony? Why did undergraduates at Oxford and Cambridge fixate on certain aspects of their life within these peculiar educational institutions? And finally, what place have these institutions occupied in British culture, social structures, and mindsets?

In seeking answers to these questions through a dissection of Oxbridge undergraduate culture, this book pays careful attention to broader historical forces of the late nineteenth and early twentieth centuries. Rather than being merely an examination of quaint undergraduate traditions or interesting and amusing anecdotes, this book explicitly and self-consciously relates the study of Oxford and Cambridge to the histories of professionalization, imperialism, gender relations, adolescence, sexuality, and politics. While each of these histories is covered to varying degrees in the pages that follow, it is my hope that the reader will leave this book with an understanding not only of how these institutions functioned as incubators for a national elite but also of how they function as indicators or gauges of historical forces and change more generally.

Acknowledgments

One of the pleasures in completing any kind of writing is being able to thank those who have provided, along the way, intellectual, financial, or emotional support. I therefore offer the following expressions of gratitude to those who have influenced this work and helped to make it a book worthy of being read.

In a project of this nature, universities and colleges obviously figure prominently in any list of debts incurred. Trinity College in Hartford, Connecticut, provided me with a superb undergraduate education that made it possible to pursue graduate study at the University of Toronto. Toronto supported me financially with generous fellowships and assistantships, an outstanding faculty, and a wonderfully stimulating intellectual environment that convinced me that academic life was well worth pursuing. I have had the opportunity to teach at several fine institutions, all of which have supported me financially and sustained me intellectually. Trinity College and Sweet Briar College provided me with wonderful collegiate teaching experiences in my first few years out of graduate school. Texas Tech University gave me an institutional home from 1999 to 2004. The Department of History there is a lively and stimulating place, full of sharp minds and bright students. I am especially grateful for the support provided to this project by two chairs of the history department (Allan Kuethe and Bruce Daniels), the College of Arts and Sciences, and the Provost's Office (and, most particularly, the assistance of Vice Provost Jim Brink). Finally, I wish to thank the University of Vermont, which in 2004 presented me with a wonderful opportunity to join their faculty and to return to my native New England.

I am equally indebted to the institutions that have provided the subject matter for this book. At Oxford, I am grateful for the assistance I received at the Bodleian Library, the Oxford University Archives, the Brasenose College Archives, the Magdalen College Archives, and the New College Archives. Simon Bailey and Robin Darwell-Smith (at the University Archives and Magdalen College Archives, respectively) shared their vast knowledge and expertise willingly and answered my many queries. I would also like to express my gratitude to Mansfield College and Worcester College, which provided me with places to stay and, in the case of Mansfield, with a formal affiliation that I continue to cherish. At Cambridge, I would like to thank the staff at the Cambridge University Library, the Cambridge University Archives (most notably Elisabeth Leedham-Green), and the archivist at Emmanuel College. I am also grateful to Jesus College for providing me, during several summers, with very fine accommodations and a congenial social environment. The staffs at the Sterling Memorial Library and Seeley Mudd Library also kindly granted me access to their facilities so that I could consult Yale University's superb collection of Oxford ephemera.

A number of fine historians (many of whom also happen to be good friends) have influenced and contributed to this project, and I welcome the opportunity to thank them here. At various points, I have benefited enormously from the comments, insights, and encouragement of Jeffrey Auerbach, Mark Curthoys, Carol Engelhardt, Margot Finn, Martin Francis, Dan Healey, Matthew Hendley, Matt Houlbrook, Kali Israel, Tim Jenks, Dane Kennedy, Marjorie Levine-Clark, Trevor Lloyd, William Lubenow, Maureen McCarthy, Patrick McDevitt, Cecilia Morgan, Alison Prentice, Ellen Ross, Greg Smith, Tori Smith, Reba Soffer, Christopher Stray, and Angela Woollacott. Many of my colleagues at Texas Tech were also instrumental in helping me complete this book, especially Tita Chico, Colleen Fitzgerald, Will Gray, Randy McBee, Aaron Meskin, Jeff Mosher, Patricia Pelley, Jose Santos, Alice Sowaal, Ron Rainger, and David Troyansky. Stephen Heathorn has been my closest confidant in the profession since we first met in graduate school. He has read numerous drafts of this book and urged me to complete it at a time when I was dragging my feet just a bit. Richard Helmstadter allowed me to first pursue a very different version of this project as a doctoral thesis at the University of Toronto. His guidance, support, and tireless letter writing are appreciated more than he knows. Carol Helstosky and I chose to pursue the same career paths shortly after graduating from college. Her brilliance as a historian and her guidance through the process of completing a book continually remind me of why I value her so very much. Susan Pennybacker first inspired me to pursue British history and has been a steadfast supporter, a passionate critic, and a dear friend for eighteen years. Barbara Todd has been a wonderful example of the scholar-teacher since I first met her as a Toronto teaching assistant, and her perceptive insights (many of which have been offered over very pleasant dinners in London) have made this a much better book. Finally, Chris Waters has been, in the years that I have known him, a fine mentor, a consummate professional, a first-rate critic, and a provider of fine accommodations in Oxford.

I am also deeply grateful to Indiana University Press for taking on this project. I would especially like to thank my editor, Richard Higgins, who has been remarkably supportive throughout the publication process. His comments, insights, and willingness to track down an elusive Cambridge University Athletic Club runner are appreciated greatly. Furthermore, Shoshanna Green's expert copyediting has made this a much cleaner book and saved me from several unfortunate errors. Any that remain are, of course, my own. Along the way, Marilyn Grobschmidt, Jane Lyle, Janet Rabinowitch, and Robert Sloan have all contributed to the final product. I am most thankful for the perceptive readings the manuscript received from Carol Dyhouse, Erika Rappaport, and one anonymous reviewer. The insights of these fine historians expertly guided me as I revised the book and have improved the final product dramatically.

Friendships in several countries and on two continents have sustained me through the occasional trials of researching and writing this book and have provided many necessary diversions. My summers in England are regularly brightened and enlivened by the time I spend with Steve and Katharine McGuire, and their assistance has been instrumental in helping me complete this project. During my years in Toronto, Jane Harrison and Charlie Trainor always provided me with a second home, great companionship, and many fine meals. Sarah Neill continually reminded me of why a stop in Boston on my northward journeys was always a necessity. Janice Duggan has been a superlative friend through the entire process: her support, sense of fun, and keen intellect and wit have meant more to me than I can say. Since I first met them in Lubbock, my close friendship with my colleagues Stefano D'Amico and Aliza Wong, and more recently their son Luca D'Amico-Wong, has sustained me and enriched my life immeasurably. Without their support, sense of perspective, good humor, and sympathy, life in Texas and, more especially, the process of completing this book would have been much less bearable. They may, in fact, be as happy as I am that it is now done.

Most importantly, I wish to acknowledge the support and assistance of my family. My parents (Donna and Ted Montgomery and Paul and Barbara Deslandes) and my sisters Deb Davidsohn and Dawn Millett and their partners, Michael and Davies, have never questioned my idiosyncratic interests and passions, have provided me with places to stay for long stretches of time, and have fully supported my scholarly pursuits. With this in mind and as a symbol of how important the contributions of my family have been to this endeavor, I lovingly dedicate this book to my nephews, Andrew Paul Davidsohn and Matthew Peter Davidsohn.

Oxbridge Men

Introduction

The educated classes and the government alike were obsessed with the status of England's ancient universities in the late nineteenth and early twentieth centuries. Driven by a desire to understand the place of higher learning (and what form that learning should take) in a society rife with dramatic economic, social, and cultural changes, many authors ruminated, in the pages of the great periodicals like the *Fortnightly Review,* on the place of the liberally educated and masculine undergraduate in the modern world. In March of 1901, for example, one contributor to *Blackwood's Edinburgh Magazine* published a review of William Tuckwell's *Reminiscences of Oxford* under the broad title of "Oxford in the Victorian Age." Within this piece, ostensibly an assessment of the literary merits and veracity of Tuckwell's book, the reviewer discussed the impact on the university of several important nineteenth-century developments, including the rise of science, debates about evolution, and the theological controversies that emerged as a result of the Tractarian movement and John Henry Newman's conversion to Roman Catholicism.

This anonymous author also commented specifically on the more sharply focused intellectual and competitive environment that came to dominate at Victorian Oxford after the implementation of a series of reforms in the 1850s, noting in particular the ways in which these years represented a dramatic departure from the "lethargic . . . eighteenth century," when academic laxness and undergraduate licentiousness, according to many different observers, ruled the day. With the changes of this period came, according to the reviewer, several key developments that resulted from curricular reforms, the rise of new academic exercises, and changes to the academic staff of the various Oxford colleges: "The intellectual atmosphere became clearer, a fresh breeze stirred in dust-covered corners, and the best of those who were fated to shape the nation's destiny were taught to feel that their career must be based upon active intellectual work."[1]

While the author of this piece clearly recognized the value of the transformations of the nineteenth century, he also lamented the excessive emphasis within modern Oxford on professionalism and competition: an "evil influence" that had, for this observer, "penetrated far too largely into the spirit of the university." Only by rejecting this slavish devotion to winning honors and acquiring professional credentials in favor of a "wide and general training," he asserted, could the university hope to redeem British manhood and become, once again, a "nursery of good citizens, a great center of solid and broad-based national influence," and "a citadel of sound and comprehensive learning." This rejection of an insidious "professional insolence" also entailed a questioning of the "modern prevalence of athleticism" and the "contagion of the competitive mania" that accompanied it. In the end, the reviewer sought a return to what he perceived to be older values, according to which undergraduates prized their training as healthy citizens by embracing the "abnegation of self" and the "abiding sense of comradeship and discipline" that made "them the bulwark of the nation."[2]

With these words, the author of "Oxford in the Victorian Age" weighed in on one of the hot political and intellectual issues of the day as he criticized his university for modernizing too quickly and embracing a competitive ethos that he deemed potentially destructive to the British nation and the men who made it great. In so doing, he highlighted, from a contemporary perspective, the two substantive themes that dominated the mindset of the late Victorian and Edwardian Oxbridge man and that permeate the individual chapters of this study: the role that the universities played in fostering, recasting, and perpetuating the values of a distinctive educational elite and, more importantly, in forming British masculinities. These twin, and inextricably linked, roles for the university took on particular significance for undergraduates between 1850 and 1920, a period of tremendous change both for Oxford and Cambridge and for the men who passed three or four years there ensconced in a state of what many described as "inexpressible pleasure."[3]

While Oxford and Cambridge had always trained clerics, educators, orators, and scientific men, their status as institutions altered considerably in the years after 1850 as a socially (as well as academically) acceptable education became increasingly important to members of the British professional elite, who ran the government as politicians and civil servants; administered the empire as colonial bureaucrats in India, the Caribbean, and Africa; and dominated as lawyers, boarding school masters, university lecturers, college fellows, and clergymen.[4] Part of this education consisted of the formation of an elite *esprit de corps* that encouraged a sense not only of masculine community but of superiority. Nowhere was this tendency more apparent than at public schools like Eton, Harrow, Rugby, and Winchester, institutions that began as a result of radical reforms in the 1840s, '50s, and '60s to emphasize a curriculum that had at its core the formation of character (often through participation in team sports), the perpetuation of class status, and the study of classical languages and literatures.[5] This agenda also informed, in a slightly modified form, the goals of reformers who sought, during a period of British global hegemony, to make the universities more relevant to national interests by fostering what historian Reba Soffer has labeled an ethos of leadership premised on notions of service to "God, country, and good."[6] These changes, which were part of a broader transformation of intellectual life and occasionally resisted by antediluvian college tutors who clung to older models of academic and spiritual mentorship, were accompanied by several other crucial developments in this period that rendered the universities more "modern" and had, as we shall see, a profound impact on the undergraduate sense of self.[7]

The years between 1850 and 1920 were characterized first and foremost by the triumph of the competitive ideal in British education (a development highlighted even by detractors like the author of "Oxford in the Victorian Age"). Beginning with the formation of government-sponsored University Reform Commissions in the 1850s, which opened college fellowships and scholarships to competitive examinations, the ideal further developed within the universities through activities ranging from an intricate, and still extant, system of examinations for degrees to annual rowing contests.[8] A concurrent development was an increasing (if never entirely ascendant) professionalization of the corps of academic dons at Oxford and Cambridge and the emergence of an explicit link, in the popular imagination, between university education and professional credentials.[9]

Several other changes also made this period transformative for England's ancient universities. First, these institutions gradually embraced a more secular outlook by admitting, in the 1850s, students who did not subscribe to the Thirty-nine Articles of Faith of the Church of England and, by the early decades of the twentieth century, abolishing compulsory chapel attendance altogether.[10] Modernization also entailed a dramatic expansion of the curriculum and the introduction to the undergraduate course of study of new academic disciplines such as physical and moral sciences, modern languages, and modern history, which were integrated with the more traditional subjects of classics and mathematics.[11]

Further developments altered, albeit in limited ways, the composition of an undergraduate population that principally consisted, during these years, of public school–educated men, drawn primarily from the professional middle-class families of Britain and, in general terms, strongly committed to the ethos of national and imperial leadership that the universities promulgated.[12] With the nation's vast empire still expanding, university-educated Indians being incorporated into the governing structures of the Raj, Oxford and Cambridge gaining increased international stature, and travel now becoming possible by steamship, the names of colonial students and foreigners began to appear with much greater frequency on matriculation lists, especially after the 1870s.[13] Similarly, feminist agitation and liberal reform, beginning in the 1860s, led to increased calls for the higher education of women. While they remained formally excluded from full membership in the universities during the period explored in this study, they were able to assert their presence through the establishment of separate women's colleges (or societies, as they were more correctly known at Oxford) in the 1860s, '70s, '80s, and '90s and by attending lectures, sitting university examinations, and generally participating, in circumscribed and often chaperoned ways, in the public life of these ancient communities.[14]

These broad intellectual, curricular, and institutional shifts were not the only transformations that Oxford and Cambridge men negotiated as they constructed a distinctively student-oriented culture and helped to fashion the modern undergraduate type.[15] The youthful, Oxbridge identities that they created for themselves also built on a series of dramatic developments in the history of male gender identities. British masculine ideals, a set of culturally contingent and often rigid discourses that prescribed proper behavior and profoundly influenced the ways in which men lived their lives and saw themselves not only within college walls but also in the broader world, underwent a dramatic transformation over the course of Queen Victoria's reign. For the middle and upper middle classes, the most dramatic transformation occurred at around the same time that the reform of England's ancient universities began. During the 1840s, '50s, and '60s, the focus in definitions of British manliness (as a specific type of gender ideology) shifted away from conceptions dominated by an evangelical Christian ethos that privileged earnestness, self-sacrifice, sensitivity to those less fortunate, and contemplative piety to a model, more familiar to early-twenty-first-century readers, that emphasized physical strength, muscular development, the stiff upper lip, adventure, fortitude, and action.[16] This transformation, identified by David Newsome as a move from "godliness and good learning" to "muscular Christianity," signified the nineteenth century's most crucial break with earlier constructions of male gender identities.[17]

A number of other developments in the years between 1850 and 1920 also had a profound impact on the articulation of upper-middle- and middle-class masculinities. The cult of domesticity and the ideology of separate spheres that so many historians of British women have admirably documented in their work reached its apogee at the beginning of this period.[18] The domestic realm, as both a sanctuary from the hardships of modern life and a vital site in the construction of class identities, had, as John Tosh has recently noted, a far greater impact on definitions of middle-class masculinity than most gender studies scholars have previously assumed. Advice manuals directed at both women and men, personal letters, and diaries were replete (at least until the final decades of the nineteenth century) with references to the masculine pleasures of the hearth, the importance of paternal involvement in childrearing, and the significance of a secure, well-appointed, and morally sound home in solidifying the British man's independent status.[19]

While the home and the private sphere may have been important to the formation of middle- and upper-middle-class male subjectivities in the mid-Victorian period and later, the years after 1870 tended to be characterized by an emphasis on what Tosh has called "a flight from domesticity."[20] In the final decades of the nineteenth century, the demands of empire, the dynamics of international competition, and worries about the health of the superior British "race" prompted the rise of an exaggerated masculine culture in which militarism was valorized, imperial adventure (reflected not only in colonial conquest and administration but also in activities like big-game hunting and mountain climbing) was elevated to near religious significance, and the virtues of physical fitness and athleticism were extolled. Organizations such as the Boy Scouts (f. 1907), organized sport,

and magazines directed explicitly at youthful male audiences popularized
some of these notions and highlighted the process whereby gender ideals
entered the popular imagination through various cultural forms.[21]

At the turn of the century, the bold claims for the superiority of the
British man as an aggressive, competitive, and powerful figure were thrown
into question by several direct challenges that produced a state of crisis or
unease.[22] Anxieties were generated, first and foremost, by the vocal demands of British feminists, who, in addition to wanting access to higher
education, also questioned the validity of the separate spheres ideology,
called for the reform of property and divorce laws, and even pressed for the
vote. Discussions of sexual behavior also entered into debates about the
state of British manhood. Fears of the contaminating influences of prostitution and the problem of masturbation prompted a social purity movement that sought to modify and limit the ways in which men acquired
sexual experience. Furthermore, an increased awareness of the destabilizing
dangers of homosexuality prompted discussions in which same-sex desire
was feminized and the "boundaries of masculinity," as Angus McLaren has
noted, were vigilantly policed.[23] This period of crisis culminated in the
outbreak of the First World War, which, instead of reaffirming traditional
masculinity by allowing men to prove their manhood in battle, only added
to a state of gender crisis in which male and female roles seemed to blur
even more as women entered the workforce and men often returned home
not as heroes but as emasculated amputees or victims of shellshock.[24] By
the conclusion of this conflict, the visions of Victorian manhood outlined
above, which had remained dominant for nearly two decades after the
queen's death in 1901, were forever altered.

* * *

Rather than simply assuming that these momentous historical developments affected the ways in which students at Oxford and Cambridge
saw themselves and the world they inhabited, without examining how
they did so, this book explores the psychic, cultural, and social formation
of elite masculine identities within institutions about which much is assumed in British historiography but very little is fully understood. At its
core is an attempt to explore the ways in which the broad contours of
Victorian and Edwardian history and the discourses of British masculinity
influenced the lived experience of Oxford and Cambridge men. It is not
only concerned, however, with adding nuance to studies (generally of other
topics, like the use of gendered discourses in colonial India) that remark
on a "veneer of an 'Oxbridge' training" without interrogating critically

what that training entailed or how it influenced elite worldviews or masculine perspectives.[25] It also charts how undergraduates negotiated, in often contradictory and conflicting ways, the changes of the nineteenth and early twentieth centuries; how they embraced, frequently altered, and occasionally rejected prevailing notions of what it meant to be a man in a society that seemed to be preoccupied with the subject; and, finally, how they influenced British culture and society in both direct and indirect ways.

With these broad points in mind, the years between 1850 and 1920 are identified within this book as a period of coalescence for Oxbridge culture. Many of the traditions that continue to be associated with student life (and directly relate to the historical developments outlined above)—including athletic competitions and the particular brand of manliness that they inspired, the Unions (or debating societies), extravagant May Balls, annual examinations for degrees, the Oxford or Cambridge "manner," and the assumption that an education of this sort fitted one for a position of power—originated during the nineteenth century and were consolidated during the years under examination here. As such, they might be characterized as recently "invented traditions," to borrow a much used but still very useful concept from Eric Hobsbawm.[26] In representing these new traditions as time-honored and long-established, elite Britons in the late nineteenth and early twentieth centuries sought to mark a mythic continuity with the past that legitimated their cultural, political, and economic power and authority.[27] In point of fact, the decline of the traditional landed aristocracy, the rise of professional society, and the growth of meritocracy all meant that new elite traditions had to be created to accommodate the growing hegemony of the upper middle classes. As the "universities [and prominent reforming dons] successfully transformed a set of values, encoded in the concept of 'liberal education,' into a licensing system for a national elite," undergraduates created a culture of their own which complemented, and even occasionally challenged, these curricular and intellectual developments.[28] Within such a climate, student rituals and traditions reinforced new insider/outsider distinctions and dichotomies of inclusion and exclusion that were absolutely vital to preserving elite status in a changing world.[29]

This elite Oxbridge undergraduate was frequently represented as the epitome of the self-assured British man prepared to take on his role as a leader in the world beyond the college gates. For the Oxford or Cambridge student, elite status was gendered, specifically and unsurprisingly, as male. The emphasis on the acquisition of professional credentials and the competitive spirit that marked the universities as modern training grounds for imperial and domestic leaders also marked the undergraduate as a particular type of privileged man: confident in his status, removed from the potentially contaminating influences of femininity, and certain of his future place within the nation. The benefits that accrued to these undergraduates by virtue of their economic, social, and political status were, for much of this period, enjoyed exclusively by men. For these young men, the rhetoric of masculinity in the late Victorian and Edwardian periods was *the* prevailing vocabulary of power in imperial Britain. This vocabulary of power was complicated, however, on numerous occasions by its intersection with the rhetoric of class, race, and national identity.

For Oxbridge undergraduates, maintaining their privileged position in British society meant asserting the masculine, elite, and racially exclusive character of the experiences they considered most formative in their lives. This was particularly true as they faced challenges posed by an increasingly vocal and critical feminism, the wealth and social status of certain members of the industrial middle classes, international economic and military competition from the United States (and, after 1870, Germany), the growth of an organized and politicized labor movement, and the presence of colonized peoples within the metropole.[30] Definitions of the university as a male space, the importance of discipline, examinations, and athletic traditions in articulating male identities, and concerns about minimizing the influence of outsiders within this context all pointed to just how intimate and precarious the connections were between class, racial, national, and gender identities. As this book illustrates, the unprecedented attention that Oxbridge undergraduates paid to individual and national conceptions of manhood helped to create, as much as reflect, the pervasive culture of uncertainty, anxiety, and instability that marked the tumultuous decades around the turn of the century.[31] The masculine crisis of this period disproportionately affected the upper and middle classes precisely because they had placed so much stock in articulating their privileged position in society through an invocation of certain languages of masculinity, which this book attempts to untangle.

In this study, then, I take very seriously Joan Scott's reminder to consider "how social institutions [have] incorporated gender into their assumptions and organizations."[32] Despite the existence of some recent work that examines the cult of the athlete at the ancient universities or the concept of friendship as it was fostered by organizations like the Cambridge Apostles, this book represents the first sustained attempt to apply the recent insights of gender and sexuality studies scholars to the history of these important institutions.[33] Students at these universities in the latter half of the nineteenth century frequently used notions of gender and sexual difference to distinguish between the social spaces of Oxford and Cambridge and the outside world.[34] Gender did not, however, function merely at the level of discourse for students keen to articulate their distinctive educational experience and particular brand of masculinity.[35] Rather, it informed nearly every facet of life within these institutions. For the Oxbridge undergraduate, clearly influenced in profound ways by the gender ideologies of muscular Christianity and imperial leadership, male identities were formulated in a complicated web of rituals, activities, relationships, *and* discursive constructions and categories.

Within such a climate, which produced a remarkably varied gendered landscape, there were both dominant and subordinate forms of masculinity.[36] Athletes, reading men, aesthetes, and sporting or gambling men, to mention but a few of the distinctive brands or styles of masculinity present at Oxford and Cambridge in the late Victorian and Edwardian eras, all coexisted (sometimes harmoniously and sometimes not) within the precincts of these two cities.[37] These various gender identities need to be linked, in any consideration of the ancient universities, to sexuality. As did the different masculine styles, various forms of desire and modes of sexual expression functioned simultaneously within these distinctive environments. Although scholars and popular readers have tended to probe the ways in which same-sex desire permeated these homosocial environments, I treat this form of sexual expression as one location on a broad continuum of desire.[38] Same-sex eroticism and activity were increasingly proscribed as concerns about the dangers associated with homosexuality escalated near the end of the nineteenth century, thanks to the intervention of sexologists, legal scholars, and medical practitioners. While undergraduates may have operated within an environment in which homoerotic yearnings could be given full vent, it is important to remember that the socialization of the elite male undergraduate entailed a vitally important education in heterosexual romance and heterosocial contact; this feature of the student experience is illuminated in my detailed examination of college boat races in chapter 5.

* * *

The environments within which Oxbridge undergraduates lived, played, and studied functioned as sustainable, tradition-bound, and identifiable cultural systems with distinct guideposts, language, rituals, hierarchies, organization, iconography, and symbols.[39] My understanding of what scholars mean when they use the term "culture," a word that the critic Raymond Williams asserted was "one of the two or three most complicated . . . in the English language,"[40] builds on recent work in anthropology, cultural studies, and, what was labeled more than a decade ago by Lynn Hunt and others, the "new cultural history." The cultural history approach privileges a close and multilayered reading of texts, pictures, and actions; an open-mindedness to what those readings reveal; and a general eschewal of grand narratives and simplifying social theories.[41] In doing so it builds on a definition of culture, promoted by the anthropologist Clifford Geertz, which sees human beings as "animal[s] suspended in webs of significance" that they themselves have spun. It is these webs that constitute culture for Geertz. Cultural analysis is not, within this formulation, "an experimental science in search of law but an interpretive one in search of meaning" which places at the fore the explication of "social expressions" that are "on their surface enigmatical."[42]

Within these "webs of significance," undergraduates created, perpetuated, and transmitted their values and perspectives through a set of ritualized activities (including examinations, degree ceremonies, and the acquisition of furniture for college rooms) that were traditional in meaning and profoundly gendered (as rites of passage that signified, for the Oxbridge student, the transition from boyhood to manhood) and that produced, in the words of French sociologist Pierre Bourdieu, "coherent and distinctive systems of cultural references and ethical or political values."[43] The universities were thus loaded with tremendous significance, both corporate and personal, for the men (and women) who regularly passed through them. With this point in mind, ceremonial locations such as the Sheldonian Theater at Oxford and the Senate House at Cambridge, college rooms and dining halls, city streets and athletic fields are viewed, in this study, as crucial sites: spaces that are not merely inhabited or utilized but, rather, invested with meaning through cultural practices that transformed specific geographical locations into symbolically important places.[44]

What follows, then, is an analysis of the social expressions, rituals, and meanings assigned by undergraduates to specific physical and psychic spaces that views these universities together as a cohesive cultural unit: a site of identity formation in which the unique and elite character of this particular brand of education served to differentiate or distinguish those privileged enough to experience it from virtually everyone else in British society.[45] Rather than focusing on those issues that separate Oxford and Cambridge as institutions within this period, I point to their remarkable similarities and points of convergence, focusing on shared undergraduate values, ideals, views, and lifestyles that united junior members at either institution more than they divided them as intervarsity rivals. My use of the term "Oxbridge" throughout this study should be read, then, as a deliberate choice, reflecting my conviction that these institutions must be treated in tandem as specific milieus, not as isolated communities of scholars untouched by outside forces and blissfully unaware of the kinds of cultural reproduction that they were fostering.[46]

* * *

In focusing on the experiences, ruminations, actions, and foibles of students themselves, this book seeks to return the history of Oxford and Cambridge to the undergraduates who (in an era prior to extensive graduate education) constituted, in the words of one student journalist in 1888, the "life and spirit" of the university.[47] While the voices of undergraduates have been frequently obscured, or underplayed, in studies of the universities, it would be an overstatement to compare this recovery project to Edward Thompson's rescue of poor stockingers, Luddite croppers, and handloom weavers "from the enormous condescension of posterity."[48] Ultimately, the voices of Oxbridge undergraduates were frequently heard, especially as they assumed their "rightful" places in the British ruling class as policy makers, legislators, and colonial district officers. Still, the historical project inaugurated by Thompson has tremendous implications for this study. His insistence that class (and one might extend this insight to the study of gender as well) is defined by individuals as they live their own history, and that it is as much a cultural as an economic formation, has provided a general methodological base for this and other recent studies that have taken the middle classes and British elites as their primary focus.[49]

To reconstruct the world that Oxbridge undergraduates inhabited and the meanings they attached to it, I have relied on several different types of sources. First and foremost are the 196 magazines, newspapers, and reviews that were produced by Oxford and Cambridge undergraduates between the years 1850 and 1920. Some historians have recognized that publishing activity among junior members of the universities acted as a benchmark of the normal functioning of student life, but this book represents the first systematic attempt to examine fully this rich and underutilized body of sources.[50] Although they were generally produced by a small minority within the undergraduate population, their broad dissemination among students in college common rooms, as well as their timeliness, renders them far superior to most of the other sources that are usually consulted by those interested in examining undergraduate life.[51] Among the most prominent of these are the voluminous autobiographies and memoirs that were produced by Oxford and Cambridge graduates in the Victorian and Edwardian eras. Though these books are certainly not avoided in the pages that follow, they are approached critically as "contrived writings that attempt to create order out of their subjects' lives," to borrow from the words of one historian of the American undergraduate experience.[52]

My emphasis on student magazines, newspapers, and reviews is not merely the result of an archival whim or a firm conviction about the utility of one type of source over others, however. It is also based on the observations of several contemporary writers, who commented on the importance of these publications to people interested in learning about the inner lives of Oxford and Cambridge undergraduates. In one essay on undergraduate literature that appeared in the *Saturday Review* in 1857, for example, student magazines were described as "curious specimen[s] of the kind of thoughts and language current among the young men who are now preparing at those seats of learning, to fill offices in Church and State," while in an idiosyncratic little pamphlet published in 1899, they were seen as gauges of pervasive cultural values and telling indicators of those "burning questions of the hour" that preoccupied the undergraduate population.[53]

The periodical publications produced at these institutions, which continued throughout the nineteenth century to be viewed as "trustworthy" and "fair exponents of the modern university mind," ranged in form and content from serious literary reviews (which predominated from 1850 to 1870) to the ephemeral and largely humorous, if not wholly silly, pamphlets that were produced with great frequency after 1880 for springtime boat race festivities.[54] Publications of this sort, occasionally rendered problematic by the frustrating anonymity of authors and editors, were one of the many locations in which undergraduate identities were formulated, defined, and recast during these years. In exploring these sources, then, this book pays particular attention to the ways in which the language that appeared in the published organs of the undergraduate population conditioned how students understood their college experiences.[55] The ideas and concepts that undergraduates drew on, and occasionally created, in their writings were thus not mere reflections of a specific mentality but, rather, crucial to its formation.[56]

Naturally, the identities that were articulated in the pages of student publications were not divorced from broader cultural and social forces or the general categories of gender, nation, race, class, and ethnicity. Frequently, the unique, masculine, and elite character of the universities of

Oxford and Cambridge was predicated on the existence of groups who could be and were excluded from the traditional undergraduate world. Women, non-Anglicans (before 1871), non-whites, and the working classes (often appearing as simplistic caricatures in student publications) were, as we shall see, central to the process of self-representation and identity formation for undergraduates between the years 1850 and 1920.[57] While this notion of "otherness" has perhaps been overused recently in historical studies and rightly criticized as deterministic, it still retains some value as an explanatory concept in this consideration of undergraduate identities and the ways in which Oxbridge men saw their world as heavily reliant on strict boundaries of inclusion and exclusion.[58] In representing themselves, undergraduates also, however, drew on ideas about their position in society as members of an elite, as part of a youth culture which often sought to define itself in opposition to the authority of the university, as fundamentally British in their conception of nationhood, as remarkably distinct and separate from members of other universities, and as individuals educated and destined for greatness. An emphasis on difference, uniqueness, specialness, and separateness allowed undergraduates to culturally construct a superiority that had accrued to them through material, economic, and educational benefits as members of Britain's increasingly dominant professional elite.

Newspapers, magazines, and reviews functioned on several other levels as well. They provided valuable news, articulated codes of behavior, defined undergraduate space, instructed new students through a variety of prescriptive mechanisms, censured authorities, and helped to unify disparate undergraduate populations. Editors often pointed to this multiplicity of functions in their introductory issues. When, for example, the *Bulldog* first appeared at Oxford in 1896, its editors noted their intentions to represent both the unified and fragmented experiences of Oxford men. In contrast to its larger, and more established, competitors (the *Oxford Magazine* and the *Isis*), the *Bulldog* expected to "deal more fully with some phases of undergraduate life than has yet been attempted" and depict the "devotees of every cult and disciples of every school."[59]

Periodical publications also amused undergraduates and represented, in fact, a distinctive brand of humor writing that served a variety of explicit functions in these complex cultural systems. Depictions of dons and other university officials, parents, members of the working classes, foreigners, and, most importantly, women were often meant to elicit laughter from undergraduate readers who routinely peddled exaggerated stereotypes of outsiders to humor their mates and to mark their separation from the broader population. Understanding why images of women students, who had been essentially neutered (or masculinized) by their pursuit of an intellectual life, were funny to those men operating within the universities provides insight into the values, attitudes, and concerns of undergraduates who seemed resolutely determined to preserve the masculine status of Oxford and Cambridge. Humor, then, never served an indeterminate or wholly frivolous purpose. For these students, the ability to recognize the joke in a clever quip, an artfully drawn cartoon, or a funny poem was one hallmark of their insider status at the universities and signified another rite of passage that they had to negotiate as they made the transition from boyhood to manhood. Throughout this book, then, humor is analyzed as a device used to express discontent or consternation, to ridicule inappropriate behavior, to police gender and sexual boundaries, and to construct images of undergraduate life that contributed to the formation of corporate identities.[60]

While the words of students, as they appeared in these often amusing undergraduate publications, constitute the main source for this study, I do not allow these documents to rest alone. This book, in fact, draws on several other types of material in reconstructing the rarefied world of the Oxbridge man. The experiences and imaginings of undergraduates are also re-created here through an examination of personal letters, diaries, disciplinary records, matriculation registers, administrative papers, visitors' guides, accounts from the popular press, and a vast array of university memoranda, flysheets, and advertisements. While I am principally interested in examining students' words, artistic expressions also figure prominently in the pages that follow. Cartoons and photographs provide enormously rich evidence of undergraduate attitudes and preoccupations. They also serve one other vital function by providing a detailed record of what the world these young, privileged men inhabited actually looked like. In this way, visual evidence allows the reader to more fully understand the finer points and intricacies of Oxbridge public and private spaces.

* * *

Before proceeding with the main substance of this book, it might be useful to describe in general terms some of the basic features of student life by looking at what a typical undergraduate day and week might have looked like for much of the period covered here. Undergraduates at either institution matriculated as members of both the university at large and an individual college—or, after the 1860s, an organization (called a delegacy at Oxford and a syndicate at Cambridge) responsible for overseeing those students who, for financial or social reasons, elected not to join a college. This federation of individual colleges within the universities meant that students identified both with the broader institutional communities of Oxford and Cambridge and with colleagues within the more intimate surroundings of the colleges, which often possessed their own distinctive cultural identities.[61] The intention here is not to minimize distinctions that existed, for example, between the intellectual climate of King's College and the intense athleticism of Jesus College at Cambridge, but rather to focus on the ancient universities, and the kind of lives that students lived within them, as whole entities. While much occurred within the perimeters of the colleges, as we shall see, the Oxbridge man's interaction with fellow undergraduates was not limited to this setting; students at the ancient universities intermingled in societies, clubs, and athletic teams and, more informally, at private parties and university-wide celebrations.

Undergraduates most commonly attended the university for three to four years, and during each year spent three eight-week terms in residence and the remainder of their time on vacation. During vacations they might travel or, more often than not, catch up on reading (required by an examination system based in part on independent study) not done during the academic term. All Oxbridge men generally resided in the colleges of the universities. In the 1850s and 1860s, provisions were also made for undergraduates to reside in licensed lodging houses, which were regulated by the universities, but most continued to take rooms in a college for at least their first year. The college, as the primary residential space, was the focus of much activity, and it functioned in ways that resembled, somewhat paradoxically, both a family environment and a men's club. Social activities, reading, attending lectures and meetings with one's tutor or supervisor, exercise, and entertaining dominated the undergraduate's time "up." The Oxford or Cambridge student lived in a set of rooms that he rented and decorated according to his own tastes. In these surroundings he read, took notes, received and entertained guests, and ate the private, smaller meals of breakfast and lunch. All undergraduates were generally required to appear in their college dining halls for supper, attend chapel (or a roll call for those who were not members of the Church of England) at around 8:00 A.M. each morning, and be in their colleges by the time the gates closed at a prescribed hour (usually between 9:00 and 10:00 P.M.).

The average day, at a glance, looks rather leisurely. Mornings usually consisted of breakfast, at which one might entertain guests, followed by a lecture or two and a few hours of reading. Lunch was generally quick and might also be followed by some reading. Later afternoons were often spent, especially in the years after 1860, taking some form of exercise: an organized sport, a brisk walk, or, as the century progressed, a ride on a bicycle. After tea, students might read again for a while before dinner. Many spent the hours after dinner entertaining or being entertained. Drinks were often involved on occasions where students served dessert to mates in their college rooms. Junior common rooms, as communal spaces, also provided opportunities for socializing, especially at night, but also during the day. Similarly, organizations such as the famous debating societies known as the Unions often held evening meetings that many students attended, looking to them for companionship and social contacts. Undergraduates who showed some restraint might, before retiring, return to their books for an hour or two.

While most days were dominated by these general patterns, there were particular times in the undergraduate career when the central preoccupation might be more academic than social, or vice versa. During the annual intercollegiate boat races that occurred in the late spring and became especially popular social occasions after 1880, those undergraduates not facing exams found their time dominated almost exclusively by entertainment and visits from family members and sweethearts. Alternatively, undergraduates who found themselves confronted by the examinations that so dominated the scholastic side of life at Oxbridge, and were the sole measure of academic success, often found little time to do anything but study or catch up on neglected reading. Successful university athletes might place undue emphasis on the importance of sport in their education, sacrificing both the academic and social sides of college life for the sake of victory.[62]

An Oxbridge education in this period was defined as much by socializing and acquiring a level of well-roundedness as it was by academic learning. This particular form of residential life not only prepared students for a future of social, political, and economic leadership but ensured that they had the contacts and social skills necessary to assume such roles with confidence, aplomb, and sophistication. Just how undergraduates saw this education, and the significance they attached to it as a specific kind of masculine experience, will become apparent in the remainder of this book.

1

Constructing Superiority:
The University and the Undergraduate

In 1861, an anonymous contributor to *Great Tom,* an Oxford magazine devoted to discussions of university life and contemporary politics, characterized the experiences of the undergraduate as "extremely peculiar." He elaborated further by establishing an explicit connection between peculiarity and privilege in British society: "there is something extremely peculiar in gathering together from all parts of a kingdom, the very *elite* of that kingdom—the young, the noble, the wealthy, and the talented."[1] Echoing these sentiments twenty-nine years later, a contributor to the long-running Cambridge magazine *Granta* observed that "undergraduates, it has been justly said, are a people apart. It is not everybody who can understand them. Their traditions are peculiar, their vocabulary is both peculiar and extensive."[2]

These brief, if hyperbolic, descriptions of ethnographic separateness, distinctive linguistic markers and cultural traditions, and peculiarity functioned for late-nineteenth- and early-twentieth-century undergraduates as crucial signifiers of elite status: collective acts of consecration, to borrow from Pierre Bourdieu, "aimed at producing a separate, sacred group."[3] As examples of a broader process whereby Oxford and Cambridge students sought to attach a range of complex meanings to the specific activities, experiences, and ceremonies of university life and articulate the superiority of their youthful masculine perspective, impassioned assertions of this sort situated them within both the circumscribed boundaries of the university and larger national and imperial communities. Rather than taking as givens the undergraduate's strong emotional attachment to the university as a gathering place for the "very elite" of the "kingdom" and his elevated status within British social and gender hierarchies, I explore, within this section of the book, the various ways in which student journalists, memoirists, and artists defined the social spaces they inhabited and differentiated the Oxbridge man from broader British and international populations.

In describing how undergraduates fashioned the universities into highly gendered little worlds characterized by intense institutional loyalty, specific notions of male time and space, and carefully articulated visions of male solidarity, this study challenges the traditional practices of historians of higher education. Instead of privileging curricular developments, institutional milestones, or administrative shifts in chronicling the emergence of the modern university, I rely here on undergraduate visions: perspectives that highlight how the unique and exclusive character of these institutions was as much the product of distinctive cultural practices and strategies as it was the creation of government-sponsored commissions or reforming dons.

As they reinforced the special position of the ancient universities in British society and delineated their exclusive character, undergraduates maintained rigid distinctions between elite university insiders and marginalized outsiders by erecting cultural barriers that often mirrored those separating different social classes, races, and genders in late Victorian and Edwardian Britain. The presumptive superiority of men, the professional classes, and the British nation and "race" were, within such an environment, premised on corresponding assumptions about the inferiority of a whole range of other groups, including women, the working classes, non-whites, and non-Christians.[4] The creation of this "magical boundary" between insiders and outsiders in undergraduate culture underpinned, reinforced, and ultimately reflected more general structures of power relations in British society.[5] This tendency to differentiate between the included and the excluded was thus not simply a quaint byproduct of university life or the myopia of misguided adolescents. Rather, it was part of a broader tendency that was manifested in a variety of other cultural settings during this period: imperial legitimacy and racial hierarchies were maintained, for example, in India and Africa through the creation of segregated social clubs; some two hundred thousand elite men sought, by the end of the nineteenth century, to reinforce their authority and find masculine refuge in hundreds of exclusive organizations; and boys in public schools found comfort and status in the rituals and accoutrements of organized sport and secret societies.[6]

The fact that these newly fashioned, and increasingly exclusive, definitions of the university and the undergraduate emerged between the years 1850 and 1920 was no mere coincidence. As the universities grew in strength and stature and became more modern institutions, undergraduate culture acquired a sense of permanence, timelessness, and importance (reflected, as Sheldon Rothblatt has noted with reference to the early nineteenth century, in the creation of debating societies, athletic organizations, and dining clubs) that added to the already considerable level of confidence possessed by Oxford and Cambridge men.[7] A more important component of the rise of modern undergraduate culture was, however, the dramatic articulation of a distinctive and highly stylized ethos of superiority, a development that corresponded directly to the expanding role these institutions played in nurturing an elite, professional meritocracy. This chapter reveals that the process of creating and perpetuating such an elite was something more than academic and organizational for undergraduates and extended well beyond curricular changes that sought, as Reba Soffer has noted with reference to the introduction of modern history, to educate this new ruling class for positions of leadership.[8]

While certainty and assurance became, within this period, hallmarks of the successful university man, it is also possible to argue, as I do in subsequent chapters, that assertions and reiterations of superiority, distinctiveness, and difference also betrayed fundamental insecurities about just how long this status could be maintained. An increasingly organized and vocal feminist movement demanding (among other things) access to higher education, growing uncertainties about the permanence of the British empire, and the blurring of distinctions between the business and professional classes all meant that Oxbridge undergraduates felt the need to articulate more fully who they were and how they fit into the broader structures of British society.

Creating a Sense of Place: The Architecture of the University

The buildings, grounds, and gardens that make up the physical environments of Oxford and Cambridge acquired a range of specific meanings in the nineteenth and early twentieth centuries that assisted undergraduates, as members of an emerging meritocratic elite, in actively creating a sense of place whereby they imparted, in the words of Sheldon Rothblatt, "special virtue[s]" and "qualit[ies]" to hallowed and sanctified locations.[9] Brick and mortar, grass, trees, and flowers served, then, at a most essential level, as distinguishing hallmarks of what many saw as special environments. Sentiments of this sort were expressed routinely in reminiscences and commentaries about the ancient institutions. Alfred Noyes, for example, an Oxford man who revisited his old college in 1907, commented explicitly, and somewhat forlornly, on the visual pleasures of his "beautiful" university: a geographically and historically specific place characterized by "time-worn towers," "the warm gold dusk of the meadows," and "gay-coloured barges" on the Isis.[10] Cloistered buildings that served as reminders of ecclesiastical traditions and church connections, expansive lawns and impeccably maintained gardens, and river banks lined with boat houses and barges were just some of the distinguishing features of these astoundingly attractive educational settings; they set them apart and elicited comments from tourists, visitors, and prospective students alike.

The buildings, streets, and churches of these ancient seats of learning were, for many observers in the years between 1850 and 1920, also charming and evocative reminders of the nation's rich history. Joseph Wells, an admirer of Oxford architecture and antiquities, commented in 1920, for example, on the ways in which the "two old English Universities" possessed innumerable "memories of the days of old."[11] R. W. Livingstone (a Hertford College undergraduate from 1900 to 1903), in a discussion of his alma mater penned in 1907, established more explicit connections between the British past and the physical aging of the graying buildings of Oxford; the structures were "inscribed," in his estimation, with rich historical meaning and populated by the "incongruous and unfamiliar ghosts" of "Protestant and Papist, Roundhead and Cavalier, Jacobite and Hanoverian."[12] For Livingstone and many others like him, Oxford was a central player in the nation's great historical dramas, which included, among many other acts, the Reformation, the English Civil War, and the Jacobite rebellions of the eighteenth century.

Undergraduates, in discussing the physical spaces that they inhabited, emphasized not only their links with the glorious events of the past but also their peculiar position as the heirs of an important legacy of national leadership. For Oxbridge men, understanding British history did not simply provide them with vital moral lessons and instructive examples of how they might best administer the nation and the empire.[13] It also established an unbroken line of patrilineal descent, whereby the masculine virtues of prominent national figures were transmitted, as if by magic, from generation to generation in college halls and other hallowed spaces.[14]

Two nineteenth-century students focused, in particular, on the role that common meals in college halls played in cementing relationships between elite men. In the first instance, Edward Jupp, an Oxford undergraduate who entered Christ Church in 1868, wrote the following description in a letter to his younger brother at the beginning of the Michaelmas (autumn) term: "I dine in the most splendid Hall in the world, hung all round with the pictures of the great men who have been at Christ Church. 300 men often dine there, and I shall have to say a Latin Grace one week."[15] George Nugent Bankes, who will appear several times in this study, was more colorful in delineating the special qualities of the King's College, Cambridge dining hall: "it is a grand thing to feed where so many great men have fed before; to reflect that their Hall formed part of their daily life, and that the attendant associations possibly had great influence on their after career; and from the latter, because it is equally grand to think that I may have a future Archbishop on my right and a Lord Chancellor on my left."[16] Both accounts established a connection between the three hundred or so undergraduates dining in a college hall and their symbolic (and in some instances actual) "ancestors," in effect cementing the elite bonds that were thought to exist between different generations of Oxbridge men united in their reverence for these sanctified social spaces.

The links between this glorious past and the visions of professional and proactive masculinity that dominated the Oxbridge undergraduate's life after about 1850 were sometimes made even more explicit. Ralph Durand, the author of a 1909 book on Oxford manners and history, commented specifically on the power of architecture to unify busy and active men when he wrote, "so long as Oxford's stately colleges preserve even a semblance of their ancient form, they will have power to bring us in some degree into communion with those who lived and worked, thought and played within their walls." At a time when the university occupied a significant role in the training of imperial civil servants, Church of England clergymen, educators, and authors, Durand highlighted the connections between these men and those who preceded them, in effect creating a vision of symbolic descent for professional men that mimicked, in a way, the structures of aristocratic inheritance. With specific reference, once again, to the bricks and mortar of college walls, he noted, "they remind us of men who took their part in moulding the history both of this Empire and of that great nation across the Atlantic which England begot and lost.

... They remind us of men who have worked for the Christian Church and the Christian Faith. . . . They remind us of men whose written word still lives and will outlast the walls that sheltered them."[17] Such rich historical associations set Oxford and Cambridge apart from more recently established and less prestigious seats of higher learning, like the University of London (formally created in 1836), by marking them as peculiarly elite institutions with distinctive, and almost mythical, traditions and social bonds.[18]

The University as a Little World and the Rhetoric of Emotion and Attachment

The very act of occupying such revered and historically significant space for three to four years (the usual length of time it took to complete a degree course) served for undergraduates as an important unifying experience and helped to foster an enduring sense of community among university men. Upon entering the "sacred" buildings, grounds, and gardens of the various Oxford and Cambridge colleges, undergraduates were immersed in a world that they sought to make their own in a variety of complicated ways.[19] The universities, then, as social structures and incubators for a national elite, were dynamic spaces: sites of meaning in which undergraduates forged complicated, intersecting, and occasionally contradictory identities. The attitudes and perspectives of these men, as objects of study, are important and often neglected historical artifacts that illuminate how elites in late imperial Britain situated themselves within overlapping social, racial, gender, and sexual hierarchies.

The significance that undergraduates attached to these peculiar gathering places for "the young, the noble, the wealthy, and the talented" was most often reflected in the systemic attributes that students routinely assigned to these ancient institutions. Descriptions of the universities as small and self-contained societies appeared frequently in a variety of different places, helping to establish the notion that the university was, indeed, a distinct "little world." Often revealed in the most fragmentary of ways, this idea dominated throughout the Victorian and Edwardian eras, and examples of its use, in the student press and elsewhere, abound. At Oxford in 1874, for example, one undergraduate contributor to the *Shotover Papers* identified the word "university" as a "diminutive of *universe,* a little world."[20] Other terms were also used to convey similar ideas. Phrases and words like "small world," "world of," and "microcosm" appeared repeatedly in undergraduate descriptions of the spaces they inhabited and reinforced, for students and outsiders alike, the consuming nature and en-compassing quality of life within these institutions.[21]

Undergraduates, in defining the universities as little worlds, drew ex-plicitly on concepts that they had used at institutions like Harrow, Eton, and Winchester to describe the experience of being a public school boy, a background that the majority of Oxbridge men in the late Victorian and Edwardian periods shared upon matriculating.[22] Often employed in both settings to emphasize the separate and unique character of these institu-tions, these concepts were vitally important in cementing elite status and separating the included from the excluded in the later nineteenth century. This tendency to view school and university attendance as a totalizing experience also reflected just how important associational life was to the formation of masculine identities in this period. Public schools and col-leges were crucial, not only because they fostered the admired, and often overstated, manly attributes of bodily strength, fortitude, and the stiff up-per lip, but also because they erected barriers to the outside world, effec-tively shielding the young elite man from dangerous forces that, if allowed to infiltrate, would inevitably produce chinks in his armor of masculinity. These little worlds thus functioned, in an era when anxieties about male gender roles occupied a prominent cultural place, as manly fortresses that separated boys and men from their homes, domestic responsibilities, and ultimately the moderating and potentially contaminating influences of the so-called "real world."[23]

While undergraduates drew on a variety of ideas and concepts to con-vey the uniqueness of the university as a little world, they most frequently resorted to depictions that emphasized the youthful vitality of these im-portant social spaces. Dons (college fellows who had both teaching and pastoral responsibilities) young and old alike appeared in student descrip-tions of university society, but they were often seen as peripheral charac-ters, emblems of a distinctive variety of British manhood that functioned as a minor life force within a world dominated by postadolescent exuber-ance. The "university society" of junior members most often excluded the little worlds of dons, which had, as their focal points, the senior common rooms and high tables of various colleges.[24] Within this society, students were depicted as an essential ingredient for a complete university; in an era when the ideal of the research institution was barely perceptible in Britain,[25] undergraduates considered Oxford and Cambridge simply de-void of any purpose without their junior members.

Oxbridge journalists and memoirists, in describing these institutions during vacations (when they fell, according to Charles Dickens the younger, into a "long torpor"),[26] often conceded, as one Oxford man did in 1888, that the "life and spirit [of the universities] ebb and flow as Undergraduates come up and go down."[27] Occasionally, this relationship between the energy of the student and the lifeblood of the university was characterized as symbiosis. Desmond Cooke, another Oxford undergraduate, commented specifically in 1903 on the disadvantages of visiting his institution during the summer months when he highlighted for the readers of the *Oxford Point of View* the relationship between the university's essential character and the presence of undergraduates:

> [Everywhere] an air of incompleteness, as of a scene set but lacking the actors, for if men be a city, how much more are men a College. It might be said that now is the time to see the city, when there is no gauntlet of staring undergraduates to be run in each quadrangle, and when poetic reveries roused by the sombre piles are not shaken by discordant shrieks of comic songs or the fitful murdering of a piano. But this is to make false use of sentiment: for the undergraduate is a part of Oxford, discord a part of the undergraduate. Oxford in the Long Vacation is far from being Oxford.[28]

At no time was the impact of the absence of undergraduates more apparent to Oxbridge students than when Britain found itself at war in 1914. Oxford and Cambridge men, junior and senior members alike, readily volunteered for battle. The male undergraduate populations of both institutions were significantly reduced as a result of this massive surge of patriotic enlistment.[29] At Cambridge, for example, the number of male undergraduates dropped from a high of nearly four thousand before the war to 575 by the Easter term of 1916.[30] Students themselves were well aware of what this cataclysmic event meant for the universities. One undergraduate contributor to the Oxford paper *'Varsity* commented, in the autumn of 1914, on the diminished level of activity around the university. Clubs ceased to exist, the Union society became "a corpse galvanized into a hideous semblance of life," and "real Oxford" became only a memory. In this instance, Oxford's very existence was called into question by the absence of an abundance of youthful undergraduates. This particular state of affairs presented problems, especially for new students: "The Freshers that come up this year, with no knowledge of the Oxford that is gone, know nothing of the joys that once were so powerful here. They, too, live a life subdued and quiet, hushed into the grey tones of an aimless monotony. The great god Pan is dead: and now Oxford is no more."[31]

Just as the university was deficient in some way when undergraduate members were absent, the student was also at a loss when away from the institution. The little world of the university was, for students, the standard by which all other things were judged. For the young man in these circumstances, the university replaced the family or the school in the formation and articulation of gender and other social identities. This perspective is betrayed in the phrase "go down," still commonly used by undergraduates at both Oxford and Cambridge to denote leaving the university, whether at the end of a term or upon completing a degree. The metaphor reveals their somewhat skewed symbolic and geographical interpretation of the world (especially among those who departed the university for northern locations). Arthur Clement Hilton, a Cambridge undergraduate from 1869 to 1873, offered the following explanation of this particular worldview: "the University man always goes 'down'; his *locus* is the headquarters of the earth, and everywhither 'goes down' from it."[32]

This special vocabulary and unique, if faulty, interpretation of the world betrayed not only the egocentrism of youth but also a level of insularity, privacy, and secrecy that was thought essential to the preservation of elite status and masculine privilege in later Victorian and Edwardian Britain. For John Aston, an Oxford cartoonist who produced, in 1902, a small book of sketches detailing various features of university life, the shared cultural legacy and common attributes of university men became most apparent to the undergraduate upon "going down" (fig. 1.1). In one of his cartoons, athletic events, sociability, study, and leisure are all given pride of place by a departing undergraduate who recalls his college days, in his dreams and the caption accompanying the illustration, by remembering with fondness the "secret" rites and traditions that set him apart from others in the wider world. Perspectives of this sort were not confined to the period under examination here; Barbara Rogers noted them in the 1980s when she conducted a sociological study of men's organizations and institutions in Britain. According to Rogers's highly entertaining and informative account of the bastions of British male privilege, the "key to elite private education" (in which she includes Oxbridge) was a matter of "'school-approved' accent and mannerisms" as well as "expectations, ways of relating to 'superiors,' equals and 'inferiors', shared topics of conversation, shared knowledge of certain sports or certain people, shared likes and dislikes . . . a shared culture."[33]

While the forlorn looks of the departing undergraduate in John Aston's drawing reflect his strong attachment to the university as a formative social space, they also betray another element of the undergraduate identity that was forged at Oxford and Cambridge in this period. Upon being

XII. GOING DOWN.

'Still on her spire the pigeons hover :   Drumming her old ones forth from town,
   Still by her gateway haunts the gown ;   Know you the secret none discover ?
      Ah ! but her secret ? You, young lover,   Tell it—when you go down.'

Fig. 1.1. John Aston's artistic rendering of the mournful undergraduate "going down." *Varsity Sketches* (Oxford: Holywell, 1902), p. 12.
By permission of the Bodleian Library, University of Oxford, shelf mark Per. G.A. Oxon c. 203(7).

initiated into this world, the student was expected to establish deeply rooted emotional attachments to the university that were permanent, not fleeting. The memories that college life fostered and the distinctive imprimatur that these institutions were thought to leave on Oxbridge men were frequently described, in a world preoccupied with delineating the boundaries separating insiders from outsiders, as enduring marks of status. Their "sunny association[s]" with the university kept, in the words of Dickens the younger once again, the lives of members of this privileged group "the sweeter"[34] and reminded them of a "sacred fire" that burned in the hearts of all for whom it was an "inestimable privilege to conjure up recollections of the[ir] best and fairest days."[35] "The remembrance of days gone by,"[36] and the identification with one's university or school that recollections of this sort represented, irrevocably bound the Victorian and Edwardian ruling class together, especially as education at socially acceptable institutions became more important in defining elite status and securing a place for these young men in professional hierarchies.

The university, then, was not only a place for study, play, and sociability; it was an institution to which students should wholeheartedly pledge their commitment. In a number of instances, students and former students alike used images of Oxford or Cambridge as a stern but nurturing mother to underscore the notion that the university was worthy of both adoration and respect. This kind of reverence appealed, in the late nineteenth and early twentieth centuries, to an upper-middle-class sense of chivalry that emphasized, among other things, tradition, honor, loyalty, duty, muscularity, and a revived enthusiasm for the medieval tradition of courtly love.[37] Edward Hugessen Knatchbull-Hugessen, a Magdalen College, Oxford undergraduate from 1847 to 1851, addressed this issue specifically in a memorial (first published in 1879) to the influence of his alma mater in which he linked manly worth to institutional loyalty: "I believe a man to be worth very little indeed who, on leaving the University, does not carry away with him feelings of veneration and love for her which only end with his existence."[38] The interplay here between womanly nurture and manly responsibility clearly points to the various ways in which the university, as a space that was routinely interpreted through a highly gendered lens, could be both intensely masculine and surprisingly feminine (and even domesticated) at the same time.

Alma mater was also invoked by one 1877 contributor to the *Cambridge Tatler* who, in describing the return of students for the final term of the academic year, offered the following advice to his fellow undergraduates: "Alma Mater—She opens her arms joyfully to receive you all back, and the majority, I am sure, return her embrace with interest. Of course you are glad to come back to her; at least, if you are not, you ought to be ashamed of yourself. It would be unnatural if you were not glad."[39] Clearly, the university world became, for many, a surrogate family dominated by a welcoming and affectionate (if abstract) maternal figure. This familial metaphor was commonly used to encourage and naturalize the strong attachment that many men felt to their universities by comparing the return to Oxford or Cambridge to a return home after a long absence. Its use, however, also betrayed certain contradictions or tensions in undergraduate culture. Despite, as we shall see, a very strong tendency among Oxbridge men to view the university as a masculine retreat from the domestic sphere that figured so prominently in middle- and upper-middle-class culture throughout the nineteenth century, many students were never entirely comfortable dispensing with the reassuring imagery of the home in describing environments that they viewed as essential to their development as men. Rather than fully rejecting the private sphere of their mothers, sisters, cousins, and aunts or discussing the university as a primarily public space, they sought to fashion a peculiarly masculine private sphere in which the mythical presence of alma mater replaced the real nurturing presence of female relations and friends.

The transference of allegiance from home and mother to the broader world of manly responsibility and activity began, as historian John Tosh has noted, at the public school and marked, for men of the upper and middle classes in the later nineteenth and earlier twentieth centuries, the transition from boyhood to manhood.[40] In some instances, the women left behind by departing sons and brothers felt the psychological impact of this transition nearly as strongly as the young men who were experiencing it firsthand. Edward Jupp (the Christ Church undergraduate) received a letter from his mother in October of 1869 that commented, among other things, on the wretched quality of the autumn weather, which she assumed was mitigated for her son by the "warm welcome of Alma Mater" that he received upon returning to her for the Michaelmas term. Such knowledge, she admitted, was not entirely comforting, precisely because it revealed her son's progressive straying from the family fold: "You must allow the other Mater to be a little jealous, as I hear you were so delighted the end of the 'Long' had at last arrived."[41] As a substitute for family and a marker of the young man's arrival at a new stage of life, the university came, in this account, to serve all his needs: emotional, social, and bodily as well as educational. Identification with alma mater, and all that it involved, marked the experience of university life as unique and special not only for students but also for parents and siblings, highlighting the extent to which Oxbridge men acquired elite status at both an individual and a familial level.

Defining Male Time and Space and the Uniqueness of Oxbridge

The little world, the nurturing capacity of alma mater, and the commitment and loyalty she was depicted as inspiring remained important features of a collective undergraduate sense of self throughout the later Victorian and Edwardian eras. Common identities were also constructed, however, in more mundane ways. Repeated references to such things as the division of the academic year into three eight-week terms, the importance of masculine companionship, the specific demarcation of male time and space within the university, the foreignness of these and other customs to outsiders, and the uniqueness of undergraduate dress all helped to further elaborate notions of Oxbridge distinctiveness.

The academic year was divided for undergraduates between term time, when they came up to the university, and the vacations (or "vacs"), when they generally did one of three things: return to their family homes, travel abroad, or pursue further studies, either independently or as a member of what were commonly known as reading parties.[42] The significance of this division of time was reflected in the pages of student magazines, newspapers, and reviews, which routinely noted the ebb and flow of the undergraduate calendar with articles alternately titled "Au Revoir" and "On Coming Up."[43]

For Oxbridge men, the contrasts between the activities of term time and those of the vacation were most often understood in gendered ways.[44] The majority of undergraduate chroniclers emphasized masculine companionship and pursuits in their descriptions of life during the academic year, while feminine company and romantic crushes tended, in most depictions, to dominate vacations. Reginald Stephen Copleston, a Merton College undergraduate from 1864 to 1869, emphasized this bifurcated worldview when he compared university life to the pleasures of home in the *Oxford Spectator* in 1867: "We are going from the stern hardihood of Oxford, to the warm welcomes and bright firesides of home; to a mother's quiet enquiries, or a sister's eager admiration; to all those ordinary affections which some of us perhaps have been foolish enough to despise."[45] Beyond simply reinforcing prevailing ideas about the division of middle- and upper-middle-class worlds into public and private spheres, this admiration for the home reveals one side (the celebratory) of the profoundly ambivalent and ever-changing relationship between the Oxbridge man, his family, and the domestic sphere. Undergraduates' responses to home and family vacillated between the poles of quiet celebration and violent hostility, depending on both personal circumstances and the momentous cultural shifts in the nineteenth and early twentieth centuries that influenced male responses to what Martin Francis has recently called the "frontier of domesticity."[46]

Many students viewed female companionship as an essential and desirable alternative to the company of undergraduate men.[47] In Copleston's words, it tempered the influences of an all-male society and restored manly vigor by allowing men "in gay ball-rooms, and merry country houses" to "regain the long pined for society of the unenfranchised sex." Rather than eschewing heterosocial contact, Oxbridge students, more often than not, saw it as a vital corollary to the homosocial relations of school and college. Heterosexual romance, courting, and liaisons, not romantic friendships with other men, dominated the sexual development of most undergraduates. This emphasis on heterosociability became, as we shall see in subsequent chapters, nearly as vital to the formation of undergraduate identities as class status or personal wealth. Regulated contact with women at specified times (especially during vacations) was, for Copleston and others, an essential component in the development of a man's character. To reject or denigrate such companionship was, in his eyes, to subscribe to a "mock manliness" that was antithetical to the true Oxford spirit. According to Copleston, readers of the *Oxford Spectator* needed to work hard during the term time so that "they might have full leisure to pay their homage and reap their reward before the throne of Beauty" during vacation periods and thus assume their rightful position as men at home as well as within the university.[48]

While this tendency to associate vacations with leisure and feminine companionship dominated throughout the period under examination here, the somewhat vague "stern hardihood" that Copleston associated with Oxford in 1867 acquired, after the 1880s, a range of more specific meanings that drew explicitly on emerging concepts of upper-middle-class masculinity and emphasized even further the gendered division of time. Descriptions of the term often relied in these years on language that equated immersion in the life of the university with a professional vocation or the impending responsibilities of a breadwinning adulthood.[49] In discussing the usual routine at Oxford, one correspondent to the *Cambridge Observer* characterized the various preoccupations of the undergraduate in the following way: "Some of us think of the near approach of Schools [final examinations] and of the responsibility of life; others, whose interests center elsewhere, return to their old vocations on the river and the tow-path, and so on."[50] In a 1907 foreword to a small and short-lived Oxford paper called the *Pageant Post,* the activities of a regular summer term (April–June) were described not only as vocations but in ways that drew on a masculine imagery of battles, male honor, and heroism: "For the last eight weeks he has played his inimitable part in the wear and tear of *'Varsity* life—he has waged the battle of the ball upon the cricket field—he has upheld the honor of his College on the river—whether in the boat itself or amid the mad chaos of humanity in wild rush upon the river's bank—he has indulged in the day dreams of youth as some well cushioned punt bore him in utter abandonment along the Cher [a smaller Oxford river]; perhaps in more serious vein he has entered the list for victory in the schools."[51]

Characterizations of this sort, building as they did on prevailing notions of the male/female divide, assisted undergraduates in defining the university as a distinctively masculine and elite social space. University-wide regulations that excluded women from degrees until 1920 at Oxford and 1948 at Cambridge and college restrictions that limited women's movements within college quads and courts clearly reinforced this notion, but the demarcation of university precincts as male or masculine was never simply a matter of statutory restrictions.[52] Rather, Oxbridge spaces acquired meaning and significance through a whole range of cultural practices, including, but not limited to, the establishment of boundaries that separated the university from other social spaces and, in the process, created often-rigid divisions between 'varsity (university) men and all others.[53]

Within this context, meals in college dining halls, examinations, boat races, and annual rituals, such as the singing of Latin hymns from the tower of Magdalen College, Oxford at dawn on May Day, functioned simultaneously as customs that marked the undergraduate's progression through the terms and as social practices that separated him from the broader population. Undergraduates positioned themselves as knowing insiders by emphasizing their particular role as interpreters of these "sacred mysteries" of Oxbridge life. This point was underscored at Oxford in 1914 in an article appearing in *'Varsity* that portrayed the undergraduate as an intermediary between the male world of ideas and political discussion and the female space of the family home, a "messenger who carried in vacations to clever and admiring sisters" glimpses of the intellectual life of the college common room.[54]

Nineteenth- and early-twentieth-century undergraduates undertook a similar role when they wrote "Oxford or Cambridge Letters" home to describe the ins and outs of student life to admiring female relatives and sweethearts.[55] They even went so far, on certain occasions, as to produce specific pamphlets that described university customs to the women in their lives, a group characterized by one 1903 contributor to the Oxford paper *Isis* as "psychologically incapable of understanding [Oxford's] life and true atmosphere," in ways that carefully marked the differences between male and female spaces.[56] An example of this particular brand of university literature from 1874 begins in the following manner: "Our Mothers and sisters know very little of our school life, they know still less of our life at Oxford. Many would write them word if they could, more if they had time. Why should we not jot down pencillings of Oxford ways and Oxford scenes in a form that our Mothers might read, our youngest sisters understand. We will try."[57] These attempts to communicate the complexities of university life to mothers, sisters, cousins, and aunts allowed male undergraduates to articulate their privileged position, display their knowledge, and reinforce certain male prerogatives that enabled them to move at will between the worlds of the university, the home, and society at large.

Amusingly naive female relatives and girlfriends were not the only ones whose failure to comprehend the peculiarities of the Oxford or Cambridge "manner" had consequences for the undergraduate. The quizzical gaze and observations of any visitor unfamiliar with university traditions made Oxbridge men aware of the advantages they possessed over tourists, interlopers, and transient intruders alike. One contributor to the *Vacuum,* an ephemeral Oxford publication, put it this way in 1900: "It is at these moments that one enjoys that thrill of pride and consciousness of superiority; when one understands that one forms a part of that magnificent whole which these poor wanderers have come to see; that what to them is the scene of one short visit is to us a second home."[58]

Undergraduates often went to great lengths to expose the deficiencies of external observations and commentaries, reinforcing, in the process, the gulf that existed between the included and what one contributor to the Oxford *Shotover Papers* pointedly labeled in 1874 "outsiders."[59] Particular ire was reserved for novels about 'varsity life written by non-university men, which, the *Tatler in Cambridge* indignantly protested in 1871, more often than not "misrepresented" undergraduates and expressed "the most astonishing [and presumably wrong] Ideas" on "the Modes and Manners of our life here."[60] According to the critiques penned by students and old boys alike, the Oxbridge experience could not be fully understood without an intimate knowledge of the university's inner spaces. Non-university writers' lack of a proper perspective led most often to obfuscation or imprecision. An 1898 discussion of university novels that appeared in *Macmillan's Magazine* and was written by George Saintsbury (a Merton College, Oxford undergraduate in the 1860s) sustained this particular style of critique by employing a whole range of insider/outsider dichotomies: "Laymen writing about law and clergy, ladies writing about parliament or clubs, Frenchmen writing about England, Americans attempting to imitate the vulgar speech of England,—all these are by-words for slips and errors. But it is doubtful whether the unhappiest of them ventures on such a perilous task as a man who is not of the University writing about the University."[61] An even more forceful critique appeared in *'Varsity* in 1901. In an article titled "Local Colour," descriptions of Oxford written by non-university men as well as impertinent women are said to lack an essential "soul" that can only be captured by matriculated members: "The externals they may get with fair exactness, but the heart of the picture is absent, and the difference is the contrast between an old master and a spurious one."[62]

While undergraduates clearly used the medium of the student press (as well as other writings) to set off their world as unique and special, they also did so in more concrete ways, most notably through the use of physical markers such as dress. In this regard, students were assisted in fashioning Oxford or Cambridge as specifically male spaces by regulations that required them to wear academic caps and gowns, a carryover from the universities' monastic origins. In J. R. Seeley's 1863 student guide, written for the benefit "not of actual students only, but of all persons who may contemplate entering the University of Cambridge," cap and gown were said to be required "on all occasions when the student acts in the character of a member of the University." This included a variety of settings: "at Chapel, at the public dinner in Hall, and at all College lectures, at all University lectures, on all public occasions in the Senate-House and in the University Church . . . [and] in visiting the Masters and Tutors in the College and the officers of the University."[63] Throughout the period under examination here, undergraduates were also generally required to wear cap and gown in the evenings and on Sundays so that they could be easily identified by university officials in areas that were ambiguous, occupied potentially by both town and gown (streets, bars, music halls, etc.).

Although undergraduates resisted this and other disciplinary measures, they made the best of these requirements by appropriating the cap and gown as a visible symbol of their student identity. For junior members, this garb not only represented an imposed standard of dress but also functioned as a reminder of university privilege, an important identifier of their insider status, and a badge of masculinity. As a mark of distinction the gown represented to freshmen their first taste of university manhood.[64] Alfred Henry Lawrence (a Trinity College undergraduate from 1884 to 1887) underscored this point in his *Reminiscences of Cambridge Life,* which was privately published in London in 1889. Identifying the donning of cap and gown as a noteworthy moment, Lawrence wrote, "Returning from my walk it was time to put on Cap and Gown for the first time in real earnest, and pay a visit to my Tutor."[65] In both artistic depictions of "the freshman" and a humorous ode entitled "To My Gown" which was written, in 1874, by Gordon Campbell (an Exeter College, Oxford undergraduate from 1871 to 1875), the cap and gown figured prominently as a signifier of manly rank and status:

> O gown in which I first began
> To be a bona fide man,
> Until the day of my degree
> My one companion thou must be.[66]

In addition to performing these functions, caps and gowns also represented one of the many Oxbridge traditions that had to be comprehended and mastered by new students. For senior undergraduates and outside observers alike, the freshman's inability to fully grasp the intricacies of sartorial etiquette was a potent reminder of his greenness. Helpful hints to freshmen not only instructed them in how to wear the academic costume but also reminded them of their lowly status in the student hierarchy. Charles Dickens the younger was careful to instruct freshmen on this matter, in his "Dictionary of the University of Cambridge," in a way that emphasized the young man's transition both from boy to man and from outsider to insider: "Having arrived, one of the first things is to get a cap and gown, which have to be worn in a peculiar way; the latter with the loop inside, and the former so placed on the head that the wearer can see one of the four corners (there is only one way of doing this)."[67] This level of sometimes humorous, but always very precise, prescription regarding caps and gowns continued to be a regular feature, well into the twentieth century, of the books, pamphlets, and magazines that were directed at new students. In a 1909 guide for freshmen written by Oxford undergraduates, discussions of the etiquette of this particular form of dress figured prominently: "It is considered one of the seven deadly sins to wear an ordinary tweed cap with a gown, or to use a walking stick with a gown."[68]

The donning of somewhat anachronistic garb helped to unify disparate undergraduates, but it also served, like the Oxford or Cambridge letter and the critiques of university novels discussed above, to differentiate the included from the excluded, the knowledgeable from the ignorant. The separation of insiders and outsiders reinforced the social, economic, and political clout that many of these young men, as members of Britain's ascendant professional classes, possessed. This general tendency functioned, then, as an important cornerstone in the construction of Oxbridge distinctiveness and superiority by ensuring informally that the secrets of the "club" were carefully protected. This protection was repeated in the legal and medical professions, politics, and the exclusive and homosocial clubs of London and other cities that became such important haunts for upper-middle-class men in the late nineteenth century.[69]

Definitions of the Undergraduate

Oxbridge men were, in socio-economic terms, drawn chiefly from the higher ranks of British society.[70] Contemporary observers, like one 1857 contributor to the *Oxford Critic and University Magazine,* generally agreed that "as a rule" late Victorian and Edwardian undergraduates were "gentlemen,"[71] meaning that they were firmly upper-middle-class and usually from a professional or minor landed family with an income in excess of £300 per annum. Such families constituted anywhere from 2 to 11.6 percent of the population between the years 1867 and 1904.[72] While these labels and statistics reflected irrefutable material prosperity and genuine political and economic power, their meanings in undergraduate culture were never entirely stable. Class, as a modern category of identity, should never be seen simply as a reflection of economic conditions or circumstances (and therefore an essentialized or real "thing"), but rather as the product of a whole range of "subsidiary characteristics," cultural practices, and discursive formulations.[73] To illustrate this point and to build on the assertions of such historians as Patrick Joyce and Dror Wahrman, I analyze, in the remaining pages of this chapter, how junior members of the universities defined themselves and discussed, in always mutable and occasionally contradictory and inconsistent ways, the categories of middle-class, professional, gentlemanly, and British in the magazines, newspapers, reviews, and memoirs that they produced between the years 1850 and 1920.[74]

Where Oxbridge undergraduates saw themselves in the class structures of British society is somewhat difficult to determine. They seemed generally certain of their position as an elite, but whether the values of that elite were aristocratic in origin or the product of the "great middle class" remained open to some interpretation and reconsideration in the years after 1850. As definitions of elite status shifted with the gradual decline of the aristocracy in the later Victorian period,[75] students struggled to position themselves somewhere between an ineffectual, and perhaps antiquated, landed elite and the excessively philistine and pragmatic business classes. They did not entirely reject the latter in favor of the former but rather sought to chart a middle course in which it was possible to incorporate elements of both while articulating a newly fashioned professional identity: in effect, constituting themselves as a privileged segment of British society whose capital, as historian William Lubenow has noted in his recent study of the Cambridge Apostles, "was in their imagination, their education, and their talent."[76]

This attempt to chart a middle course was clearly in place by the 1860s and 1870s, when undergraduates seemed to shy away from the aristocratic labels that occasionally appeared in descriptions of Oxbridge men in the 1850s.[77] This transformation to what might be described as a middling worldview can be seen in one description of the Cambridge undergraduate that appeared in the magazine *Momus* in 1869. In a snippet of advice that was published in the third and final issue, the contributors (who included E. H. Palmer of St. John's College, G. Anderson Crichett of Caius College, and Walter H. Pollock of Trinity College) reminded undergraduates about to attend the annual Oxford-Cambridge boat race in London to behave in a self-controlled, respectable, temperate, and thoughtful manner. In describing the probable scene and the attendant temptations of the metropolis, the authors of this editorial offered one vision of who the Oxbridge man should be:

> LONDON will be filled with undergraduates from both universities. Let every man remember that to him is intrusted some small share of the fair fame of his own University. It is not every man who can contribute to a victory in the boat race, but every man can bear his part in winning for his University a greater triumph, the *triumph of self-control.* By those very ancients from whom we have borrowed the practice of athletic contests, Temperance was numbered among the four cardinal virtues. . . . The man who yields to the frivolity of a music-hall, the excitement of brawling in public, and the allurements of vicious society, shews that he has not only a diseased moral nature, but a defective understanding.[78]

In this case, the Cambridge student, as an upstanding member of the middle class, was expected (in theory if not in reality) to serve as an exemplar of the university's manly ideals and spirit of self-control when confronted by the licentious and frivolous allures of both working-class and aristocratic London (the latter signposted throughout this article by the author's references to "vicious society"): a powerful rhetorical formulation, articulated in late-eighteenth- and early-nineteenth-century evangelical tracts, prescriptive literature, and other cultural artifacts, that held at least partial sway until the First World War.[79] This notion that the Oxford or Cambridge student fell somewhere in the upper half of the social hierarchy and epitomized virtuous British manliness remained dominant throughout the Victorian and Edwardian eras. One 1903 discussion of the Oxford undergraduate, for example, characterized him as "neither tall nor short, neither of aristocratic birth nor ignobly bred."[80]

While the description of the Cambridge undergraduate that appeared in *Momus* makes it clear that the values of the industrial bourgeois, the gentlemanly capitalist[81] involved in finance, banking, or insurance, and the professional (all of whom possessed middle-class status of one form or another) could overlap and intersect in this period, it is important to note that undergraduates consistently identified their social status, in the years after 1870 or so, in several more precise ways that highlighted their position within the upper reaches of a broadly construed middle order. In a short article that appeared in the *Granta* in 1889, a father's profession was described as the best gauge of a student's social position. In this case, the range of occupations in which the *pater* (the nineteenth-century middle and upper classes often used this Latin word for "father") might be engaged firmly positioned the undergraduate in the upper reaches of the social hierarchy (but not at the very top) and included "country gentleman," "Member of Parliament," "legal luminary," and "Merchant Prince."[82]

The professional elite was clearly ascendant in British society by the early decades of the twentieth century, so much so that it constituted for one contributor to the *Isis* a new "upper class."[83] As neophyte members of this class, undergraduates were keenly aware of the advantages a degree might confer upon them. Indeed, between the years 1900 and 1913, 84.02 percent of Oxford graduates entered one of three occupational categories: the civil service (including local government and the colonial civil service), education, or the traditional professions of the clergy, law, and medicine.[84] For Oxbridge men, then, the universities were something more than institutions of higher learning. They were vitally important incubators, "nurser[ies] of statesmen, rulers and good citizens" that provided well-rounded and fully integrated professional educations and ensured the perpetuation of a new kind of elite status.[85] George Nugent Bankes (a King's

College, Cambridge undergraduate from 1879 to 1883) used an industrial metaphor to convey the same idea in a book of reminiscences that he published in 1883. Of himself and the fellow students on his college "staircase" he observed, "we are a regular factory of bishops, statesmen, judges, and what not *in futuro.*"[86]

Ideas of this sort were clearly at work in the mind of one author who published, in 1873, an article on medical training at Cambridge in the *Cantab,* a short-lived magazine of fiction and non-fiction. From his perspective, the ancient universities were peculiarly suited to offer "good training and advantages of association" to Britain's future medical doctors, who had tended, prior to this period, to be educated either at the Scottish universities or in hospitals such as St. Bartholomew's in London.[87] He saw the location of medical training within the universities as particularly advantageous to the upper stratum of "that great middle class from whose ranks are furnished most of the candidates for the various professions." For those who chose to pursue a medical education, Cambridge not only provided practical knowledge, in the form of scientific training and expertise, but also imparted "those gentlemanly qualities which are perhaps more necessary and more valued in the medical than in almost any other profession."[88]

Although more specialized degree courses and technically oriented business careers had become more popular by the first decade of the twentieth century, most undergraduates, as gentlemen professionals and "future governors" in training,[89] envisioned themselves not as avatars of "rampant utilitarianism" but, rather, as liberally educated and self-confident inheritors of national and international power.[90] In the late Victorian and Edwardian eras, this power was often exercised by assuming imperial duties as a member of the Indian Civil Service (the organization responsible for the general administration of the subcontinent which oversaw, among other things, the justice system, road construction, agriculture, and medical care), the Colonial Service, or a missionary society. The Oxbridge man clearly operated, then, within an imperial culture that allowed him to celebrate, as a component of his racial, ethnic, and national identity, the British ability to conquer, administer, and civilize colonized peoples around the globe.[91]

One anonymous contributor to an ephemeral Oxford paper published in 1907 addressed explicitly the role of the university in the creation and consolidation of Britain's burgeoning empire and the special responsibilities of the university man as an exemplar of the imperial race.[92] Oxford's contributions to the empire were, according to this author, threefold. In addition to providing "statesmen, men of letters, and thinkers to the Mother country" and "builders and organizers of the Empire to the Colonies and dependencies," it also functioned as a "center of Imperial and even of Anglo-Saxon education." The undergraduate was peculiarly suited to undertake the "great and sustained efforts" that success in "imperial . . . work" required. In celebrating Oxford's role as the preeminent educational institution in the empire, this author also implicitly connected institutional traditions, the masculine discourse of imperial leadership, and political power in some simple concluding remarks that wishfully exhorted the university to "ever maintain her traditions and the old learning which has produced in the past that which is the most vital necessity of all—real men!"[93]

Definitions of this sort, which were dominant but never monolithically so, led to the production of a climate in which social snobbery and a keen awareness of one's status within class hierarchies, the nation, and the empire figured very prominently. These tendencies occasionally presented problems, however, for students who came from more humble backgrounds.[94] A telling comment on the social prejudices of the universities and the prevalence that the gentlemanly and professional ideals had achieved by the 1870s is contained in the memoirs of Thomas Anstey Guthrie, who had been a Cambridge undergraduate at Trinity Hall. Anstey's father was a businessman of modest means, and Anstey admits that he chose to keep his class origins a secret during his student days out of fear of how they might affect him socially: "No one there asked me what my father was, and I did not consider there was any necessity to volunteer the information. It might not have made them less friendly if I had, though I think in the majority of cases it would have produced a somewhat chilling effect at that period. One is frequently told that all prejudice against trade has now disappeared—but I doubt it."[95]

This propensity toward snobbishness as an essential cultural practice was most evident, however, when undergraduates tried to distinguish, in the writings they produced between 1850 and 1920, between "town" and "gown." The class fissures of British society (especially as they were reflected in relations between masters and servants, lodging-house keepers and residents, and shopkeepers and clients) became a staple theme in student magazines, poems, and cartoons during this period.[96] One ethnographic "study" of Oxford, which appeared in an 1868 issue of the *Oxford Spectator* and was written by Edward Nolan, a St. John's College undergraduate who matriculated in 1864, divided the city geographically along class lines and highlighted the episodes of conflict that occasionally erupted between town and gown: "Beginning from the railway station, you come to a people dwelling in houses, and buying and selling. These are not the true Oxonici, but a newer race of men; nor are they at all times peaceable, but sometimes revolt against the Oxonici; therefore a prison has been built for them near to a mound. Beyond them the true Oxonici begin."[97] For Nolan, true Oxford dwellers were members of the university and its colleges, which were situated in the center of the city and surrounded by lodging houses and places of business. The "newer race," which consisted of Oxford workers, servants, and small tradesmen, resided in the districts of Jericho and Cowley, where businesses, brothels, music halls, and working-class houses dotted the streets. These divisions reinforced the sense of separateness that Oxford men cultivated and mirrored developments in other British cities that witnessed, with the onset of industrialization, the proliferation of class-specific neighborhoods or districts and rail-linked suburbs.

The boundaries that separated the university-educated elite from their social inferiors were most clearly demarcated, however, in the comparisons that were often made between Oxford or Cambridge students and scouts (male servants at Oxford who attended to men in college), gyps (male servants who performed the same function at Cambridge), bedmakers (female housekeepers at Cambridge), and porters. As representatives of the working class, college servants functioned as foils to the admired "noble" or "gentlemanly" traits of the Oxbridge man. At a time when the participation of the working classes in the political process, in organized trade unions, and in the cultural life of the nation was on the rise (facilitated by the extension of the franchise in 1867 and again in 1884), undergraduates sought to emphasize what they characterized as the manipulative, thieving, haughty, proud, and disloyal nature of this particular segment of the British population.[98] The deficiencies of college servants were highlighted in descriptions of their excessive drinking, their powers as extortionists, their ability to make their charges' possessions and provisions disappear at an alarming rate, and their tendency to intrude into one's rooms or offer misguided advice and engage in idle chatter at unwelcome times.[99] As in all other things, however, undergraduates remained inconsistent in their descriptions of scouts, gyps, bedmakers, and porters. Despite a general tendency to denigrate the character of college staff, undergraduates could occasionally recognize the indispensable roles these servants performed as providers of food, cleaners, and, in some cases, confidants.

Class difference was also interwoven with gender difference in undergraduate descriptions of the women who provided services to the various colleges of Oxford and Cambridge. Mothers, sisters, and cousins, those individuals one returned to during vacations and entertained as visitors at the universities, represented one category of womanhood for Oxbridge undergraduates, while female servants, landladies, laundresses, and barmaids represented another altogether.[100] Both clearly served as useful foils in the construction of Oxbridge masculine identities, but the female servant performed a more varied function by reminding students of their superiority over not only women but also members of the working class. Characterized as nuisances, busybodies, and money-grubbing opportunists,[101] and occasionally more positively as combined "foster-mother[s] and maid[s]-of-all-work,"[102] this particular version of femininity contrasted sharply with the domestic tranquility, sweet naiveté, and attractiveness of its upper-middle-class counterpart. For undergraduates, a picture was always worth a thousand words in conveying cultural assumptions. Images of bedmakers, or "bedders" as they were sometimes called in the university vernacular, served to reinforce these points by emphasizing the age, misshapenness, and "roughness" of these women, thus marking their class difference (fig. 1.2). In the end, what distinguished these female servants above all else was their ambiguous position; while the services they provided were essential to the maintenance of the universities and their members, their status within these institutions always remained curiously marginal.

As well as pointing to the elite origins of the student body and highlighting what the undergraduate was not, student authors in the nineteenth and twentieth centuries often sought to identify his more positive attributes, which included, in a generalized sense, his manliness, his gentility, and, above all else, his Britishness or Englishness. The conflation of English and British is intentional here, since the application of English attributes to Britons did not generally present many problems for university men, even those from Scottish, Welsh, and Anglo-Irish backgrounds. The terms "Britishness" and "Englishness" were often used interchangeably by Oxford and Cambridge undergraduates, although they tended to use "English" to refer to the admired attributes or "personal" and "communal" traits of Britons, particularly elite Britons.[103] In descriptions that served to both identify admired attributes and prescribe proper behavior, undergraduate journalists and memoirists alike often located the Oxbridge man at the pinnacle of imperial Britain's gender, racial, and national hierarchies.

THE BEDDER.

Fig. 1.2. The "rough" Cambridge "bedder" as she was depicted in Frank Rutter's book *'Varsity Types: Scenes and Characters from Undergraduate Life* (London: R. A. Everett, 1903), p. 146. Illustration by Stephen Haweis. By permission of the British Library, shelf mark 012331.h.41.

On one occasion in 1871, G. L. Reves, a contributor to the *Tatler in Cambridge,* used a common and long-standing element of British nationalist discourse—Francophobia—in comparing the elite boys and young men of Britain with their French counterparts.[104] According to Reves, the British were superior to their continental foes for three reasons: their "strong Feelings of chivalrous respect for Women"; their "hereditary Loyalty to the Institutions of their Country"; and their "Reverence for their Church and their God." His article "French Novels" goes even further in delineating those attributes that separated the British from the French. Whereas the English youth was best known for his fondness for "manly sports," the French adolescent was characterized first and foremost by his indolence and debauchery. In the words of the author, "The Class of Young men who make *England* famous for their Boat-Races, their Cricket-Matches, and their Pedestrian Feats, make *France* notorious for their shameless, Mode of Life."[105] In this instance, gender, class, and national identities merged and morphed as the undergraduate sought to make sense of himself, his culture, and his activities. Definitions of upper-middle-class manliness were predicated on a conception of Englishness that privileged physical activity, reverence for British institutions, and loyalty. British women, as revered creatures, were the proper recipients of a chivalrous respect that was absent among both French men and members of the British working class. And patriotism, as one true measure of masculinity, set the Cambridge man off as superior not only to the French but also to most Britons.

According to the *Rattle,* an Oxford magazine devoted principally to rowing matters, the traits identified by Reves were not exceptional. Rather, they were those that the "ordinary" student, as the perfect embodiment of the model English gentleman (circa 1886), possessed. In ways that served to reinforce, once again, the connections between class, racial, and gender identities, the author of "The Ordinary Undergraduate" described his subject as the "best model of the ordinary English gentleman." In addition to identifying the gentleman as a peculiarly English creation, this author also enumerated several of his traits. "Bodily activity, manliness, generosity, and evenly-balanced, if not brilliant, intellect" were highlighted as his most "salient features," while "enthusiasm, congeniality, and a vein of chivalry" were thought to "complete the picture."[106] In setting these traits up as ordinary, the author prescribed a particular code of behavior for his readers that many willingly embraced as an identifiable marker of a privileged social status. These traits were conveyed visually in a simple but telling image published in the *Granta* in 1889. Confidence, exuberance, enthusiasm, and bodily activity were easily marked, for readers of the Feb-

Fig. 1.3. The Cambridge University Athletic Club runner as paragon of undergraduate masculinity. *Granta* 1, no. 6 (February 22, 1889), illustration between pp. 8 and 9.
By permission of the British Library, shelf mark P.P. 6058.i.

ruary 22 issue, by the Cambridge University Athletic Club runner's muscular body, handsome face, and self-assured stance (fig. 1.3).

Occasionally undergraduates, as exemplars of Britishness, needed to be reminded of their obligations to their race, their nation, and their gender. In calling for greater enthusiasm at Cambridge in 1899, when the country was at war in South Africa and national confidence seemed to be faltering, one undergraduate contributor to a short-lived Cambridge publication called the *Snarl* admonished Britain's best and brightest for not living up to their potential. While this author clearly recognized that Cambridge, as a "great colony of young Englishmen," was the "best school for life in the world" and an incubator of imperial greatness, he also lamented inaction and apathy among Britain's ablest men, who possessed, in his opinion, "blood, muscle, and brain in quality superb; in quantity well-nigh unlimited."[107] Few Oxbridge men acquired positions of power without paying a price: indefatigable enthusiasm, a willingness to approach every task with British pluck, and an unfailing optimism became for the undergraduate not only hallmarks of youthful exuberance but national and imperial duties.

While definitions of the ideal undergraduate, as the epitome of national greatness, seemed remarkably constant throughout this period (which attests to just how successful undergraduates were in attaching a sense of permanence to these labels in an era of cultural consolidation for members of the professional elite), some important changes did occur as the nineteenth century progressed. First and foremost, perhaps, were the ways in which these definitions acquired a more specific racial meaning. British society placed an increasing premium on its whiteness as contact with racial "others" (in Africa and Asia particularly but also within the imperial metropolis) became more commonplace. Historians have noted that middle- and upper-class national and gender identities were reconfigured in Britain as racial attitudes hardened in the years after the Indian Mutiny of 1857 and the Morant Bay Rebellion of 1865, incidents in which non-white colonized peoples revolted against British colonial authority in India and Jamaica respectively.[108] Undergraduates expressed their racial identities in a variety of interesting ways. Two examples from Oxbridge men reflect the significance of this shift.

An 1861 undergraduate poem about the Oxford University Volunteer Rifle Corps (a volunteer militia), published in an annual volume of Oxford and Cambridge verse entitled *College Rhymes,* celebrated the superlative masculine traits of the British military leader (as embodied in the form of the Oxford volunteer).[109] His ability to hold steadfast in defense of empire and to treat others with equanimity and respect figured prominently in the first stanza:

> WE volunteers, defenders true,
> Will keep peace while we can,
> In ev'ry clime, of ev'ry hue,
> Man is our brother man.

While older notions of the equality of souls, which had informed anti-slavery rhetoric at the beginning of the century, continued to influence racial attitudes in this period (and in this poem), the reader was assured in a later stanza that any sense of universal brotherhood that may have existed between different races and nations could be quickly dispensed with in the event of war:

> But if fierce foes
> With War's fell woes
> Our island home attack,
> Our patient ire
> And rifle-fire
> Shall hurl th' Invader back.[110]

It was the ability to maintain this precarious balance between righteousness and defensive preparedness, and to know which response was required when, that differentiated British men from more volatile, emotional, irrational, and ultimately effeminate colonized peoples.[111]

While racial invective was noticeably absent in this poem, later observers of both Oxbridge and British masculinities readily constructed taxonomies of manhood that drew explicitly on hierarchies of race. By the end of the nineteenth century, racial and masculine identities had become inextricably linked in undergraduate culture. These links were made readily apparent to Cambridge students in 1899 when some of them were chastised by a short-lived publication called the *Screed* for behavior that transgressed carefully prescribed, if not always entirely explicit, boundaries. In the article in question, a piece entitled "Manners Maketh Man" that sought to admonish undergraduates for disruptive and rude behavior in Cambridge theaters, the author resorted to imperial imagery to convey the "foreignness" of excessive unruliness and the impropriety of such actions in British institutions. He maintained, "In truth, the scenes we have witnessed there [at the theater] lately remind us very much of Savage South Africa with its howling Matabele and Kaffirs, but not of a company of those whom we call by courtesy—English gentlemen."[112] Savagery is contrasted with courtesy to describe the difference between the behavior of those within the university at home and of "native" inhabitants of the South African outpost—but not, tellingly, to describe the Afrikaners of European descent against whom the British were actually fighting during the Boer War (1899–1902). Contemporary imperial conflicts thus entered undergraduate discourse in a way that reminded readers of an important political and military crisis while accentuating the distinctive features of the British gentleman that students were thought to embody. Contrasts such as these also bolstered a foundering sense of British superiority at this time, as fears for imperial security, the quality of the British army (and consequently British manhood), and the white race escalated.[113]

* * *

Just as the universities fashioned them into "men of activity, responsibility, and common sense,"[114] undergraduates fashioned themselves, through a range of cultural practices, into an identifiable elite and isolated, categorized, and effectively excluded a broad range of outsiders. Exclusivity, superiority, and dominance became organizing principles in undergraduate culture between the years 1850 and 1920 and served to reinforce not only the Oxbridge mystique but also the status of 'varsity men as future statesmen, imperial leaders, and paragons of British masculinity. Such bold assertions also served, as we shall see, to obscure multiple insecurities about the status of elite British men as well as the British nation and empire. The Oxbridge undergraduate never functioned in splendid isolation, then, removed from the cares, status anxieties, and social dislocations and conflicts of Britain's modern industrial society. Rather, he was suspended in a complicated web of class, racial, gender, and ethnic identities that revealed just how much a part of this broader social fabric he was. By demarcating the university as a male space, emphasizing the rhetoric of emotional attachment that their alma mater inspired, and speaking a slang-laden language, undergraduates ensured that the universities remained subjects of eternal fascination and speculation and, in the process, that the Oxbridge man assumed his rightful place at the top of the British social hierarchy. While the definitions offered above held considerable sway in undergraduate culture and determined, in large part, the ways in which students presented themselves to the wider public, there were of course alternative visions of both the university and the undergraduate that challenged these dominant paradigms. Still, by establishing the basic contours of the undergraduate worldview, this chapter has enumerated those features of a shared culture that helped to determine the ways in which Oxbridge men made sense of the activities that dominated their lives as university students, Britons, and future imperial leaders.

2

The Transition from Boyhood to Manhood

Oxford and Cambridge students, in defining the universities as nurturing spaces, were not simply referring to the role that these institutions played in preparing Britain's imperial leaders for national service. They were also highlighting a more immediate, and arguably more essential, transitional function. It was within these "sacred nurseries of blooming youth"[1] that "fresh scions" arrived as "boys" and were, according to one 1891 contributor to the *Granta,* "new-fashioned into men."[2] The progression that the Oxbridge student made from boyhood to manhood while at college functioned as a crucial unifying experience for undergraduates between the years 1850 and 1920. Despite a diversity of interests, personalities, social and educational backgrounds, and even masculine styles, Oxford and Cambridge men, who ranged in age during this period from eighteen to twenty-four, all had to negotiate their way through the unwieldy limbo of late adolescence and early adulthood, a developmental stage characterized by the Reverend H. G. Woods, in a sermon he delivered to Oxford undergraduates in 1885, as a "critical time" and by social scientists, such as the American psychologist G. Stanley Hall, as both a personal disruption to the young man experiencing it and a potential social problem.[3]

For men from the upper middle classes, whose rising rates of attendance at public schools and universities, longer periods of financial dependence, and ample time for leisure and entertainment extended the experience of youth in the latter half of the nineteenth century, this brief period of life was a crucial and occasionally troubled one.[4] Neither boy nor fully developed man, the undergraduate occupied an ambiguous position in the society from which he sprang. Even though he enjoyed a "new freedom" and was generally "conscious of new responsibilities," his "action[s]," which one 1884 account described as "neither onerous nor unpleasant," always occurred within the safe environment of the university and were never "without guidance."[5] This sense of being betwixt and between, neither a fully independent man nor a completely dependent child, was expressed in numerous ways by undergraduates who seemed only too conscious of what the anthropologist Victor Turner has termed their "liminal" status. Oxbridge men were in a period of transition, during which they simultaneously withdrew "from normal modes of action," behaved defiantly, and were initiated into the responsibilities, rights, and privileges of elite British manhood.[6]

While other historians of the universities, including John Darwin, Reba Soffer, William Lubenow, and Sheldon Rothblatt, have recognized how these institutions functioned as a "threshold for entry"[7] into the adult world for professional men, the gendered, generational, and psychic implications of this transition have generally evaded much scrutiny. The incremental journey toward maturity was marked for undergraduates—and perhaps for other Britons, who may have experienced these transitions, depending on their class background, through apprenticeships or military service—by a series of informal initiations and rites of passage that signified a distinctive stage of life and delineated those masculine traits that distinguished younger from older men.[8] The gender identities that were constructed during this period of the Oxbridge man's life were thus highly age-specific and marked most prominently, as J. A. Mangan has noted with reference to the rise of athleticism at the universities in the later nineteenth century, by intergenerational conflict, opposition, and confrontation between fellows and students, fathers and sons.[9] As they asserted the superiority of youthful masculine visions, increasingly valorized in the later Victorian and Edwardian eras, undergraduates frequently pointed to the deficiencies and inadequacies of college tutors and deans. The years after 1850 were thus marked by more conflict, not less, between dons and students, a "parting of ways" that may have begun in the late Georgian period but became, by the final decades of the nineteenth century, a dominant characteristic of the gendered worldviews of Oxford and Cambridge men.[10]

The undergraduate's incremental progression toward manhood, as we shall see, occurred most frequently in college rooms. Decorated according to personal tastes, these symbolically important spaces helped him cope with his initiation into manhood by allowing him to express his individuality, assert his independence, and enjoy the pleasures of a living environment that, ostensibly, he alone controlled. If, as John Tosh has argued, manhood in the nineteenth century was attained in part by setting up a new household, surely the mimicking of this adult activity within the transitional institution of the university served as a dress rehearsal for the subsequent show.[11] As we will see, however, college rooms also functioned in another capacity by providing undergraduates with a space in which they could subscribe to, and indeed even create, a broad range of historically specific masculine styles, poses, or, in the words of Graham Dawson, "imaginings" that gave "shape, purpose and direction" to their lives as men.[12]

Boys or Men? The Worlds of the Public School and the University

Most Oxford and Cambridge colleges drew the majority of their students from the reformed public schools: elite institutions intended to prepare boys from the middle and, most especially, the upper middle and upper classes for productive lives as British leaders.[13] In addition to emphasizing, in the late Victorian and Edwardian periods, the knowledge of classical languages and literature that was a prerequisite for university admission and elite status more generally, these institutions fostered, especially after the middle decades of the nineteenth century, a spirited sense of community, chivalry, loyalty, teamwork, conformity, and the "manly" virtues of physical strength, stoicism, and anti-effeminacy.[14] To a certain extent, the elite sensibilities and identities that were forged at the public schools were further developed in the universities. Yet, while the parallels are certainly undeniable, historians of this period must not assume, as historian of sport J. A. Mangan and others have done, that the universities operated as mere finishing schools for these quintessentially English institutions. Rather than elucidating, this scholarly tendency has obscured differences in meaning and hindered our general understanding of how Oxford and Cambridge functioned in the formation of elite male identities in the late nineteenth and early twentieth centuries.[15]

Undergraduates certainly recognized the continuities that existed between public schools, on the one hand, and universities, on the other, where Eton, Harrow, or Winchester "old-boys" easily mixed with what the privately educated Cambridge student Alfred Henry Lawrence somewhat jealously identified as "troops of friends ready made."[16] They seemed, however, more interested in highlighting those features of the university experience that served to demarcate the boundaries separating the ideological and social spaces of these distinct little worlds. Student journalists and memoirists, for example, routinely used the theme of personal freedom to distance university men from public school boys. Undergraduates at Oxford and Cambridge, while clearly subject to collegiate and university discipline (as we shall see in chapter 3), enjoyed a life generally free from the intervention of masters, prefects, or head boys. Despite the existence of statutory restrictions that prohibited him, for example, from frequenting public houses, the life of the Oxbridge man was, on the whole, less encumbered than that of the public school scholar. He was free to attend lectures at his own discretion, to entertain independently, and to avoid the tyranny of athleticism, if he so desired.[17] In the words, once again, of Alfred Henry Lawrence, a 'varsity man, upon matriculating, was firmly "'within the gates.'" "Hard restrictions as to going here or going there, doing this or doing that" were nearly absent, and "with very slight exceptions" students were granted an almost "boundless liberty."[18] While this relative freedom from restrictions was vital in helping the undergraduate feel as if he had progressed to another stage of life, equally important were the expanded opportunities that residence in a college presented for uninterrupted private study, contemplation, and rest within one's own rooms, which George Nugent Bankes described as his "headquarters" and base of "operations."[19]

It was thus understood by most undergraduate contributors to student magazines, newspapers, and reviews that although institutions like Eton, Harrow, and Winchester might have molded boys into responsible adolescents capable, as senior students, of self-discipline, it was the experiences of university life that "converted," according to Trinity College, Cambridge undergraduate Hugh Reginald Haweis, the "puny youngster . . . into the muscular man."[20] One Pembroke College, Oxford graduate confirmed this generally held belief when he tried, in 1883, to explain several disturbances that occurred at the college in the spring of that year. Referring explicitly to the metamorphosis that undergraduates underwent at university, he attributed these disciplinary violations to the inexperience and exuberance of younger students who, when they "come up here, . . . are little better than boys for their first year or two."[21]

Acquiring the "glamour of manhood,"[22] as it was labeled in one instance, naturally entailed more than simply stating that the universities were places inhabited by "real" men who, according to Trinity College undergraduate (1857–1861) and Cambridge Apostle George Otto Trevelyan, not only grew in "stature and in grace" while in residence but also achieved a "conscious[ness] of power" and a "burning for the strife" that allowed them to succeed "in the field of life."[23] Undergraduates, as men of ambiguous status caught somewhere between the society of fully functioning adults and the complete dependence of childhood and early adolescence, were especially preoccupied with separating from their boyhood pasts as they traversed the long and winding road to maturity. The repudiation of what one historian of American masculinity has termed "boy culture" occupied a prominent place in the lives of Oxbridge undergraduates, who often stated emphatically their need to discard the vestiges of boyhood and behave in an age-appropriate manner.[24]

The student press often warned undergraduates, especially those who were new to the universities, that boyish behavior and intellectual immaturity remained out of bounds at the 'varsity, where, according to one 1870 contributor to the *Oxford Undergraduate's Journal,* "gentlemen ought *always* act as gentlemen."[25] The editors of the *Undergraduate,* an Oxford paper dedicated to providing, in a sometimes caustic manner, general news to students, chastised "a brace or so of freshmen," in February of 1888, for bringing the amateurish practices and "manner of their school debating societies" into the hallowed halls of the Oxford Union, an organization that functioned as a training ground of sorts for orators and statesmen.[26] In a more revealing example from 1911 of this tendency in undergraduate culture, a poem entitled "Visions of Childhood" in the ephemeral Oxford paper *Why Not?* took some eccentric and flamboyant undergraduates to task for appearing in public with teddy bears tucked under their arms, a practice that tellingly betrayed their inability to discard the toys, accoutrements, and gender ambiguity of childhood.[27] This tendency, brought to life most vividly by the character of Sebastian Flyte in Evelyn Waugh's 1945 novel *Brideshead Revisited,*[28] defied what the poet knowingly described as the usual course of events in the unfolding life of a young man. Undergraduates who "fondle[d] and caress[ed]" teddy bears instead of rejecting boyhood toys and the doting mother did so to "obtain a cheap [a]nd nasty notoriety" by "behaving worse than any babies would." In the process, they also defied the normal course of adolescent development by engaging in behavior that was doubly problematic because it was both puerile and effeminate.[29]

Student journalists scrutinized "teddy bear fondling," boyish debating styles, and excessive boisterousness precisely because they were keen to enumerate accepted codes of behavior within communities that relied extensively on peer approval and validation. These behaviors were, however, also criticized because they dangerously blurred the boundaries that were thought to distinguish the amateurish concerns of boys from the business of real men.

The Hierarchy of University Men

The undergraduate progression toward manhood was not just a matter of repudiating the boy culture of the public school or fully embracing the maturity one was thought to acquire at matriculation. Oxbridge men, like their non-university counterparts, leaped through multiple hoops as they marched toward full maturity. During these three or four years, under-graduates underwent a number of smaller transitions as they transformed from boys into men. Incremental developments marked each phase of the young man's university career and served to underscore the piecemeal manner in which male gender identities were (and are) always acquired. As they progressed from freshmen to senior men, Oxbridge students were reminded of both the hierarchical structure of university culture and the various stages that marked the male life cycle from infancy to old age.

As a freshman, one contributor to the *Cambridge Terminal Magazine* asserted in 1859, the undergraduate entered a period of liminal infancy in which the "little exuberances . . . [of] . . . school and home were worn off"[30] and the excitements of a new world were discovered. Edward Nolan, a St. John's College undergraduate who matriculated in 1864, identified among Oxford "freshers" a general tendency to make mistakes; spend, drink, and eat excessively; and waste time as they struggled, during their first few terms, to find a social niche: "In this age he is very much given to games and he passes many hours in playing with other naughty boys, who teach him wicked words, and encourage him to do what he ought not."[31] The freshman was also, according to a 1901 contributor to the Oxford paper *'Varsity,* plagued by an unrefined personality that tended toward extremes: "boundless in self-confidence or woefully timid—in either case making the same mistakes as his predecessors have made for generations."[32]

As the freshman acclimatized to the university, he entered a boy-stage in which his primary preoccupation was to choose, once more in the words of Edward Nolan, his "line in life."[33] In entering his second year the "'fresher' of last term . . . emerged like a butterfly from his chrysalis state of 'fresherdom,' and . . . put on the glory of the second-year man," parad-ing it "with great eclat before those in whose seat he himself was one short year ago." This evolutionary process continued apace as the undergraduate got closer to leaving the university and entering what was identified in a 1908 article in *'Varsity* as the "great world" of manhood.[34]

Senior undergraduates, as they entered their final years at the 'varsity, were characterized by their focus on more adult concerns. Chief among these new preoccupations was the migration from college rooms out to "digs" or lodgings (in houses that were licensed by the universities but run, usually, by local landladies) and the looming prospect of final examinations. By his last year, the Oxbridge undergraduate usually had found his social niche and position within the complex hierarchy of student culture. In progressing from a "weedy freshman" to a "complete fourth-year man" he asserted a greater degree of independence, eschewed an almost slavish reliance on peer approval, and prepared himself for the hardships of life that awaited him.[35] The senior man was distinguished by his comfort, quiet, and confidence. He demonstrated his position as an established and wise member of the undergraduate community in the contents of his room and his relaxed interaction with college peers, according to the author of a 1902 article on student life simply entitled "Evolution":

> He has accumulated a quantity of crockery that bears his College coat-armour, and a long and dense array of photos crowds his mantel-shelf . . . ; his socks have taken a character for comfort and warmth rather than lightness and open-work. For him is the joy of the loose Norfolk jacket, the négligé tie, and the general impression of carelessness, combined with a certain neatness that still prevails. He is no longer dependent on his neighbour, he has learnt to think for himself, and by the time that he moves into "digs" a corkscrew is the only indispensable article of furniture. He has no longer to make an impression on his fellows: that has been done for good or ill, and he smokes his "birds-eye" without any regard for the opinions or tastes of his friends.[36]

Although the particular fashions discussed in this passage changed over time, the characterization of the senior student as independent, certain of himself, poised, and settled endured throughout the late Victorian and Edwardian periods.

Self-assurance and comfort thus signaled the young man's arrival at the pinnacle of his undergraduate career and his readiness for life beyond college walls. At the end of their journey, undergraduates saw themselves as adequately prepared, indeed anxious, to take on the responsibilities of manhood and engage in the activities of the "cold grey world." Even at the conclusion of their university careers, however, full manhood remained something that they had to continually strive for. A successfully completed B.A. did not mean that one's masculine identity was fully developed, a fact of life underscored in an article entitled "The Parting of the

Ways" that appeared in the Oxford paper *Isis* in 1908. In this case, university students were seen to just be reaching the threshold of manhood when they were awarded their degrees: "In all the fresh-won glory of a B.A. hood they stride away, leaving boyhood forever behind them and setting their faces in the direction of manhood." The freedom and liberty of college, while important to the formation of masculine identities, could pale for some in comparison to the hallmarks of "self-dependence and self-reliance" that were acquired after the undergraduate went down and began "to earn his own bread and butter." It is clear, from this and other accounts, that the prevalent notion of "man as breadwinner," an important feature of adult masculine identities since at least the nineteenth century, informed undergraduate perspectives on what "real manhood" in a professional society ultimately entailed.[37]

The undergraduate did not have to travel this difficult and winding road from freshman infancy to senior-year maturity to life in the world alone. In nearly every instance, the camaraderie and the communal nature of the college existence, as well as the emphasis on hierarchy and initiation that characterized male culture in Britain generally, ensured that the Oxbridge man received abundant advice, both wanted and unwanted, on how to negotiate these complicated rites of passage. Texts, published with an eye to the needs of the young man who aspired to attend one of the ancient universities or to those of a more general readership, provided advice not only on admission standards but also on how new students might assimilate quickly. The "Dictionary of the University of Cambridge," published in 1884 by Charles Dickens (the novelist's son and namesake), functioned in this capacity when it warned readers, in a brief statement, against joining members of the local community in boisterous Guy Fawkes Day celebrations: "Any Freshman . . . who does not wish to air his greenness, will avoid . . . blackguard rowdyism."[38] Words of wisdom tended, however, to come more frequently from senior colleagues (either final-year students or recent graduates) who, by virtue of their elevated position in the undergraduate hierarchy of men, felt obliged to offer their assistance to freshmen and did so, quite routinely, in the pages of student newspapers, in guides published explicitly with the new student in mind, and through word of mouth.[39]

Forceful reminders or warnings of the joys and pitfalls of university life were offered as "words of kindly advice," "hints to freshmen" (sometimes punctuated by illustrations), and instructive or didactic parables (fig. 2.1).[40] These remarks ranged across a broad spectrum of issues, but tended to focus on topics related to the dangers of overconfidence or ex-

Fig. 2.1. John Roger's artistic "Hints to Freshmen," from his enormously entertaining and popular *A Cambridge Scrap-Book* (Cambridge: Macmillan, 1859), pp. 2–3. By permission of the British Library, shelf mark 1322.m.25.

cessive cleverness, the irritations and impropriety of excessive "shop talk" (discussions related to academic study in particular), styles of dress, and college and university discipline.[41] In addition to enabling the freshman to succeed in undergraduate society, these hints also offered the occasional kind word of support during what could be a stressful time. A "Word of Welcome" that appeared in the Cambridge magazine *Granta* in October of 1905 reassured new students that the "self-consciousness" they were experiencing in this "entirely new society" was something that could be easily alleviated as long as they took full advantage of the "admirable guide[s]" at their disposal and remembered to respect Cambridge "convention."[42] Similar well-meaning attempts at easing the freshman's transition to university life frequently appeared in the student press. Often intended to offer new undergraduates, just "out of swaddling," helpful words to the wise, these useful remarks emphasized men's various social obligations and highlighted the ways in which Oxbridge students viewed manhood, as they did professional credentials and wealth, as something that could be acquired by proactively and aggressively shedding boyish pleasures and assuming manly responsibilities.[43] In a leading article that appeared in an 1892 issue of the *Granta,* for example, the new academic year was inaugurated with a simple "[w]elcome to Cambridge" for freshmen in which they were encouraged to "quit" themselves "like men."[44]

"Old Fools" and "Relics": Generational Conflict and the Formation of Masculine Identities

Unequivocal assertions and dramatic eschewals aside, undergraduates were genuinely caught between two worlds. On the one hand, they were certain that their claims to manhood trumped those of public school boys, while on the other, they remained painfully aware of their dependent and inferior status as junior members of institutions that placed them under the disciplinary watch of college fellows, tutors, and deans. As they attempted to deal with this contradiction, undergraduates produced images of dons that betrayed both an age-specific conception of manhood and a characteristic degree of youthful arrogance. Dons were cast, within the hierarchy of masculine attributes, as representatives of an older and decidedly inferior version of manhood, whatever their chronological age. In this formulation, the vigor and vitality of youth were contrasted sharply with a vision of the college fellow that emphasized his advancing years, physical degeneration, "donnishness," and failure to fully assume the "true," public responsibilities of adulthood. Thus, despite the presence of reforming college tutors like Oscar Browning at King's College, Cambridge who sought to fashion college tutors into spiritual fathers and affectionate older brothers, the lines separating dons and undergraduates were sharply demarcated, not blurred, at the ancient universities during the late Victorian and Edwardian periods.[45]

Older men, represented most frequently in undergraduate writings about college dons but also in their descriptions of recent graduates and elder family members, functioned as useful foils for Oxbridge students who were struggling to assert their independence and challenge what African historians Stephan Miescher and Lisa Lindsay have called "senior masculinity."[46] Representations of dons acted as reminders of both the statutory restrictions and the academic requirements that prevented undergraduates from achieving full manhood within the universities; recent graduates symbolized the loss of carefree days and the sometimes unpleasant and burdensome responsibilities of adulthood; and elder uncles and fathers, as the principal sources of financial support for most undergraduates and the ultimate voices of authority, reminded Oxbridge men of just how limited their claims to freedom really were. The tensions that marred relations between undergraduates and these various representatives of older manhood were part of a broader propensity in male culture to assert autonomy by rejecting and denigrating the authority of others and casting off, in the vaguest of Freudian terms, father figures who were, paradoxically, both strangely attractive and potentially threatening. Undergraduates' reactions to these different groups, then, were part of a broader progression toward manhood that was as much psychological as it was physical, cultural, or social.[47]

College dons were especially targeted as representatives of this older variety of manhood after the 1860s and 1870s, when their average age began to increase. While 42 percent of Oxford dons were under thirty in 1874, only 12 percent were so young in 1900. Similarly, the number of dons over the age of fifty increased dramatically during the final decades of the nineteenth century. By 1900, nearly 25 percent of teaching fellows had reached their sixth decade of life, up from a mere 3.5 percent in 1874. The reasons for this are really quite simple. Beginning in the late 1860s, colleges at both Oxford and Cambridge began to alter centuries-old statutes that made celibacy (and hence bachelorhood) mandatory for fellows. Prior to these changes, dons were generally recent graduates, often in holy orders, who retained their fellowships only until they found a suitable parish living or alternative career. With the changes that accompanied what Sheldon Rothblatt has called the "revolution of the dons," a college fellowship became an end in itself rather than simply a step on the way to securing a respectable church income. Dons, according to A. J. Engel in another study of academic life, were transformed within this period into a professional corps of college teachers, often married, whose careers in Oxford (or Cambridge) lasted a lifetime rather than just a few postgraduate years.[48]

These increasingly professionalized college tutors were frequently held up, in the articles, poems, and cartoons that appeared in the undergraduate press, as convenient examples of a particular type of weakened or tarnished manhood, as "uninteresting," aloof, hypocritical, suspicious, and "crumbling decrepids."[49] One contributor to the Oxford magazine *Great Tom* articulated this sense of difference when he observed in 1861 that "too great a gulf between the Undergraduate and the Don" exists "to permit much cordiality."[50] Seven years later, T. H. White of Oriel College described the don, in the pages of the *Oxford Spectator,* as "a stranger; . . . almost an animal of a physically different class; a being to be treated with a distant severity generally, with a splendid condescension sometimes, with a friendly interest never."[51]

Other representations of the gulf between undergraduates and college fellows often drew the reader's attention to the perceived inadequacies of dons as men. Their tendency to delay or permanently eschew the natural course of masculine development by remaining in the college environment rendered them, in the minds of many undergraduates, no longer men but merely dons, a separate category of existence altogether. "Even dons, we know, were Men once," one contributor to the *Isis* noted in an article on undergraduate athletic successes published in 1892. The editors of *'Varsity,* another Oxford paper, also chose to highlight these distinctions when they published a leading piece in their October 21, 1902, issue simply titled "Dons and Men."[52] Undergraduates' usage of the term "men" to describe themselves alone pointed to a myopic worldview that placed students at the center of the universe and relegated the don to a position of secondary importance. It also, however, reinforced a masculine hierarchy that privileged late adolescent vigor and identified manhood not only as a specific stage of life but also as a psychic and emotional space that only a select few were allowed to inhabit.

These "flowers of England's youth," as undergraduates were described in one Oxford publication of the 1870s, were thus thought to be vital to energizing the university as a masculine space and making it appealing to outsiders.[53] Lord Alfred Douglas, the insufferably snobbish and unstable lover of Oscar Wilde and a Magdalen College, Oxford undergraduate in the early 1890s, adopted this theme when he underscored the physical and sexual attractiveness of students to women and men alike in an 1892 article that he wrote for his homoerotic journal *Spirit Lamp*. In "An Undergraduate on Oxford Dons," he maintained that it was only natural for visitors, in "coming to a place full of beautiful things and charming young men," to "take no interest in such a thing as a Don, who represents to them the gloomy and dull part of Oxford life." Tourists in this university town, according to Douglas, looked not "for an ugly bearded Don with a black gown and an important air, no, but for a merry boy with a fresh face under his straw hat and a flower in his coat."[54] This erotically charged, and sometimes subversive, emphasis on youthful beauty as Oxford's chief attraction served to deepen the divide that separated the fresh and merry young men from the dreary, dull, and hairy dons of age and experience.

Douglas's focus on physical strength and facial attractiveness occupied a prominent place in a society that became, in the final decades of the nineteenth century, increasingly obsessed with fitness, athletic competition, and the health of the nation, especially in the aftermath of the stunning military defeats that marred the early stages of the Boer War.[55] Students at Oxford and Cambridge considered their vigor, leanness, and alertness to be telling markers of their vital importance to the future of the British "race," especially in contrast to the lethargy, stoutness, feebleness, and indigestion of older men.[56] The stress on health and fitness also foreshadowed what would become a central feature of nationalist discourses about the vitality and importance of the upper-middle-class, athletic, and youthful body at the onset of the First World War.[57]

Thus, while undergraduates could respect both younger college tutors with "manly forms" and older dons who, according to the *Cambridge Tatler* in 1877, delighted in "a fine stalwart young fellow" who worked hard "for his college, both with his head and his muscles," most Oxbridge men viewed dons, in this period, with a critical or suspicious eye.[58] The administrative and academic power of the college fellow, tutor, dean, and university official was almost always seen as a threat to youthful manhood. Undergraduates, in the student press and other writings, expressed a general distrust of all dons, regardless of chronological age or athletic propensities, and in doing so they fostered generational tensions and emphasized the impossibility of egalitarian friendships between these two segments of the university community. One contributor to the Oxford *Shotover Papers* articulated this sentiment unequivocally in a fictional letter to his tutor, published in 1874, which began with a simple apology: "Forgive me if I say that I can scarcely bring myself to regard you as a Friend." For this author, the don's distance from the undergraduate meant that true friendship between the two was impossible: "It seems little short of sacrilege to couple the hallowed name of Friendship with yours; for you yourself can hardly be ignorant of the fact that there is not one of the 25 men entrusted to your charge who would not rather seek advice from the merest acquaintance than from you." The "merest acquaintance," precisely because he shared a similar perspective and occupied the same position in the masculine hierarchy, was more likely to provide some real "sympathy" and not look upon the solicitation of advice as an "impertinent intrusion."[59]

The inability of dons to respond adequately to the intellectual and emotional needs of undergraduates, alluded to in the simple reference to "impertinent intrusions," may have, in fact, been a result of the professionalization of academic life. Some undergraduates, by the late nineteenth and early twentieth centuries, clearly saw dons as opportunistic careerists who were only far too willing to eschew the moral and pastoral responsibilities of their positions to gain personal or professional advantages. In these contexts, then, the "ivory tower" critique of academic life emerged and coalesced, permeating descriptions of both donnish masculinity and the relationship between students and college fellows. In a 1908 poem entitled "A One-Sided Friendship," a contributor to the Oxford magazine *Magnum* warned readers not to expend energy on establishing friendships with dons (in the hope that they might, for example, improve their chances on examinations), reminding them that college fellows who willingly befriended undergraduates usually had ulterior motives. In a humorous final stanza, the likelihood of reciprocal and mutually beneficial friendships between dons and students was questioned:

Fellow-victims, beware! Do not make the mistake
That a Don is as ready to give as to take.
No! His affable conduct *in term* is the stake
Which he plays for his private immunity's sake—
When the *term ends* he's not worth a rap.
It is worth a Don's while to be friendly to *you,*
But it has no advantage from your point of view;
He may save his own skin, and a ragging or two,
But if *you* are in trouble, *he* won't pull you through.
A Don is the DEVIL—verb.sap.

This poem as a whole functioned as a prescriptive warning about those dons, labeled "notorious worm[s],"[60] who never had the best interest of students in mind and abused their roles as disciplinarians and examiners alike by needlessly and callously punishing or failing undergraduates.[61] According to this perspective, true camaraderie, as opposed to the façade of friendship that characterized relations between some tutors and their charges, could only be achieved among junior members of the universities. The ethics of teamwork, commitment, connection, selflessness, and friendship that, on the surface, united undergraduates were almost entirely absent in selfish dons, whose own sense of brotherhood was corrupted by their exercise of power.

Undergraduate disdain for dons sprang, in large part, from the fact that they functioned as obstacles to adulthood and reminders of the Oxbridge student's liminal status. As impediments to the assertion of undergraduate independence, this particular group of older men were described in Douglas's 1892 article as wholly uninteresting and "perpetually in [the] way." According to the young aristocrat, they prevented undergraduates from "cultivat[ing] their intellects by reading in their own way, or express[ing] their joy in life by making a noise or doing some other equally irrational and delightful thing."[62] The tension that he described between constraint (represented in the form of the don) and freedom characterized, in a very real way, the progression from boyhood to manhood for the Oxbridge undergraduate and allowed him to articulate some of his concerns about the ambiguities, difficulties, and uncertainties associated more generally with later adolescence.

Undergraduate Sanctuaries: Rooms and the Elusive Quest for Independence

While undergraduates frequently complained about the restraining influences of dons and, as we shall see in the next chapter, institutional discipline, they also sought to carve out for themselves an independent, manly existence in student clubs and societies and college rooms. As retreats that allowed them to evade the watchful eyes of dons, these important social spaces afforded Oxford and Cambridge men with numerous opportunities to indulge in the pleasures of associational life and engage in a particular form of male sociability that was vital not only to the formation of masculine identities but also, as a diverse range of scholars including Matthew Hilton, Paul Rich, and Mrinalina Sinha have noted, to the preservation of elite status.[63]

The university debating societies (known as "Unions" and housed in their own buildings, containing libraries, large meeting rooms, and various private spaces) functioned as gentlemen's clubs of a certain sort and, according to an 1856 contributor to *Great Tom*, "noble monument[s] of . . . Undergraduate energy and wealth."[64] It was within these social spaces that Oxbridge students felt, according to the author of an article on the Union Society that appeared in an 1858 issue of the *Cambridge Terminal Magazine*, "an indescribable sense of freedom" and were able to experience the pleasures of unhindered male camaraderie. Despite the fact that college fellows could and did join the Union Societies as members, a Union was described as an indisputably undergraduate space: "no dons cast their malign influence over its sacred sofas and academic shades—no savage proctor dares profane its sacred threshold—no sycophant porter informs of fines on entrance of its gates in boating straw." Indeed, it was "this freedom, the pride of every Englishman, which constitute[d]" the "indescribable charm" of these organizations and contributed to their significance as institutions broadly symbolic, in this particular description, of British national greatness.[65] These societies were also indisputably male. Women could be admitted as guests on special occasions throughout the period under examination here, but they were excluded from full membership at both Oxford and Cambridge until the 1960s.

By far, however, the most important social spaces inhabited by undergraduates at both institutions, and assumed to be theirs alone, were residential in nature. Rooms in colleges or, after the 1850s in Cambridge and the 1860s in Oxford, private lodging houses functioned as retreats for solitary study, entertainment, or relaxation. Until after the Second World War, when increased student numbers necessitated that suites be divided into single units, most undergraduates occupied sets of rooms, usually consisting of a sitting room and a bedroom.[66] An American undergraduate who matriculated at Trinity College, Cambridge in 1859 assigned the following dimensions to a fairly typical suite of Cambridge rooms: "our friend's domain consists of a front room about fourteen feet by thirteen, looking into the court-yard, a back room not quite as wide, and a small dark cupboard called a gyp [servant's] room, where miscellanea are kept."[67] Anna Florence Ward, a sister of Magdalen College, Oxford undergraduate William Ward and an acquaintance of Oscar Wilde, visited Oxford for Commemoration Week in June of 1876 and recorded in her diary a sketch and description of her brother's college rooms: "very pretty indeed."[68] While Ward's were a bit grander than most (including two sitting rooms, one of which housed a piano), her drawing reflects a fairly common separation of living and sleeping space and general configuration of sofas, tables, and chairs.

These spaces provided for many the illusion, at least, of manly independence, domestic tranquility, and individual masculine space, a theme highlighted in the reminiscences of George Nugent Bankes. In *A Cambridge Staircase*, Bankes commented explicitly on the "intense feeling of satisfaction" that he experienced upon entering his college rooms at the start of a new term. His lodgings at King's were "really comfortable" precisely because they represented a "place where one has made one's surroundings for oneself, and has not the feeling of living there on sufferance; where you can order servants who are not paid by others, can get up when you like, feed when you like, and go to bed when you like."[69] These spaces were also important, for Bankes and others, because they afforded opportunities to exercise masculine power. Men admitted women only on invitation, which served to underscore the latter sex's marginal status within the universities more generally. Undergraduate lodgings, then, whether shared or single, one room or multiple, afforded Oxford and Cambridge students with opportunities to supervise, however minimally, their own servants, create an individual space that bore the hallmarks of distinct tastes and interests, and fashion a sanctuary where it might be possible to shut out the rest of the world. Residential life, while subject to the restrictions of college statutes and university regulations, came to represent for many an independent status, the attainment of relative (if somewhat circumscribed) freedom, and an opportunity for self-expression lacking both at school and within their home environments.

Locating, outfitting, and maintaining college rooms required the undergraduate to assume certain adult responsibilities and functioned as an additional rite of passage that he negotiated in making the transition from boyhood to manhood. While bursars and other college officials frequently assigned rooms to matriculating students, they were allowed a degree of personal discretion in making housing decisions. Edward Jupp, a Christ Church, Oxford undergraduate, discussed the possibility of a move to new college rooms in a letter to his father in 1869. In an attempt to convince the *pater* that moving was a good idea and secure from him the required sum of £60 to pay for the appraisal and purchase of the room's contents, Jupp offered a very positive description of his intended surroundings: "These rooms are so good that I may be very likely to keep them for the rest of my career; and so avoid the trouble and expense of another valuation. I think I said they were in the New Buildings, rather high up, and rather far from Hall and Chapel, but large, airy and quiet; besides the scout, though a less amusing fellow than my late one, seems better in other respects."[70] While the senior Jupp, as the chief provider of funds, had the final say in this decision, his son was able to exercise a level of personal initiative that corresponded roughly to what was expected of men of his age and social class.

Those undergraduates who began their university careers living outside of college walls were often confronted with more complicated decisions, simply as a result of the array of options available to them. On learning that he had been admitted to Trinity College, Cambridge in the fall of 1884, Alfred Henry Lawrence had to decide several things about his lodgings. Was he, for example, willing to live over a shop? Did he prefer a private door or a shared entrance? In the end, he wrote in his *Reminiscences of Cambridge Life,* he "settled to take the rooms on the first floor over Cave's, the boot shop in Sidney Street." This decision was not, for Lawrence, an easy one because he was required, as part of the deal, to "take an extra bedroom." In return for this small sacrifice, however, he acquired a "sitting room . . . of good size," a location "close to the college," and a "private door," which facilitated greater freedom of movement.[71]

Most undergraduates did not, however, make this kind of decision until they searched for outside lodgings during their final year of studies, an experience that became increasingly common in the years after 1860. Migrating out of college, as the undergraduate author of "Evolution" indicated, required the first of many adult choices the student would make about his future. The full exercise of independent decision-making powers in this case was, of course, circumscribed by the strict university rules formulated specifically for these in-town dwellings and enforced by a Lodging House Delegacy in Oxford and a special Syndicate in Cambridge.[72] These dictated, for example, where an undergraduate could search for accommodation and how he should conduct himself once in residence. The initial period of searching for "digs," the term most commonly applied to out-of-college lodgings,[73] could be exciting and full of promise as the young man established new relationships with landladies and servants and experienced, according to a 1901 contributor to *'Varsity,* a "freedom from limitations of time and space decreed by the wisdom of a discreet [college] founder."[74]

The quality of the rooms that undergraduates like Jupp, Lawrence, and the author of the piece in *'Varsity* occupied varied enormously, depending on several different factors. Wealthy colleges (such as Trinity and St. John's at Cambridge, which had, in the early part of the twentieth century, annual incomes around £50,000) generally possessed superior physical resources, which usually translated into more varied housing options for students.[75] Furthermore, undergraduate residential space might be opulent or spartan depending on the student's financial circumstances and the magnanimity of his parents or guardians. Despite these variations, most undergraduates managed to acquire certain necessities in one way or another. College rooms generally required a small sofa, several chairs for dining or drinking tea, a table, bookshelves, a desk, a reading chair, a bed, and the various decorative accoutrements students felt were necessary to express individual senses of style. Photographs, prints, and, on occasion, original works of art were prominently displayed on the walls of many rooms and often occupied a place of pride in the undergraduate's heart. Similarly, mementoes of sporting successes such as oars, cricket bats, and college sweaters might also be displayed. Books were another important furnishing, although their nature depended on the intellectual and artistic proclivities of the individual student.[76]

The acquisition of these various items was for many undergraduates an important step toward adulthood. Most, of course, arrived with cherished items from their home and school, but many had to avail themselves of the services of local merchants to complete their furnishings. Delightful descriptions of shopping permeate some memoirs written by Oxford and Cambridge men. While these descriptions tended to emphasize the necessity of shopping, the pleasures of consumption were never far below the surface. Although shopping, as Erika Rappaport has so astutely reminded us, was constructed as an urban female pleasure in this period, men could not escape its allure.[77] Oxbridge undergraduates, as ambiguous beings, vacillated between the emotions of pragmatism and ecstasy as they purchased items for their rooms and, in so doing, betrayed the fragility of the divisions that separated the masculine from the feminine, particularly in adolescence.

A full array of responses to the modern consumer experience appear in sources of interest to the historian of Oxbridge undergraduates. George Nugent Bankes's descriptions of shopping, for example, tend more toward the businesslike and the pragmatic. In his book *Cambridge Trifles; or, Splutterings from an Undergraduate Pen* (a collection of essays first published in the *Cambridge Review*), Bankes lists, in a fairly straightforward fashion, the items he acquired for his rooms upon coming up for the start of a new academic year. These included "a centre table, a sofa, a piano, a small table with wonderfully situated flaps, and enough chairs to seat a small temperance meeting." In his discussion of second-hand shops, he clearly emphasizes frugality and resourcefulness. Within these shops, scattered throughout the city of Cambridge and catering principally to the student market, he found "an armchair, a bookcase, and a writing-table, all undeniable bargains, and all capable of being put into good working order after a little judicious exercise of the hinges, drawer-handles, and other component parts."[78] For Bankes, commercial transactions were also markers of masculine status and swagger. In another description of consumer purchases, Bankes emphasized his progression from boyish awkwardness to manly confidence in his interactions with Cambridge storekeepers: "I was a little awkward at first in my commercial transactions, but the lordly air with which I can now go into a grocer's shop and order in a pound of short sixes, or grumble on the recent rise of a halfpenny in the pound in the price of sugar, surpasses description."[79]

While Bankes's depictions were common enough, equally prevalent were more sensual celebrations of the pleasures associated with searching Cambridge shops for bargains and pleasing decorative items. Alfred Henry Lawrence, for example, reveled in entering Cambridge shops that were highly popular among undergraduates. At Farren's, on the King's Parade (an important Cambridge thoroughfare that runs past King's College and is, to this day, home to numerous retail establishments), he "ordered two engravings for [his] room, Millais's 'Gladstone,' and Calderon's 'Captain of the XI,'" which, according to his reminiscences, he "had decided on having." Lawrence most clearly departed from Bankes's pragmatism by discussing these purchases as the fulfillment of certain desires. Calderon's print, for example, had taken his "fancy when in the shop window the previous May," while he had admiringly and longingly viewed the original of Millais's portrait "some years previously in the rooms of the Fine Art Society in Bond Street." In both instances, long-term wants were met through a single act of consumption. The considerable pleasures (aesthetic and otherwise) derived from this purchase were conveyed in a final sentence that illuminated the importance of these selections as artistic and decorative choices: "The boy Cricketer, with bat in hand, made an excellent companion to the 'Gladstone,' hanging one on each side of my fireplace."[80]

The joys of purchasing did not, however, come cheaply. Undergraduates relied on funds from a variety of sources to support them during their years at the 'varsities. While some possessed independent incomes, most students counted on senior family members to foot the considerable bills associated with university education. At a time when most members of the professional middle classes earned yearly incomes between £250 and £1,800 (with only the very richest segments of the upper middle classes earning more), the cost of a year at Cambridge, including rooms and miscellaneous purchases of consumer durables, ranged between £150 and £400, depending on college and lifestyle.[81] Oxford was similarly expensive. The author

Compton Mackenzie remarked on costs in a set of reminiscences he penned for the magazine *Oxford* in 1938. Referring to his own college days (Mackenzie was an undergraduate from 1901 to 1904), he observed, "I should say that the average man's allowance at Magdalen was £300 a year, but Magdalen was considered an expensive college. If one took the University as a whole £180 to £200 was what it cost the average undergraduate, or rather his father."[82]

Given the expenses associated with a university education as well as the considerable consumer demands of young upper-middle-class men, it is not surprising that issues of finance figured prominently in both undergraduate minds and the pages of university magazines and newspapers. As Oxford men like Edward Jupp and Compton Mackenzie noted, pleas and requests for money occupied a central place in students' relations with their parents. J. R. Seeley, the Cambridge don and historian, revealed a general awareness of this dynamic in his 1863 *Student's Guide to the University of Cambridge,* in which he noted, "It will very rarely be found that a young man of any sense goes wrong on money matters when a proper confidence exists between himself and his parents on this point."[83] In an 1892 edition of this book, by T. F. C. Huddleston, parents were offered the following advice: "The more kindly a well-disposed and sensible young man is treated, the more careful he will be, and the more anxious to shew that he can control his expenses."[84] University officials went to great lengths to understand the financial relationship between father and son, if for no other reason than that their own livelihoods partially depended upon it.

Such financial harmony was not, however, the norm. Students often resented the degree of control that their fathers, grandfathers, older brothers, uncles, or trustees were able to exercise over them, a fiduciary reality that served to further underscore the undergraduate's curiously semi-independent position as a young man caught between two worlds. Undergraduates were, not surprisingly, often dissatisfied with the amount of money they had at their disposal. Parents' and other relatives' lack of generosity was regularly bemoaned in the student press. The frequent mentions of occasions when "Daddy wouldn't fork out"[85] or a visiting uncle offered his nephew only "half-a-crown"[86] pointed to some of the ways in which elder male relatives could be viewed primarily as financial agents. Tensions that arose over money matters underscored the generational conflict between men and the difficulties produced by the undergraduate's continued reliance on the familial purse.

The financial universe of the undergraduate was rendered even more complex and problematic by the ready availability of credit from Oxford and Cambridge merchants and tradespeople. Huddleston instructed parents to look not only to their sons' clothing for signs of extravagance and excessive expense but also to their "tailor's and hosier's bills," which were often appended to the account inquiry conducted by undergraduate tutors each term.[87] Undergraduates might therefore avoid making the painful request for family funds by taking advantage of the generous credit that was extended alike to Oxford and Cambridge men and to members of the upper and middle classes throughout the country.[88] Colleges, too, extended a type of credit to their students in the form of battels, which effectively allowed them to charge food, beverages, and college services to an account to be settled according to the regulations of the college bursar.

Undergraduate references to credit and its terms appeared with some regularity. Occasionally, students protested what they deemed to be extortionate prices or practices. In 1865 at Christ Church, Oxford, for example, 108 undergraduates signed a petition alleging that "the prices charged for certain articles by the Butler are such as to cause universal dissatisfaction." Among their complaints were the cost and quality of bread and butter provided at meals and the "dinners and . . . beer . . . supplied in hall."[89] Undergraduates sometimes also sought to warn new students of the need to keep full accounts in dealing with local merchants who, on occasion, engaged in unscrupulous actions like price inflation or bill padding, or sold to students without the university's permission. In the "Editorial Notes" section of the Oxford *Undergraduate,* for example, freshmen were instructed in November of 1888 to "take warning, and look upon receipts (if they have any) as their most valuable possessions."[90]

More often than not, however, undergraduate discussions of credit or business practices betrayed immaturity and carelessness regarding financial matters. Few commentaries focused on the importance of fiscal responsibility or the necessity of punctual payment. Rather, students tended to dwell on the comparative hopelessness of their financial arrangements or the humor of debt. In an advertisement for a parody of Edward Fitzgerald's popular translation of the *Rubaiyat of Omar Khayyam,* published in 1913 by J. G. Brandon Thomas, an image of an Oxford merchant welcoming an easily enticed undergraduate is accompanied by a verse about the "seeds of credit" which, in an attempt to amuse, emphasizes a spending pattern familiar to more than a few undergraduates.[91] Undergraduates did generally recognize that setting up accounts and learning to deal with debt were important steps in a young man's life,[92] but their occasional unwillingness to pay bills may have reflected a more serious ambivalence about assuming the mantle of adulthood and a degree of callousness bred through privilege.

Undergraduates routinely portrayed themselves as people who willfully disregarded notices of debt and the persistent entreaties of bill collectors, whom they referred to colloquially as duns.[93] Their sometimes blatant lack of respect for local merchants and tradesmen was partly the result of traditional town/gown antagonisms and class frictions. To some extent, undergraduate journalists and poets who wrote of such things were simply verbalizing a basic human tendency toward procrastination. They also poignantly displayed the slippage that sometimes occurred between the categories of professional responsibility and aristocratic shiftlessness, idealized types of masculine behavior that informed, to varying degrees (as we have seen), the class identities of Oxbridge undergraduates. Attitudes of this sort were chiefly possible, however, because of a general understanding, encoded in university regulations, that one's father, not the individual undergraduate under the age of twenty-one, was ultimately accountable for debts incurred—a fact underscored in one 1872 poem by the Cambridge student Arthur Clement Hilton in which the perverse joy derived from irritating the *pater* (as a crucial representative of an older, but financially indispensable, variety of British manhood) was duly noted:

> Bills get higher, higher, higher,
> and the parent's wrath is dire.
> His son's resolute endeavour
> Not now to pay nor ever,
> Making him scold and swear and roar.[94]

Like the rooms themselves, financial arrangements to pay for what was contained in them pointed directly to the liminal nature of university life, the ambiguities of the transition from boyhood to manhood, and the difficulties that university and college officials encountered in trying to manage the pitfalls of liberal credit.

On occasion, these liberal credit arrangements led to financial problems for Oxford and Cambridge students, when extravagance and overspending led them into debt. A merchant, a tradesperson, or even a college unable to get results by appealing to the authority and purse of parents or guardians could call in the highest administrative levels of the university: the Chancellor's Court at Oxford and the Court of Discipline at Cambridge. At Oxford, foreign students, undergraduates with independent incomes, and men who had reached the age of majority were the most likely to be called before the Chancellor's Court for non-payment. The debtor was presented with a summons that included a copy of the unpaid bill, the names of the plaintiff and the defendant, the cost of the summons, and the costs incurred by the proctor (a university official responsible for overseeing disciplinary matters) and his servants in locating the undergraduate. Papers from the Chancellor's Court, housed in the Oxford University Archives, reveal interesting information about the frequency with which such cases were heard. Between 1865 and 1905, the Chancellor's Court at Oxford handled, on average, between eighty and a hundred cases a year. Debts generally ranged, in this period, from £1 to £20 and in some extraordinary instances totaled upward of £50.[95] In most cases, undergraduates ran into problems with three groups of merchants: tailors, stationers, and booksellers. One undergraduate, an Indian student by the name of Kudur Shama Rao, incurred, between 1915 and 1918, debts in excess of £50 by purchasing clothing (including a lounge suit and silk handkerchiefs), books (including numerous works by Oscar Wilde), and cycling gear. In cases such as Rao's, the court generally ordered either that the creditors be paid directly or that a plan be created for payment in installments, closely monitored by the proctors.[96] While clearly indicative of some of the difficulties inexperienced young men faced in monitoring their finances, these extreme examples also reveal not only the enticements of the modern consumer society for men as well as women but also the considerable pressures many undergraduates felt to conform to the expectation that their rooms (and their bodies) would function as visible markers of style and substance.

College and lodging-house rooms, decorated with furniture, artwork, and books often purchased on credit, occupied, then, an undeniably central place in the culture of the undergraduate and the formation of Oxbridge identities, especially in an age of increasingly conspicuous consumption.[97] Ownership of the objects within these pseudo-homes functioned as an important marker of manly upper-middle-class status, and the pleasure students took in it is reflected in, for example, George Nugent Bankes's discussion of "my 'things'" and the pleasures of stirring "my coals in my fireplace with my poker."[98] In this way, domestic spaces served, as Leonore Davidoff, Catherine Hall, and John Tosh have all noted in their work on the nineteenth-century middle classes, as crucial a role in the formation of masculine identities as the much-lauded and frequently studied public sphere.[99] Drawing on cultural meanings attached to a range of homosocial spaces, including men's clubs, dens, and hunting lodges,[100] Oxford and Cambridge undergraduates constructed, in the words of one contributor to the *Shotover Papers* in 1874, "every room . . . [as] . . . a paradise accommo-dated to its respective inhabitants."[101] Depictions of the warming pleasures of the hearth, the comfort of the reading chair, and the familiarity of one's pipe all served to mark the room as a place of freedom, refuge, and respite.[102]

College and lodging-house rooms, as masculine spaces, also possessed, however, a range of aesthetic, sexualized, and gendered meanings that point to just some of the ways in which homosocial worlds could become contested and fractured spaces, challenged not just from outside but from within. These were spaces of creativity and self-fashioning: warm and wel-coming retreats in which undergraduates' personal tastes were expressed and individual identities were styled. In an article that appeared in the *Undergraduate* in November of 1888, rooms were seen as telling indicators of a man's personality and demeanor: "It is an old proverb that one can tell a man by his friends, but at Oxford we might with almost as much truth substitute rooms for friends. The decoration of rooms affords an endless scope to the creative genius of the occupier; and in many cases the taste displayed in furnishing and ornamenting rooms would excite admiration of the greatest art connoisseur."[103]

Rooms, personal possessions, and individual tastes were often con-nected with particular "sets" or "types," which included, among others, the rowing man, the dressy man, the dramatic man, and the gambler. Sto-ries and articles about them thus provided undergraduates with opportu-nities to address variety in what could be a fairly homogeneous popula-tion.[104] While variations over time certainly existed, four stock characters dominated throughout the Victorian and Edwardian periods: the aesthete, the athlete, the reading man, and the "blood" or sporting man. Each pos-sessed his own distinct attributes and carefully decorated suite of rooms. Descriptions of the personal tastes of these undergraduate types provided students with an important vocabulary of difference that enabled them to discuss the various masculine styles or poses that Oxbridge men assumed. Masculine and feminine attributes were thus routinely ascribed to a range of material objects in an attempt to establish the connections between gender identity and decorative choices, a point reflected in an 1888 pam-phlet that described one fictional undergraduate's rooms as being "fur-nished with an exquisiteness of taste that betrayed no effeminate proclivi-ties or aesthetic excrescences."[105]

The possession of certain things thus became a symbol not only of wealth or status but also of gender identity.[106] In the descriptions of rooms that appeared in the undergraduate press, a definite, but occasionally unstable and blurred, hierarchy of masculine attributes emerged. The majority of undergraduates undoubtedly valorized those who conformed more generally to the hearty ideal of late Victorian and Edwardian muscular manhood, while denigrating aesthetic and enervating excesses. However, this ideal was not always rigorously emulated. Some slippage between categories clearly occurred, reflecting perhaps a level of masculine ambiguity that deserves further scholarly pursuit. While upper-middle-class notions of respectable consumption demanded that Oxbridge men "avoid a look of coldness, meanness, or inhospitability on the one hand, and of redundance and display on the other," prescriptions of this sort did not absolutely preclude experimentation as undergraduates exercised their newly found privileges as semi-independent shoppers.[107]

Discussions of the specific relationship between masculinity and the selection of rooms and furnishings appeared in both university memoirs and articles intended to instruct undergraduates on the important matter of decorative schemes. The rooms of the aesthete (an undergraduate with artistic proclivities, an interest in fashionable clothes and furnishings, and a commitment to the pursuit of a life full of beauty) were the ones most frequently held up to public scrutiny. As a symbol not only of decorative excess and feminine propensities but also of sexual ambiguity, the aesthete was a sometimes problematic reminder of the slippage that could occur between the masculine and the feminine, the manly and the unmanly, in a homosocial world. In describing each man on his Cambridge "staircase," George Nugent Bankes offered the following description of his aesthetic neighbor Hayling (probably a pseudonym), whose rooms were fitted out in a "lavish manner . . . in the early English style—new paper, new dado, curtains that wouldn't fit anywhere else, & c." As an arbiter of the latest fashions, Hayling kept Bankes up on "the last moves in taste."[108] While Bankes was clearly aware of the ways in which the aesthete could be derided in undergraduate culture as an example of masculine transgression, he asserted that tolerance, not persecution, dominated on his close-knit staircase, where the "community of life . . . destroyed . . . [the] barriers" between the reading man, the rowing man, and the aesthete. Harmony between the different masculine poses of the undergraduate world predominated in Bankes's vision of Cambridge life, in which all men shared alike and had no "compunctions as to using each other's things indiscriminately" or in "associating with each other's friends and trying to adapt ourselves to the different kinds of company that we thus find ourselves brought into." In this case, gender differences between men were celebrated, not feared, indicating the kinds of diverse reactions that could be elicited, even in an environment where hegemonic models of masculine behavior held considerable sway.[109]

Another response to the aesthete, from roughly the same period, reveals an entirely different reaction to this particular masculine style. The author of "Rooms," an article that appeared in the *Undergraduate* in 1888, displayed little tolerance for this undergraduate type, lambasting him for his gender non-conformity and transgression of appropriate masculine boundaries. In this instance, the aesthete's pursuit of a more effeminate way of life rendered his sexual and gender identities ambiguous and betrayed his failings as a "true" man. Rather than being described in the usual masculine frame of reference, the aesthete's rooms were characterized by an excessively feminine décor that bore a striking resemblance to a "lady's boudoir." The inhabitant of these rooms was identified by his fondness for "women's society" and the general adornment of "not only his rooms but his person." His "refinement" was expressed in his choice of accoutrements: "He will have a few good pictures . . . he will also have, as a rule, a piano, it is sure to have pretensions to prettiness, . . . there will be one or two picturesque armchairs, a lamp, whose subdued light pays a gentle tribute to its owner's complexion, a spray of peacock's feathers, and possibly a handsome album on the table."[110] Generally elegant, useless, and decidedly effete, the "objets" of the boudoir tellingly revealed tastes that were both feminine and foreign, anathema to the undergraduate sense of masculine propriety. Montague Compton, an Oxford undergraduate, also established a connection between gender identity and furniture in a 1908 issue of the *Oxford Point of View* in which he noted, "Nothing betrays effeminacy so surely as a mannered bookcase."[111] Whether he was described as "the dressy man," "Algernon Languish," or "bombastes furioso,"[112] the aesthete, distinguished by his "gay apparel," his "bellowing waistcoat," or the "soupcon of powder on [his] vacuous face,"[113] functioned throughout this period as a fraught figure, either celebrated as a wonderful example of undergraduate diversity and refined taste or denounced as a dangerous symptom of a society gone "soft" and feminine.[114]

Other masculine types, generally considered to be less problematic, also appeared in undergraduate descriptions of college rooms. As reminders of the "vertical cleavages in Undergraduate society,"[115] these men and their rooms served not only to delineate different segments of the university community but also to highlight the more desirable, and less questioned, varieties of late Victorian and Edwardian manhood. As in the case of the aesthete, however, words of condemnation for excesses could be interspersed with approving descriptions that revealed a certain level of tolerance for individual eccentricities and a modicum of gender experimentation.

The athlete, as the most valorized of masculine archetypes, appeared frequently in discussions of undergraduates and their rooms. The disposition of one athlete on Bankes's Cambridge staircase, a student of moral science whom Bankes called Milstead, was revealed in his love of cricket and running and his "most wiry and athletic constitution." The "silver and pewter pots of all shapes and sizes" that formed "the chief decoration to his rooms" functioned, for Bankes, as telling indicators of Milstead's athletic prowess, competitive successes, and indisputable gender identity. In sharp contrast to the precision with which the aesthete Mayling's rooms were outfitted, the rooms of the athlete were characterized by a "general chaos," the result of its resident's "habit of putting anything down anywhere whenever he comes in." The athlete was frequently characterized, in ways that reflected his revered status within the masculine hierarchy, as chummy, a real man's man who was, in Bankes's terms, "a very pleasant companion, and a capital sort of fellow."[116]

The consumption of food in these college rooms complemented decorative schemes in marking the gender status of its inhabitant. In Bankes's description of his Cambridge neighbors, Hayling's "aesthetic breakfast" was marked out as feminine, domesticated, and ultimately frivolous, comprising, as it did, "cocoa, toast and some ingenious and delicate concoction got out of the cookery book," served on "old blue china." In contrast, Milstead's athletic breakfast, "consisting entirely of substantials, and not infrequently washed down with beer instead of tea," was something beyond hearty: indisputably manly in quantity, completely functional and utilitarian, in accordance with "the old forms of [athletic] training."[117]

The athletic body, frequently celebrated in undergraduate culture, was often contrasted not only with that of the aesthete but also with the less sturdy type of the intellectual or reading man, rendered slim and farsighted by mental exertion and irregular or excessively spartan meals (fig. 2.2). Reading men constituted that segment of the undergraduate population most diligent about their studies. On occasion, these men bordered on the intellectually pretentious and were sometimes caricatured in the student press for their mildly irritating tendency to engage in shoptalk.[118] The intellectual man on George Nugent Bankes's staircase, a student he gave the pseudonym of Westbury, was a hard-reading mathematical man and a "regular perambulating encyclopaedia." His rooms were "like most ordinary rooms, except they are invariably tidy," a reflection of the reading

A READING MAN.

Fig. 2.2. A contemplative and bespectacled "reading man," from the anonymous *Types* (Cambridge: Redin, 1894), p. 5.
By permission of the Syndics of the Cambridge University Library, shelf mark Cam.d.894.9.

man's quest for order and desire for efficiency.[119] However, Bankes characterized his businesslike attitude as effective and ultimately inoffensive, and his tidiness was not precious, effeminate, or frivolous but, rather, entirely in keeping with the increasingly popular upper-middle-class masculine goals of academic achievement and professional success.

The digs of the reading man were also scrutinized by the author of "Rooms," who characterized them as homey, practical, and ultimately orderly. Masculine domestic pleasure, marked by the presence of books both for examinations and for personal enjoyment, a "good lamp," and "comfortable armchairs," emerged as a prominent theme. The author, however, went beyond simply delineating the contents of the reading man's rooms. He also sought to situate him in the university hierarchy of masculine attributes by referring directly to the peculiarities of the aesthete's "boudoir," indicating the ways in which the transgressions of this undergraduate type could be used as a benchmark in measuring the masculinity of other students. With specific references to commercialized pastimes (mountain and hill climbing, hiking, and smoking) closely associated with male culture and increasingly popular in the later Victorian and Edwardian periods, the author of this piece provided readers with a telling gendered comparison: "Here the carpet will not scorn the muddy boots of the visitor—as sometimes happens in the case of the boudoir—nor will the curtains resent the fumes of a cigarette."[120]

One final undergraduate type—the "blood"—frequently described in the pages of memoirs and student papers alike, also served to police the boundaries of appropriate male behavior and identify the varieties of undergraduate masculinity. The blood, like the aesthete, functioned at the margins of Oxbridge masculine society. He often possessed aristocratic lineage; was enamored of the sporting life, especially when it came to hunting; and was generally devoted not to intellectual pursuits but to physical pleasure.[121] The rooms of the blood (or the "sporting man," as the author of "Rooms" labeled him in 1888), were again contrasted with those of the aesthete. While the masculinity of the sporting man was never questioned in the ways that the aesthete's might be, the article held his general character up to public scrutiny and declared it somewhat deficient in its excess and roguishness. Comfort, contrasted with the frills and fuss associated with aesthetic decorative schemes, served again as a defining marker of the manliness of the sporting man's rooms. Occasionally, these spaces were distinguished by "a smell of alcohol" and the presence of "siphons and soda bottles." Hunting crops, pairs of fencing foils, and packs of cards were other decorative features of these rooms, broadly reflective of the oc-

cupant's predilections. A prominently displayed "collection of photographs of actresses and society beauties" not only betrayed a devil-may-
care attitude and hinted at a reckless association with women but also
clearly identified the sporting man as a heterosexual.[122] In this way, the
aristocratic excesses of the blood were mitigated by his unwavering commitment to and pursuit of the opposite sex, a point reflected in Frank
Rutter's 1903 book *'Varsity Types* in which a sporting man (a fictional character by the name of Arthur Patrick Reginald Chivers Nocence) is described as the founder of the "White Camelia Club," an organization devoted to the entertainment of actresses and dancers at dinners, teas, and
luncheons.[123]

As Oxford and Cambridge students assigned gendered attributes to
their lodgings and possessions and the decorative choices of their peers,
they delineated definitions of masculine styles that were cropping up in
other places in the late Victorian and Edwardian eras. Criticisms, for example, of the aesthete's effeminacy stemmed from concerns about the
strengths of British men more generally and a fear of the feminine that
accompanied the rise of the women's movement near the end of the nineteenth century. This phenomenon, commonly labeled a crisis of masculinity, generated more precise and hardened definitions of what constituted
proper male behavior, especially in an era when the concept of manliness
as an emotive and spiritual state of mind gave way to codes of masculinity
that emphasized physicality, fitness, and bodily strength. This preoccupation with identifying specifically gendered forms of behavior and defining
what was normal for men was most apparent in the emerging social scientific discourses associated with psychiatry, sociology, and sexology. Irregular gender and sexual behavior was especially scrutinized, according to
historian Angus McLaren, in offices, laboratories, and courts as medical
men, scientists, and jurists sought to stigmatize dangerous forms of male
sexual behavior (transvestism and homosexuality being but two examples)
and demarcate the appropriate "boundaries of masculine comportment."[124]

If the decorative choices of Oxbridge men are any indication, however,
typologies of masculine behavior and gender hierarchies were also created
at more mundane levels in British culture. Descriptions of rooms served
to establish, police, and in some instances challenge gender boundaries in
ways that paralleled the regulatory tendencies inherent in the more formal
definitions of inversion, perversion, and irregularity that emerged in the
writings of sexologists. It must also be noted, however, that this tendency
to compartmentalize, marginalize, and contain certain forms of behavior
could be resisted, especially by young men who struggled themselves with

the strictures of normative and hegemonic definitions of what constituted real or genuine masculine behavior. Within this world, then, we see two clear patterns emerging. First and foremost is the evolution of stereotypes, seen most clearly in undergraduate comparisons between the aesthete and the athlete, that came in the twentieth century to be used to separate "queer" from "normal" men. We also, however, see the imprecision with which these categories operated in homosocial worlds. This is not to say that undergraduates rejected normative models or that these educational environments were not in fact oppressive for the men who transgressed the boundaries of masculinity and were considered more and more irregular as time went on. It is, however, to suggest that we should not lose sight of the ways in which these categories operated as overlapping, not distinct, entities.

The emphasis on sociability that runs through these descriptions points to one final, vital function that rooms served in undergraduate culture. While clear and telling indicators of social status, tastes, and identities, undergraduate lodgings also provided spaces in which Oxbridge men entertained others and practiced important masculine social skills. The ability to entertain independently was a requirement in undergraduate society and symbolized further the freedoms as well as the distinctiveness of college life. Fraternizing in one's place of residence with fellow undergraduates constituted a major form of sociability within both universities and afforded students with opportunities for camaraderie, revelry, and the repayment of social debts incurred while in college.[125] Entertaining in one's rooms also constituted, however, an important element of the gender performances that undergraduates enacted daily. When an undergraduate welcomed others into his carefully decorated, and highly gendered, personal space, he was inviting guests to imbibe, and possibly embrace, a particular masculine style. In this way, small parties constituted an easy opportunity for Oxbridge men to traverse not only different geographic spaces but also different forms of social identity in environments that were liminally perilous and safe at the same time. Furthermore, these activities paralleled, on a junior scale, dinners in one's home and, more importantly, the sociability of the London men's clubs which became important focal points for many of these young men later in life.[126]

While small gatherings, usually not involving a full meal, were generally the norm, larger parties called "wines" (especially popular in the years before 1880), where guests could partake of "fruit, dried and fresh, cakes, and biscuits, with decanters of wine" and perhaps musical entertainment, were occasionally thrown in undergraduate rooms. Charles Dickens, in his 1884 "Dictionary of the University of Oxford," noted the sometimes boisterous nature of these events. The frequent singing of choruses from popular ditties, he observed, promoted "good-fellowship immensely, as is evidenced by the walnuts and biscuits which will begin about this time to fly fitfully across the room." Most undergraduates, however, for reasons of expense (Dickens estimated in 1884 that a large wine party could run between £5 and £6) and decorum, stuck to the smaller version of this event, which entailed inviting a "few [friends] at a time to come into one's rooms after Hall [dinner], where a mull of claret, and two or three bottles of wine and a small dessert will provide the most comfortable and rational form of social stimulus."[127] This smaller event became the dominant form of entertainment in undergraduate rooms by the end of the Victorian period. The author and Oxford alumnus Compton Mackenzie confirmed this in the article on undergraduate life that he wrote in 1938: "The private 'wine' of which one reads so much in University novels of Victorian days was already practically extinct when I came up, though in my first term it was the habit of freshmen to invite one another to drink port after Hall in their different rooms."[128]

The importance of pleasure, social intercourse, and the enjoyment of conversation on such occasions was made abundantly clear in undergraduate celebrations of these events, which frequently constructed them as crucial episodes of masculine intimacy, revolving around the enjoyment of physical and oral pleasures in the form of drinking and smoking (fig. 2.3). The Cambridge undergraduate Alfred Henry Lawrence commented on this dynamic in his 1889 *Reminiscences of Cambridge Life,* in which he noted the convivial pleasures of social gatherings: "One thing that made this term pass so pleasantly was that my most intimate friends came so often in the winter evenings to see me. Very often after Hall was over and the night set in, they would return with me to my rooms for tea and coffee, perhaps also to indulge in some games of draughts or chess."[129] The warming intimacies of friends, tea, and coffee were charged in this and many other instances with homoerotic overtones, reflecting the multiplicity of meanings that undergraduates could assign to these events. Such occasions were, however, rendered less problematic or potentially disruptive to the gender order, in both the illustrations and Lawrence's description, by direct or indirect references to men gathered specifically for sporting or competitive purposes (to play cards or chess, or to celebrate athletic victories).

The homosocial nature of these soirées appealed to undergraduates, who saw them not only as opportunities for sociability, and perhaps homoerotic sensuality, but also as occasions to celebrate their independence and,

FIG. 2.3. John Roger's 1859 depiction of college fare and conviviality. *A Cambridge Scrap-Book* (Cambridge: Macmillan, 1859), p. 6. By permission of the British Library, shelf mark 1322.m.25.

according to an 1898 contributor to the *Isis,* "learn much . . . about the charms of the theatre, the eloquence at the Union [and] the sermons at St. Mary's" from their colleagues.[130] The informality of these activities made them prime ways to delight in the pleasures of the unhindered company of men, secure the bonds of friendship, and underscore their separation from the society of women, which could restrict their actions with ceremony and protocol. In one instance in 1877, the *Cambridge Tatler* contrasted the discomfort of a "dinner party of modern society" with the warm conviviality of a "quiet little meeting of six or seven of your best friends." The former was characterized most prominently by the donning of the requisite "tight suit of black and shiny boots" and the fact that enjoyment was entirely contingent upon "the partner who may be allotted to you and whether she is agreeable or not." The little dinner in college rooms, however, was free from such burdens. Here undergraduates could wear "everyday clothes" and "speak out [their] real opinions to any and everyone of [their] company, without laying on the gloss of social mincing politeness, and revive pleasant recollections of by-gone times in a pleasant manner."[131] Clearly, then, the latter was perceived favorably as an unencumbered opportunity for male bonding. The society of women was used in this case to contrast masculine informality and dialogue with a feminine social rigidity and discomfort seen as broadly representative of an occasionally hostile and destabilizing outside world.

* * *

The undergraduate's transition from boyhood to manhood was thus as problematic and troublesome as it was exciting and invigorating. Students, in reacting to the circumstances of university life, tried to make further sense of their position as young men caught between the certainties of boyhood and the responsibilities of adult manhood. As they negotiated this journey, they found themselves reminded of their status time and again. In coping with their precarious position, they often tried to give an impression of confidence that, not surprisingly, frequently came across as arrogance. In so doing, they denigrated age and experience, showed disrespect for those older and younger than themselves, and struggled to formulate gender identities and find niches and sanctuaries which they could call their own. As we move to the more specific features of student life scrutinized in subsequent chapters, we discover that reminders of the undergraduate's ambiguous status and the trials and tribulations of transition were everywhere: in college statutes and university regulations, in examinations, and even in leisure.

3

"Your Name and College, Sir?"
Discipline and Authority

In E. M. Forster's posthumously published novel *Maurice,* the eponymous central character and his loving companion Clive Durham encounter the dean of their Cambridge college as they attempt to sneak out of the city on a motorcycle with a side car. By ignoring the pleas of this angry official, who demands that they stop and explain why they are skipping lectures and using a prohibited mode of transportation, they set themselves up for a serious disciplinary reprimand, which Maurice indeed receives the next morning when he is summoned to the dean's office. During this meeting, he is reminded that "yesterday you cut chapel, four lectures . . . and hall," chastised for his impertinence, and sent down—suspended—until he agrees to write the dean a letter of apology.[1]

In this simple scene, Forster introduces readers of his compelling novel to a system of institutional discipline, encoded in written and unwritten rules and standards of conduct, which carefully ordered the university experience and regulated the activities of students at both Cambridge and Oxford. Nearly every facet of college life, from dining to interpersonal relations, was monitored or controlled in some way through an intricate combination of statutes and punishments that included, according to authors of an 1892 guide for Cambridge students, "fines, confinement within the walls of the College in the evening, rustication (dismissal from the

University for one or more terms or part of a term . . .), and expulsion from the University."[2] These rules, often medieval in origin and made more stringent as student numbers began to increase in the early decades of the nineteenth century, remained omnipresent in Oxbridge undergraduate culture until after the First World War, when it seemed strangely inappropriate to carefully regulate the activities of men who had witnessed the horrors of the trenches.[3]

Disciplinary requirements such as compulsory chapel, described in an 1863 student's guide to Cambridge as an "ordeal by which the steadiness of a man's character and industry may be tested,"[4] did more than regulate the lives of undergraduates, police boundaries, and demarcate the regimented social order of the university, however. Like the trials entailed in making the transition from boyhood to manhood or, as we shall see in subsequent chapters, the experience of undergoing examinations or participating in boat races, these rules and regulations provided undergraduates with opportunities to cement a distinctively youthful and occasionally defiant vision of British manhood, predicated on a spirit of both competition and opposition. While senior members, particularly those who occupied collegiate fellowships, were also expected to adhere to a fairly strict system of discipline and fulfill a range of statutory obligations,[5] it was the undergraduates at Oxford and Cambridge colleges who were most profoundly affected by this form of careful surveillance and what Michel Foucault has called the "control of activity."[6]

In reacting to and, in some instances, resisting university and college statutes, undergraduates cast themselves, sometimes simultaneously, as rebellious sons, aggrieved parties, and sexually mature, assertive young men about town. The reactions detailed in the following pages functioned as microscopic acts of rebellion against the strictures of a society that was, as we have already seen, both liberating and confining.[7] Undergraduate transgressions of statutory boundaries and the caricatures of university proctors and college deans (the officials responsible for overseeing disciplinary matters by monitoring the behavior of all persons *in statu pupillari*[8]) that routinely appeared in both magazines and memoirs represented discernible points of conflict between younger and older men. In opposing authorities who attempted to limit and regulate their independence, boisterousness, camaraderie, and, in some cases, sexual development, undergraduates at Oxford and Cambridge, like the youth of Britain more generally, sought to subvert the traditional order of things and thus assert their arrival at a new stage of life. Conflicts over disciplinary matters between college and university officials, undergraduates, and occasionally townspeople also represented, however, struggles over the ownership of public and private space within the university. In attempting to regulate prostitution, for example, proctors sought to control not only the undergraduate's sexual development and experimentation but also his access to the public, sexualized spaces of Oxford and Cambridge streets.

These battles contributed, in a frequently dramatic fashion, to the ways in which junior members of the universities articulated their masculine identities. Manhood was acquired in this setting not only on the playing fields and in college rooms but also in Oxford and Cambridge thoroughfares and alleyways, spaces that were, in the words of Lynda Nead, not just "passive backdrop[s] to the formation of identity, but . . . part of an active ordering and organizing of . . . social and cultural relations."[9] Undergraduates, then, in discussing disciplinary actions and threats of official retribution for unsanctioned activities, were doing more than simply highlighting the differences between youthful manhood and the "decrepitude" of college and university officials or celebrating successful attempts to evade disciplinary action as manly victories, similar in form to athletic achievements. They were also consciously delineating the ways in which these contests between officials and undergraduates represented a complex struggle over place that was part of a broader quest for modern, urban subjectivities in a world where upper- and middle-class men thought cities, and the sensual and consumable opportunities and pleasures associated with them, were theirs for the taking.[10] In Cambridge's Senate House and Oxford's Sheldonian Theatre; in pubs, restaurants, and hotels; in city streets and in college rooms undergraduates used the policed and monitored university landscape to forge gendered, sexualized, and classed senses of place and self.[11]

The Structures of University Governance, Authority, and Discipline

Oxford and Cambridge, like other educational institutions in Britain, regulated the lives of students to ensure that the institutions' academic, moral, and spiritual goals were achieved. Unlike most schools and universities in the nineteenth century, however, these privileged bastions of higher learning possessed an unparalleled level of self-government, autonomy, and influence, which they had held since at least the fifteenth century. This unique position, derived in part from the connections that existed between these ancient foundations and the established Church of England, enabled them to exercise authority over town residents, as well as graduate and undergraduate members, in the name of promoting public safety and creating a morally upright environment conducive to "learning and the maintenance of good order and discipline."[12] Governing bodies at the universities had, for example, the right to license and control ale-houses, set standards for weights and measures, monitor or prohibit entertainments, legislate with respect to markets and fairs, and regulate prostitution well into the nineteenth century and, in some cases, to the end of the period discussed in this study.[13] Oxford and Cambridge also wielded considerable influence in local and national politics through direct representation in Parliament, a privilege only abolished in 1948 at the end of more than a century of franchise reform. Furthermore, the political activity of university alumni as members of Parliament, cabinet ministers, and prime ministers meant that there was always a voice in government protective of Oxbridge interests.

The evolution of this system of university governance was thus closely related to general national developments. In an effort to maintain religious and political conformity in the century following the Henrician Reformation, for example, university statutes and governing structures were formalized. At Cambridge under the direction of John Whitgift in 1570, and at Oxford under the chancellorship of Archbishop William Laud in 1636, the structure of authority and chain of command were codified in statutes that would dominate institutional government for the next three and a half centuries.[14] With the reforming impulses of the 1850s came certain attempts at rationalization under the auspices of the University Acts for Oxford (1854) and Cambridge (1856). This legislation slightly altered and modernized bureaucratic structures, but continuities with the past remained glaringly apparent. At both institutions, the supreme authority in affairs of government, discipline, and finance rested with the university chancellor or, as was usually the case, his resident representative—the vice-chancellor—who was assisted in maintaining order and enforcing statutes by several deputies, chosen from among the heads of colleges.[15]

While the day-to-day affairs of university government were securely in the hands of these officials, graduate members of the universities were responsible for decisions on larger administrative and procedural matters.[16] At Cambridge, all M.A.s in good standing were entitled to sit in the Senate and, at Oxford, in Convocation. These bodies, when assembled, voted on decrees, changes in statutes, and all forms of legislation affecting the government of the university. At both institutions, smaller specialized councils (known as Congregation at Oxford and as the Electoral Roll at Cambridge) also played a role in governance. Each body, made up of university officials and M.A.s who resided within one and one-half miles of the center of each city, was responsible for voting on all legislation before it proceeded to either the Senate or Convocation, thus giving an effective administrative voice to the dons.

The most elite layers in these bureaucratic structures were the Hebdomadal Council at Oxford and the Council of the Senate at Cambridge, each composed of the chancellor and vice-chancellor, the proctors, various college heads, and several elected members. The two councils' responsibilities were similar, and were effectively summarized in the 1888 *Historical Register of the University of Oxford*. In addition to advising the chancellor and vice-chancellor, these bodies also "deliberat[ed] on all matters relating to the maintenance of the privileges and liberties of the University, or to the due observance of its statutes and customs, and generally . . . consider[ed] and discuss[ed] every measure lending to the improvement or benefit of the University before such measure should be submitted for the approval of the whole academical body in Convocation assembled."[17] Over time, the matters discussed in council varied. Issues like changes to the curriculum, examinations, honorary degrees, the elimination of Greek as a requirement for admission, and the status of women within the universities all received some attention.[18]

Undergraduates, while clearly affected by these larger policy decisions, were most concerned with those aspects of university governance related to the enforcement of codes and statutes and the maintenance of discipline. Both institutions relied on the medieval office of the proctor and the authority of the Chancellor's Court (at Oxford) and the Court of Discipline (at Cambridge) to prosecute and censure those who had violated one or more of the myriad rules and regulations. The proctors, as we shall later see in greater detail, came to symbolize for students the structures of university hierarchy and discipline, the authority of the statutes over their lives, and their ambiguous and liminal status within the university. They thus featured prominently as looming figures in undergraduate culture, a fact revealed in countless humorous images of them chasing undergraduates through the streets or confronting them as they leisurely strolled with pipe in hand or a woman of "questionable" origins on their arm (fig. 3.1). Their primacy as representatives of institutional authority was underscored by their academic garb, which consisted of a special gown, a hood, and a distinctive and prominent clerical collar. In maintaining student discipline, junior and senior proctors were assisted by deputies known as pro-proctors and a group of proctors' servants who functioned as a university police force and were identified colloquially as "bulldogs."

When the violations of university statutes and regulations were par-

Fig. 3.1. The thrill of the proctorial chase, as illustrated on the cover of the Oxford magazine *Bulldog* 1, no. 1 (February 28, 1896).
By permission of the British Library, shelf mark 1866.a.17(21).

ticularly grave or beyond the purview of either the proctors or college authorities, cases involving members of the university *in statu pupillari* could, as a last resort, be referred to the courts of discipline that fell under the direct jurisdiction of the university chancellors. Even though it was infrequently used, the Chancellor's Court in Oxford possessed powers that were quite extensive in their reach: "jurisdiction in almost all cases, whether civil, spiritual, or criminal, in which scholars or privileged persons resident within the precinct of the University were parties."[19] The Court of Discipline in Cambridge was similarly equipped and, like its counterpart in Oxford, had the "power to punish by deprivation of degree, expulsion from the University, or by rustication, or by any lighter sentence."[20]

The extraordinary measures and powers that allowed officials, for example, to limit the interactions between undergraduates and undesirable townspeople bolstered the authority of the universities as hierarchical and multilayered bureaucratic structures and highlighted for all Britons the national significance of these institutions and, more generally, the privileges of the educated classes. The rules and regulations associated with these systems of discipline also demarcated and differentiated official spaces and reminded undergraduates of how these little Oxbridge worlds operated as administrative units, exercising a remarkable degree of control over students' activities and movements. As we shall see in the next section, however, the meanings of the rituals of governance that the universities sponsored in supporting these systems could be contested. Struggling to assert their independence, articulate concerns about serious matters, and formulate masculine identities, students frequently lampooned and disrupted these rituals in public acts of defiance and written expressions of discontent.

Representing Authority to the Undergraduate

While the mechanisms of disciplinary control were most apparent to students who encountered proctors and college deans when they violated some statute or regulation, certain community-oriented activities at Oxford and Cambridge displayed, for participants and observers alike, more generalized features of the structures of university governance. The ceremonies that accompanied Matriculations, Convocation and Senate meetings, Commencements, and Commemorations provided brief glimpses of a pageantry that symbolized institutional authority and prerogatives, displayed university and college hierarchies, and functioned as a ritual of inclusion and exclusion. These ceremonies also delineated the boundaries that separated women from men, junior members of the university from their senior colleagues, and the different visions of manhood that coexisted within these environments from one another.

Many of these ceremonies also functioned as rites of passage for the undergraduate. All men, for example, were admitted to the privileges of university and college membership at Matriculation, a ceremony that usually occurred within two weeks of the freshman's arrival at Oxford or sometime during his first term at Cambridge.[21] At this event, which was presided over by the vice-chancellor, the names of undergraduates were entered into the register of the university and the newly admitted member was "bound," in a quasi-contractual way, "to observe all the Statutes . . . as far as they concern[ed] [him]."[22] For the undergraduate, this event marked his admission to the university as a junior member and enhanced his sense of progression from boyhood to manhood. In submitting to the rules and regulations of the university, however, the undergraduate also agreed to a partial and occasionally problematic extension of schoolboy regulations that smacked of paternalism and opposed the Oxbridge man's burgeoning independence.[23]

The various ceremonies that occurred at the conclusion of the academic year also underscored the authority of university officials and the position and status of undergraduates within the institutional hierarchy. The most important of these occasions were those at which degrees were granted. Undergraduates who had completed the necessary requirements (success in examinations, residency, and the payment of fees) were admitted to the B.A. in distinctive ceremonies that were progressive in nature and peculiarly formal. In the first step, a formal notice or petition (known as a supplicat) granted members of the university permission to take leave of their present status and proceed to a higher level (undergraduate to B.A., B.A. to M.A, etc.). Next, aspiring B.A.s and other degree recipients were invited to participate in the Commencement ceremony itself, a specifically masculine rite of passage that emphasized tradition and relied extensively on a series of carefully articulated father/son metaphors.[24]

At both institutions, the candidate was formally guided through the ceremony by an "elder" (usually a representative of his college and referred to, at Cambridge, as the candidate's father or praelector) who led him by the hand to a dais occupied by the vice-chancellor and the proctors. At Cambridge, candidates were presented for their degrees in groups of four or five, and each remained symbolically linked to his "father" throughout the ceremony by gripping a finger on his right hand, a gesture that was simultaneously infantile and sexualized.[25] At Oxford, the presenter "grasp[ed] the hand of the candidate or one of the candidates with his right, then [said] 'Most distinguished Vice-Chancellor' (and bow[ed]) 'and you, excellent Proctors' (bowing to each in turn), 'I present to you . . . '"[26] After this important ritual of presentation, candidates were exhorted to uphold the statutes of the university, exercise their rights and privileges judiciously, and, in the process, quit themselves like men.

Degree Day ceremonies, and many of the other formal occasions that marked the academic calendar, did not function exclusively as symbolic theaters of display that reinforced hierarchy and authority and delineated the boundaries between governors and the governed. They also presented undergraduates with opportunities to act as something more than passive degree recipients or quiescent observers. Frequently, students at Oxford and Cambridge chose these occasions to make their collective presence known, assert their youthful brand of exuberant manhood, and lay claim to official university spaces. In utilizing these ceremonies as opportunities to air grievances against university and college officials alike, undergraduates extended, into a very public forum, the tensions, disagreements, and differences of opinion that sometimes developed between junior and senior members.

At Oxford, undergraduates most frequently expressed their discontent with university officials at the Encaenia, a ceremony more commonly known as Commemoration (the Oxford equivalent of what at Cambridge was simply labeled Degree Day) that occurred during the final weeks of the summer term and honored both the original founders of the university and honorary degree and prize recipients with public orations and ceremonial processions.[27] The event was held in the Sheldonian Theatre and was dominated by graduate members of Convocation who, by virtue of their elevated status within the university, had an automatic right to enter. Undergraduates were reminded of their marginal or peripheral position by being required, along with "lady" spectators, to present admission tickets and sit in galleries far away from the area of activity and place of power, often referred to as the "pit."[28] While gender relations were never challenged by such an arrangement, due in large part to the fact that female guests at this event were required to be "introduced" by male members of the university, this conflation of youthful manhood with feminized spectatorship undoubtedly reinforced for undergraduates their inferior and ambiguous status.[29]

To counteract the negative effects of this marginalization, and in the process assert the importance of their bold masculine presence within the university, students "enlivened" these dry, formal occasions with what Charles Dickens characterized, in discussing the Degree Day ceremony at Cambridge, as "more or less witty and appropriate remarks from . . . the gallery."[30] Undergraduates regularly attempted to intrude into proceedings by employing the enduring practice of heckling.[31] At the Oxford Encaenia, again dissected by Charles Dickens in his 1884 "Dictionary of the University of Oxford," "the undergraduate [let] loose [his] satire upon the Proctors." Those awarded honorary degrees were greeted and "saluted with appropriate chaff and large cartoons hung over the gallery, which [became] the subject of exciting struggles between the exhibitors and the Pro-Proctors keeping order." Likewise, those who offered speeches, including the undergraduate awarded the Newdigate Prize for English Verse, became "the butts of kindly satire of a stereotyped kind" as they "ascend[ed] the rostrum."[32]

These disturbances, which were characterized more by amusing jokes and pranks than by violent disruptions, remained a prominent feature of both the Encaenia and Degree Day ceremonies throughout the period examined in this study. The unruly and boisterous behavior of undergraduates on these occasions was not merely an assertion of youthful bravado or a simple attempt to get honored guests to recognize the youthful galleries. Contained within these humorous acts were more serious messages about the abilities of undergraduates to disrupt and unsettle figures of authority and briefly subvert Oxbridge institutional and masculine hierarchies.

Displeasure with, and even disgust and outrage at, university and college officials could be conveyed at these ceremonies in numerous ways. At Cambridge in 1870, for example, a group of students friendly with Arthur Clement Hilton, a St. John's College undergraduate from 1869 to 1873 and editor of the Cambridge magazine the *Light Green,* boisterously interrupted the proceedings of a ceremony in which the Greek archbishop of Syros and Tenos was to be awarded an honorary degree. Hilton and his friends took their position in the gallery of the Senate House, a "special resort" characterized by Robert Pearce-Edgcumbe (the author of a short biography of Hilton, who was a Cambridge contemporary of his), as a space where undergraduates have "the best possible view of all the proceedings, and are free to their hearts' content to banter their friends as they proceed to their degrees." Edgcumbe went on to describe the disruption in colorful and evocative terms:

> just when the Public Orator was enlarging upon the character and qualification of the Greek Archbishop, the Archbishop happened to drop his

handkerchief, and stooped down to pick it up. The current song of the day whistled by every street urchin was called *The Grecian Bend,* and Hilton seeing the Archbishop stooping down shouted out *"The Grecian Bend."* The whole gallery full of undergraduates fell at once to singing *The Grecian Bend.* Someone on the dais below explained to the Archbishop that the song was sung in his honor, thereupon the Archbishop commenced bowing to the undergraduates singing the popular song with increasing fervour, so that the roar of hilarious voices in the gallery became tremendous. The dignitaries on the dais below had to pull up the Archbishop and stiffen him, but it was a long while before anything approaching quiet was restored.[33]

The archbishop's inability to grasp the hilarity of the situation under-scored, for the Cambridge undergraduates in attendance, the uniqueness of both formal and informal traditions and ceremonies. He was the butt of this spontaneous prank, and his ignorance was manipulated to reinforce several distinctive components of the student worldview. The prelate, of course, represented the unknowing foreigner to whom undergraduates and senior members alike compared themselves and their insider culture. His innocent attempt to stoop and retrieve his wayward handkerchief also pro-vided the men in the galleries with an entrée into the proceedings. By disrupting the ceremony, inserting humor into an otherwise solemn occa-sion, and seizing the opportunity to embarrass their superior, Hilton and his followers undermined, however briefly, the authority of the officials on the dais, appropriating official spaces for their own purposes.

The irreverence of undergraduates sometimes became too much for of-ficials, transgressing boundaries of decent behavior and threatening the universities' reputations. Their anger and retaliation were not simply ex-pressions of displeasure, but rather pointed reminders of the effectiveness of these disruptions as a means of subversion. The language used in casti-gating junior members for their boisterousness on these occasions was of-ten suffused with disappointment and tension. In 1865, the vice-chancellor of the University of Cambridge expressed deep regret at the activities of undergraduates at "the presentation of Honorary Degrees and . . . the reci-tation of Prize-Poems in the Senate House." This event, he lamented, had been "seriously interrupted by the noise and derisive observations made in the galleries." In articulating his desire that such an occurrence not be repeated, the vice-chancellor struggled to convey to undergraduates the importance of maintaining decorum on such occasions by appealing to their "right feelings": "At a moment when the University is acknowledg-ing the merits of successful competitors for academical distinction and awarding its honours to persons of eminence, it seems to be especially desirable, and in accordance with every generous feeling, to abstain from any conduct which can mar the effect of the ceremonial."[34] In this instance, at least, undergraduates had succeeded in diminishing the power of university ceremonies and challenging authority, and their success is succinctly conveyed in the vice-chancellor's plaintive appeal.

Officials and outside observers often condemned, perceptively and knowingly, immoderation and excessive rudeness at university ceremonies as both ungentlemanly and an unpleasant vestige of schoolboyishness, a characterization that they knew would force undergraduates, keen to eschew these traits, to sit up and listen. One Oxford tutor, in an anonymous memorandum about Commemoration published in 1876, appealed to the "good sense and gentlemanlike feeling" of all undergraduate members of the university. This brief document, in its call for moderation, also defended the rights of undergraduates to engage in these displays of sanctioned disorder as a specifically English "liberty" that "no one desires to abridge." Its tone is, however, largely recriminatory. By questioning whether or not obstreperousness and disruption should be tolerated in any meeting of gentlemen, this shrewd tutor drew explicitly and skillfully on undergraduates' conceptions of themselves and anxieties about their progress through the various stages of manhood:

> Gentlemen you are all by position, the great majority of you in feelings and habits. I call on you then to discountenance and (which you can best do) to put down this practice. I do not refer to the fact that if the Authorities see fit, they can suppress it by severe punishment. Such an argument might be good to schoolboys, but is unworthy of Gentlemen. . . . you can be independent without insolence, and humorous without being vulgar.[35]

Limitations and demands for moderation functioned as potent reminders of how the hierarchy of the university was structured and where undergraduates figured into it. Attempts to curtail spontaneous interruptions of ceremonial occasions also reinforced authority while still offering moments of conflict in which the struggle for independence and the transition to adulthood were enacted and symbolically affirmed.

These grander rituals and ceremonies established a general context of hierarchy and authority within the universities. Undergraduates had little contact with the higher reaches of this hierarchy, and what contact they had was primarily collective, occurring within the anonymity and safety of the crowd. At times, however, they found themselves individually confronting the power of the university or the college. Such encounters with proctors and deans over matters of discipline were the student's most direct and potentially dangerous interaction with authority. The threat of fines or expulsion figured prominently in the undergraduate mind and regulated his actions. Dreaded meetings with college deans and the specter of proctorial intervention remained constant and defining features of undergraduate life and culture at Oxford and Cambridge well into the twentieth century.[36]

College Discipline and the Undergraduate

Oxbridge men were expected to adhere to disciplinary regulations and systems of governance at both the university and the collegiate levels throughout the Victorian and Edwardian eras. Each college had jurisdiction over its finances, appointments, and undergraduate members, independent both of other colleges and of the larger corporate body. Within these smaller institutions, fellows, deans, bursars, and masters governed according to statutes and rules of conduct described in one 1873 handbook for Oxford students as "domestic in . . . character, allowing in some respects of closer restraint, and in others of greater elasticity."[37] Because the college functioned as the primary residential space, dining center, and locus of social activity for undergraduates, they tended to have more frequent and prolonged contact with collegiate officials than with representatives of the university.

The Cambridge statutes formulated after a further round of parliamentary reforms in 1877 illuminate the general principles that guided collegiate discipline throughout this period. At Clare College, those *in statu pupillari* were instructed to "carefully observe the statutes, orders, and regulations of the College . . . attend the appointed lectures . . . show respect to the Master and others who are in authority over them, and . . . conduct themselves in a quiet and orderly manner."[38] More specific regulations were also in place at the colleges of both universities during these years. Collegiate authorities monitored several prominent areas of undergraduate life, including college entertainments occurring within the confines of undergraduate rooms, academic progress, the movement of students in and out of colleges and lodging houses, and chapel attendance and religious life. The specifics of college discipline at Brasenose College, Oxford, as recorded in the diaries of Falconer Madan (a prominent fellow and long-time chief librarian at the Bodleian), reveal some of the more salient features of how this system of regulations worked during the 1870s,

1880s, and 1890s and functioned as a site of conflict for undergraduates and dons who routinely struggled over the control of space and mobility.

In policing undergraduates, college officials focused their attentions on student rooms, the Oxbridge man's "home away from home" and site of entertainment, social interaction, and general conviviality. Concerns about the activities of Brasenose undergraduates in college rooms appeared frequently in the diaries that Madan kept during his years as a tutor. In November of 1877, for example, in a fairly typical scene from the period, an undergraduate by the name of John Bruce was reprimanded for sponsoring an informal dinner. In an attempt to evade a rule which stipulated that suppers for more than four not be served in college rooms, this particular host had ordered a lunch for twenty, kept the food with the assistance of a servant (who, Madan observed, was to be "severely reprimanded" for his complicity), and later in the evening served it to his guests. While not particularly raucous, indeed "in the main very respectable and even fairly quiet," the party remained a violation of regulations and represented a very particular sort of struggle over college spaces that symbolized more broadly the tensions between students and dons. The partygoers, in this instance, tried to avoid detection by "refus[ing] to admit the Porter when sent up, and turn[ing] the lights out when Watson [another college tutor] came in person."[39] Partly as a result of these attempts at evasion, John Bruce was gated (confined to college after dinner) for the rest of the Michaelmas term by Brasenose authorities.[40] Deans and fellows also carefully monitored entertainments and student behavior outside rooms but within the college. Misbehavior in the dining hall, public drunkenness, fighting, pranks, and nefarious or unsanctioned club activities that reflected not only the excesses of undergraduate life but genuine points of conflict, all appeared in Madan's diaries as issues of disciplinary concern.

A perhaps more pressing worry for college officials was the freedom with which undergraduates came and went. Rules dictating the hours during which students were required to be in either college or lodgings, while varying somewhat between institutions and over time, were universal features of Oxbridge discipline. At Cambridge, college gates were generally locked at 10:00 P.M., while in Oxford they were locked closer to 9:00 P.M. (regulations that were liberalized, at both institutions, in the 1940s and 1950s and finally, in the later 1960s, abolished).[41] Once the gates were shut, students were prevented from leaving the colleges, though they might be granted permission to enter as long as they arrived before midnight. Entrance after midnight was forbidden under most circumstances and could result in a rather severe reprimand from one's tutor or the college dean and a fine.[42]

Similar regulations also limited the movement of junior members in and out of town. Undergraduates were expected, for example, to arrive punctually at the beginning of each term, and required to have an exeat (permission for leave) to travel away from the cities of Oxford and Cambridge for more than a day during term. Problems might indeed arise when undergraduates failed to meet these expectations or deliberately tested the limits of the college dean's patience. Madan's diaries are sprinkled with references to students who disobeyed these rules: "[Thomas] Warner and [Francis?] Wollocombe gated for coming up (1) on *Sunday* (2) on *Sat-y* instead of on Friday. Gated (1) for a week after 9 p.m. (2) for 4 days after 9 p.m. . . . Sent for because late in returning on January 26: [Archibald] Rooper, 1st time, nothing done; Kearsley, 3 days (poor excuse) gated, at 9 p.m.; [Edward] Marshall, (mistook the day) gated for a week at 9 p.m.; [Walter] Barnes, gated for a week at 9 p.m."[43] These simple references highlight the complications associated with regulating undergraduates who felt themselves to be at a stage of life that entitled them to the masculine privileges of free and easy movement, unhindered travel, and unrestricted access to the pleasures of the modern world.

Undergraduates who neglected to return to their colleges in a timely fashion may have been suffering from fits of absentmindedness or youthful irresponsibility, but their actions might also be interpreted as miniature rebellions in which they protested and resisted, in sometimes outrageous ways, attempts to control their movements. One boisterous incident at Brasenose College in November of 1879 provides an especially useful illustration of the tensions that could arise between undergraduates and college authorities over issues of entertainment and the freedom of movement. In this case, four men, two of whom were no longer members of the college, created quite a stir when they draped the statue in the college quad with the bedclothes of John Menzies, a second-year undergraduate, "and routed (?) about [Frederick] Hayes & [Edward] Twopenny." Obviously drunk after a dinner the entire group had attended, one of the culprits, William Stirling, "also set the College notices on fire." In a final act of destruction on this evening, Hayes's lamp was smashed against the bedecked statue. In this case, the disciplinary options pursued by the college, while not extreme, certainly packed a considerable punch and reflected the severity of this misbehavior. Stirling was banned from participating in any activity in the college, including attendance at dinner in hall, and confined to his lodgings after 9:00 P.M.; Arthur Cunninghame was to be kept out of college during the next term if he failed moderations (an intermediate examination), and was also gated after dinner each evening; and Arthur Harter and Mountifort Longfield, the two former members, were to "be prevented from entering Coll. after 9 P.M."[44] In this case, violations of collegiate discipline and a blatant disregard for other Brasenose men resulted in a form of punishment that limited the perpetrators' mobility and the opportunities they had to associate freely with their peers.[45]

Disciplinary measures at the collegiate level did not go unnoticed by undergraduate journalists interested in rooting out official excess, harshness, and injustice. The editors of the Oxford magazine *Blue,* for example, described compulsory chapel and college closing times in 1893 as "possibly the two most vexed questions, affecting the undergraduate weal."[46] Observations and complaints of this sort frequently invoked the familiar theme of "don as obstacle" and indicated a general dissatisfaction with restrictive college rules that in effect policed masculine camaraderie. One contributor to the Oxford paper *Isis* illustrated this in 1896 when he contrasted the youthful flexibility of undergraduates with the obstinacy of an older don whose inflexibility stood in the way of nighttime pleasures and, by extension, full manhood: "Perhaps the earliest moral lesson instilled into us in our youth is the Twelve o'clock Rule. One would think Cinderella had been specially designed by 'Varsity authorities to prepare the young idea for future restrictions. Night after night that heart-rending tragedy is enacted in this domain of Learning. Many are the revels untimely brought to their close; many the good stories clipped in their telling—and all this to comply with the inexorable obstinacy of the unreasonable Don."[47]

Deans, as the figures entrusted with the most burdensome responsibilities for upholding collegiate statutes and regulations, also functioned as effective symbols for undergraduate journalists interested in questioning authority, challenging disciplinary structures, or positioning the Oxbridge man in a hierarchy of generation-specific masculine attributes. In lampooning and lambasting these officials, undergraduates highlighted the peculiarities of institutional discipline, further underscoring the uniqueness of the Oxbridge experience and the distinctions between insiders and outsiders that figured so prominently in student worldviews. An example of the form these attempts at humor took appeared in a May 1877 issue of the *Cambridge Tatler.* In this instance, contributor Walter Frith (a Trinity Hall undergraduate from 1875 to 1880) burlesqued a Jesus College garden party, intending to both amuse and undermine by depicting the dean of the college (Edmund Henry Morgan) as weak and infantile.[48] In a fictional tennis match between the dean and the college steward, he described Morgan as having "completely lost control over his temper," flinging "his racquet with violence at the Steward." At a banquet later in the day, in the words of our creative undergraduate journalist, the dean was "found crying inconsolably in a corner, because somebody had poured a brandy and soda down the nape of his neck, and as he himself said with truth, 'He felt very wet.'"[49] Morgan took particular offense at this characterization; John Willis Clark, the university registrar and a collector of undergraduate ephemera, described him as "furiously angry."[50] In the end, he threatened immediate disciplinary proceedings against Frith and others unless they offered a public apology. Morgan's intemperate reaction might be attributed to personal idiosyncrasies, but it must also be read as a reflection of the power journalistic suggestions such as these were thought to possess and the need officials felt to regulate them.

Challenges to college authority, in this case, resulted in the harsh imposition of discipline. Thomas Anstey Guthrie reported that Morgan and other college officials "resented it so strongly that [they] insisted on *The Tatler* being suppressed, its printer 'discommonsed,' or forbidden to carry on business in Cambridge, and Frith himself being sent down for a term."[51] Ultimately, that edition of the paper was reprinted without the offending article and with the addition of a substantial apology from the publisher and printer, who most certainly recanted under the threat of a loss of business. Such disciplinary intervention also rang the death knell for the *Cambridge Tatler,* unable to withstand the long arm of university censorship.

The ability to survive the rigors and dangers associated with college and university discipline signaled, then, the uniqueness of the Oxbridge man, much in the way that compulsory games and the occasional pain associated with them at school were seen by some contemporaries to be a "necessary initiation into manhood."[52] Encounters with college and university officials were frequently discussed in terms of confrontation and struggle, terms that echoed the sentiments of the pervasive athletic ideal. The prevailing discourse valued the fight well fought and the ability to conquer adversity, celebrating robustness, healthy aggression, and good-natured bravado.

The "thrill of the chase" and the fear of being caught became common themes in undergraduate discussions of these episodes of generational conflict and tension. While detection might have seemed inevitable, undergraduates often saw resistance, or at least good humor, as an essential part of the game. This sense of fun was revealed in a 1906 Oxford cartoon by

Graham Hoggarth, in which an undergraduate "hauled up" before the dean for dunking a fellow student in a college fountain responds to the dean's queries about which part he took "in the disgraceful affair" with "the left leg, sir" (fig. 3.2). Depictions of this sort were undoubtedly intended to render a serious situation humorous. They also conveyed a peculiarly undergraduate perspective by privileging acts of open, if honest, defiance and contrasting the superior physical form of the youthful undergraduate with the slouching, pot-bellied, and balding figure of the college dean. In the final, and most substantial, section of this chapter, we turn to a more detailed study of some of these themes by analyzing relations between undergraduates and proctors.

University Discipline, the Undergraduate, and the Proctor

The relationship between the undergraduate and collegiate discipline (personified in its most obvious symbols, the dean and the don) was generally similar to the one that developed between the undergraduate and the structures of university discipline. This system, represented most poignantly by the image of the proctor as ominous threat and looming predator, was reinforced through a whole range of symbolic gestures and ceremonies that not only reminded the undergraduate of his status within the university hierarchy but also demarcated institutional authority and the "internal mechanisms of power" that rendered Oxford and Cambridge uniquely British and elite.[53] These mechanisms also served to distinguish these institutions from the new civic universities like Birmingham and Manchester, which were less residential in character and generally devoid of such precise rules and regulations.[54]

The publication of disciplinary codes in student handbooks, and in particular the presentation of statute books to undergraduates at Matriculation, referred to by the editors of the *Chaperon* (an Oxford paper published in 1910) as the "annual injunction," served nicely to explicate the structures of authority. This latter event, a highly gendered ritual in which students were symbolically reminded of their obligations to alma mater and encouraged to live up to their responsibilities as British men, established the broad contours of a system that regulated their activities for the three or four years they were in residence (fig. 3.3). Routine ceremonies of this sort functioned, on the one hand, as contrived attempts to assert authority, but on the other, as central defining experiences in the creation of unified undergraduate identities.

While undergraduates quickly forgot the minutiae of their statute

HAULED BY THE DEAN.

THE DEAN : 'So you confess that the unfortunate young man was carried out to the fountain and there immersed. Now, Mr. Brown, what part did you take in this disgraceful affair ?'

MR. BROWN (*meekly*): 'The left leg, Sir.'

Fig. 3.2. Graham Hoggarth's rendering of an undergraduate encounter with a dean. *Cap and Gown: Varsity Humours by G. Hoggarth and Others* (Oxford: Holywell, 1906), p. 13.
By permission of the Bodleian Library, University of Oxford, shelf mark G.A. Oxon 4° 219(16).

books, they were routinely bombarded with printed notices that reminded them of the rules and regulations governing their lives. Usually published in the form of a broadsheet, and posted in various public places, including on bulletin boards located outside the porters' lodges of the colleges (where they appear to this day), these notices delineated the jurisdiction of the university as comprehensive and far-reaching and functioned sym-

THE ANNUAL INJUNCTION.
ALMA MATER: "Be Good."

Fig. 3.3. A symbolically charged depiction of the annual presentation of statute books to undergraduates. *Chaperon, or the Oxford Cher-ivari* 1, no. 1 (October 15, 1910): 3. Nothing can be discovered about the artist; the name "Helen Robinson" is most likely a pseudonym.
By permission of the Bodleian Library, University of Oxford, shelf mark Per. G.A. Oxon. 4° 293.

bolically as visible representations of university authority. These messages from the proctors explicitly identified their audience as "undergraduate" or "junior" members of the university, and were carefully worded to convey an appropriate level of sternness.[55]

To ensure that undergraduates complied with this multitude of rules and regulations, which prohibited activities ranging from smoking in public to frequenting hotel dining rooms and bars, proctors engaged in a nightly ritual of "rounds" that enabled them to observe students as they moved about town. William Everett, the American undergraduate who matriculated at Trinity College, Cambridge in 1859 and received his B.A. in 1863, described the ritual for an American audience in a series of lectures he delivered in Boston in 1864. He drew attention, first and foremost, to the dress of the proctors and their bulldogs in discussing their nightly perambulations: "A procession is seen advancing, consisting of a master of arts in full academicals, with white tie and bands, and behind two stalwart men, their coats ornamented with a profusion of buttons." This form of constant vigilance, referred to by Everett and others as "proctorizing," served to unsettle the undergraduate by "reprehending all offences against University discipline and public morality."[56] The visible presence of proctors in the streets of these university towns, especially during the evenings, functioned as an indispensable device for maintaining these intricate systems of discipline and authority.

Order was maintained or preserved through various other means as well. As we saw in chapter 1, undergraduates were identified, and consequently monitored and controlled, by the requirement that they wear an academic cap and short gown. Specific notices issued by the proctors enumerated the times and occasions when these garments were required. Cambridge proctors in 1890, for example, reminded those "persons *in statu pupillari* that they are required . . . to wear academical dress *in the streets* at all times on Sundays."[57] In the manuals passed from proctors to their successors (an underutilized and tremendously instructive source for historians of the universities), it is possible to catch glimpses of how academicals were seen by these agents of institutional discipline as instruments of regulation. In one case the proctors pinpointed two specific benefits to be derived from vigilance in enforcing the rules relating to cap and gown: "(1) It gives the undergraduate a sense that they are liable to discipline. (2) It gives a convenient pretext for dealing with elements of possible disorder, that are not yet absolutely disorderly."[58] While the undergraduate dress codes were somewhat relaxed by the early twentieth century (allowing students, for example, to carry their gown instead of wearing it and to appear without their cap), a general expectation that undergraduates would at least wear their gowns after 9:00 P.M. remained constant between the years 1850 and 1920.[59]

Despite the fact that undergraduates often embraced the cap and gown as a badge of manhood, they could also call them instruments of repression and refuse to wear them, either as an act of protest or, as Reginald Stephen Copleston identified it in 1868, as an expression of "deliberate contempt for authority."[60] In discarding these articles of clothing, either out of displeasure or as a matter of convenience, undergraduates ran the risk of detection. Indeed, violations of the regulations regarding these items were, for much of the nineteenth century, the most common disciplinary matter dealt with by the proctors. Charles Shadwell, an Oxford proctor for the 1874–1875 academic year, noted in his records 290 infractions, 191 of which involved "beaver," the term for appearing in public without cap and gown. At a time when the undergraduate population numbered only 2,460, this was a significant figure.[61] Stories of "getting caught" without these key items were equally prevalent and highlighted for Oxbridge men, often in instructive terms, their vulnerability to fines and other forms of punishment. In a poem entitled "A Fine Tale" that appeared in the Oxford paper *Undergraduate* in 1888, for example, a "careless young student" out for a nighttime stroll is caught without cap and gown by a junior proctor on the "prowl," who forces the offending undergraduate to bring "two large silver pieces" to his room the next morning.[62]

Undergraduates and university officials also struggled over several other disciplinary matters, including prohibitions on various forms of entertainment thought by proctors and deans to contaminate or disrupt the education and moral development of young men. Disciplinary authorities had two predominant concerns: to minimize problems arising from independent and unregulated forms of entertainment, and to maintain a proper distance between town and gown by policing public and private spaces. While undergraduates, as we have seen, reinforced class divisions by positioning themselves above townspeople in the social hierarchy, the disciplinary structures in place at Oxford and Cambridge ensured that interaction between these two groups remained minimally distracting or corruptive.

Most prominent among these regulations were those that restricted the circumstances in which undergraduates might entertain, dine, or drink out of college or lodgings. Generally, bars and public houses remained off-limits to Oxford undergraduates throughout the period examined here. Cambridge seems to have been slightly more lenient, allowing occasional visits to these places of liquid refreshment. The forceful wording of these regulations serves as a general barometer of the disciplinary climate. In an 1870 memorandum issued by the Cambridge vice-chancellor, for example, undergraduates were not encouraged to avoid such places or urged to abstain from patronizing them, but rather were "forbidden" to "give or join in giving an entertainment at a Tavern, without the permission of their College Tutor."[63] Even dining outside of the college or lodging house was regulated. An Oxford memorandum issued to freshmen at matriculation in 1904 explicitly denied undergraduates the right to visit restaurants,[64] although, as the proctors noted in 1897, on "reasonable occasions" special permission might be granted for private dinners in respectable establishments.[65] Injunctions against entering a tavern or public house without permission did not, however, keep undergraduates from doing so. Between 1910 and 1920, proctors at Oxford caught some 620 students in "bars" without permission, illustrating the extent to which undergraduates were willing to risk disciplinary action to claim the public spaces of this university town and thus assert their full status as men.[66]

Disciplinary records at both institutions are full of routine requests for permission to sponsor a dinner for a group of friends, an athletic team, or a society or club. The papers of the Oxford proctor Charles Shadwell contain numerous requests of this sort, submitted by college tutors on behalf of interested undergraduates or by students themselves. Generally simple, these brief notes usually drew on some precedent in their appeals. Exeter College fellow and tutor William Walrond Jackson wrote, for example, in a note to Shadwell, "Mr. Miller has asked me to write to you on the subject of the 'Adelphi' club. The club was allowed a dinner . . . two years ago— and has so far as I recollect always dined together once a year with the leave of the Proctors."[67] The potential for misbehavior on such occasions did not go unnoticed by proctors, who recognized the need to take measures to ensure that the rules of propriety were observed. At Oxford, for example, the proctors' manual for 1887 offered the following words of advice: "before granting leave to any party to dine at any hotel, the Proctors should obtain the names of 2 or 3 (or more according to the size of the party) who are to be held responsible and heavily fined in case of any disturbance taking place."[68]

Precautions of this sort did not alter the simple fact that undergraduates and officials frequently disagreed about what constituted proper or appropriate behavior. In fact, despite official attempts to maintain a certain level of decorum, undergraduates could and did behave appallingly on occasion. One Cambridge case from 1893 illustrates this point particularly well. In early May of that year, a group of undergraduate members of the

Crescent Club, a Trinity Hall organization, and their guests dined in the Bijou Rooms on Peas Hill, a city center street. At about 11:00 P.M., a number of the participants entered the adjoining house, in which "Professor Middleton, his wife, and other ladies were lodging." The events that ensued are best recounted in the words of the proctors: "The men rushed up and down stairs yelling and kicking at the ladies' bedroom doors. A maidservant was knocked down and hurt, and a parcel was carried from the sitting room into the Bijou rooms where it was found the next morning. The men were unable to open the house door to let themselves out, so the door was burst open by friends outside: The bell handle was wrenched off, and a window broken." Considering the violence of these actions, the disciplinary measures taken were decidedly lenient, reflecting the benefits that could be derived from a system of discipline peculiar to the ancient universities. Had the event involved non-university men, legal action would have undoubtedly followed. Aside from apologizing to Professor Middleton, the ten club members who sponsored the event were "ordered to repair the damage to one of the doors &c., and in addition each member was fined two guineas and gated for three weeks."[69] While certainly an extraordinary case, this episode represents one extreme form of undergraduate entertainment and illustrates some of the various ways in which disciplinary officials meted out punishment.

Violations of this magnitude were uncommon. Infractions that occurred in restaurants or following private parties tended to be minor and did not usually involve, according to one Oxford proctor in 1855, "cases of gross immorality" or "incivility."[70] While these forms of entertainment might be viewed as problematic annoyances by the proctors, they were generally containable and did not ultimately threaten prescribed patterns or ideals of class relations and gender divisions. The mingling of undergraduates with undergraduates did not represent a significant deterioration of the barriers that divided town and gown or man and woman and was generally considered, despite occasional points of conflict over what constituted appropriate behavior, to be a normal part of masculine socialization. Activities of this sort did not, in most cases, violate the guiding principle of proctorial discipline, identified in 1904 for undergraduates with a simple statement: "The Proctors exercise a general supervision over the conduct of Undergraduates; and this supervision extends to the company which they keep and the places which they frequent."[71]

These systems of discipline tried various means to enforce good undergraduate behavior. Statutory reforms in the nineteenth century, in part a response to the excesses of the raucous gambling and drinking undergraduate of the late eighteenth century, forbade attendance at or participation in public horse races within the precincts or neighborhood of the university.[72] Regulations were also established to police or limit other forms of entertainment—such as theaters, public dances, music halls, and, as they became more common around the turn of the century, cinemas—that brought the Oxbridge man into contact with the outside world. Undergraduate attendance at popular theatrical and musical performances worried proctors, and other university officials, for several reasons, most prominently because it threatened to blur class distinctions. One proctor, writing in 1905–1906 of the Empire Music Hall on the Cowley Road in Oxford (a working-class neighborhood), observed, "[t]his Music Hall . . . presents some difficulties. The class of entertainment & of the audience do not make it a very desirable place for undergraduates to attend. And the Elm Tree Public House opposite is frequented by a very low class of men & women."[73]

Since most undergraduates behaved, according to one Oxford proctor in 1897, "in an orderly manner,"[74] both universities tended, by the turn of the century, to allow decorous and well-mannered students to attend performances unchecked. Still, when the maintenance of propriety dictated, proctors did indeed intervene. At Cambridge in 1905, for example, bad behavior at the New Theatre became a focus of special attention for university officials. On this particular occasion, the proctors, in trying to ensure that undergraduates conducted themselves in a gentlemanly and class-appropriate fashion, "sent a strongly worded protest to the managing director of New Theatre . . . in consequence of the toleration of ribald and even lewd remarks and of disgraceful behavior of the undergraduates frequenting his theater." To reinforce this point, the university registrar, John Willis Clark, delivered a speech to patrons of the theater early in the May term, warning them of the penalties for bad behavior.[75] The onus in this case, however, was placed not on the students but on the director of the theater, who was coerced into supporting institutional discipline primarily out of a desire to maintain the good favor of a university that had the power to place such establishments out of bounds to undergraduates.[76] Oxford proctors also attempted to exert control over local theater owners in order to maintain proper social space between junior members of the university and residents of the town, suggesting in 1912 that cinemas provide better lighting and a block of "special seats for *men,* to which alone u.g.s [were to] be admitted."[77]

The Oxford proctor, concerned with seat arrangements and social contact in the cinemas that were springing up around the city by the second decade of the twentieth century, echoed in his complaints general anxieties voiced by moralists and social purity reformers alike about theaters as sexualized spaces. As Tracy Davis has noted, theaters and music halls, with their erotically charged performances and storylines, and the districts within which they were located constituted a "geography of erogenous zones" in the Victorian and Edwardian city.[78] Public theaters and cinemas, and the female stars who performed in them, became sites and objects of sexual fantasy for men in both London and the university towns of Oxford and Cambridge. This taste for actresses and music hall performers was developed through the "Theatre Notes" sections of some long-running undergraduate periodicals, such as the *Isis* at Oxford and the *Granta* at Cambridge. The actress as object of sexual desire, emblem of urban modernity, and subject of undergraduate fantasy was also celebrated regularly on the cover of the *Oxford and Cambridge Illustrated*.[79] This erotically charged attraction to actresses and a general assumption among undergraduates that they were sexually accessible is reflected in proctorial records that are peppered with references to students caught "stagedoor loitering," as E. D. Babcock of Worcester College, Oxford was in 1913, or "waiting for, accosting and walking about with [a] Pantomime actress after [a] performance at [the] E. Oxford Theatre," as G. A. B. Chester of St John's College was in 1911.[80]

Given these circumstances, it is not surprising that proctors enforced regulations that were intended to "protect" undergraduates from "loose" women and prostitutes, who were thought to be particularly susceptible to these new forms of entertainment and often conflated (wrongly, as Tracy Davis has found) with professional actresses.[81] University officials were always anxious about the "problem" of prostitution, especially, as Philip Howell has noted, Cambridge proctors in the years prior to the passage of the Contagious Diseases Acts. But their concerns strengthened in the later nineteenth century as middle-class women's roles in public became less circumscribed; as Oxbridge undergraduates felt themselves threatened by the presence of female students; and as gender roles, especially in the eyes of university men and other members of the upper middle and middle classes, became less certain. Within such a climate, jurisdiction over debased women, especially when justified as a necessity in regulating male undergraduates, remained a sanctioned instrument of patriarchy and a way of thwarting modernity's incursion (embodied in this instance in the form of the professional actress, the prostitute, and the female undergraduate) into these ancient male institutions.[82]

This preoccupation with the fantasies and sex lives of Oxbridge men, reflected in the public and private discussions that university officials had about deviant sexual acts between students and townswomen, also contributed to what Jonathan Ned Katz has labeled the "invention of heterosexuality."[83] The reminders of the dangers of prostitutes (a category of womanhood often defined in this context in rather imprecise ways) and the proscriptions of contact with them that proctors and others issued had built into them certain assumptions about the naturalness of the heterosexual impulse. The concept of this impulse emerged first in the writings of sexologists like Richard von Krafft-Ebing and Havelock Ellis but was reinforced through a variety of distinctive cultural and social practices at the ancient universities, including, as we shall see in chapter 5, athletic ritual. Proctors attempted to demarcate the sexual boundaries that separated immoral acts (liaisons with prostitutes, loose women, and female members of the working classes more generally) from respectable ones (romantic idylls involving, for example, sisters of college friends who visited at sanctioned times of the year) and helped to construct an ideal of heterosociability that valorized some forms of sexual contact over others but always assumed that the impulses they sought to regulate were "normal."[84]

Official concerns about sexual activity among undergraduates and assumptions of the naturalness of the heterosexual impulse are evident in the discussions of public entertainments that punctuate the proctorial record. Performances by the Oxford city band, for example, elicited an interesting response from proctors in 1905–1906: "In the Summer Term in particular the band in the evening was a favourite place for promenade or loitering by young women and girls, often very inclined to lark with any young men there. Many u.g.s were in the habit of loitering at the band, or getting into conversation with girls or indulging in familiarities."[85] Officials saw these exchanges as a significant, if largely natural and unavoidable, problem and took appropriate measures to ensure that such meetings were detected and dealt with, in effect limiting undergraduates' access to marginal women who functioned for men about town as objects of sexual fantasy and, as Judith Walkowitz has recently noted, occasionally harassment.[86]

Institutional attempts to limit such flirtations spilled over into other areas which may, at first glance, appear to be entirely unrelated. Officials were concerned about undergraduate modes of transportation throughout the period examined in this study.[87] Their worries were exacerbated by the emergence of motor vehicles and a masculine motoring culture, a development that led proctors to devise a series of elaborate regulations governing undergraduates who either owned or hired cars. Even though only a limited number of students had access to this new and expensive technology, associated in late Victorian and Edwardian Britain with upper-class luxury, university officials still felt the need to issue periodic notices that reminded undergraduates not "to keep any form of motor-car or motor-cycle without leave."[88] What most concerned the proctors were the erotic possibilities inherent in car ownership. Automobiles were modern conveyances that traversed public spaces and enabled the undergraduate to flee proctors easily, but they were also intensely private (especially when driven off-road) sites of sexual contact. Cars thus complicated the proctor's job by making it more difficult to regulate mobility, morality, and divisions between male and female space and between town and gown. Oxford proctors in 1905–1906 worried that associations with "flighty girls of lodging-house-keeper status" were "largely due to the fact that motor cars have made it easy to range further afield."[89] Likewise, at Cambridge, immorality was seen to be on the rise in 1913–1914 largely as a result of the "increasing facilities afforded by motor cars and punts,"[90] which, it was assumed, allowed furtive encounters away from the watchful eyes of university officials.

Proctors' policing of heterosociability and heterosexual contact was, of course, most apparent in their attempts to regulate relations between undergraduates and prostitutes. Disciplinary records reveal a preoccupation with the dangers of prostitution, a desire to contain it, and a concern with carefully articulating the boundaries of sexual propriety. This fixation, however, was expressed primarily in rhetoric, not in actual prosecutions. Cambridge figures, in fact, reveal a general decrease in the number of committals to the Spinning House, the university prison to which women discovered or suspected to be prostitutes were confined. In 1850, for example, forty-seven women were committed to the Spinning House for offenses related to prostitution. By 1870 the number had fallen to fourteen, and in 1880 and 1890 the figures were two and five respectively.[91] This decrease was due primarily to the gradual erosion of university jurisdiction over such matters, as the municipal governments of Oxford and Cambridge assumed greater responsibility in the later nineteenth century. By the 1890s, the authority of the university to monitor the activities of suspected or known prostitutes was ceded to borough councils and independent police forces, resulting in a tendency on the part of proctors and deans to pursue and discipline undergraduate offenders more vigorously.[92]

This real decline in institutional power was also accompanied by an escalation in the discourse of sexual predatoriness that dominated discussions of these "dangerous" women in disciplinary records.[93] Proctors throughout the 1890s and the early decades of the twentieth century indeed saw prostitutes as a very real and disruptive threat, a view made abundantly clear by the catch-phrases and buzzwords used in university memoranda and other documents. For example, an 1892 notice reminded senior members of the University of Cambridge of their peculiar moral obligations: "It is highly important that the University authorities should be able to keep temptation as far as possible out of the way of the young men under their charge, especially in the evenings—and it is highly important also that the streets should be kept in such a state of decency that young women of modest character may be able to appear in them without risk of annoyance."[94] Alarmed appeals also appeared in the more private records of disciplinary officials. In the handwritten instructional manuals that the Oxford proctors passed among themselves in 1887 and 1897, for example, they reminded one another that "it is one of the most important duties of the Proctors to keep the streets clear of prostitutes."[95] Similarly, lengthy discussions of "houses of ill-fame," the most notorious of which were under proctorial surveillance, and general observations about perceived "increases in immorality" among the undergraduate population reveal the level and extent of these anxious ruminations between 1890 and 1920, as well as a prurient fascination with this vice that served, ironically, to make sexual experience with a prostitute central in student culture.[96]

This regulation of undergraduate sexuality and sexual activity, which was primarily concerned with limiting physical contact with women of "loose" character, also served to define the university as a male space. Disciplinary officials were not, however, solely fixated on heterosexual liaisons. Although they are unusual, incidents at both institutions reveal the furor that could be created by same-sex eroticism. These cases appear in the records after male homosexual relations were criminalized in 1885 under the Labouchere Amendment to the Criminal Law Amendment Act. As J. R. de S. Honey has noted, suspicions about male friendships and a general fury about "indecent acts" between boys and men only became a prominent and pressing concern for public school authorities after 1880.[97] The same seems to have been true of the universities, where in the 1860s two chums who lived together could be described as cohabiting "like husband and wife" without raising suspicions.[98] As the category of the homosexual or, to use Havelock Ellis's language, the sexual invert developed and was constructed as a threat to normative gender and sexual identities, which privileged the stiff upper lip and compulsory heterosexuality, proctorial vigilance increased and intense relationships between young men were more carefully scrutinized.[99] Disciplinary systems at Oxford and

Cambridge were thus implicated in the marginalization of same-sex desire as a deviant category of human sexuality, a point reflected in their tendency to label relations between men unnatural while liaisons with prostitutes became simply "undesirable flirtations"[100] that occurred in recognized sites of heterosexual opportunity and pleasure: city streets and alleyways, theaters, music halls, and cinemas.

In two cases from the disciplinary records of officials at Oxford and Cambridge, the concerns about relations between men are clear, despite the fact that sexual acts are never mentioned explicitly. The series of allegations and quasi-legal proceedings that emerged from a case involving an Emmanuel College, Cambridge undergraduate in 1905 are instructive.[101] In this instance, "two boys in town" accused the student in question, Hugh Gonin, of committing "unnatural offenses" with one of them. Despite the fact that this allegation was made before the chief constable, the Police Court turned the case over to university officials on account of insufficient evidence: "the case could not be taken into the Police Court in the absence of any evidence from a person who had been an eyewitness and not concerned." This, however, was not the only reason no criminal charges were filed. University privilege and the symbiotic relationship that was established between the proctors and municipal police protected undergraduates and senior members alike from prosecution on more than one occasion. Oxbridge regulations and statutes, extralegal devices that underscored the unique and privileged position of these institutions in British society, constituted a peculiar system of discipline that safeguarded the reputation of the universities as much as it punished.

While concerns about the moral character of undergraduates were clearly at work here, attempts to regulate sexuality were also driven by a desire to maintain distance between the various social classes in the public spaces of university towns. One of the boys involved in this instance, for example, was of a "notoriously bad character," and his very separateness from the university made his testimony suspect. The undergraduate implicated was not, however, considered entirely beyond reproach despite his repeated proclamations of innocence. The proctors noted several telling factors in considering this case before passing it on to college adjudicators: "the story has got out without any attempt at blackmail; and the undergraduate had been mixed up with a similar case in 1903, where again no positive and independent testimony was obtained."

Oxford proctors also expressed concern about sex between men. In 1914, the vice-chancellor and proctors issued an obscurely worded letter to heads of houses (presidents or provosts of colleges) that highlighted, however obliquely, some of their anxieties. They began their carefully worded warning in the following way: "the attention of the V.C. & Proctors has recently been called to certain serious dangers which may arise to u.g.'s from the practice of employing masseurs." Without specific reference to any instances of obvious misconduct, the proctors requested that undergraduates "not be permitted to use the service of masseurs, either in their rooms or elsewhere, except under the certificate of one of the medical practitioners of the town." One proctor, Arthur Spenser Loat Farquharson, discussed a specific incident, which may have prompted this letter, in a later commentary: "the evil was very odious, & I had a written confession from an u.g. (under seal of confidence) before I took it to the V.C. As far as I know it was confined to one College, but involved at least two men."[102]

These cases reflect the way that the system of university discipline was fixated on moral issues. The indignation that suffused Farquharson's written statements was also present in proctorial comments about a case of "immoral relations with a boy" in 1911, involving St. John's College, Oxford undergraduate L. G. Pocock. In this instance, sexual misconduct was punished not with fines and "gating," as when undergraduates were caught with known prostitutes, but rather with immediate expulsion. Pocock, according to disciplinary records, was "given two hours in which to take his name off the books of the University."[103] Differential treatment of this sort unwittingly sanctioned heterosexual license while vilifying same-sex desire.

The undergraduate's exploration of his sexuality might be viewed within several different contexts. Increased sexual activity in late adolescence and early adulthood was, of course, a simple function of normal physical development, and the patronization of prostitutes was a common enough feature of late-nineteenth- and early-twentieth-century masculine society. Sexual relations with prostitutes were also symbolically important to the oppositional and relational definitions of the self that allowed Oxbridge men, as occupants of a higher social status, to assert their dominance over women and members of the working classes by purchasing their bodies.[104]

The largely working-class and lower-middle-class women (usually servants or shop clerks) that undergraduates had relations with were not, of course, simply passive recipients of their youthful sexual advances or, in some instances, aggression. Prostitutes were active agents in the exchanges associated with commercialized sex and regularly sought out clients in Oxford and Cambridge streets by "nudging them, at night . . . to attract their attention," as Daisy Hopkins (a Cambridge woman) was said to have done in 1891.[105] More important were those instances when prostitutes actively resisted proctorial jurisdiction by either running away or fighting back. The Spinning House committal records at Cambridge are full of references to such acts of resistance, which ranged from the use of disrespectful language to physical altercations. One prostitute active in the 1850s, a woman by the name of Jane Harrison, was described as someone who "used very bad language" and was often "very violent" when confronted by proctors. Similarly, when Sarah Crowe was arrested she "gave very great trouble and caused much disturbance," according to the proctors (who obviously stood to gain by exaggerating these episodes). Daisy Hopkins, who worked in the late 1880s and 1890s and had some notoriety, was reported to have "behaved badly on being sentenced" after her arrest in 1891.[106]

Other women, involved sexually with undergraduates but not necessarily prostitutes, attempted to use the systems of justice at the universities for their benefit. Between 1871 and 1926, for example, several paternity cases involving undergraduates and local servant women were heard by Oxford's University Justice Court, which adjudicated cases against townspeople and university men alike involving crimes against property and sexual offences. In 1891 and 1897, respectively, Annie Parsler and Elizabeth Prior lodged paternity suits against Joseph Storer Clouston (an undergraduate at Magdalen College) and Ernest Brocklehurst (an undergraduate at Brasenose College). While both claims were summarily dismissed due to the unfair and heavily weighted nature of university justice, which relied on a whole set of class biases about the unreliability of college and lodging-house servants, such actions do reflect an attempt to challenge the prerogatives of men and the university. In the end, however, the University Justice Court and institutional privilege won out, further sanctifying heterosociability and the heterosexual impulse by delimiting as appropriate, and largely trouble- and responsibility-free, a certain type of sexual access to the "lower orders" that had figured prominently in elite worldviews for centuries.[107]

Undergraduates also utilized the disciplinary encounters with proctors as moments of self-assertion in which they attempted to claim independence and challenge, sometimes openly, the codes of conduct that governed life at the university. Resistance to these regulations can be seen in two distinct types of responses. The first were direct challenges to proctorial authority. In attempting to evade detection or, more significantly, avoid punishment, students pursued a number of strategies that highlight the confrontational tenor of relations between disciplinary authorities and junior members. The most common means of resistance was to give a false name to authorities upon being found either in a "house of ill-fame" or in the company of what officials labeled a woman of "questionable modesty."[108] This made follow-up and prosecution difficult for the proctors and enabled the undergraduate to remove himself from the embarrassing situation unscathed. Of course, authorities took precautions to prevent such evasions. The Oxford proctors observed in 1902–1903, for example, that "in the case where the penalty is heavy, the Proctor with the Marshal or Servants should escort the Undergraduate home, and verify the name and address. The most common case of this kind is that of an Undergraduate caught with a woman."[109]

Undergraduates caught in these situations might choose to be less bold and run away to avoid capture.[110] Two Oxford students in 1903, for example, were successful in fleeing when they were noticed by the proctor on duty in the company of two "undesirable" girls (ages fifteen and seventeen). The proctor, C. E. Haselfoot, in reporting the incident to the controller of the Lodging House Delegacy, noted how the undergraduates escaped: "The Undergraduates separated from the girls as soon as they saw they were detected, hailed a cab and drove off so rapidly that our servants were unable to follow them." The girls involved in the incident were unable to afford the expense of a cab, and were consequently apprehended.[111]

Undergraduates might also attempt to explain their predicaments to authorities. In one instance, a medical student of "Eurasian birth" offered a legitimate excuse for visiting the residence of a well-known Cambridge prostitute. The student, who is identified only as Nair (probably Chettur Ramunni Nair, a non-collegiate student who matriculated in 1891), admitted that he had visited the residence at Brown's yard but that it had been at "the request of a young woman named Barker, whom he had treated as an out-patient at Addenbroke's [hospital] and had afterwards met and spoken with in the street." Furthermore, it was noted, "[h]e maintained that his visits to her in Brown's yard had been paid simply as a medical student, in order to study further, and prescribe for, her case." While this explanation was found to be plausible, the student disappeared from Cambridge in disgrace and his name was withdrawn from the Non-Collegiate Students' Board.[112]

Most efforts at evasion were unsuccessful. Nonetheless, students' attempts to conceal or obscure activities they knew to be in violation of university statute, aside from functioning as acts of self-preservation, also represented partial attempts to test the policing capabilities of the proctors and undermine their sense of control. Incidents of this sort were not, of course, simple episodes of resistance. They also represented important points of conflict between students and university and college officials who waged masculine, and oftentimes generational, battles over working-class female and male bodies. These struggles, which occurred in the sexualized spaces of these university communities, frequently entered undergraduate culture through a variety of written and artistic forms that simultaneously challenged the authority of the proctors and deans and reified the central role of heterosociability in student life. These depictions and discussions of illicit liaisons and amorous meetings also emphasized the importance of transgression and the thrill of engaging in prohibited activities while reminding undergraduates of the potential dangers of the proctorial sting.

In a "Perverted Proverb" that appeared in the Oxford magazine *Bump* in 1909, for example, surreptitious contact with "girls" featured prominently as an act of subversion and provided readers, who themselves may not have engaged in such activities, with an opportunity for titillation. The author of this piece assigned pride of place, in one simple line, to the ability of undergraduates to pull the wool over the eyes of authorities: "A girl in one's digs is worth two in a taxi."[113] In so doing, he elevated in significance the role of heterosexual escapade in the extracurricular lives of Oxford and Cambridge men. Proctorial interruptions were also frequent subject matter for undergraduate artists who sought not only to amuse their audience with humorous scenes from undergraduate life but also to demarcate sexual spaces, challenge proctors, and emphasize the central role of heterosexual contact in undergraduate culture. A series of Cambridge sketches in 1906, for instance, illustrated a fairly typical scene in which an undergraduate was caught, on a park bench, in a compromising position with a woman whom he identified as his cousin to avoid punishment.[114] Such seemingly simple and innocuous attempts at humor reminded undergraduates of the risk that a proctor and his bulldogs, dressed in their easily recognized regalia, would interrupt a pleasurable episode with a formal interrogation. They also worked alongside the proctors' obsession with policing undergraduate sexuality to reinforce an increasingly prevalent heterosexual ideal, present in a variety of different cultural forms, including popular literature, music hall theatricals, and early silent films.[115]

Images of Proctors in Undergraduate Culture

The peculiar circumstances of the undergraduate's extended transition to manhood produced a number of unique tensions, as we have seen, over issues of control. Within the climate of hostility that marred relations between students and dons, proctors were used, sometimes literally, as punching bags by undergraduates lashing out against the constraints of institutional statutes and regulations. As representatives of an older and inferior variety of manhood and barriers to mobility and sexual opportunities, these officials were often the targets of derision and wrath in student newspapers, magazines, and memoirs. As divisions between adolescents and adults became more clearly demarcated later in the nineteenth century,[116] Oxbridge journalists and memoirists represented proctors in increasingly negative ways as spoilsports, foilers of fun, and competitors. In so doing, they not only exacerbated generational tensions but also sought to undermine the fatherly status of these highly contentious figures.

Hatred and disgust (always exaggerated for humorous intent) were common themes in descriptions of the proctors. Francis G. Stokes, a Merton College undergraduate from 1872 to 1876 and contributor to the usually caustic Oxford magazine *Shotover Papers,* did not, for example, hold back in an 1874 characterization of the proctors: "there exists amongst us a loathly and detestable class of beings who, under the name of 'Proctors,' ply their dreadful trade, urged either by the greed of pain, or by a fearful misanthropy which ever compels them to be in constant warfare with their species."[117] Similar sentiments were expressed in other publications. *Ye Rounde Table,* a magazine for both Oxford and Cambridge students published in the late 1870s, saw fit, for instance, to describe the proctors as "much-hated."[118] Proctors and bulldogs, as troublesome agents of discipline, were to be assiduously avoided. Undergraduates were advised by Frederick Sanders Pulling (an Exeter College undergraduate from 1872 to 1875) in 1874, again in the *Shotover Papers,* to "run as you were mad" upon noticing these despised officials.[119] A contributor to the Oxford *Clown* described them in 1891 as "poisoners of merry laughter," and an undergraduate journalist writing in the *Oxford Tatler* in 1886 said they were worthy of shunning in the open street.[120]

Such sentiments could be carried to extremes in, for example, undergraduate wishes for proctorial illness.[121] One particularly exaggerated expression of the animosity that relations with these officials occasionally produced appeared in the *Undergraduate* in 1888 when the editors surmised that the former senior proctor must indeed be "a man of considerable courage," because he "was seen walking down the High in broad daylight without a bodyguard. We should have thought that after his notable reign he would not have cared to shew his face for a year or so."[122] This anonymous observer drew on undergraduate memories of a particularly harsh disciplinary year to humorously remind readers of the excesses and abuses of their chief opponent, whose power was tellingly revealed, for Oxbridge students, in the fines that proctors charged undergraduates for getting caught "in [a] secluded spot with [a] town girl" (£5 in 1911) or frequenting a tavern (£1 in 1912).[123]

The power of the proctor to punish resulted in what were sometimes very real and sometimes exaggerated expressions of fear of getting caught. Most frequently, these anxieties were revealed in clever undergraduate depictions of the proctors' nightly rounds or "beats," when they roamed the streets, "search[ed] houses of ill-fame," and visited pubs, billiard rooms, and hotels to ensure that students were not engaging in proscribed activities.[124] Threatening representations of proctors warned undergraduates about the dangers of transgression as they provided them with a convenient bogeyman, against whom these young men waged both real and imaginary battles as they acquired the credentials of imperial leadership. By exaggerating the threats that marked this progression, then, they increased the thrill of surviving confrontations with the proctor, which functioned as important metaphors for the broader contests between age and youth and manhood and boyhood that figured so prominently in Oxbridge undergraduate culture.

As tensions between dons and students intensified in the years after 1880, due in large part to the increase in the average age of college fellows described in chapter 2, menacing representations of proctors as "insidious" and "hovering" watchdogs ready to "take any man at a disadvantage" appeared with much greater frequency.[125] Oxbridge journalists also described the proctors' actions with words that emphasized their policing functions and highlighted their ability to limit the undergraduate's mobility in both Oxford and Cambridge public spaces and his sometimes treacherous march toward manhood. Junior members, for instance, were described in several different Oxford papers in the 1880s and 1890s as being "pursued" and captured, or warned to "beware! for brand-new Proctors all around there be!" These terms conjured images of impending grave danger.[126]

The severity of these characterizations was particularly apparent in several articles whose authors referred to the proctors as a pestilence. In one submission to the *Isis* in 1893, they were labeled "the pestilence which walketh in darkness," and thirteen years later, this sentiment was repeated by another Oxford undergraduate in a poem entitled "The Nightly Pestilence" that began with a simple and unambiguous line: "THERE is a Fear that stalketh here the unheeding steps of men."[127] Artistic renderings also characterized the proctors as menacing predators. A cartoon in a 1905 issue of the *Granta* depicted the proctor as an *aeroprog,* a mythical flying beast with eyes on the back of his head and dangerous talons capable of capturing undergraduates caught enjoying a prerogative of manhood—in this instance, smoking (fig. 3.4). Depictions of this sort simultaneously reinforced what for many was a unifying feature of the undergraduate experience just as they delineated evenings as a potentially dangerous and terrifying time of day when manly transgressions (often cast as defiant acts of youthful heroism) and, occasionally, illicit acts were most likely to be detected and punished.

* * *

The mechanisms of control and moral regulation that were in place at the ancient universities functioned as important sites of conflict for undergraduates and officials as the former struggled, between the years 1850 and 1920, not only to assert their own position and challenge the latter's in highly stratified institutional hierarchies but also to formulate gender and sexual identities. As potential threats to the stability and harmony of these institutions, undergraduate bodies and actions were carefully monitored by officials interested in limiting student access to public spaces which might prove, in one way or another, to be corruptive. By imposing these limits, officials not only angered undergraduates, who responded in forceful and sometimes agitated ways, but also demarcated the boundaries between moral and immoral activities and normative and "queer" identities. Attempts to police the sexuality of the Oxbridge undergraduate (along with a range of other aspects of student life) resulted, perhaps unwittingly, in a valorization of heterosexuality that became an important feature of university culture during this period.

Restrictions on the undergraduate's movement and his ability to socialize or engage in sexual activity all marked the ambiguity of his status as a man caught between the more extreme controls of schoolboyhood and the presumed freedoms of adulthood. Undergraduates, as they struggled against and challenged these attempts at control and transgressed statutory boundaries (both real and symbolic), engaged in acts of miniature rebellion and self-assertion. In dealing with the regulations that these systems of discipline imposed upon them, students at Oxford and Cambridge also forged an identity, predicated on their inferior status within these institutional hierarchies, that was peculiarly their own. Coping with and sometimes evading the proctor, the dean, and the rules that figured so

"BEASTS THAT MIGHT HAVE BEEN."

THE ÆROPROG.

(With apologies to "The Sketch.")

Fig. 3.4. The proctor as menacing beast. "Beasts That Might Have Been," *Granta* 18, no. 396 (March 11, 1905): 121.
By permission of the British Library, shelf mark P.P. 6058.i.

prominently in their lives served to unify undergraduates and give expression to feelings of adolescent solidarity and manly camaraderie. Managing or circumventing college and university rules and finding ways to claim the public spaces of Oxford and Cambridge as their own were steps that undergraduates took on their march toward manhood, giving them opportunities to prove not only the superiority of their youthful perspective but also the legitimacy of their particular vision of masculinity.

4

Those "Horrid," "Holy" Schools: Examinations, Competition, and Masculine Struggle

In 1908, the producers of Nestor's cigarettes published an advertisement in the Oxford paper *Isis* that drew on a common undergraduate experience—the intensely public posting of examination results that occurred several times each year at the ancient universities and other institutions of higher learning around Great Britain. In trying to get undergraduates to purchase "their exquisite Egyptian cigarettes," and thus engage in the male pleasures of smoking, the fine print announced, with resonant words, "Nestor passes with Honours" (fig. 4.1).[1] By linking an intensely rigorous academic activity—taking exams—with other crucial moments in the undergraduate's life, including microscopic acts of disciplinary transgression (such as public smoking), the advertiser drew explicitly on several defining experiences discussed in the two preceding chapters of this study. This entry of the examination list into popular culture also highlights the extent to which these competitive exercises had entered the consciousness of Oxbridge men and of Victorian and Edwardian Britons more generally, both as measurements of academic success and professional credentials and as highly masculinized activities.

Students and dons at both universities, as well as a whole range of

Why do Connoisseurs Smoke

Nestors?

BECAUSE they are the best.

BECAUSE they have 32 years unrivailed reputation.

BECAUSE they are manufactured of the finest Tobacco the world produces.

BECAUSE they are guaranteed free of all added flavouring and harmful drugs.

BECAUSE of their delicious natural aroma, due solely to quality.

BECAUSE the smoker does not pay for an elaborate box, but for the quality of the goods inside the box.

BECAUSE they can be purchased all over the world at any Tobacconists or Stores.

BECAUSE there are no heavy intermediate profits connected with the sale.

BECAUSE the consumer thus benefits by increased quality, as no manufacturer can buy his trade and give the best quality.

BECAUSE they can be purchased in all sizes and qualities from 6/10 to 18/- per 100.

BECAUSE they are smoked by Members of the Royal Family and the leading aristocracy in Great Britain.

"Nestor passes with Honours."

NESTOR
The Exquisite Egyptian
CIGARETTES
(Nestor Gianaclis, Cairo)

Fig. 4.1. The examination list as advertising gimmick. *Isis*, no. 379 (February 8, 1908): 121.
By permission of the Bodleian Library, University of Oxford, shelf mark Per. G.A. Oxon. 4° 145.

outside observers, regularly commented on the importance of these academic tests of intellectual merit during the seven decades that passed between the curricular and administrative reforms of the 1850s and the conclusion of the First World War. In an 1863 *Student's Guide to the University of Cambridge,* for example, J. R. Seeley, the famous don and historian, celebrated the invigorating, youthful, and competitive nature of the Tripos (or Honours) examinations in a lengthy discussion of academic life: "Into these [examinations] flock annually the ablest young men . . . who during their University course have received all the instruction that the best Tutors, and all the stimulus that a competition well known to be severe, can give. . . . The contest is one into which the cleverest lads in the country enter [and] it may safely be affirmed that even the lowest place in these Triposes is justly called an *honour.*"[2] Even before Seeley penned these comments, competitive examinations had become, in the words of one 1859 observer, "matters of . . . much interest and importance not only to those whose future success in life depended upon them, but to the public in general."[3] Popular interest was further fueled, throughout this period, by numerous articles in the periodical press that discussed and debated the general value of competitive examinations and by the regular publication of test results in national newspapers such as the *Times.*[4]

This rise of competitive examinations has functioned, for many, as an important benchmark in the history of nineteenth-century Britain.[5] As devices that fostered the growth of a meritocratic society and elevated, to an unprecedented level, the culture of intellectual competition, these important academic exercises (which originated first at the ancient universities) promoted, as Harold Perkin and Reba Soffer have both noted, a professional ethos that prepared members of the British elite for careers in public service.[6] Indeed, reforms to the examination systems of Cambridge and Oxford (beginning, respectively, in 1747 and 1800) antedated, and largely set the stage for, such historically important developments as competitive public examinations for colonial and domestic civil service appointments and Robert Lowe's Revised Code for Education of 1862, which instituted "payment by results," tying the level of state aid to elementary schools to students' performance on tests of reading, writing, and arithmetic.

Most historians of Oxford and Cambridge, in exploring the momentous changes that teaching and learning underwent at these institutions between the years 1850 and 1920, have tended to focus on the form and content of examinations or the disciplines that provided their subject matter. In general terms, this work has addressed questions associated with administrative and structural changes and the expansion of the examining bodies that accompanied the late-nineteenth- and early-twentieth-century diversification of the curriculum. The work of Sheldon Rothblatt, and more recently that of Andrew Warwick, are two notable exceptions to this general rule.[7] In his explorations of the early nineteenth century, Rothblatt has noted the utility of examinations as "controlling devices" that served to discipline a student body which was, in the late Georgian and early Victorian periods, increasingly independent, peer-oriented, and activity-driven. In other work, he has identified a general undergraduate reluctance, during the pre-1850 period, to fully embrace the success ethic and the imperative of competition associated with examinations, a tendency almost entirely absent in the decades following the administrative and curricular reforms of the 1850s.[8] Rather than focusing on the form, content, or subject matter of the examinations, I explore, within this chapter, undergraduate reactions to a process, probing, specifically, the role these academic exercises played in the formation of class and gender identities.

Whether they described it as a severe test of character capable of pushing even the ablest of young British men to their limits, a foreboding and horrific ordeal, or a simple mechanism for determining merit and progress, Oxbridge students saw the examination as a defining moment. These aspiring members of Britain's professional society fashioned the act of sitting exams into a particularly manly endeavor and a specific act of masculine "consecration and recognition."[9] In many ways, this need to bolster the gendered significance of examinations was not simply the product of the economic, social, and cultural changes that accompanied the rise of professional society and its attendant emphasis on individual merit and accomplishment. It also sprang from a need to preserve male prerogatives at institutions that were frequently characterized as under siege by women, who in the 1870s began to attend the separate female colleges of Girton and Newnham (at Cambridge) and Somerville and Lady Margaret Hall (at Oxford) and in the 1880s came to sit examinations themselves and thus appropriate, challenge, and occasionally subvert the meaning of a process that Oxbridge men assumed was theirs alone.

A combination of forces converged, then, to transform what Henry Latham characterized in 1877 as a strongly held "belief in the sanctity of examinations" into a newfound "article of creed" that accorded a special place to the ethics of ambition and success.[10] The emerging professional ethos of the latter decades of the nineteenth century represented a newly fashioned version of British masculinity premised not so much on the traits of godliness and good learning or even muscular Christianity (though these were certainly part of it), but rather on notions of proficiency, competence, intellectual and psychological as well as physical fortitude, and unimpeachable character.[11] For the majority of male undergraduates, who in this period were from neither aristocratic nor industrial/entrepreneurial backgrounds, gender identities were increasingly predicated upon their future status as colonial administrators, government officials, civil servants, doctors, lawyers, and clergymen and their accompanying notions of public service, mission, and national obligation. Within such a context, examinations functioned as something more than academic milestones. Like purchasing a cap and gown, receiving university statutes, or furnishing one's rooms, they became, for undergraduates, a crucial marker of the transition from boyhood to manhood. The anxious ruminations of student journalists, which simultaneously combined assertions of supreme confidence with expressions of insecurity, are thus read in this chapter as consternation about not only a particular process but also the undergraduate's status as a man, his professional future, and his position in increasingly complex, and perhaps less certain, class and gender structures.[12]

The Structure and Form of University Examinations

A system of examinations for degrees has always existed in some form at England's ancient universities. Reform of this system, in the century and a half after 1747, was intended to restore academic rigor to a process that had degenerated, according to one Oxford observer, into nothing more than "mere ceremony" and "farce,"[13] a point echoed in a somewhat hyperbolized description by John Scott, the first Earl of Eldon, of his examinations in 1770. Eldon maintained, in his discussion of the experience, that the exam (which he also described with the word "farce") consisted of two simple questions: "I was examined in Hebrew and in History. 'What is the Hebrew for the place of a skull?' I replied 'Golgatha.'—'Who founded University College?'—I stated, (though, by the way, the point is sometimes doubted), 'that King Alfred founded it.'—'Very well, sir,' said the Examiner, 'you are competent for your degree.'"[14] The modernization of the universities in the nineteenth century, in part a response to this egregious slip in standards, led to a general increase in rigor.[15] The introduction of new formats, an increase in the amount of required written work, and the formalization of classes or ranks all served as important hallmarks of this shift.

This transformation of the examination systems at the ancient universities involved both structural and philosophical changes. These were characterized most significantly by an emphasis on the principles of standard-ization and competition. Cambridge led the way in reforming its curricu-lum, instituting new requirements a full fifty years prior to Oxford. In 1747, Cambridge introduced a more formalized Mathematical Tripos ex-amination, reflecting both a predilection within the university for that discipline and its ability to resist the precipitous decline in academic standards experienced at Oxford in the eighteenth century. At around the same time, the value of ranking candidates came to be recognized, and distinct classes were created in 1779. With these changes also came a gen-eral shift away from oral disputation toward written work.[16]

The system for determining Honours at Cambridge fostered greater individual competition among the undergraduates at that institution. In addition to being divided into the classes of Wranglers, Senior Optimes, and Junior Optimes, examinees were also ranked (in published lists) ac-cording to their performance within each class. Oxford rejected this prac-tice in the first decades of the nineteenth century, for fear that it might deter students from pursuing an Honours course.[17]

At Oxford, the Examination Statute of 1800 provided the initial im-petus for reform. These new regulations established standards, formalized the office of the public examiner, encouraged further the study of Latin and Greek, and, as at Cambridge, outlined provisions for awarding distinctions to exceptional candidates. Written work here, too, was an integral part of the process and became a major preoccupation for examiners and under-graduates alike.[18] While in Cambridge the Mathematical Tripos garnered the most prestige, the Oxford course of classical study, known as Literae Humaniores and devoted to the study of the Greek and Latin languages, rhetoric, moral philosophy, and, increasingly after 1830, ancient history, Greek and Roman authors, and moral and political science, emerged as the most prestigious area of study.[19] This was the most crucial curricular dis-tinction between the two institutions for much of the nineteenth and twentieth centuries. By the 1810s, both institutions had begun the process of diversifying their curricula. Changes at Cambridge in the 1810s and 1820s allowed undergraduates to pursue discrete courses of study and ex-aminations in law and classics. By the 1840s and 1850s, written competi-tive examinations, now a firmly entrenched feature of undergraduate edu-cation, had achieved unparalleled importance. This general development was accompanied by the introduction of a series of tests in several new subject areas. Cambridge in 1848, for example, introduced exams in moral science and the natural sciences, while Oxford in 1850 created separate fields of study in mathematics, natural sciences, and jurisprudence and modern history.

The evolution of new academic disciplines and shifts in intellectual life influenced the incremental and piecemeal introduction of new subjects and topics.[20] Gradually, the exclusive dominance of the study of mathematics and the classics gave way to an increasingly diverse curriculum that included modern history, a discipline finally granted an independent place when it was separated from the study of jurisprudence in the 1870s. By the early decades of the twentieth century, the new social sciences, including anthropology, economics, and political science, had achieved an elevated status within the universities as Honours courses, which meant that students could now read for degrees in those areas.[21]

If the early nineteenth century was marked by the introduction of formal written exams and the resuscitation of the academic prestige of the ancient universities, the second half of the century witnessed the regularization of the examination system. By the 1850s, the rigor of this system had been established as a common feature of the undergraduate experience with nearly universal resonance, although a decreasing but still significant percentage of the student population continued to take an ordinary degree (called the Poll at Cambridge, and the Pass at Oxford) or left with no degree at all.[22] To remain in the university, one had to proceed through the appropriate hoops. Thus, every undergraduate had, at several points during his time up, to subject himself to the academic scrutiny of the examiners. In the set of detailed lectures that William Everett delivered before a large and inquisitive audience at the Lowell Institute in Boston, the ambitious American undergraduate, who spent his years at Trinity College, Cambridge, immersed not only in study but also in a range of extracurricular activities, enumerated his (fairly typical) encounters with exams. Over the course of his three years at Cambridge, Everett submitted to three examinations for university scholarships (in 1860, 1861, and 1862), a preliminary examination to measure academic progress (in 1861), two final sets of examinations for Honours in two separate fields of study (mathematics and classics), and a number of college and university examinations for various prizes and awards.[23]

It is apparent, from Everett's account and others like it, that undergraduates encountered numerous tests of character and mind shortly after making the choice, or having it made for them by their parents, to pursue a university education. The university commissioners in the 1850s determined that open and competitive examinations were the best way to gauge and reward excellence and force "the Tutor and the Pupils to aim high" by awakening a spirit of "noble emulation."[24] To ensure that these aims were accomplished, examinations, faithfully accepted as true tests of excellence, were administered to choose suitable candidates for scholarships. These constituted the motivated undergraduate's first brush with the system that would come to dominate his academic life. Junior members of the university were not, however, tested only to determine their eligibility for scholarships. Some individual colleges, as well as the universities, also required that their students sit entrance examinations prior to or shortly after matriculation. Similarly, periodic tests of academic progress became an increasingly prominent feature of college life after the 1860s.

These periodic assessments were not the most worrisome to undergraduates. Anxiety and stress were generally reserved for the more substantial and university-wide degree examinations. These marked particular milestones in the Oxbridge man's academic career. George Nugent Bankes discussed the preoccupying and solemn nature of these exercises when he commented, in his 1881 collection of essays, on just how distracted by examinations an undergraduate could become: "I cannot talk of much, as my conversation would be a bore to my companions. I can think of nothing but statistics, Trigonometry, and Higher Algebra; I sit in moody silence . . . everything I do in some way forces itself into an illustration of one of [these subjects]; my only amusement consists in setting myself test papers and not being able to do them."[25]

Bankes pointed in this account to the ways in which examinations functioned as momentous occasions in the undergraduate's academic career. Administrative and statutory peculiarities, which students regularly discussed in their writings on the subject, served to reinforce this sense of specialness. The undergraduate, for instance, was examined at prescribed times during the year (after 1882 in May at Cambridge and usually in late May or early June at Oxford) that were announced publicly in circulars similar to those issued by university officials to remind undergraduates of disciplinary regulations.[26] Oxford and Cambridge journalists reinforced this point when they described the month of May in *Ye Rounde Table,* a magazine directed at students at both universities, as a "time for much," during which "the Schools [the Oxford term for Honours examinations] begin."[27]

These exercises were also rendered momentous by the purpose-specific buildings in which they were held and the requirement that undergraduates wear, within those buildings, the "academic dress of cap and gown," a point underscored by one contributor to the student newspaper *'Varsity* in 1914 who noted, as the examinations began, "this week is full of dark coats and white ties."[28] (Regulations specified that undergraduates must wear not only cap and gown to their examinations but also "sub-fusc," a dark suit with a white shirt and a white tie.) The Senate House in Cambridge, an important official building, functioned as the chief location for examinations until a new building was constructed in the early twentieth century to accommodate increasing numbers. Oxford had responded earlier to the strain placed on the buildings of the old Schools, located in the Bodleian Library, by erecting between the years 1876 and 1882 an imposing edifice designed by the noted Victorian architect T. G. Jackson. This new building, prominently located on the High Street, betrayed upon sight the significance attached to examinations. Its sheer opulence (it was once unflatteringly described as a "Marble Palace") and the carved images which grace the front entrance, depicting both learning in an abstract sense and the ritual of examinations more specifically, make this point abundantly clear.[29] The symbolically charged "sculpted Three, above the New Schools' gate" reminded Alfred Denis Godley, a Magdalen College fellow and tutor, of the tests of character that undergraduates were subjected to beyond these impressive gates and the potential for failure that exams entailed.[30] For undergraduates at both institutions these facilities were "sacred buildings" in which fearful "spectres" were faced and frightful "ordeals" endured, and from which they emerged, depending on their performance, into complete happiness or "utter despair."[31]

The degree examinations that were administered within these buildings followed a similar pattern at both Oxford and Cambridge after 1850. The first step for the Cambridge man was an exercise known as the Previous, or sometimes, more colloquially, as the Little-Go. Arthur Clement Hilton described it in a November 1870 letter to his mother as "the most disagreeable business I was ever in for."[32] The equivalent examination at Oxford was known as Responsions. All candidates, whether Honours men or Pass or Poll, were tested within their first two terms in Latin and Greek grammar and literature, the gospels, Euclid, and algebra. Cambridge undergraduates pursuing the Poll degree, which became a separate route distinct from the Tripos examinations after 1858, were required by the 1870s to undergo a second exercise known as the General Examination for the Ordinary Degree, which tested further their knowledge of scripture, the classics, algebra, and some elementary principles of science and mechanics. Honours candidates were not required to sit this examination but were expected to write additional papers after the Previous that tested, primarily, their knowledge of mathematics (in keeping with earlier Cambridge tra-

ditions which elevated this subject above all others).[33] The Poll B.A.'s final
obstacle was the Special Examination, which focused on a specific subject
area, such as law and modern history, natural science, or theology. The
Tripos man proceeded after the additional papers to the Tripos examinations that, like the Final Schools at Oxford, determined his academic fate
and the quality of his degree.

Examinations became, in the nineteenth century, tests of considerable
duration that required stamina, fortitude, and stability of candidates hoping for success. William Everett, in an attempt to convey this point to
his American audience in 1864, described very particularly the examined
undergraduates' need for food: "O, many are the luncheons, mighty the
dinners consumed in these eight days. Science must be fed. The most un-
compromising appetites I ever saw were among my most learned and successful friends in England."[34] Such exertions also required advance warnings and reminders. One 1893 contributor to the *Isis* prepared his comrades
for the impending hardships of examinations with a quip that served to
shock, amuse, and steel: "Fast approaches the time when despondent candidates think grimly of how they might circumvent their torturers."[35]

At either institution, these tests took place over several weeks (alter-
nating between intervals of work and rest) and often required candidates
to respond to set questions for three to six hours each day and, at Oxford,
to submit to a viva voce (oral) examination.[36] The Mathematical Tripos at
Cambridge required a special kind of stamina (though all Tripos examinations followed a version of this general format by the latter decades of the
nineteenth century). Within the period under consideration here, undergraduates sitting it first faced three days of preliminary papers. During an
interval of one week to ten days, these papers were read and a list of those
who would be allowed to proceed to the remaining five days of examinations was posted. If successful, the undergraduate might emerge at the end
of this ordeal with the distinct honor of being named Senior Wrangler, a
result that was announced with much fanfare when the "lists of successful
candidates [were] nailed to the Senate House door."[37]

The pressures that mounted during such intensive periods of work
were considerable, and exams, as we shall see, could take their toll. One
key to achieving a positive result was the ability to withstand certain challenges, such as the public display of results in the pages of the *Times*. These
wider broadcasts occasionally elicited grumbles from undergraduates who
disliked having their shortcomings revealed. In one case, an editor of the
Oxford *Undergraduate* managed to attack examiners, the *Times,* and the
utility of examinations in chastising the officials for delays in the publica-

tion of results: "WHAT a slow lot are these examiners! Six weeks had passed and we had forgotten all about Honour Mods., when in the *Times* and other public prints, there appear, quite unauthorised by ourselves, our names arranged in a very invidious order."[38]

Success was not, however, guaranteed to those who managed to maintain heartiness or impermeable constitutions; the ability to endure the considerable pressures of examinations and the public display of one's success or failure were only, in fact, part of the formula. All undergraduates, no matter how talented or intelligent, could expect to work for Honours, if they chose to pursue that route. Preparations often consisted of individual and small group sessions with one's tutor, attendance at lectures, independent reading and study during both academic terms and vacations, and, often, tuition with a private tutor (referred to as a coach) who might help the less than diligent examinee cram for the final crunch or assist the more conscientious student in maximizing his potential.[39] Stamina and strength were thus required not only to survive what William Everett called the "intellectual struggle to which the physical efforts accompanying the fiendish barbarities of the prize-ring are as child's play,"[40] but also to withstand the rigors of intense preparation that preceded the examination period.

Examinations and Undergraduate Culture: Symbol and Meaning

The success with which examinations were absorbed into undergraduate culture is underscored by the substantial number of references to them that appeared in student magazines, newspapers, and other published and unpublished material during this seventy-year period. While university officials determined the structure, form, and content of examinations, the meanings assigned to them were almost uniquely the product of a preoccupied undergraduate population that, as we discovered in chapter 1, saw itself as the human lifeblood of the university: a guiding force without whom these institutions were incomplete. Even when undergraduate views of examinations coincided with those of senior members of the universities, such a self-image meant that students privileged their own perspectives. What mattered most to the Oxford or Cambridge man was not the disciplinary function of the Tripos or the Schools but rather the ways these mechanisms for testing undergraduate academic progress could be manipulated symbolically to allow undergraduates to vent competitive spirits; formulate, express, and preserve gender identities; and articulate some of the primary concerns of late adolescents on the cusp of manhood.

The extent to which examinations were foremost in the minds of students at both institutions between the years 1850 and 1920 was reflected in a variety of significant ways. The simplest of these were the frequent reminders and warnings of impending examinations that were scattered throughout a multitude of undergraduate publications. Routine calendars and schedules, like those that appeared regularly on the cover of the *Oxford Tatler* and announced in painstaking detail the date, time, and location of examinations, highlighted each week's academic exercises.[41] The more creative Oxbridge journalists wove frequent references to examinations into their many publications by offering fellow students clever bits of advice on how to succeed in them and reminding readers of the particularly harrowing nature of these exercises. One common feature of these publications, the use of the test question as a quasi-literary device, also tellingly and simply betrayed the extent to which undergraduates could become preoccupied by examinations. In a piece that appeared in the Cambridge publication *Momus: A Semi-occasional University Periodical,* humorous hints or admonitions were phrased in a form most familiar to the magazine's readers. The first of these asked, "Find the value of the continued fraction caused by a bull in a china-shop?" while another, explicitly critical of college disciplinary regulations that required students to attend religious services, asked the fictional candidate to "Shew that the inclination of the dons to a man varies inversely as the square of his inclination to morning chapel?"[42]

Reminders, warnings, and the frequent use of the examination-style question might have been enough to create an aura of significance around the Triposes or the Schools. Undergraduates did not, however, stop there. A whole range of humorous poems, anecdotes, and cartoons about examinations were employed to bolster the symbolic importance of these exercises and to communicate the pervasiveness of performance anxiety. A. P. Poley amusingly conveyed to readers of *Ye Rounde Table,* in 1878, the concerns generated by impending examinations. In the "Notes" section of the paper, Poley wrote, "The Agricultural Show and the Schools begin in June. It is expected that for the benefit of the uninitiated some first-class specimens of ploughing will be exhibited."[43] In this instance, humor was found in the pun on "ploughing" (Oxbridge slang for academic failure) and the fears felt by the men about to go through the experience of university examinations. This culture of anxiety existed simultaneously with a culture of celebration that elevated the status of examinations as crucial tests of character. Academic exercises, within this context, became gauges of professional masculinity which could measure the candidate's competitive spirit, endurance, stamina, strength, diligence, ability to overcome adversity and rise to any challenge, gentlemanly proficiency, and, as it became a more central feature of life for the late-nineteenth- and early-twentieth-century elite classes, merit.

The examination affected nearly every facet of undergraduates' lives. Like most of the activities Oxford and Cambridge students engaged in, examinations presented unique opportunities for community building, a process of vital importance in the formation of elite identities at the universities. Cambridge undergraduate Christopher Wordsworth, for instance, detailed the need for companionship and the importance of friendship in the months leading up to the Tripos. To combat the effects of test anxiety, which he characterized as feelings of "uneasiness and restlessness," this author procrastinated by spending "a large portion of time in the rooms of friends, whose sympathy and advice [were] eagerly courted."[44] The demands of work in this case produced not only avoidance but also an opportunity for camaraderie. University journalists also reinforced this spirit of manly comradeship by proffering genuine advice to students about to undergo the experience of examinations. In an October 1889 issue of the *Oxford Examiner,* for example, undergraduates were instructed to allow rational thought to prevail on their initial encounter with an examination paper. The author, an experienced examinee, observed, "The first thing I have noticed is how hard all papers look at first sight, but the majority improve on acquaintance; it is only the few that remain obstinately unfamiliar to the end."[45]

Certain ritualized activities associated with examinations were equally important in promoting this sense of masculine community. The simple act of gathering for Finals and anticipating their start functioned as a unifying experience for Oxford men, a point emphasized in a 1914 issue of *'Varsity* with a brief reference to the halls of the Schools, which, on examination days, were "crowded with men listening intently while bells ring."[46] Awaiting the results of the examinations also presented undergraduates with an opportunity for social bonding as well as a chance to collectively celebrate their successes and mourn their failures. A wide range of evidence confirms the significance to students of the posting of results. "Very large crowd[s]" frequently gathered near the sites where "class lists" were posted, and if the examinations had been particularly difficult, it was not, according to Alfred Henry Lawrence, uncommon to see undergraduates "weeping and gnashing their teeth" on these occasions.[47] The rough-and-tumble nature of the proceedings in the Senate House when the results of examinations were announced was discussed by William Everett, who

completed the Classical Tripos in 1863. Everett noted that during the celebrations, the Senior, Second, and Third Wranglers were lauded with "tumultuous, furious and insane" cheers fit for great heroes. The melee that
ensued when copies of the lists were distributed from the gallery by the
proctors was described by Everett as a chaotic opportunity for men to test
their physical limits once again: "The proctors in the gallery . . . scatter
[the lists] to the multitude below. . . . the scuffle, the trampling, the crush-
ing of caps and cap-bearers in a shapeless mass, the tearing of gowns, coats,
and the very papers that come slowly floating down, beats any tumult I
ever saw, except the contention for coppers of the Irish beggars on the
wharf of Queenstown, before the tug-boat leaves for the Cunard Steamer."[48]

This tendency to cope by enlisting the support of others and to celebrate successes collectively helps confirm the significance of examinations
to the construction of male gender identities. As an experience endured in
the company of other men, and removed from the presence of women,
examinations served the same functions as do masculine rituals in non-in-
dustrial societies, where, anthropologists have observed, male friendships
center on activities as opposed to specific moments of intimacy.[49] While
examinations could be constructed as ordeals meant to be endured in soli-
tude, they could simultaneously reaffirm the importance of masculine
friendship in forging not only gender identities but also a sense of shared
masculine power, solidarity, and influence: a "common spirit and energy"
that allowed undergraduates to act as "one great band of brothers" in the
world.[50] This point was further underscored in an illustration, drawn by
John Roget and entitled "Degree Time," that highlighted the communal
nature of examinations and the ethics of success and failure as key components in the definition of upper-middle-class professional masculinities
(fig. 4.2). Again, by drawing on a reserve of shared experiences, which were
nearly unique in their formality and hallowed specialness to the Oxbridge
educated, these men were able, both during and after university, to refer
back to that sense of commonality that was so integral to the perpetuation
of elite status.

Examinations as tests of character functioned, within this context, as
rites of passage that marked a range of psychological, social, and physical
transitions for the young student. Upper-middle-class masculinity in the
Victorian and Edwardian eras was something that one acquired. For undergraduates in this period, as we have seen, the university provided a
space in which the vestiges of childhood were discarded in favor of a hard-
won but discernible mantle of manhood. The Tripos, for example, was
routinely seen to signal the end of a particular stage of life, reminding

Fig. 4.2. John Roget's depiction of the pleasures and anxieties of degree examinations. *A Cambridge Scrap-Book* (Cambridge: Macmillan, 1859), p. 19.
By permission of the British Library, shelf mark 1322.m.25.

undergraduates of the uncertainties of the future and the realities of the adult world. The end of the undergraduate's academic career (unless he took up a college fellowship), punctuated as it was by final examinations, meant farewell to a familiar way of life. For Alfred Henry Lawrence, the transition was marked by a series of simple events that he chronicled in his 1889 *Reminiscences of Cambridge*. Upon learning that he had passed the General Examination for the Poll degree, he ran off to tell "friends the 'good news' by telegram and by word of mouth"; enjoyed a ball "in the evening"; and "on the following morning . . . packed up [his] goods and started for home."[51] Arthur Clement Hilton reflected on these transitions with rather more sorrow and anxiety when he compared the undergraduate's second May term, that "most enjoyable period of Cambridge life" when the student is "without worry," with his final May term, when examinations cast "shadows of impending departure to the realities of life."[52]

Within this framework, these academic exercises were invested with truly transformative potential. Undergraduates marked the passing of the years with references to the increasing amounts of work required of them as they moved closer to these intellectual milestones. In the Oxford magazine *Shotover Papers,* the progression toward manhood embodied in this scholastic journey was specifically likened to crossing a bridge with a number of academic trapdoors.[53] In an 1855 periodical entitled *Oxford Wit,* the carefree nature of the first years of university gradually gave way to a (sometimes temporary) single-minded seriousness.[54] Preparation for examinations, just like the responsibilities of manhood which the undergraduate would have to assume in the years after college, often necessitated solitary and independent study, competition with others, delayed gratification, planning, and occasional bouts of melancholia.[55] Rational choices about whether to pursue leisure or serious work also represented a conflict between two forms of activity that helped to determine masculine identities for upper-middle-class men—participation in athletics and the acquisition of professional credentials, which success in examinations was thought to confer. In a cartoon that appeared in the Oxford magazine *Chaperon* in 1910, undergraduates were poignantly reminded of the difficulties of this decision with an image that portrayed the tensions between these two choices (fig. 4.3).

This transition from boyhood to manhood also, however, occurred in public and functioned, to borrow a concept from feminist theorist Judith Butler, as a gender performance.[56] The extent to which an Oxbridge man could withstand the pressure of the "thousand eager eyes" that watched him undergo this transformation not only was a measure of his manhood

OCT. 22, 1910.   THE CHAPERON, OR THE OXFORD CHER-IVARI.   15

' BETWEEN TWO FIRES.'
(With apologies to the famous picture.)

Fig. 4.3. The difficult choices of undergraduate life. "Between Two Fires," *Chaperon, or the Oxford Cher-ivari* 1, no. 2 (October 22, 1910): 15.
By permission of the Bodleian Library, University of Oxford, shelf mark Per. G.A. Oxon. 4° 293.

but also served to affirm, as John Tosh has noted in examining other public accomplishments, the status of his family.[57] The neglectful undergraduate unable to recognize the magnitude of the event might find himself disappointed or, worse yet, a failure as both student and man.

The embrace of the ethics of ambition and success that accompanied the rise of professional masculinity in Oxbridge undergraduate culture did not come without costs. In an era when manhood was constructed as a hard-won honor, achieved through struggle in the face of adversity, it is not surprising that examinations were elevated in significance as tests of manly character and moral fiber, detestable trials and ordeals which had to be endured under the watchful eye of the examiner, described in one undergraduate poem in 1866 as the "learned Black hood."[58] Students, in their private reflections and public pronouncements, attached these meanings to them by employing a range of images and descriptive metaphors that reinforced the ideals of competitive manhood circulating among the middle classes in a number of western societies during the nineteenth century.[59]

Torture was one theme used by undergraduates who wanted to force-fully characterize Oxbridge academic requirements as tests not only of scholarly progress but also of manly undergraduate mettle.[60] An amusing description of the process that appeared in the *Shotover Papers* in 1874, purporting to be a historical account of "human sacrifices" at Oxford, took the metaphor of torture to an extreme. Beginning with the statement that "the University was founded to encourage the practice of human sacrifice," the author of this piece continued with a detailed account of examina-tions as sacrificial rituals in which "wretched beings . . . [c]lad in robes of blackness to signify the hopelessness of their case" are brought into "the presence of the sacrificing priests" and "obliged to write, write, write."[61] In humoring his readership with parody, this author contributed to the construction of examinations as assessments of both the undergraduate's knowledge and his ability to withstand the trials of manhood.

Undergraduates also drew on images of bodily discomfort and meta-phors of illness in describing the difficulties associated with examinations. An Oxford poem that appeared in the magazine *Great Tom* in 1861 builds up, in several stanzas, to a characterization of "The Schools" as nearly un-bearable physical burdens. Drawing primarily on the language of affliction to make its point, this poem describes the "solemn trial" of Schools as "[a] running-wound—a constant boil . . . an intermittent ague."[62] In another Oxford example, again from the *Shotover Papers,* examinations are depicted somewhat more simply, but with the same effect, as "ordeals" which "[jar] on the nerves of those operated upon."[63] Images of ailments, imprison-ment, and unparalleled misery regularly appear in descriptions of the proc-ess of sitting exams. The experience could produce anxious "tremor[s]" or, as it was known at Cambridge, a physical condition identified as "Tripos Fever," a sickness caused by stress.[64] For young men in an increasingly competitive professional society, the anxieties associated with examina-tions, however overstated, were not to be taken lightly. The extent to which this language of the exam as ordeal had appeal across institutional boundaries and represented, in essence, a shared set of cultural traditions can be seen in an "Oxford and Public Schools Intelligence" column that appeared in the *Cambridge Tatler* in March of 1877. In this instance, an Oxford correspondent reported that Smalls, and especially the viva voce, were an "awful ordeal . . . where three dread beings in a large room request the terrified Fresher to construe a piece of Virgil."[65]

Other descriptive metaphors employed by student journalists and memoirists served to exaggerate the demands of Oxbridge academic require-ments, and of Britain's meritocratic society more generally, and heighten their importance as transformative markers of status. Precisely because the examination punctuated a transitional moment in the lives of professional men and represented a genuine milestone, a whole range of acute anxieties could be and were projected upon it. The colleges of Oxford and Cambridge functioned, then, as curious liminal spaces that allowed, and to a certain degree sanctioned, the expression of sentiments of this sort.[66] As "little worlds" in which undergraduates occupied a status betwixt and between the full burdens of manhood and the carefree days of boyhood, the universities tolerated experimentation and the expression of doubt far more than did most professional contexts, where hard and fast rules about expertise and mastery predominated (at least in theory).

Undergraduates frequently invoked images of horror in discussing some of the insecurities and concerns about the responsibilities of adulthood that the experience of the Schools or the Tripos might generate. Their fears could, for example, take on a semi-human form as grotesque and ghoulish bogeymen (as they did in the Oxford magazine *Bump* in 1899 and 1902) capable of unsettling, at any moment, even the most prepared examinee and disrupting the masculine privileges and pleasures of university life (fig. 4.4).[67] An 1893 undergraduate description of the Tripos brilliantly employed this device by describing the Honours examinations as a "devastating monster which has for many years dwelt in our midst, propounding riddles and devouring all who cannot provide satisfactory answers."[68] Undergraduates also pointed to the ways in which their worries and fears could follow them to bed or even, in one intentionally amusing and provocative 1888 example from the Oxford paper *Undergraduate,* prompt students to commit suicide by throwing themselves into the River Cherwell (a smaller tributary that feeds into the Thames).[69] Descriptions of dreams and nightmares were used to express pressing concerns about failure and its various implications by invoking sinister or demonic images. The toll that examinations could exact was outlined in Christopher Wordsworth's humorously intended letter, written from his perspective as a "disconsolate" examinee, to the *Tatler in Cambridge* in 1871:

I have been so wretched you can't imagine—I really think you would hardly know me if you met me in the Streets. Whenever I try to read (which of course is now absolutely necessary) I see the word TRIPOS in flaming Letters all across the Page of wherever I turn my Eyes—and perhaps worst of all when I try to shut them. The same Nightmare follows me to my Coach, and even in Hall the Dishes remind me of *Liddell* and *Scott* and of the Notes to *Aristophanes.*[70]

The Imp of Schools.

Fig. 4.4. John Aston's illustration of the haunting nature of examination anxiety. "The Imp of Schools," *Bump*, no. 4 (May 23, 1902): 11.
By permission of the Bodleian Library, University of Oxford, shelf mark Per. G.A. Oxon 4° 198.

This general practice of elevating the significance of examinations to nearly absurd proportions (by, for example, welcoming death as an alternative to the misery of Responsions, as one Oxford correspondent to the *Cambridge Tatler* did in 1877)[71] highlighted the magnitude of the challenge they presented. By an implicit association, it also pointed to the undergraduate's singular ability to surmount obstacles of this sort in an admirable display of masculine strength and character. If undergraduates were combating ghoulish demons and monsters, in slumber and in the examination room, they could describe themselves as heroes.[72] At a time when British popular culture, especially boy culture, was replete with stories of daring challenges on the battlefield or the playing field and colonial confrontations with racialized others, it is not surprising that undergraduates would resort to a similar imagery of struggle and strife in describing their various trials.[73] The popular meanings of examinations were forged within this cultural framework. The Tripos and the Schools were simply modified versions (albeit highly domesticated and structured ones) of the colonial adventure in Africa or the harrowing land and naval battles in which the hero proved himself worthy as both man and Briton.[74] Like the characters that appeared in stories published in the *Boy's Own Paper* (f. 1879) or in the fictional works of G. A. Henty and H. Rider Haggard, undergraduates were expected to overcome, with aplomb, ordeals that had the potential to reduce them, according to one contributor to the Oxford paper '*Varsity,* to a state of "sheer helpless terror" or leave them "quite unmanned."[75] Examinations, then, like the encounters with wild animals and "savage cannibals" that permeated juvenile literature during the period of high imperialism, could emasculate those who succumbed to stress and anxiety. Success in either venue, however, affirmed masculine strength, as in the case of the Cambridge poet who spoke of the Little-Go as a test of character "manfully withstood."[76]

Success in examinations and achieving an Honours degree at one of the ancient universities also became an important mark of competence for those young men whose professional futures lay in the colonial administration of India or Africa. Conquering the rigors of the examination system proved not only the mental abilities of the future colonial official but also his physical strength, fortitude, and "pluck." As "future governors" and "builders and organisers of the Empire" (descriptions offered fifty-one years apart in the Cambridge *Lion University Magazine* and the Oxford *Pageant Post,* respectively), undergraduates acquired much from academic exercises that allowed them to prove themselves as gentlemanly conquerors and competent administrators.[77] The stamina, fortitude, and academic accomplishments that the Tripos or the Schools fostered became signature traits that made the Oxbridge man an imperial leader and differentiated him, according to one 1899 undergraduate author in the Cambridge magazine *Screed,* from colonized peoples.[78] Examinations within an imperial context, then, acquired a racial significance that served to reinforce assumptions about not only the Anglo-Saxon's intellect but also his peculiar ability to withstand competitive challenges. The Oxford and Cambridge graduates who played a major role in the Indian Civil Service often took the ideas that they had developed about competitive examinations at these institutions with them to the subcontinent. This is abundantly clear in the attitudes of Anglo-Indian administrators who, in the 1880s, opposed the further extension of employment opportunities to native Indians because they believed Indians lacked the competitive qualities that were required for senior positions in the I.C.S.[79]

Other strategies as well helped undergraduates define examinations as peculiarly masculine activities. In several cases, students drew on the ideology of separate spheres and notions of male and female space to differentiate these academic exercises, the "real paramount business" of university life, from leisure and the pleasures of female companionship.[80] Undergraduates about to encounter examiners were reminded in an 1865 poem, for example, to "not think which maid is the fairest," and in a 1914 article in the Oxford paper *New Cut* to leave behind favorite dates for books.[81] The problems encountered when Oxford and Cambridge men let these feminine distractions get the best of them were outlined in a discussion, that appeared in an 1892 issue of the *Isis,* of a pen that flowed prolifically when it was directed to produce panegyrics extolling the virtues of feminine beauty but was incapacitated when it was expected to write answers to examination questions.[82]

The characterization of examinations as a male preserve was part of the broader propensity in undergraduate culture to define most things feminine (especially women as the equals of men) as beyond the bounds of the university. This tendency was exacerbated, near the end of the nineteenth century, as women began to enter the universities, in a limited capacity, as students. By defining the university as masculine, undergraduates sought to shore up their defenses against female students, who were, by the 1870s, demanding that the ancient universities admit them fully to examinations. In February of 1881, the Cambridge Senate voted overwhelmingly to admit women to both the Previous and the Tripos but not to the examinations for the Poll degree. The women's results were to be published separately and they were, of course, not allowed to formally take degrees. Despite the ease with which the Senate passed this measure (398 to 32 votes), gender relations at Cambridge from then to 1897, when the university and, more especially, undergraduates voted overwhelmingly against admitting women to degrees, were marked by repeated attempts to preserve the gender-specific character of the institution by carving out rigidly delineated masculine spheres of activity.[83] The climate of change and reform which marked the years between 1850 and 1920 tended to produce reactions which sought to preserve tradition in the face of change by carefully demarcating who the true insiders and outsiders were.

It is in this light that we need to understand examinations as one of the many homosocial arenas where men were able to prove their masculinity vis-à-vis other men. Exams functioned, for one 1861 contributor to the Oxford magazine *Great Tom,* as a holy ritual in which men "learn to bear what men have borne before."[84] In *'Varsity* nearly fifty years later, "the man who has just emerged from Final Schools" was described as having "borne," in the company of other men, both the "tyranny of the examiners" and the "heat and burden of the week."[85] When undergraduates invoked the language of struggle and proof in observations about examinations (William Everett characterized the "life of a Cambridge student [as] a fight" in his 1864 lectures on university life),[86] they frequently likened these academic exercises to other all-male preserves, especially the military. The student undergoing examinations might, for example, be described, as in one 1899 article, as a "warrior" with a "manly brow" who not only submitted to the demands of a rigorous educational test but "struggled for degrees" on the battlefield of the examination room and performed in the process what one 1866 poet described as "valiant deeds."[87] Images of a fight well fought and a war courageously waged were of inestimable value in delineating the admired attributes of the examination warrior.[88]

Even the sacrifices required to succeed in these life battles were characterized as peculiarly masculine hardships. Preparation for examinations meant renouncing the companionship of one's chums, teammates, and fellow rabble-rousers, not to mention curtailing a whole range of extracurricular activities. Undergraduates increasingly saw examinations, in the latter decades of the nineteenth century, as the true business of Oxbridge life, and considered self-denial and the ability to know when leisure was permissible and when work was required distinguishing hallmarks of university manhood. While the cessation of enjoyment might be only temporary, it marred the undergraduate's time up at the university and figured prominently in the depictions of examinations considered here. Verse again worked its usual magic in the undergraduate press by pointing to the sacrifices students liked to associate with their preparations for examinations. In "A Schools Ditty," published in the *Rattle* in 1887, the academic requirements for the Oxford B.A. were portrayed as necessitating banishment "from every social joy,"[89] while in an 1896 "Ballade of the Mods. Man," published in the Oxford paper *Bulldog,* the narrator (a second-year undergraduate) lamented not only his anticipated poor showing but the curtailment of fun in his life: "I've given up rowing and footer [football], / My pleasures grow daily more scarce."[90] For one 1898 contributor to the Cambridge paper *Bubble,* the self-denial involved in preparing for the Classical Tripos entailed leaving pipes untouched and forgoing quarts of beer.[91] Giving up the pleasures of male camaraderie was characterized as one of the chief drawbacks to preparing for examinations. Discussions of these periods of abstinence from the male pleasures of tobacco and alcohol contrasted sharply with exhortations to seize enjoyment with other men while it was possible to do so. In preparing undergraduates for the publication of the lists of examination results, the *Pink for the May Week,* an ephemeral boat race magazine, reminded readers to fully participate in male culture while they were still able to enjoy it: "'let us eat, drink, and be merry, for to-morrow—,' well no—next week—the lists come out."[92]

The anxieties that the examination process generated were not, of course, merely responses to the sometimes exaggerated challenges of these manly trials. Rather, they were the product of genuine concerns about how Oxford and Cambridge men were being prepared for adulthood. Examinations for male undergraduates acquired significance in the world beyond the university as training exercises for a range of possible careers.[93] Success in the degree examinations, which came to function after the 1860s as "professional testimonials," could assist the ambitious in acquiring a position in the church, education, law, medicine, or the civil service.[94] Writing on the importance of examinations in determining the professional futures of Cambridge undergraduates, William Everett observed, "with many of them, their livelihood as schoolmasters, or clergymen, depends on their success in scholarship; with others their early introduction into law or Parliament."[95] While the knowledge acquired may have been superficial, quick thought, articulate presentation, self-assured confidence, and the patina of culture all became hallmarks of the elite educated man, attributes encouraged and valued by members of the various professions at this time.[96]

Undergraduates, of course, readily adopted the commonly held belief, articulated in one instance by Charles Dickens the younger, that "the chief value of University studies . . . will be in teaching them to perceive what they have yet to learn when they leave the University for the world."[97] The curriculum, with its important cornerstone of competitive examinations, contributed to undergraduate confidence, which was also bolstered by an entire cultural system premised on assumptions of superiority. Along these lines, Greats (the Literae Humaniores) were described in a 1909 issue of the Oxford *'Varsity* as a "School of intrinsic merit" that stood "alone as the best test of a man's ability."[98] In another instance, an undergraduate poet who attempted to provide "Advice to Scholars" observed, "[a]nd he who takes a first in Greats / masters the secrets of the Fates."[99] As tests of manhood, then, examinations functioned as useful devices in steeling undergraduates for professional futures.

Even the few undergraduate critics of the examination system, who questioned the overall effectiveness of these academic exercises in measuring or assessing merit or decried the rise of the professional ethos, readily noted the utility of the values and moral lessons that these exercises imparted. The author of an 1889 *Granta* article entitled "Tripos Fever," for example, commented explicitly on the character-building properties of examinations even as he questioned their efficacy as tools of assessment: "there must be something that is good in the contest and the emulation and the victory—something that remains when Scleicher's 'Comparative Grammar' and the 'Calculus of Variations' are forgotten. That we can allow."[100] Similarly, a 1909 contributor to *'Varsity*, despite his reservations about the validity of examinations as professional credentials and the practicality of the material that students were required to master, still found himself able to contend that "no work done in any school is thrown away, even when a few months after the examination not a word of it is remembered. . . . the training is admirable, and Oxford without the Schools, with all their unpleasantness, is unthinkable."[101] This author saw students who were able to harness their competitive impulses and succeed in the face of adversity as successful professional men, whose ability to thrive under pressure, maintain an aggressive spirit, and win fitted them to lead both nation and empire.

Examinations, Masculine Status, and Familial Pride

With such meaning invested, it is not surprising that overt expressions of anxiety occupied a prominent place in undergraduate representations of this experience. The stress produced by examinations is apparent even in a casual reading of student publications. Anxious admissions of doubt were not, however, merely the result of worry about stress or academic failure.

They also pointed to the precarious relationship between these measurements of academic success and the formation of masculine identities, concerns about familial reputation, and continued discomfort with the ambiguity undergraduates encountered as they moved from the safety of their circumscribed little worlds to the uncertainty of their future adult lives.

Poignant expressions of concern appeared in discussions about disappointing one's family or sweetheart. Manhood, for the Oxbridge undergraduate, entailed certain responsibilities, not the least of which was ensuring that female relatives and admirers were happy and content. Within such a context, examinations functioned not just as important rites of passage or professional testimonials but also as opportunities to display one's intellectual abilities and masculine prowess to potential financial dependents. In conveying information to female relatives about their academic progress, Oxbridge men frequently assumed a protective and reassuring role. Undergraduates might write to female relatives with verve, confidence, and even condescension about their work. Arthur Clement Hilton, for example, reassured his mother in 1870 that he was "working very hard," while Edward Jupp, just a few years earlier, instructed his sister not to "be alarmed about the result" of his examinations.[102] In addition to preparing men for their professional futures, then, examinations (like the annual intercollegiate boat races to which female relatives and friends flocked each spring) provided undergraduates with opportunities to delineate the correct sexual order. Controlling the flow of information about both examinations and boat races served to reinforce male power and the proper heterosocial dynamic, in which men interpreted their homosocial environment to female outsiders while maintaining the boundaries between male and female worlds.

Students keen to display their intellectual merits, preparedness for the future, and professional prospects to potential mates also worried about the impact failure might have on their chances in the game of love. One contributor to the *Cambridge Terminal Magazine* in 1859 wondered, "Oh, if I am plucked what will *she* say?"[103] Similarly, in a poetic "letter" to his "darling Kate," which appeared in the *Isis* in 1892, an undergraduate sent down after failing to pass his examinations agonized over what the implications of this might be:

I'm down for good. My heart is sore.
And well-nigh broke. How dare I
Inform your people I'm no more
In statu pupillari.[104]

Undergraduates worried that the women who cared about them would be reduced to tears of shame and despair. Their fear reveals a specific view of the gender and sexual order in which the world of women revolved around the vicissitudes of masculine activity.

Undergraduates were not concerned only with women's reactions to academic failure; the prospect of their fathers' reactions also caused stress and tension. The undergraduate expressed both respect and disdain for this central figure in his life, who simultaneously occupied the roles of stern disciplinarian and taskmaster, breadwinner, and paragon of masculinity.[105] Concerns about pleasing one's father represented an ultimate expression of the precariousness of the undergraduate's position as a man. His financial dependence, professional uncertainty, youth, and need for familial approval made him dread this man but also yearn deeply for his support. Students expressed their worries in terms which focused on the "wrath of the sire" or the "governor's horror,"[106] while they saw success not only as a personal accomplishment but also as a general triumph that served to perpetuate family prestige and reaffirm the father's masculine and, in many cases, professional status. Thomas Anstey Guthrie, a Trinity Hall undergraduate in the 1870s who had been involved in the production of the *Cambridge Tatler*, reflected on his lackluster performance on the Cambridge Tripos in a way that highlights the impact a father's approval or disapproval could have on the still uncertain late adolescent. Writing many years after the experience, he noted somewhat sadly, "I had miraculously escaped a downright disgrace, but I felt that I was none the less a failure. Which, indeed, was my father's feeling a little later."[107]

The writings of students' relatives reveal a similar preoccupation with the future. The concerns that examinations generated for worried parents were summarized in an 1864 pamphlet by John Williams, rector of a Banbury parish church and an alumnus of Jesus College, Oxford, entitled *Is My Son Likely to Pass?* While he begins by reminding undergraduates in a "Prefatory Letter" of the disappointment, tears, and discredit failure might bring upon a family, Williams devotes most of his pamphlet to a discussion of the concerns of the "anxious parent of our modern undergraduate" who "enquires, with the practical sagacity of middle or advancing life, into the probability of success that his son may anticipate in the schools."[108]

These practical considerations and anxieties about a son's future prospects punctuated a series of letters and published appeals written by Samuel P. Downing, a Wiltshire vicar, in the early 1880s. The subject of these missives and pamphlets was Reginald P. N. Downing, his only child and an Emmanuel College undergraduate who matriculated in 1877 and achieved a less than stellar record during his years at Cambridge. University proctors punished him in 1880 for several indiscretions, including giving a false name to a bulldog upon being questioned about his actions in a Cambridge street.[109] His father was also worried about his abilities as a student, and wrote to the Emmanuel College tutor William Chawner in early June of 1880 to express concern that Reginald was simply "not reading sufficiently."[110] Samuel was thus anxious about his son's work ethic and his general state of mind. Indeed, his concerns were validated when the time came, in February of 1881, for Reginald to sit the Classical Tripos exam. According to a Cambridge doctor, T. Hyde Hills, the younger Downing suffered from an acute "attack of Mania" which lasted from the twenty-first to the twenty-third and rendered him "totally unable to leave his room" and incapable of performing "any kind of mental work for some time" (Hills suggested two or three weeks), indicating just how destructive examination anxieties could become.[111]

While the elder Downing's persistence in corresponding with college officials about his son's progress was perhaps exceptional, the concerns he had about Reginald's performance were not necessarily extraordinary, especially as high-quality university degrees became increasingly important in securing top professional jobs, particularly for those from more humble middle-class backgrounds.[112] This helps to explain the intensity of Samuel Downing's response to the events that occurred in February and March of 1882, when Reginald finally completed the Classical Tripos but had his name removed from the list of examination results for cheating. According to his father, the younger Downing was charged "by the Senior Examiner, Mr. [Henry Edwin] Savage [a Corpus Christi College fellow from 1878 to 1885], with having obtained access to the Philology papers, and substituted answers, written in his own rooms, for those which he had previously given in."[113] Despite a good deal of evidence related to this episode, it is somewhat difficult to determine what actually occurred. Sources in both the British Library and the Cambridge University Archives do, however, clearly indicate questionable actions on the part of both Cambridge officials and Reginald himself.

Whatever the details of the case, the examiners and the vice-chancellor determined, in late March of 1882, that Reginald had "used unfair means to obtain a place in the Classical Tripos." Their verdict set in motion a conflict largely spurred on by Samuel Downing's year-and-a-half-long struggle to clear his son's name and to enlist the support of others in his cause.[114] The appeals and letters written by Samuel, Reginald, and some of their somewhat shadowy supporters served a variety of functions beyond simply enumerating the facts of the case. As pieces of evidence, they highlight not only the peculiarities of the Downing family but also the broader emotional, social, and cultural significance assigned to examinations by members of Britain's professional classes. Three discourses predominate in these writings: the language of outrage and spirited defense, the language of English liberty, and the language of professionalism, which was dominated by masculinized conceptions of familial pride and occupational prospects.

Samuel Downing invoked the language of spirited defense and outrage in his first critique of the actions of university officials, published in April of 1882, which functioned for the author as a morally unambiguous "appeal of the weak against the strong."[115] Downing's concerns about the attacks on his son were exacerbated, in this instance, by his sense of powerlessness (highlighted through his use of a politicized language of disenfranchisement) in the face of such considerable foes, men he saw as engaging in a conspiracy against Reginald.[116] To emphasize his outrage at these events, Samuel often referred to his son's shock at being accused of such horrible misdeeds. In a March 6 letter to William Chawner, the elder Downing relayed Reginald's words to college officials in a fairly skillful attempt to establish his innocence: "he assures me that he is entirely innocent of the deception attributed to him, and certainly it seems an altogether incredible thing that he could either have conceived or executed such an act."[117] Sentiments of this sort were also echoed in testimonials offered by various supporters of the Downing family. In one example, the Reverend Anthony Huxtable (a friend and clerical colleague of the elder Downing who was rector at Sutton Waldron from 1835 to 1871) defended Reginald as a morally upright young man, incapable of devious acts: "I might bear my humble testimony that judging you by your manner of life from your earliest youth, which has been passed in this village and under my eyes, as it were, I believe such a charge cannot possibly be substantiated against you for I had never heard or noticed a single moral defect in your character."[118]

Many of the letters and pamphlets written on Reginald's behalf accorded moral force to their strong words of defense and protestation by coupling them with appeals to the traditions of English liberty, justice, and gentlemanliness. Samuel Downing, for example, made sure to let university officials know, on several occasions, that they fell a bit short of the mark as gentlemanly upholders of British law and order. In a letter to William Chawner on April 20, 1882, he asked, pointedly, for a "fair and open enquiry" into the allegations against his son and for a formal occasion where Reginald might answer the charges against him, present contrary evidence, and defend his honor. "It is altogether contrary to the spirit of the English nation to allow such an appeal to be made in vain." In one of his published appeals he included a testimonial from a former Cambridge professor and examiner, who supported this point and chastised the college for its "perfectly monstrous" behavior and for actions "contrary to the spirit and the most elementary maxims of English law."[119]

The inability of these officials to uphold the standards and apply the rules and regulations of English jurisprudence proved, for Reverend Downing, their inadequacy as gentlemen, a deficiency he tried to drive home on several occasions between the spring of 1882 and November of 1883. In April of 1882, when he and his supporters were trying most feverishly to get the university's decision overturned, Downing resorted to the language of gentlemanly conduct in questioning the motives of the examiners, who, he maintained, as "Christian gentlemen" of a certain stature and standing in the British nation, should have been driven by something other than self-interest.[120] By challenging their willingness to uphold the standards of English law, Downing called into question the professional credentials of the Cambridge examiners and, by extension, their claims to manliness. Similarly, the former professor who demanded that the younger Downing be allowed an opportunity to defend himself observed, "this should be done . . . not only as a matter of justice to him, but to the character of the authorities of the University, for fair play and manly straightforward dealing."[121]

The connections between professional prospects, the ethics of fair competition, upper-middle-class masculinity, and familial respectability were nowhere more apparent than in the third and final set of preoccupations that pervaded the materials produced in support of the younger Downing. From the very beginning, Samuel Downing and everyone else who weighed in on the case emphasized the long-term implications of denying Reginald his place on the class list, and consequently his degree. In his first published appeal, Reverend Downing wrote of the "overwhelming nature of the calamity, which had thus befallen [his] son" and reiterated several times the gravity of the charges facing Reginald.[122] In justifying his public airing of grievances against the university, the elder Downing observed, "the accusation is such a serious one, and involves, if not disproved, such an utter destruction of all my son's prospects in life, that I now venture to appeal to you." He was concerned to clear his son's name, and by extension his own, in order to prevent a "bad impression" from being "produced amongst all his acquaintances, and society in general."[123]

This concern with honor, respectability, and familial pride, especially as it related to Reginald's ability to achieve full manhood by acquiring an appropriate professional position, pervaded testimonials and letters of support written in his behalf. In a speech that he delivered before a committee established to investigate the Downing case in May of 1883, Herbert Newman Mozley (a lawyer who was the nephew of John Henry Newman and a King's College undergraduate from 1857 to 1861) forcefully demanded restitution for Reginald, who, he maintained, had been deprived of his university affiliation on the basis of "unfounded and gratuitous" charges that led the examiners and other authorities to make "hasty and inconsiderate" decisions with long-term implications. In calling for a reversal of the earlier decision, Mozley explicitly connected academic performance, professional prospects, and masculine accomplishment: "I maintain that Mr. Downing's name must in equity be restored to the List from which it ought never to have been excluded, so as to enable him, as far as possible, though with diminished chances, to do something for himself in life."[124]

The persistence of the Downing men and their various supporters paid off in the end. In the spring of 1883, the university agreed to reexamine the evidence on both sides of the case by appointing a committee of referees charged with deliberating carefully on the sequence of events surrounding Reginald's disgrace. After several weeks, these referees determined that the evidence submitted against the younger Downing was insufficient and recommended to the Council of the Senate that the degree that he should have been awarded in the spring of 1882 be immediately conferred, "as if his name appeared on the [Classical Tripos] list." On June 18, the Council took these recommendations to heart but went one step further, when they "directed" that the younger Downing not only receive his degree but also have his name "restored to the list." Council members, in justifying their actions, noted that "unless his name appears on the list, he will be much embarrassed in his future career," indicating that they were not only aware of the professional implications of failure but also possibly influenced by some of Samuel's forceful rhetoric.[125]

On November 27, 1883, the Downing case was finally resolved when the Senate, having reviewed the matter, passed a Grace that restored Downing's name to the Classical Tripos list ("bracketed ninth in the Third Class") and awarded him his degree.[126] In the weeks leading up to the vote, supporters and opponents alike published their views in printed notices that were circulated not only in Cambridge but also throughout the nation. Reginald Downing himself weighed in on the public debates that occurred over his future. In a printed letter (published on November 15 and addressed to the vice-chancellor but really directed at the examiners and intended for mass circulation), Downing expressed his desire to prove his innocence: "I shall never feel really happy or satisfied in this matter, until I have convinced the Examiners themselves (as I know I shall eventually) of my innocence of the charges which they have formulated against me." In an attempt to gain further votes in the Senate, he labeled the efforts of the examiners to defeat the Grace an attempt to stonewall him and reminded the vice-chancellor and other readers of the severity of what his attackers were trying to do (in language that once again invoked images of financial hardship, professional ruin, and failed manhood): "The Examiners, perhaps, never realized what it meant for a young man just starting out in life to put such a millstone about his neck."[127] By playing this particular card, Reginald knew that he could tug at the heartstrings of men whose own professional futures (and claims to masculinity) and those of their sons were equally precarious and subject to ruin by allegations that were ultimately difficult to substantiate and maintain.

* * *

The rise of professional society in Britain profoundly influenced not only the way credentials for positions of power were measured but also the way gender identities were formulated for one group of upper-middle-class men—Oxford and Cambridge undergraduates. Examinations, as the primary means through which academic achievement and professional qualifications were assessed, acquired a broad range of meanings that illustrate just how significant these exercises became to students at both institutions between the years 1850 and 1920. The Tripos at Cambridge and the Final Schools at Oxford, especially, prepared them for their futures as leaders in affairs of state and empire, served as disciplinary devices that structured the work patterns of dons and undergraduates alike, and tested the knowledge that the Oxbridge man had acquired through tutorials, lectures, and independent study. They also, however, operated as rites of passage that marked the male undergraduate's transition from boyhood to manhood and functioned as one of the many sites in which the professional masculine identities of Britain's "real men" were forged.[128] Examinations served, then, to differentiate undergraduates, as members of a new professional elite, from society at large. In effect, a process that was routinely characterized as frightening, bewildering, harrowing, and steeling served a crucial unifying function by providing a shared experience that Oxbridge men carried with them into public life.

By effectively using language and imagery that constructed examinations as horrific ordeals, tests of character, and sacred masculine rituals, undergraduates succeeded in creating a pervasive culture of extreme competition and struggle whose victors could be described in supremely masculine terms, much like brawny athletes, scrappy soldiers, and plucky adventurers. Undergraduates, in employing an exaggerated rhetoric of trial and suffering, used the experience of exams to underscore their ability to succeed in the face of adversity, master a body of knowledge, manfully sacrifice pleasure, and compete intellectually. Strategies of this sort helped to define this exercise as a masculine activity, especially important as female undergraduates began to sit examinations in the 1870s and 1880s, and bolstered the accomplishment of completing a degree course.

While assertions of confidence abound in these descriptions, there is, of course, much evidence here to indicate that these young men were a supremely insecure lot. Undergraduates fretted excessively about the possibility and implications of failure and feared the loss of camaraderie that accompanied the end of one's student years, an end that was marked, as we have seen, by the experience of taking final examinations. In a society where family position and social status no longer absolutely guaranteed access to a position of power, the Oxbridge man, along with his family, also worried about what his future might hold. Concerns about professional prospects (directly correlated to academic performance) only intensified the importance of the examination as a gauge of masculinity. Indeed, by attaching the meanings that they did to examinations, undergraduates betrayed a level of anxiety about their position as young elites in British society which, on occasion, appeared to fly in the face of the ideals of middle- and upper-middle-class masculinity, based as they were on notions of superiority, assurance, and absolute certainty. In glossing over these contradictions by overstating the rigors of the process, undergraduates created a discursive space in which anxious ruminations seemed natural, warranted, and even heroic—not unmanly or cowardly. In so doing, they also pointed to the struggles that young men faced as they underwent the transition from childhood to adulthood and negotiated the complicated, fractured, and occasionally contested gendered landscapes of the late nineteenth and early twentieth centuries.

5

"Impervious to the Gentler Sex?"
Boat Races, Heterosocial Relations,
and Masculinity

In 1911, the English author Max Beerbohm introduced readers to a world of parties, revelry, and athletic spectacle in his novel about Oxford life, *Zuleika Dobson*. The narrative of Beerbohm's satirical book focuses on the arrival of the main character for a visit with her grandfather, warden of the fictional Judas College. Zuleika's visit occurs during the summer term (also known as Trinity term at Oxford), when female visitors came in droves to these all-male institutions to enjoy the usually warm weather and the public events of university life. Zuleika's poise, her inspiring beauty, and her indomitable spirit prompted nearly every undergraduate who came in contact with her to fall deeply in love with the stunning young stage actress. She could even divert the attention of rowers assembled for a race on the river Thames (or Isis, as it is known in Oxford): "For the moment, these eight young men seemed to have forgotten the awful responsibility that rested on their over-developed shoulders. Their hearts, already strained by rowing, had been transfixed this afternoon by Eros' darts. All of them had seen Zuleika as she came down to the river; and now they sat gaping up at her, fumbling with their oars."[1] With a humorous and oblique metaphorical reference to the male sexual organ, Beerbohm describes Zuleika's uncanny ability to distract those around her.

The brawn, overdeveloped shoulders, and oars in Beerbohm's characterization of the rowers surely function as crucial aesthetic markers of one
dominant vision of British masculinity. Contained within this description,
however, are also hints at the ways in which studying sport enables us to
explore both the psychological dynamics of gender identity formation and
the sexual implications of athletic ritual.[2] With this point in mind, I consider, within this chapter, several important questions: What role did the
sexual dynamics of athletic ritual play in constructing masculinity during
the late nineteenth and early twentieth centuries? To what extent can athletic rituals be interpreted as a component of the ideological, cultural, and
social processes that contributed to the emergence, near the end of the
nineteenth century, of the modern concept of heterosexuality? How does
one interpret homoerotic desire in this context? And, finally, how does a
detailed examination of athletic ritual enhance our ability to understand the
complexities and uncertainties of late-nineteenth- and early-twentieth-
century gender relations?

To answer these questions and move the study of public school and
university athleticism beyond a simple delineation of admired masculine
traits and the various ways in which sport reinforced and confirmed them,
I undertake, in the pages that follow, a particular sort of case study by
focusing on one component of the male undergraduate experience at the
universities of Oxford and Cambridge between the years 1850 and 1920.
Specifically, I analyze the annual springtime boat races that pitted crews
from the individual colleges of these universities against each other on the
river. The social buzz of dinners, dances, and theatrical performances that
accompanied these river spectacles presented opportunities for the ritualized display of university athletic prowess. They also, however, constituted
important social occasions at which a very high premium was placed on
the interaction between male undergraduates and female visitors. It was at
these events that the gender and sexual order, as Oxford and Cambridge
male undergraduates perceived it, was delineated through an emphasis on
the distinctiveness of male space within both the university and the world
at large and the primacy of heterosexual relationships in defining upper-
middle-class masculinities.[3]

Athleticism, Masculinity, and the Creation of Sexual Identities

These athletic spectacles emerged as one component of the "games mania"
that permeated elite (and to a certain extent, popular) education in Britain
by the end of the nineteenth century, as is ably demonstrated in the work
of J. A. Mangan and others. Sport was intended to foster such traits as

loyalty, unwavering integrity, and discipline. For Britons living at the end of Victoria's reign, a strong and athletic body became the signature trait of the masculine archetype. Within the public boarding schools and the older universities, participation in sports such as rugby, cricket, and rowing differentiated the manliest of men from those whose interests strayed beyond the corporeal.[4]

The male athlete in the latter years of the nineteenth century was admired not only for his well-developed physique and his manly demeanor but also for his expertise in the formalized rules and codes of conduct that came to dominate the sporting world during this period.[5] The agencies and officials responsible for making civil service appointments in Britain's professional society considered such attainments both admirable traits and vital professional qualifications. In this way, as Patrick McDevitt has observed in his discussion of Gaelic team sports in late-nineteenth-century Ireland, the obsession with athleticism often served a variety of complicated ideological functions.[6] Games encouraged conformity, precision, and teamwork, attributes necessary to professions that began to rely in the nineteenth century on ability and aptitude as measured by public, competitive examinations. Prowess in and a conversational knowledge of sports such as rowing signaled the attainment of a level of education, culture, and status that was deemed essential for "statesmen, rulers and good citizens."[7]

These developments had rather profound implications for the gender and racial identities of Oxbridge men, whose influence in the civil service (both domestic and colonial), the law, and other professions after 1850 was unparalleled.[8] Working hard, mastering skills and techniques, and attaining a manly competence became hallmarks of a new kind of professional and imperial masculinity in the latter decades of the nineteenth century that emphasized the superiority of the white, well-trained, and strong male body.[9] Undergraduates' general acceptance of this vision of masculinity was reflected both in the meanings they assigned to university examinations and in the descriptions they offered of the "average" undergraduate. By the turn of the century, gone, for the most part, were definitions of the Oxbridge student that highlighted inherited (or, indeed, aristocratic) privilege. The university man in a professional society became, in the words of one Oxford undergraduate writing in 1901 for the popular periodical *'Varsity,* a "m[a]n of activity, responsibility and common sense" capable of meeting the challenges of adulthood and imperial leadership.[10]

The emergence of the athletic ethos near the end of the nineteenth century did not reflect merely a shifting conception of manhood or a growing emphasis on professionalism. The ethos was also intended as an exclusionary device that marked off male arenas of activity, knowledge, and expertise in an era when British women were challenging these very exclusions through an array of organizations committed to securing legal reforms, higher education, and the vote. At Oxford and Cambridge, where women's colleges first appeared in the late 1860s and 1870s, the threat posed by female undergraduates to the masculine culture of these institutions was met with several responses designed to underscore male privilege and reinforce what were seen as proper gender relations. The development of a specifically masculine culture of sport and athletic competition was just one of the ways in which men attempted (however unsuccessfully) to counter women's increasingly public assertions of strength. Sporting ritual, in such a context, came to function for university men as a modern marker of gender difference, a venue within which it was possible to articulate fully the distinctions between male and female bodies, spaces, and cultures.

Curiously, while sporting rituals such as the boat races served to differentiate between the masculine and the feminine, they also functioned as elaborate performances in which men displayed themselves for women (and each other), partly in an attempt to spark a physical attraction. Female spectators at these events occupied a central and surprisingly multifold position as love interests, foils, and occasional annoyances. Sporting ritual thus allowed men not only to reinforce gender difference but also to highlight the separateness and complementarity of the sexes. In so doing, it made heterosexual sociability crucial to defining "normal" male sexuality and the performative (or enactive) nature of masculinity.[11] The important social rituals of the boat races thus contributed to the larger social and intellectual developments discussed in chapter 3 and identified by Jonathan Ned Katz as the "invention of heterosexuality." These developments worked alongside proctorial attempts to police undergraduate sexuality and social scientific theories that sought to define and contain "normative" and "deviant" erotic behavior. Together, they created a seemingly rigid dichotomy that helped to solidify the heterosexual's meteoric rise to hegemonic status.[12]

Defining masculinity and elevating the social significance of heterosociability was never, however, a simple or linear process. Contained within undergraduate discussions of the boat races are several important paradoxes. The most significant of these appear in the writings of undergraduates who describe the centrality of male-female relations in defining university manhood, while also expressing profound ambivalence about such relations.[13] Undergraduate discussions of the boat races betray far-ranging uncertainties about their future lives as men who would be expected to marry and assume the burdens of domestic responsibilities. Another important paradox is created by the frequent celebrations of male physical beauty that not only extolled the virtues of physical fitness (and, in so doing, reaffirmed admired male attributes) but also created a climate conducive to homoerotic longing and desire.[14] These tendencies, along with female students' attacks on the presumed masculine character of all Oxbridge institutions, reflect the extent to which the meanings assigned to the boat races could be undermined, challenged, and ultimately rendered more complex.

The boat races, then, provide a surprising array of possibilities for historical analysis. The celebration of masculine athletic prowess; the assertion of male privilege; the quest for leisure; the display of collegiate wealth, prestige, and lavish entertainments; and the requisite female companions all emerged as important features of these annual events which celebrated not only the onset of (curiously sexualized) summer weather but important cultural values.[15] In addition to providing insight into "the innermost values of [Oxford and Cambridge] culture," reading the social whirl that accompanied this seemingly fanciful activity enables a closer examination of a pivotal, if unstable, moment in the history of modern gender and sexual identities.[16]

The Boat Races in Undergraduate Culture

The association of rowing with Oxford and Cambridge has been both strong and enduring, as evidenced by its prominence in popular images of these ancient institutions. The annual Oxford and Cambridge university challenge race, first rowed in 1829, has "made the universities more widely known than anything else," according to Christopher Brooke and Roger Highfield.[17] The intercollegiate races, smaller perhaps but more complex as athletic rituals, became regular features of university life in the early nineteenth century. At Cambridge, the first college boat races were organized in 1826. At Oxford, the precise date of origin is unclear but appears to have been sometime in the 1820s as well.[18] Whatever their origins, they had become a tradition by 1900, prompting one chronicler of Oxford rowing to write, "[t]hese races are now so much a part of the natural order of things it will doubtless come as a surprise to many to find that they . . . [are] . . . the creation of the [nineteenth] century."[19]

The particular form these athletic events took warrants some consideration. Each crew comprised eight rowers and one coxswain, who sat in the bow of the boat and called strokes. The crews began at equidistant intervals on either the river Isis (Oxford) or Cam (Cambridge) and rowed to "bump" (or catch and pass; on occasion, to literally collide with) the boat ahead of them. The races were rowed over the space of one week in May or June (known as May Week in Cambridge and Eights Week in Oxford) and generally occurred in the early evening.[20] One boat would emerge as "head" of the river, indicating that its crew had either maintained the frontmost position by evading all bumps or, indeed, succeeded in catching the team that had started first in the order. Other accomplishments on the river were honored as well. Crews that succeeded in bumping the boat ahead of them four times during the week were rewarded with celebratory, convivial, and often drunken "bump suppers" in their college dining halls, where, according to the anonymous author of an 1868 book on boating life at Oxford, they would "drink of the same liquor, and smoke the same tobacco, and you will see them presently hobnobbing together, proposing each other's health, and shaking hands over 'Auld Lang Syne,' as if they had been 'chums' from youth up."[21] This general form (slightly modified and a little more gender-inclusive), along with the rules and guidelines that dictated racing procedures, survives to this day at both universities.

In their first forty years, the annual races were relatively uneventful and seem to have possessed little social significance to most undergraduates. John Venn (a prominent lecturer and preserver of Cambridge records and antiquities), in reflecting on his own college days at Cambridge in the 1850s, observed, "[n]o one went to see the boat races otherwise than on foot; society, indeed, had not clearly ascertained that Cambridge had a river . . . and I cannot recall more than a single occasion on which I met the family of any friend of mine."[22] By the end of the nineteenth century, however, coinciding with the general supremacy of the cult of the athlete, the races had become so important as to induce a near mania in the universities. In the later 1860s and 1870s, a flurry of activity began to characterize the race week.[23] Concerts, dinners, and balls became permanent features of the week, almost as important as the bumps themselves. The private balls and public dances were obviously intended to be mixed-sex, heterosocial occasions. This, naturally, necessitated the presence of the female visitors (as dance partners and dates) who became a central component of these rituals, a point discussed repeatedly by undergraduates in the student press and memoirs and signposted by numerous references to the distracting influences of "fair maidens" or "sweethearts" and sisters, mothers, cousins, and aunts.

Heterosocial mingling was also possible at special events sponsored by both Oxford and Cambridge, where the annual festivities surrounding the ceremonies of Commemoration (Encaenia) and Commencement (or Degree Day), discussed in chapter 3, were also marked by an onslaught of femininity. An 1866 contributor to the *Oxford Undergraduate's Journal* characterized Commemoration as a time when "our own countrywomen show fair and lovely as ever, and besides them we have met goodly blossoms from across the Channel and elsewhere. Half the belles of the London season seem to have migrated to classic Oxford."[24] Two years later, this event was marked for the editors by the presence of "gay dresses and pretty bonnets [which] may now be seen in unaccustomed places."[25] Anna Florence Ward, the sister of Magdalen College undergraduate William Ward, offered a female perspective on the events surrounding Commemoration week in a diary she kept of her visit to Oxford in 1876. In addition to being a bit bemused and, on occasion, a little disgusted with the immaturity of some of her brother's friends, who "squirted" a "ciphon of Soda Water" in his rooms and cheered excessively at dances, she also enumerated the elaborate social rituals of this festive occasion: concerts, teas in undergraduate rooms, the drinking of claret cup, and dances and balls that often lasted until 3:30 or 4:00 in the morning.[26] With simple comments and even drawings, then, undergraduates and visitors alike noted the significance of these occasions in underscoring the gender polarities and the emphasis on heterosociability that figured so prominently in the undergraduate worldview.[27]

As the intercollegiate races became more popular, they superseded the festivities surrounding Commemoration and Degree Day to become the primary social event of the undergraduate year. The scope of heterosocial activity available to visitors and university men alike expanded and included many of the same entertainments described by Anna Florence Ward in her diary. At Oxford in 1888, for example, there were, aside from the races, two cricket matches, a production of a play by the Oxford University Dramatic Society, and a variety of college concerts intended to "entertain our fair visitors."[28] Cambridge undergraduates and their visitors in 1895 also were busy with concerts, theater engagements, and "heaps of Balls."[29] The Footlights Dramatic Club began, in 1883, a tradition of presenting comedic performances during May Week that entertained visitors and undergraduates alike.[30] In the 1890s a Cambridge stationer noted the potential for profit in such a busy time and began to produce a small program booklet titled *May Term Festivities*.[31]

Students at Oxford and Cambridge also celebrated these occasions by producing "light" (that is, humorous) magazines and newspapers.[32] The increasing social and cultural importance of this annual event, especially as a harbinger of the modern age, was reflected in the proliferation of race week magazines in the 1880s, which, according to one outside (and older) observer, "no longer harp[ed] on a bygone century, but [were] of a flippant, racy and colloquial character that appeal[ed] to the younger generation."[33] Race week magazines frequently reflected this transition in style in their titles. Single words were often enough to draw undergraduate attention to a specific publication and, more importantly, entice them to part with a few pence. Titles like *May Bee* (Cambridge, 1884), *Ephemeral* (Oxford, 1893), *Parrot* (Cambridge, 1893), *Pink* (Cambridge, 1899), and *Squib* (Oxford, 1908) reflected the heightened level of frivolity and fun that characterized the summer term and indicated that these magazines were intended, first and foremost, to amuse undergraduates and their visitors. The editor of the *Bump,* an Eights Week magazine published for Oxford students and the tourists who flocked to the city for the occasion, commented specifically on the light-hearted nature of life during the races: "Gaiety indeed is everyone's motto, and an Eights Week paper rightly attunes itself to the merry creed."[34]

The frequent reports on boat races and the condition of the crews, which appeared in more general publications throughout the academic year, also attest to the significance of this event in undergraduate culture. Most student newspapers and magazines produced after 1860 contained regular news features and sections related to the athletic life of the university. Many reproduced cards and charts during the summer term, as the *Bump* and the *Buller* did in 1901 and 1912, respectively, which helped readers to recognize members of the various college crews while enabling them to compile their own racing statistics for a particular week.[35]

Aside from reporting results, they also recorded observations on the fitness of individual rowers and speculated about their prospects for victory. In so doing, they did not refrain from condemning those crews that appeared to be substandard. Such assessments, indeed, provide a glimpse into the sorts of masculine meanings that undergraduates attached to these activities. Typical of these reports was one column that appeared in the Oxford *Undergraduate* in 1888, contrasting one rower's fidelity, strength, and commitment with the weaknesses of several others: "We hear that Cool is suffering from rheumatism in the right arm and that it is only a deep seated patriotism that makes him stick to his work as he does. University are very bad; and Worcester are hopelessly dead: Harrison at stroke setting the worst example in the matter."[36] Discussions of races well rowed, examples of undergraduate "pluck," and narratives of impressive victories abounded in the pages of university newspapers during April, May, and June.[37] Typical of these reports was the "Boating" column from the *Blue 'Un,* a Cambridge publication from 1884. Here observations such as "the crew is strong and no doubt will turn out fast, under the able advice of Mr. Hocking. . . . Trinity Hall (I) have been very slow in settling their regular crew. . . . Swann is hardly rowing up to the mark" betray a general preoccupation with this activity and a desire on the part of readers to be kept up to date and reminded of the admirable physical accomplishments of notable rowers.[38]

The Ritual Significance of Boat Races

Simple amusement, predictions of the outcome of the races, and assessments of rowing abilities were not, however, the only functions served by discussions of the boat races. Student journalists attached particular significance to these athletic events in ways that assisted them in defining more precisely who the undergraduate was and what the culture of the university meant to him. In so doing, Oxford and Cambridge men pointed to the prominence of these contests as rituals (highlighting the manner in which they functioned as displays of masculine strength, prowess, knowledge, and skill), stressed the importance of the culture of competition to the universities, and, finally, illustrated the ways in which women's role as spectators and visitors was, paradoxically, both central and peripheral.

In establishing the significance of these events to undergraduate culture, students at Oxford and Cambridge often focused on the ritualistic components of race week in their descriptions. In nearly every case, the activity of the week was characterized as a bustling rite that celebrated the peculiarities of Oxford or Cambridge culture. Notions of their importance as annual events permeated discussions of these weeks of pleasure. One 1894 contributor to the Cambridge paper *Cam* labeled them "innocent water orgies," while another undergraduate journalist, writing in the Oxford paper *'Varsity,* observed, "of all the feasts . . . [at Oxford] . . . the most important are those held upon the river."[39] For some, these "time honored carnivals" had a nearly religious significance, as if they were aspects of a literal cult of athletic masculinity.[40] In 1904, for example, the editors of the Oxford paper *Barge* characterized the days during which the Eights occurred as the "week of weeks," implicitly comparing race week to Holy Week (the period immediately preceding Easter in the Christian liturgical calendar).[41] The *Mushroom,* a Cambridge race week magazine published in 1894, reminded students of the importance of "keeping" May Week, as if it constituted some kind of undergraduate Sabbath. Observing the holiday, of course, entailed indulgence in the nearly sacramental pleasures of "manly mirth," a fact that underscored further both the ritualistic importance of this event and its role as a defining experience in male undergraduate culture.[42]

The social actors in these rituals engaged in various modes of display and gender performance.[43] The ways in which participation and spectatorship were organized served important functions in reinforcing the divisions between insider and outsider, male and female, and undergraduate and visitor that figured so prominently in Oxbridge worldviews. In 1884, Charles Dickens drew specifically on some of these divisions in a description of race week at Cambridge that appeared in his "Dictionary of the University of Cambridge": "The races, both in the Lent and May Terms, are witnessed by multitudes of men, who chiefly frequent the towing-path, and many run with one or other of the boats; those who have further breath to spare shouting appropriate words of encouragement. The meadows on the opposite bank are sprinkled at the Lent Races and crowded at the May Races with ladies and others who prefer quiet to rushing."[44] The spatial divide of the river here separated young, vigorous, and masculine undergraduates (the "hordes of enthusiastic and bare-legged barbarians") from lady spectators and other visitors, among whom were fathers, younger brothers, and men of "weaker" constitutions.[45]

These divisions, vital components of the rituals associated with Eights Week and May Week, were also reinforced in the late nineteenth and early twentieth centuries by drawings and photographs that depicted passive spectators at the races and active undergraduates running along towpaths while exhorting their favorite crews to row harder. One slightly exaggerated image that appeared in the *Granta* in 1900 emphasized the spectacular nature of these events while also showcasing feminine beauty (fig. 5.1). Undergraduates, in detailing their own involvement in this spring ritual, liked to emphasize their active, energetic, and, ultimately, physical roles in it, even if they were not members of their college crew. George Nugent Bankes, while a King's College, Cambridge undergraduate in the early 1880s, joined the boating club not to row but to "wear the blazer" and enjoy the privilege of "occasionally going down to the river" to "see our college boat practising, or of running and shouting advice to it, when it is in for a race."[46] The dichotomy of activity and nearly passive spectatorship indicated not only the divisions between male and female but also a hierarchy of masculine attributes, with youth, virility, and constant activity at the top. It also served, more generally, as an instructive metaphor

MAY RACES.—II.

Fig. 5.1. The festive frenzy of May Week. "May Races.—II," *Granta* 13, Special
Eights Week Number (June 6, 1900).
By permission of the British Library, shelf mark P.P. 6058.i.

for the normative heterosexual relations that were intended to predominate during this intensely physical and sensualized week of athletic and
social pleasure.[47]

The participants in these rituals were thus assigned roles that corresponded to their position within the little world of the university and emphasized heterosociability and heterosexual eroticism. Readers of ephemeral May Week and Eights Week literature were repeatedly reminded of
the parts they were intended to play as actors in this important social
drama. An 1894 article on boat races that appeared in the *Cam* and discussed the crowd at Ditton Corner (the starting point for the Cambridge
race) further delineated gendered spatial divides and male and female
responsibilities at the races with the following statement: "Crew will
contend against crew, cousin against cousin. Other men's sisters will be
charming, fathers will be reminiscent, and the comfortable voice of the

proud but apprehensive May-Week mother will pervade the animated scene."[48] Women occupied, in this instance, fairly stereotypical feminine positions as charmers, comforters, and romantic rivals vying for the affection of undergraduates, while men were depicted as contenders, reminiscent "old boys," and active pursuers of both female company and boats. The sexual implications of characterizations like this one are easily determined. Men, in this formulation, competed for female sexual attention and assumed a position of dominance, while women enticed masculine advances and received them relatively passively.

Frequently absent from these discussions of female visitors as social actors during race week were the women undergraduates who attended the separate colleges established for them in the late 1860s and 1870s. Within the worldview of male undergraduates, as we shall see in chapter 6, these women held a status wholly separate from that of traditional femininity. Rather than representing potential romantic partners or even pleasant distractions, female undergraduates (especially by the 1880s and 1890s, when their numbers were increasing) were seen as threatening incursions into the male world of the university. While many attended the races, they were inconsequential, in the minds of many students, to the heterosexual spectacle of May Week or Eights Week.

Male Roles at the Boat Races

The specific roles played by men in the rituals of Eights Week and May Week require closer examination. The most celebrated position a man could occupy was that of an active, fully engaged, athletic participant—the rower. The male undergraduate could also take on the role of the active tour guide, escort, or spectator. In all instances, sacrifice and endurance were required. Members of the college crew had to endure the hardships of physical exertion, while the escort had to cope with the challenges posed by his nagging "people" (friends and family) and what he considered inane or inappropriate questions from women unfamiliar with the male world of the university. (It is important to remember, of course, that rowers were not on the river for the entire week and were also required to do their share of entertaining.)

The celebrated virtues of the male athlete will be familiar to those who know something about masculine ideals and the cult of athleticism in the late nineteenth century. In one discussion of the Oxford-Cambridge challenge race that appeared in an 1873 issue of the Cambridge *Light Blue Incorporated with the Light Green,* for example, the sixteen men of the light and dark blue crews (the colors of Cambridge and Oxford, respectively) assembled along the banks of the Thames were described approvingly as "fine young fellows . . . in splendid trim . . . all muscle and energy" about to engage in a "trial of strength and skill."[49] Frequently, such characterizations went much further in celebrating masculine strength, control, and precision. One undergraduate poet, writing under the pseudonym of "Robert Southey" in an 1891 Eights Week supplement to the Oxford magazine *New Rattle,* emphasized that the brawn of rowers was worthy of more than a passing glance from female spectators gathered in Oxford for Eights Week:

> She saw her brother in a boat,
> Exerting every muscle,
> With staring eyes and gasping breath,
> Join in the friendly tussle.[50]

While the onlooker, in this case, was the rower's sister, her admiration of her brother's muscled physique hints at one of the ways in which the erotic potential of the boat race was conveyed. In this instance, heterosexual sociability and attraction are celebrated as important cultural values in this age of university athleticism.

These annual displays of rowing prowess also provided opportunities for Oxford and Cambridge men to prove themselves as Britons. Indeed, rowers were not only superb specimens of manhood but also exemplars of British national and racial greatness. For example, one 1875 description of the Cambridge University boat emphasized the nobility and mettle of the light blue oarsmen who, in a race against an American crew, "beat their foes like British sons."[51] A "Trinity Boat Song" published in a Cambridge magazine in 1858 celebrated the trustworthiness, loyalty, and strength of certain athletic heroes. In so doing, it also pointed to the Englishness of these coveted attributes:

> Drink to the men who, so trusty and strong
> 'Midst the danger and treachery pulled her along,
> As Englishmen should, to the head of the river!
> Drink to our boat, and three beauty cheers give her![52]

The gendering of national identity, in both instances, served a number of functions. Firstly, it allowed undergraduates to place themselves at the top of a racial hierarchy within a broader imperial context. This racial hierarchy was also gendered, as historians of empire have noted. Within such a world the British as colonizers were seen to possess those masculine attributes which were also deemed essential for the successful athlete. Colonized peoples, on the other hand (with a few exceptions), were generally described in feminine terms that emphasized pliability, weakness, and receptivity to conquest.[53] British prowess in rowing could, therefore, translate into prowess in formulating imperial policy and administering colonial possessions, or so the equation went. The gendering of national identity within the university context also served to further exclude women from these milieus by ensuring that the definitions of Britons, and of the nation more generally, valorized the masculine, emphasizing in the process the sexual, social, and cultural power of men.

Accolades and praise of one's skill and brawn were not easily earned. Undergraduate descriptions of the rowers often emphasized their willingness and ability to work hard for their successes. This emphasis on exertion was, of course, part of a broader cultural phenomenon that extended beyond the cult of athleticism. Hard work, at least in theory, was also required in the years after 1850 to acquire a professional position in British society. Merit earned by applying one's physical and mental powers emerged as a central component of the professional manhood that became so common a feature of life for Oxford and Cambridge undergraduates. Celebrations of this particular cultural value abound in the undergraduate press. In 1901, 'Varsity characterized the Pembroke College crew as possessing "plenty of dash and some heavy men in the stern who do their fair share of work."[54] This hard work, sacrifice, and dedication were not, of course, exclusively in the service of personal gain and recognition; rather, according to the author of an 1891 description of an Oxford rowing man that appeared in the New Rattle, they aimed at "the honour of [the rower's] college," which oarsmen "strive manfully to support with all their strength."[55]

Militarism, celebrated in early-twentieth-century Britain in contexts ranging from volunteer rifle corps to the Boy Scouts to, as we saw in the previous chapter, university examinations, provided a vocabulary to undergraduates interested in representing rowing as another trial of manhood.[56] The pursuits of the river were easily likened to the challenges of the battlefield, as they were at the public schools, in parodies of Homer and titles that conjured explicit images of battle.[57] Undergraduates did not just row or work hard, they "battled" for their college or university.[58] In 1886 the Rattle, at Oxford, described the Torpids (the winter version of Eights Week) as a "coming struggle" and, more revealingly perhaps, as a "fight" and the "toils of war."[59] A year later, the Torpids again were portrayed as a "feud" between college "tribes."[60] In 1888 another Oxford paper spoke of rowing races as "fearful fights," and in 1890 opponents on the river were characterized as "foes" sailing in rival "fleets."[61] By inflating the importance of their exertions, then, undergraduate contributors to the student press increased the extent to which their achievements signaled manliness and situated themselves (without necessarily participating in military service) on the same cultural plane as what Graham Dawson has described as the "soldier hero."[62]

Not all undergraduates participated as rowers in these annual spring festivals, as George Nugent Bankes indicated in his discussion of his own peripheral role in the King's College boating club. Those men who were less inclined to be athletes but who generally supported the athletic ideal were still able to engage in the ritual of May Week or Eights Week, either as ardent cheerleaders (as Bankes did) or as representatives of yet another variety of university manhood—the knowledgeable host. If racing on the river was one particular form of masculine display, showing the university to one's "people" was another. Illustrating the ways in which this was construed as a masculine activity is somewhat more difficult than pointing to the admired traits of the manly athlete. Discussions of the undergraduate host's interaction with eager tourists reiterated the division between the masculine and the feminine that was so essential a part of the race week ritual. By exploring the relationship between these hosts and, especially, their female visitors, it is possible to learn much more about how Oxbridge undergraduates saw their position within the late-nineteenth- and early-twentieth-century gender order.

Undergraduates' responsibilities toward female visitors were exceptionally varied. At the very least, they were expected to provide guidance and assistance to those women who had made the trek up to the universities for one of the annual spring rituals: boat races, Commemoration, or Commencement. Undergraduates were reminded of their social obligations in printed notices and articles that appeared in student magazines and newspapers and emphasized, once again, a gendered and sexualized vision of the university world in which undergraduates functioned as active instructors and women as passive learners. The *Shotover Papers* in Oxford, for example, highlighted in 1874 the responsibilities of the knowledgeable and gracious Commemoration host, whose "privilege" it was "to expound the mysteries of Commem. to two very charming" guests.[63] Similarly, in an 1891 example from Cambridge, the author of an advice column in the ephemeral magazine *Wasp* instructed undergraduates to provide useful, if humorous, hints to visitors in need of some guidance.[64]

Female sightseers, travelers passing through Oxford or Cambridge, and inquisitive observers presented to the undergraduate host a number of peculiar challenges. Men on these occasions had to display their abilities as entertainers and knowledgeable insiders as well as show interest in what some considered the frivolous concerns and questions of their guests. Often, this manly responsibility took the form of a muted sort of chivalry which dictated that undergraduates, in assuming the mantle of manhood and its attendant sexual and social privileges, treat women with a degree of respect that bordered on condescension, and which was, as we shall see, mired with suppositions about the inferiority of female knowledge.[65]

The undergraduate host, as a representative of budding manhood, found himself confronted with numerous decisions and a variety of social obligations. His first responsibility in this capacity was, according to George Nugent Bankes in his 1881 book *Cambridge Trifles,* to greet his guests by either going "down to the station" to meet them and offering to "look after their luggage" or, in the event that his visitors came directly to his college rooms, "run{ning] out and see[ing] about luncheon."[66] Many undergraduates did not find this incursion of fathers and brothers, mothers and sisters, and cousins and aunts into their world entirely pleasant. Familial and social expectations, however, demanded that Oxbridge men be as gracious as possible. In a generalized depiction of the kinds of interactions that occurred when an undergraduate met his family at the train station, one 1878 contributor to *Ye Rounde Table* observed that he "[shook] hands with his father, . . . kissed his mother, and saluted the residuum of his family," a potentially embarrassing spectacle which, the author maintained, the student hoped to survive with "as much dignity as circumstances will allow." Above all else, this undergraduate (and probably most who would have read this piece) remained principally concerned with skillfully mediating between the worlds of home and university in ways that would impress inhabitants of both.[67] To his family, the Oxford or Cambridge student tried, through his various actions, to assert his mature status as a young man comfortable in social situations and capable of assuming the responsibilities of manhood. Before his undergraduate peers, he struggled to maintain his "cool" and avoid any embarrassment by projecting confidence and surviving this ordeal of late adolescent manhood.

While personal welcomes like this were the most important ones in introducing family members to the undergraduate's world, other, more general, greetings to visitors were extended in the student press, often in ways that directed the reader's attention to the strict gender divisions and intense heterosocial contact that figured so prominently in race week. In an introductory editorial that appeared in the Oxford paper *Meteor* in 1911, this was accomplished very simply with a single sentence that compared the fair feminine charms of visitors with the hearty masculine welcome of undergraduates: "And now to our fair visitors this week we extend a hearty welcome, and we hope they will enjoy Eights Week."[68] Other Eights Week publications elaborated on these divisions in introductory salutations that further emphasized the sexual attractiveness of female guests and the powerful gaze of male undergraduates. The editor of the *Bump* chose, in 1903, to explore some of the differences in content between a publication directed entirely toward men and one intended to welcome, court, and even seduce, at least metaphorically, "fair visitors" with their "flutter of skirts":

> At other times [the student journalist's] efforts are entirely for male consumption, and so he pours forth his views on facts and figures, speeches, schools, and dons, for the delight of *men*. They may be clever, but they are undoubtedly dull. But to-day how different! He need not bore you, ladies, with statistics, nor affront you with frivolities. Banished from his pages are the personalities in which the mere man delights, and in their place are—little poems, interesting conversations, witty and illuminating drawings.[69]

The presence of sisters, cousins, and aunts thus transformed Oxford and necessitated temporary changes to accommodate and entice women even as they disrupted the "mere delights" of men. Portrayals of fair visitors and fluttering skirts also, however, provided a certain amount of innocent titillation. Students were reminded, in these seemingly simple editorials, not only of the gendered divisions that marked university life but of the romantic potential embodied in these visits and the sexual opportunities that occasions like the boat races might present. Undergraduate attempts to contrast the rugged activities of men with the amusements of women (represented in this case by "little poems" and "illuminating drawings") might be read, then, as a commentary on contemporary sexual relations and a key component in the valorization of the heterosexual ideal, premised on notions of men as aggressors and women as willing and compliant partners, that featured so prominently in undergraduate culture after about 1870.[70]

Entertaining, enticing, and romancing female visitors also entailed extensive preparations. Undergraduates, as young men responsible for representing the university to outsiders, felt compelled on these occasions to display alma mater in her fullest glory. Again, the focus in these preparations was on impressing women and obscuring both the "ugly" side of university life and some of its more sacred mysteries. The preparations involved ranged in most cases from improving the decor of one's rooms to securing accommodations for guests and, finally, to displaying the university in all its glory by putting on a "holiday face."[71] In part, these preparations functioned as strange grooming rituals, preludes to courtship during which undergraduates put their best foot forward in trying to attract other men's sisters and distant cousins as romantic partners. These preparations also, however, represented a strange reversal of roles that pointed to the undergraduate's liminal status as a young man betwixt and between two worlds—that of familial dependence, in which he relied on parental approval and acquiesced to his relatives' continual demands, and that of the full independence of bachelor manhood. By assuming the domestic chores that visits of this sort entailed, the Oxford or Cambridge student reinforced the enigmatic ability of single-sex environments to simultaneously reinforce and blur gender distinctions.

"Fair Visitors" and Undergraduate Reactions to Domesticity and Heterosexual Romance

While student journalists instructed readers in appropriate male behavior during Eights or May Week, undergraduate reactions to the visitors who came to the universities for the bump races were enormously varied and reflected not only their liminal status as late adolescents and their desire for heterosexual romance but also their ambivalent and occasionally hostile attitudes toward family members, women, and the heterosocial world more generally. The incursion of family life, for example, into the university setting was especially problematic for undergraduates as they struggled to define for themselves a distinct adult identity. Expressions of these sentiments took on several different forms. Students could, for example, comment on the incongruities that existed between family life and the male sanctuary of the university. In the Oxford *Undergraduate,* one student journalist identified only as "T. S." used what he characterized as "unfilial" and "undutiful" language in an October 1888 complaint: "I don't know, but still I consider family parties are all very well in their proper place, but in Oxford, no I cannot bear to think of them." In this instance, the interminable dinner with an old "Varsity chum" of his father, during which the undergraduate narrator uttered a misplaced and ill-timed expletive and had a chance encounter with a woman of dubious origins, produced moments of embarrassment and irritation that highlighted the difficulties associated with any family visit and the tensions that existed between different generations of men. The uneasy meeting of these two spheres also pointed to the chasm that was thought to exist between the undergraduate's relatively independent life at the university and the constraints temporarily imposed upon the student by the presence of parents, siblings, and other relations.[72]

The presence of male and female relations alike also reminded undergraduates of the demands of domestic life and the expectation that they would assume, in the not too distant future, the financial and moral responsibilities of the *paterfamilias,* a prospect that frightened some young men of the middle and upper-middle classes. Some of them, as John Tosh has noted, rejected domesticity in the final few decades of the nineteenth century by entering Anglican monasteries, working as public school masters, serving the empire, or living in "settlement houses" such as Toynbee Hall in London.[73] This repudiation is evident in a fictitious letter that appeared in the Oxford magazine *Eights Week Opinion* in 1909. With some simple comments, the undergraduate author (identified as C. B. Gull) clearly differentiated between university life and the domestic sphere: "generally . . . all subjects of domestic interest are not likely to appeal to the average 'varsity man."[74] In the *Bump* the same year, an aunt (who might be seen as one embodiment of domesticity) is described as irritating her nephew to the point where he was "itching to strangle her."[75] Such vehemence was intended to be humorous and tap into a common undergraduate tendency to be both annoyed and embarrassed by the behavior of visiting family members. It also betrayed, however, a level of hostility that must be interpreted as a sign of the forcefulness with which at least some undergraduates were willing to eschew the demands of domesticity.

The supreme exemplar of domesticity for the undergraduate was, of course, his mother. While relationships between mothers and Oxford and Cambridge men could be tender and loving, they could also be fraught with tension. Mothers were especially trying when they challenged the undergraduate's position as a knowledgeable, independent host, emphasized the young man's social and domestic responsibilities, and reminded him of his junior status within the family. One 1895 contributor to the Oxford magazine *Octopus* characterized their demands, constant nagging, and frequent reminders, in an article amusingly entitled "What Can We Do with Mamma?" as "out of place in Eights Week." The author of this piece identified as particularly troublesome mothers' desire to visit museums or attend the flower shows that were frequently held during race week and thus draw their sons' attention away from the athletic events at the river. "Mammas" were, however, an even greater nuisance at the boat races themselves: "On the barges they ask ridiculous questions. . . . They almost invariably leave their wrap behind in one's rooms, and though the sun is scorching they will have it fetched. Refusal is obviously impossible, you hasten, as fast as your figure will permit, to do their bidding."[76] The requirement to secure an acceptable boat from which the undergraduate and his excessively needy visitors might view the races and the expense of entertaining and arranging meals, described by George Nugent Bankes in 1881 as a "reckless plunge of extravagance into the kitchen bill," were also among the trials confronted by the race week host.[77] Such episodes, whether they involved mothers, sisters, cousins, or aunts, served as potent reminders of how these unwelcome familial incursions disrupted the natural rhythm of masculine camaraderie in homosocial settings and foretold the difficulties and demands that would mar men's adult, married lives.[78]

While tensions clearly resulted from these incursions by the domestic world of mothers, sisters, cousins, and aunts, not all female visitors were, of course, unwelcome. Many undergraduates, in fact, relished the opportunities that these occasions presented and awaited these moments of heterosociability, especially when they offered the chance of forming a romantic attachment, with great anticipation. Still, descriptions of these interactions often contained expressions of doubt and uncertainty. On the one hand, undergraduates celebrated the boat races as courting rituals worthy of veneration, while on the other they worried about the presence of women who might detract from their ability to conduct the real business of university life. The undergraduate's relationship with women was indeed a complicated and conflicted one, a point reflected in the various, and often contradictory, depictions of both female visitors and, as we shall see in chapter 6, female undergraduates in the seventy-year period under examination here.

Undergraduates drew on a range of images and long-established cultural traditions in describing those female visitors to the university who were potential romantic partners. Representations, for example, that cast women as beguiling and enchanting *femmes fatales,* who possessed the ability to "bewitch," enabled male undergraduates to construct the charms of romantic partners as another difficult challenge of university manhood.[79] Female visitors, particularly those to whom it might be possible to develop a romantic attachment, were seen to possess an almost supernatural ability to make an otherwise oblivious undergraduate, according to one *Granta* contributor in 1892, "fall into a rapture of admiration" with the "slightest movement" or, according to another Cambridge student in 1868, with a simple glance.[80]

As beautiful objects, elegantly dressed and colorfully displayed, beguiling female visitors also reminded undergraduates that race week represented an opportunity to engage in activities different from those of the rest of the year, when, in the words of one *Granta* editor in 1899, "chronic murkiness" and "masculine slough" predominated.[81] Oxbridge men, on these occasions, were able to admire and court women at balls, dinners, wine parties, picnics, and teas; "proceedings" rendered, for George Nugent Bankes, "pleasant and enjoyable" by the very presence of these feminine interlopers.[82] The exchanges between students and female visitors on these occasions often resulted in greater mutual understanding that stood both groups in good stead later in life as they began the search for marriageable partners.

Visits from the "gentler sex," then, provided men with an important component in their education as gentlemen.[83] The presence of these women reminded undergraduates of the world beyond the masculine confines of the university, the pleasures of female society, and the possibility of romance in the future. This point was underscored when these female visitors left and the regular patterns of student life resumed. As one Oxford undergraduate journalist writing for the *Blue* in 1893 put it, "Sisters, cousins, aunts and the whole of the female train have melted away. . . . Our short 'Season' is over, and the thin veil of enjoyment is rudely torn down, disclosing behind it the hideous bogie of 'the Schools.'"[84] For many Oxford and Cambridge men who were beginning to think about their future lives and the responsibilities of manhood, positive romantic depictions of women might counter descriptions of female visitors (especially mothers) as bewitching taskmasters or social irritants.[85] In the end, this tendency to think and write about race week as a sacred ritual of courtship further valorized the heterosexual ideal for many undergraduates who linked the boat races with male-female eroticism. In this way, it contributed significantly to a process that was occurring, simultaneously, in the minds and writings of sexologists as they attempted to delineate the boundaries that separated different, and hierarchically categorized, types of desire.

The association of heterosexual romance and idealized attachments to female visitors with the summer term in general and race week in particular, as seen in one 1906 depiction of "An Eights Week Idyll," also provided undergraduates with numerous opportunities to reinforce what amounted to limiting and pigeon-holing views of women (fig. 5.2). Verse extolling female beauty and the benefits of love proliferated in publications produced in May and June and helped to highlight the peculiarity of that time of year. Romance, in one 1894 poem published in the *Cam,* caught an undergraduate who thought himself "impervious to the gentler sex" by surprise when he met a "maiden with the dark brown eye" during race week. Cupid's arrow, in this case, produced a sweet "bondage": a somewhat muted metaphor of enslavement used here to convey bliss.[86]

Romantic attachments to women were described, in other instances, as useful antidotes for the inevitable sadness one would feel upon leaving the university and departing the company of male companions. Women were seen to provide solace in times of trouble and offer relief from the worries of examinations and other challenges in a young man's life, functions in keeping with earlier nineteenth-century conceptions of the female-dominated domestic sphere as a refuge from life's hardships.[87] As pleasant ways to pass the time, Eights Week or May Week relationships reminded the undergraduate of what the future might hold, but they also served as sad reminders that, for most, it would be more difficult (though not impossible, thanks to gentlemen's clubs and other forms of associational life) to obtain completely unhindered masculine camaraderie in later years.

This realization, combined with the general level of undergraduate ambivalence about the desirability of heterosocial relations and the demands of compulsory adherence to heterosexuality, also resulted in several unflattering depictions of female visitors in student newspapers, magazines, and memoirs.[88] These descriptions and images were intended to contain the impact the presence of these women might have on the universities, prevent the emotion of physical attraction from overcoming undergraduates, and keep to a minimum the disruptions that mothers, sisters, cousins, and aunts invariably caused. Celebratory accounts of female visitors were thus almost always countered, in these sources, with comments that belittled their intellectual capacity, preserved male knowledge and, consequently, camaraderie, and ensured that the proper gender and sexual order was maintained. In so doing, these men aggressively asserted their power over women in a male space; and this assertion, as we shall see in the final chapter of this study, was reenacted on several different occasions in the 1880s, 1890s, and 1900s as male undergraduates expressed their (occasionally violent) displeasure with proposals that suggested women be admitted to degrees at Oxford and Cambridge. Ambivalence about women and their presence in the universities during race week was often revealed in persistent depictions of them as foolish and ignorant outsiders in dire

An Eights' Week Idyll.

Fig. 5.2. Graham Hoggarth's depiction of Eights Week love at Oxford. *Cap and Gown: Varsity Humours by G. Hoggarth and Others* (Oxford: Holywell, 1906), p. 11. By permission of the Bodleian Library, University of Oxford, shelf mark G.A. Oxon. 4° 219(16).

need of instruction. In this capacity, they served nicely as foils to the intricate male understanding of university traditions, lingo, and specialized rituals. Undergraduates exploited these images to bolster their own position as insiders and illustrate important distinctions between masculine and feminine pursuits.

One device utilized repeatedly in illustrating female ignorance and naïveté, and hence inferiority within the university, was the "ladies' letter." Male undergraduates used these fictional, and nearly ubiquitous, correspondence columns (which frequently appeared in May Week and Eights Week papers, but also in other places) to assume a female voice and confirm for readers women's (and indeed all outsiders') lack of understanding. In 1869, for example, a fictional letter from "Camilla" appeared in the Cambridge magazine *Momus.* Camilla told her friend Amelia that the winner of the quarter-mile event at the University Athletics competition had completed his race in a wholly impossible "five seconds," revealing an inadequate understanding of this important sporting event. Her description of the hurdle race as "quite pretty" established for the reader the peculiarities, and even attractiveness, of feminine sensibilities and the hopeless inability of women to recognize the significance of such firmly masculine pursuits.[89] With these brief words, undergraduates constructed sporting knowledge as a peculiarly male preserve that reinforced not only the social and political power of men but their dominant position in the sexual order.

Ignorance about the time and location of the boat races themselves pointed to the important differences between male and female pursuits and the peculiarly masculine customs of these "foreign watering places," as one contributor to the *New Rattle* labeled them in 1891.[90] In one example from an 1888 issue of the Oxford *Undergraduate,* some older women "not up in Oxford dates" who came to town unannounced, in search of an unsuspecting undergraduate relative, were duped by local townsmen and boys who preyed on their naïveté much as the Oxbridge student himself might do. Their lack of knowledge about the Eights, in this case, led them to search for their nephew in every corner of Oxford but the river.[91] Usually, however, undergraduates pointed to these deficiencies of female visitors even more explicitly. In some cases, this was accomplished by providing "Advice to Our Visitors" columns in May or Eights Week magazines that contained information laughable in its simplicity to the undergraduate but considered essential to poorly informed women.[92]

Other examples relied on more specific references to the chasm that existed between the ability of university men to converse about the finer points of varsity rowing and the faulty, if charming, comments of mothers, sisters, cousins, and aunts. In a 1907 letter to the Oxford *'Varsity,* a fictitious "Eights Week Girl" named Peggy described her first encounter with the boat races as a "rather bewildering affair." Her bewilderment was compounded by her inability to fully grasp the meanings of a perplexing array of cheers and salutes shouted by members of different colleges. The pronunciation of Magdalen College as "'Modlin'" confounded her, while more straightforward "murmurs of 'Univ' [University College], 'New' [New College], and a 'Bump'" came "within the range of her intelligence" and comprehension. "The House," the name applied to Christ Church by undergraduates, however, remained a mystery, a "riddle still unsolved." But this state of affairs, she noted, could be easily rectified. She reminded other Eights Week girls to ask a knowledgeable undergraduate for explanations. The wise Oxford man was thus portrayed as a point of access to the obscure and occasionally arcane jargon of undergraduate life. Engaging the insider, Peggy reminded her readers, would allow them to discover that "'Modlin' and 'The House' are names by which two of the colleges are known, that the undergrad seldom consents to use the recognised name of any person or thing, . . . that men who sport pink mufflers have rowed in some big race; and that four or more bumps to a college mean bump-suppers, bonfires, and general rejoicing."[93]

Several specific goals were accomplished in this simple description of the races. First and foremost, women were gently instructed to rely on the expertise of male undergraduates in negotiating their way through the labyrinth of university culture. More significantly, by asserting the authority of the male undergraduate, this author sought to counteract the destabilizing effect that the presence of female visitors might have on the sexual and gender order. Assertions of this sort appeared simultaneously with celebrations of female beauty and romantic attachments and betrayed, in the process, the unease with which undergraduates mediated between their desires for close heterosexual companionship and their need to retain the upper hand in homosocial milieus.

Alternative Visions

While most undergraduates generally subscribed to the views of the boat races outlined above, it would be wrong to assume that alternative or potentially subversive meanings were not also attached to this important undergraduate ritual. Most notable, perhaps, were those of two groups: the anti-athletic aesthetes who populated the universities in fairly sizable numbers near the end of the nineteenth century and those who derived overt homoerotic pleasure from observing these rowing spectacles and their participants (the two groups frequently overlapped). The former group generally objected to the tyranny of the athlete as a valorized style of masculinity, while the latter saw, embedded within the social drama of the boat race, same-sex erotic potential. In expressing views contrary to the ethos of athleticism, these groups articulated a more diverse conceptualization of masculine archetypes and heterosociability within the university and, in so doing, created a space in which other forms of male behavior might be expressed.

Most early critics did not condemn the cult of the athlete wholesale but, rather, issued calls for moderation. Rowers, rugby players, and cricketers were not necessarily derided. They were, however, encouraged to avoid excess. It was the opinion of these critics that Oxbridge men should strive for a well-balanced university life and pleas to this effect appeared, with some frequency, in certain undergraduate publications in the student press during this period.

Discussions of this sort were most frequent during the 1860s and 1870s, when athleticism was less firmly entrenched in university culture and therefore more susceptible to criticism. At this time, references to some of the unattractive excesses of rowing were not uncommon. The amount of exertion that the sport required was, for example, described as particularly unpleasant in the *Cambridge Terminal Magazine* in 1859.[94] In 1871, Vincent Henry Stanton, an undergraduate at Trinity College, writing in the *Tatler in Cambridge,* found the loss of individuality that accompanied submitting to the discipline of an eight especially unpalatable. The loss was, however, mitigated for Stanton by the "lessons of endurance, self-denial, and co-operation" which one might learn, "probably mak[ing] you twice the Man you would otherwise have been."[95] The authors of two separate pieces in another undergraduate organ, the *Cambridge Tatler,* complained, in March and May of 1877, of the "absorbing ailment of 'boat fever,'" which afflicted many rowers, and of the excessively cliquey rowing man, whose chief flaw was his "contempt for any and everybody who does not row."[96]

While these and other accounts pleaded for moderation and balance,[97] later anti-athletic sentiments expressed in an organ of the Oxford aesthetes, the *Spirit Lamp* (1892–1893), challenged more explicitly certain assumptions about late-nineteenth-century masculinity and its slavish devotion to the pursuit of muscle. In one instance, masculine brawn, exertion, and the unreasonable demands of the river were depicted as undesirable. The final focus was, again, on the loss of individuality that submission to a team required:

> By all means when summer is leafy,
> The air and the sunshine a feast,
> Don't train til you're brawny and beefy:
> 'Tis making a man but a beast
> But have your canoe, your outrigger,
> Your punt, and go boating galore;
> But never I counsel you, figure
> As a galley slave chained to the oar.[98]

In another general critique of the "tyranny" of the myopic, anti-intellectual athlete, the *Spirit Lamp* mourned the passing of a day when one was expected to pursue excellence in both mind and body concurrently. This discussion contained within it an aristocratic condemnation of the competitive impulses of Britain's professional society, which, in the opinion of its author, had "choked up all things; permanently severed the brain and the body, subjected either to continual coaching and cramming, and forced every man to choose between the two." This contributor to the *Spirit Lamp* openly critiqued the narrow definitions of masculinity and male beauty that dominated British culture by the end of the nineteenth century: "The effete has fallen down and worshipped the full-blooded: strong men and strong women, acrobats, prize-fighters, have been the lions of the sapless herd; and while few can be athletic in their own persons, the whole world, it seems, is gone a-sighing after the lost instinct of primal brutality."[99] This commentary was something more than a mere lament. It was one component of an attempt by a small minority of men (including Lord Alfred Douglas, editor of the *Spirit Lamp*) to provide Oxford readers with an alternative vision of manhood. In so doing, it represented an implicit challenge to the supremacy of the athlete in prevailing definitions of masculinity.

Some supporters of athletic culture realized the same-sex erotic potential in sport, a potential that was alluded to in numerous descriptions of the athlete. The attempts to establish a hierarchy of admired masculine attributes at Oxford and Cambridge were, on the surface, a bold and optimistic assertion of certainty about the supremacy of the athlete and the place of athletic ritual in delineating proper heterosexual relations.[100] In constructing a fairly rigid taxonomy of manhood and enumerating the desirable traits of the brawny and unimpeachably masculine athlete, undergraduates challenged the masculinity of those, like the aesthetes, who did not possess these traits. Within such a climate, the potential for subversion was also clearly present. Close examinations of the athlete's body, celebratory descriptions of these men as future imperial leaders, and impassioned expressions of admiration lent to the discussion of rowers and other sporting men an element of homoeroticism which could, if taken to its logical conclusion, represent a most potent threat to the power of these figures as symbols of late Victorian and Edwardian manhood. Indeed, the crisis of masculinity for late-nineteenth-century Oxbridge men resulted not only from their uncertainty about their domestic futures but also from their attempts to reconcile accepted terms of admiration in their homosocial world with the increasingly pathologized views of homosexuality (originating in both the medical and legal professions) that became ever more pervasive as the century drew to a close.[101] The athlete and, by extrapolation, the imperial leader became in this context a contradictory figure of desire on the one hand and denial and self-control on the other.[102] While his "vein of chivalry"[103] positioned him firmly within the world of heterosexual relations, his body represented a primary focus of male-male desire. He was thus positively invoked in various student publications, including the critical *Spirit Lamp*, which more than occasionally contained highly charged homoerotic celebrations of the athletic male body that drew attention to his physical attributes.[104]

Various sources yield evidence about the heterosexual/homosexual contradiction that emerged in discussions of the athlete's admirable body. In the years surrounding the turn of the century, just as social scientists like Sigmund Freud were articulating the hetero-/homosexual distinction, certain cultural practices, as we have seen, were simultaneously reinforcing and undermining this distinction.[105] In many instances, discussions of the undergraduate athlete placed him at the top of the normative sexual order while also underscoring his desirability as an object of same-sex desire. Several examples, drawn from the writings of Oxford and Cambridge students, point to some of these tensions. The impressive physique, indisputably handsome face, and general attractiveness to men and women alike of Mr. Albert Mason Stevens provided material for the *Isis*'s "Idol" column in 1907. In this case, one line suggested multiple meanings for the athlete's body: "In a word, we can recommend our Idol heartily to all Idolaters, whether for open-air or indoor worship."[106] Similar descriptions appeared in other student publications both before and after 1900. Another celebration of the athletic imperial body, in a 1902 issue of the *Oxford Point of View*, offers up an equally interesting and, perhaps, slightly less ambiguous expression of admiration. Here, these paragons of manhood are described as "splendid creatures . . . really works of art, and our only substitute for sculpture. . . . From the collector's point of view they belong to the best period."[107]

While we must use caution in speculating on the sexuality or desires of the authors of these passages without further evidence, we should not discount alternative (or even "queer") readings of these texts and images.[108] They indicate that the heterosexual ideal in undergraduate culture did not rise to ascendancy in a linear and unproblematic fashion, nor was it ever embraced completely or uncontested. At the very least, we must consider the full range of sexual meanings that might be applied to the ritual of the boat race and its participants and the ways in which homoerotic significance could be attached to what were probably intended as celebratory descriptions of unimpeachably masculine and, by extension, heterosexual traits. Multiple and, at times, contradictory readings of the athlete's physique in this period provide us with a clear indication of just how unstable the meanings attached to the late Victorian and Edwardian cult of the body could be.

* * *

By shifting the focus in the history of sport away from both institutional developments and the admired attributes of the athlete, this chapter has sought to illuminate another component of the undergraduate experience by exploring the ways in which the heterosexual ideal entered Oxbridge worldviews through athletic culture. As rituals, the Oxford and Cambridge college boat races performed a variety of functions in undergraduate society. They served to mark crucial differences between male and female culture, to delineate an insider/outsider dichotomy that was central to the process of undergraduate self-definition, and to provide a social space within which the tensions between homosocial realities and heterosocial expectations were articulated, mediated, and partially resolved.

The boat races, like other university traditions, emerged as central features of student life during a period of rapid change for both the universities and British society more generally. The mania for boat races grew just as women asserted their public presence (in education, the professions, and politics) with greater vehemence during the closing decades of the nineteenth century. In undergraduate culture, "New Women" were rendered an inconsequential threat through the reinvention (in discussions of the boat races) of a new sort of "separate spheres" ideology in which they were cast, often simultaneously, as beguiling distractions, nuisances, and romantic partners. Curiously, it was these sorts of characterizations that highlighted just how central these visitors remained to undergraduate attempts to define the university and the university man as quintessentially masculine. Without such points of reference, comparisons and contrasts were impossible. Images of women and femininity served, then, as useful foils to the various masculine images that pervaded discussions of the boat races.

These events must also be situated within the broader context of several other crucial developments. As rituals, the races served to highlight the importance of the heterosexual impulse in defining "proper," upper-middle-class masculinity, mark female undergraduates as separate and distinct beings (different not only from men but from other women), and reinforce male power. Try as undergraduates might, however, these meanings were always open to challenges and reinterpretations by anti-athletic, homosexual, and, as we shall see in the next chapter, female students. The boat races, then, were one arena in which late-nineteenth- and early-twentieth-century gender conflicts were enacted. They were also events that pointed to the profoundly ambiguous and constructed nature of the gender and sexual order as articulated by young Oxford and Cambridge men.

While the basic form of these races remains largely unaltered in present-day Oxford and Cambridge, a number of significant changes have occurred which reflect some of the broader transformations that have accompanied the "democratization" of England's ancient universities. Women's crews now vie for "bumps" on the Cam and the Isis; mothers, sisters, cousins, and aunts are often now fully recognized students or alumnae themselves; and the supremacy of the athlete has generally receded, though not disappeared, in student culture. Still, the changes of the twentieth century have not detracted from the continued ability of these annual rituals to function as markers of Oxford's and Cambridge's unique status within the British nation. Indeed, a recent description of the Eights Week Races as the "premier inter-collegiate sporting event of the year" suggests that as social rituals these events continue to function, in the words of one historian of Indian cricket, as activities that delineate, "in concentrated form, the values, prejudices, divisions and unifying symbols" of undergraduate society.[109]

6

Girl Graduates and Colonial Students

This book has explored, up to this point, the various ways in which Oxford and Cambridge students assigned specific meanings to the activities and experiences of university life and how they, in the process, forged identities that were simultaneously unified and fragmented. The British-born undergraduate, by most accounts, was a confident young man, certain of and even arrogant about the pivotal role that he played within both the university and society at large. In the descriptions of Oxford and Cambridge men that appeared in student newspapers, magazines, and memoirs between the years 1850 and 1920, the undergraduate was also considered to be immune to the contagion of the outside world, resilient in the face of threat, and capable of surmounting nearly any challenge placed in his way. Rare indeed were explicit admissions that his status as exemplar of both British manhood and the nation more generally might be precarious or artificial.

Despite such seemingly superhuman levels of confident exuberance and youthful arrogance, undergraduates at the ancient universities did face a number of challenges that ruffled more than a few feathers and undermined, in vitally fundamental ways, the certainty with which most Oxbridge men seemed to conduct themselves. Royal Commissions on Oxford and Cambridge were convened in 1851, 1871, and 1919 to implement modernizing reforms. Many undergraduates saw the growing internationalism within the universities, changes to the curriculum, and the emergence of an increasingly democratic society as genuine threats to an established and cherished way of life that they not only enjoyed but relied upon in fashioning their own identities as members of the British elite.

While Oxbridge men clearly fretted about the general implications of these reforming impulses, they were especially worried, in the years after 1870, about the consequences of several more specific developments that grew out of these changes and altered, rather substantially, the racial and gender composition of the universities. Of particular concern were recommendations by a number of prominent reformers, beginning in the 1850s, that religious tests (subscription to the Thirty-nine Articles of the Church of England) for matriculants and B.A. recipients be abolished. Parliament did abolish them in 1871, making it easier for many previously excluded groups (non-Anglican Christians, non-Christians, and, most important of all, foreigners) to attend these ancient seats of learning. This important change, combined with the relative ease of travel, the expansion of the empire, and the universities' increasing reputation and stature, created a set of circumstances that contributed to higher foreign enrollments.

Undergraduates worried, as well, about the implications of another development that occurred around the same time—the growing presence and prominence, at both institutions, of women. Beginning in the 1870s, female students began to receive undergraduate education, albeit under severely constrained conditions: they attended separate female institutions that operated independently of the men's colleges and occupied an inferior position within these university communities. At Cambridge, Girton College was founded in 1869, and Newnham in 1871; at Oxford, Lady Margaret Hall was founded in 1878, Somerville in 1879, St. Hugh's in 1886, and St. Hilda's in 1893. Privileges were gradually extended to the students of these colleges; they gained the right to attend lectures in the 1870s, to sit examinations at Cambridge in 1881 and at Oxford in 1884 (albeit in rooms separate from the men and with the results published on separate lists), and to participate in certain student organizations. In 1920 Oxford began awarding degrees to women; Cambridge did so in 1948.[1] Feminist calls for the higher education of women thus produced new institutions that altered the gendered landscape of the ancient universities and inserted a new category of womanhood—that of the "sweet girl graduate"—into the undergraduate's worldview.

Change, as it was embodied in the presence of two new groups (white and non-white foreign students and women), had to be confronted, absorbed, and accommodated in distinctive ways by Oxbridge undergraduates who, as we saw in chapter 1, defined themselves as white Britons,

Protestant Christians, imperial leaders, and gentlemen whose existence at the universities was ideologically and physically separate from the "feminine." At their most basic level, the reactions of these young men (riddled with telltale signs of anxious hand-wringing) to female students and foreigners betrayed not only the unstable nature of these definitions but also just how threatened Oxbridge students were by "sieges" from outside. In coping with these developments, male undergraduates of British ancestry tended, first and foremost, to characterize these two groups of newcomers as the very embodiment of the dangerous and destabilizing reforms that were invading the universities and threatening the precarious power and status of the British man.

Direct contact, in familiar contexts, with groups that most undergraduates considered to be other also forced them to examine, question, and strengthen the categories and dichotomies routinely used in representations of the nation and the young elite men who ruled over it and the empire. Even when their numbers were small and their position marginal, the presence and voices of foreigners and women in environments where they were traditionally either absent or decidedly silent underscored for the undergraduate the fragility not only of his own seemingly circumscribed identities but of male power and masculine hegemony more generally. Especially in the years leading up to and immediately following the First World War, female and foreign students reminded undergraduate male Britons that the nation's strong imperial position, its hold over colonial subjects, and its supremacy over other countries might be unstable. Furthermore, reversed "colonial encounters" and the incursion of women into male spaces threw into question traditional ideals and practices of imperial power and male authority and challenged the physical and psychic separateness that "otherness" so often necessitated.[2]

The fiercely contested battles and crises of confidence that were precipitated by the presence of these outsiders also tended to result in an even more exaggerated emphasis on the differences that existed between British men and their institutions, on the one hand, and foreign and female interlopers, on the other. Undergraduates responded to these momentous changes by pointing to the damaging impact members of (what we would call) minority groups might have on British institutions and, by extension, the nation, while at the same time underscoring the incompatibility of these new groups with Oxbridge milieus. They relied, then, on a paradoxical construction that predicted cataclysmic consequences of this foreign presence while attempting to minimize its impact and render it inconsequential. In so doing, Oxbridge men contributed, in compelling ways, to a cultural process whereby maleness, whiteness, and elite status (and the exclusive access to power that went with them) were intimately linked, sanctified, and preserved in late imperial Britain.[3] In the pages that follow, I chart how undergraduates adjusted, modified, and refined these categories of identity as they sought to both adapt to change and ensure that their preferred status as white men and superior Britons remained intact.

The Reaction to Female Undergraduates and the Crisis of University Masculinity

For the male undergraduate, the most profound change after 1870 was probably what Vera Brittain labeled in her book *The Women at Oxford: A Fragment of History* the "unofficial" presence of women within these university communities.[4] The numbers of female students in the women's colleges grew steadily throughout these years, reaching approximately 400 at each university on the eve of the First World War, when male undergraduate populations totaled about 3,600.[5] These women remained largely separate from male students in colleges that functioned as quasi-domestic sanctuaries and were generally located on the outskirts of Oxford and Cambridge, not, as Kali Israel has noted, in "the densely built-up center of town, where the historically male colleges are within five minutes of each other."[6] Nonetheless, they created a tremendous stir and elicited a number of interesting reactions that altered somewhat over the course of this fifty-year period but almost always contained at least a hint of hostility.

The barriers that nineteenth-century feminists encountered as they fought to expand educational opportunities for women and secure at least some of the privileges associated with university attendance have been admirably documented in the work of several prominent historians.[7] In describing the challenges they confronted, these scholars have often pointed to the opposing viewpoints of male medical practitioners and educationalists such as John Thoburn, Robert Lawson Tait, and Henry Maudsley, who predicted deleterious consequences for families and the nation in general if women taxed their minds and bodies excessively in lecture halls and college rooms.[8] Dons and undergraduates alike at Oxford and Cambridge frequently imbibed this oppositional rhetoric as they feverishly resisted the matriculation of women and their admission to degrees and struggled to preserve an institutional culture that was unabashedly inhospitable to female students, male-centered and male-dominated.

Despite these considerable insights, most scholars who have examined this important period in British women's history have not pursued the social and cultural relevance of these reactions to their fullest extent or explored their significance as telling episodes in the history of masculinity or "gender differentiation" more generally.[9] Aside from viewing them as clear examples of misogynistic patriarchy at work (which they so patently were), I utilize them, within this chapter, as flashpoints: moments of conflict and crisis during which the complexities of male (and to a certain extent female) gender identity formation are revealed and brought into high relief. Within this section, then, I attempt to answer several questions: How did male undergraduates respond to these changes, and in what ways did they try not only to hinder the advancement of women's education or maintain male privilege but to preserve masculine gender identities contingent on the principles of separation and difference? To what extent were the reactions to female undergraduates signs of the precariousness of professional elite identities, which Oxbridge undergraduates predicated almost completely on masculine prowess and the ability to compete openly, fairly, and valiantly in examinations and games? Finally, how did the presence of female undergraduates challenge or alter the heterosexual ideal that emerged, in the latter decades of the nineteenth century, as an increasingly important component of normative masculine identities and became such a crucial feature of the Oxbridge student experience? The attempts at damage control that Oxford and Cambridge seemed to engage in as women began to enter these institutions extended, as these questions indicate, beyond attempts to merely preserve the character of the universities as masculine enclaves; the universities were preoccupied with articulating and preserving individual and collective masculinities.

Before exploring in detail the nature of the Oxbridge man's reaction to women students, it is worth examining what many undergraduates labeled the mysteries of female college life. When the women's colleges emerged, they quite naturally developed their own cultural traditions, some of which were unique to these new foundations and some of which mimicked and, in certain instances, tried to appropriate or even subvert those of the older men's colleges. As Martha Vicinus and, more recently, Janet Howarth have noted, women at Girton, Newnham, Somerville, and Lady Margaret Hall developed and fostered an independent life in these newly formed institutions, and they too sought to define their college experience as peculiar and unique.[10]

Students at the women's colleges frequently capitalized on their separate existence from and inferiority to the men's colleges to emphasize their own sense of specialness and commitment to a parsimonious and almost completely unostentatious existence. In establishing this point and under-scoring the broader moral and political significance of their mission, fe-male students, as they wrote articles and editorials in their own newspapers, magazines, and reviews, highlighted the struggles that they encountered as the newest and most underfunded group in the universities. In 1882 and 1883, for instance, the *Girton Review* discussed the recurring problems of insufficient space and library resources.[11] Those who attended the wom-en's colleges in the years prior to the First World War, when female stu-dents and dons were most actively engaged in the struggle to get women a place at the table, were most likely to sound such notes.[12]

The women students of Oxford and Cambridge also forged their own distinctive undergraduate identity in more positive ways by encouraging female sociability and the formation of clubs and societies in the pages of their college magazines.[13] In the earlier years of the women's colleges, these articles and letters to the editor could take on the form of appeals for in-creased activity among students for whom the pleasures of an extracurricu-lar existence were a bit foreign. The *Girton Review* in 1885, for example, published "A Plea for Societies," urging the cultivation of "that public spirit" and "common bond of interest" which it thought essential in the creation of a cohesive and distinctive women's college culture.[14] This plea was probably more an attempt to get women at the colleges to mimic, even further, the vibrant club and society life of their brothers and cousins at the men's colleges than a specific critique of the options available to students at the time (which were considerable). Indeed, by 1884 there existed clubs and societies for those interested in moral science, history, natural sciences, music, drama, debating, tennis, the fire brigade, the gym-nasium, and literature.[15]

Female student culture, particularly among the first generations of col-lege women, was most distinguished, however, by its emphasis on aca-demic success and university examinations, especially in the years after 1881 (at Cambridge) and 1884 (at Oxford) when women were allowed to enter these annual competitions. In formulating their own undergraduate culture, students at the women's colleges were, of course, painfully aware of the world they were entering and routinely appropriated features of the male rhetoric that surrounded these academic exercises in trying to make them their own. Female students, like their male counterparts, could, for example, be consumed by the stresses of the process and comment on the dangers of overwork by using a range of illness and victim metaphors, as contributors to the *Girton Review* did on several different occasions in the 1880s.[16] Similarly, one Newnham College correspondent to the male *Cam-*

bridge Observer commented on this matter explicitly when she noted in 1892, with a myopia common among Tripos "men," that there "is but one subject of real interest, and that is the Tripos."[17]

Like Oxbridge men, female students also saw examinations as peculiar rites of passage. Edith Terry, an undergraduate at Cambridge from 1902 to 1905, described her preparations for examinations in the following way: "My most lasting memory of our studies is that we were made to feel responsible for our progress in them: we were no longer schoolgirls but adults, and we were proud of our independence."[18] While the intensely gendered meanings that men ascribed to the process were not so readily apparent here, for women and men alike the examination clearly functioned as a milestone in the journey toward adulthood.

Despite these telling points of convergence, there were some rather crucial differences in the ways in which men and women viewed the Tripos and other academic exercises, and these differences suggest reasons why men sometimes responded to these newcomers with such vitriol. As they began to sit university examinations at both Oxford and Cambridge, female undergraduates developed particular strategies for describing the process that underscored the symbolic importance of this experience in defining for these women their newfound identity as students in an institution of higher learning, while emphasizing the importance of establishing female communities in a male-dominated environment. These differences in perspective were made abundantly clear in contributions to the *Girton Review* and its Oxford equivalent, the *Fritillary*. In one instance, this divergence was revealed in a description of a post-examination fete that appeared in the Cambridge magazine in the spring of 1882. While successful examination candidates were certainly lauded at the men's colleges, communal celebrations, usually involving drink, were generally reserved for athletic accomplishments. Women's colleges like Girton, on the other hand, celebrated academic, rather than sporting, achievements at the special dinners and ceremonies that they intermittently sponsored for students. In this particular case, it was reported that Girton students honored the "three out of five candidates for the Natural Sciences Tripos [who] had gained First Class Honours" with an "enthusiastic greeting," a "candlelight procession and college songs which celebrated their success." Such occasions presented opportunities to reward those women who did "justice to themselves" and were a "credit to their college."[19] Similarly, E. E. Constance Jones (a Girton student from 1875 to 1880, and mistress of the college from 1903 to 1916), described in her memoirs the celebrations that occurred at an "Examiners Dinner" and observed that her First Class result on the Moral Sciences Tripos examination was not only a credit to her "people" but "very satisfactory to the College as well."[20] Statements like this one highlight the extent to which individual accomplishments could acquire broader significance when they were seen to further the cause of women's higher education in Great Britain.

On occasion, students at these women's institutions attempted to subvert male authority and question what had become a hallmark of the professional masculine ethos. Some, for example, were quite aware of challenging male prerogatives when they lauded, in their magazines and newspapers, their ability to succeed in a man's world, or simply outperformed the men on examinations, as Agnata Ramsay of Girton College did in 1887 when she was ranked as the top classical scholar and "the only candidate [male or female] in the first class of the classical tripos."[21] Contributors to the *Girton Review* sometimes challenged masculine prerogatives and the assertions of intellectual superiority that occasionally punctuated male discussions of the examination process. In an 1884 piece, women were deemed to be "as good as 'other men',"[22] while, in a poem published three years later with specific reference to some of the successes of Cambridge women, Jane Wilson, a student from 1886 to 1889, asserted, "For Girton has shewn us again and again / That her students can equal—nay distance the men."[23] In employing this rhetoric, women students at Girton and the other female colleges attested to the predominance of the meanings that male undergraduates had assigned to the examination system. By appropriating this language of masculine skill and prowess, however, they also attempted to alter the meaning of a process which was claimed by male undergraduates as exclusively their own. In so doing, the women of Oxford and Cambridge sought to unpack the ideological punch that the language of masculinity possessed in descriptions of examinations, just as they attempted to assert female solidarity.

Male undergraduate responses to change or to these broader, explicitly feminist, claims to equality were not, of course, uniform. On several occasions in the student press, in fact, Oxford and Cambridge men advocated the extension of full university privileges to women and seemed to agree with at least some of the women's claims. One magazine, the 1888 *Cambridge Fortnightly,* was particularly outspoken in its support of women's degrees and remains an important exception to the general rule. In an article printed in the February 21 issue, one undergraduate author even went so far as to support the idea of a "mixed" or coeducational university.[24] At Oxford, supportive statements periodically appeared advocating that women be included on the same examination class lists as men.[25]

Similarly, debate societies offered chances to express minority opinions. At the Oxford Union in 1896, Gilbert Hollinshead Blomfield Jackson (a Merton College undergraduate and a conscientious objector during World War I) openly supported the admission of women to degrees.[26]

These exceptions cannot detract, however, from the vehemence with which the majority of male undergraduates at Oxford and Cambridge opposed the presence of these newcomers. Tepid expressions of support were generally surpassed, especially during the final two decades of the nineteenth century, by a growing level of hostility as male control of the university seemed under threat and as concerns about masculine gender identities (reflected in the social preoccupation with physical fitness and with delineating the boundaries between normative and transgressive behavior) escalated.[27] The emergence of a distinctive women's college culture that prized independence from men, fostered female solidarity, and encouraged open intellectual exchange threw into question the certainties of the Oxbridge man's status not only as a man but also as a member of the budding professional elite. When these women appropriated not just masculine spaces but also masculine language, male undergraduates were reminded just how precarious their hold was on their claims to professional competency and, more broadly, social, political, and economic power.

As they attempted to cope with the social problem of the female student (a potent emblem of late-nineteenth-century feminism, the social phenomenon of the "New Woman," and modernity more generally), Oxbridge men tried, in a variety of ways, to contain the threat such women posed, make sense of their significance, and, when necessary, reconfigure gender and sexual relations accordingly.[28] The presence of female students not only challenged conceptions of the university as a male environment and threw into question certain assumptions about prescribed gender roles and boundaries, then, it destabilized the explanatory power of the categories of the masculine and the feminine and forced Oxbridge men to think more precisely about how the labels of male and female operated in their unsettled times.[29] Furthermore, the three standard categories of women—relatives and girlfriends, servants, and prostitutes—were, as we have seen, central to the formation of masculine identities; but when women entered the university as female students, these categorizations had to be realigned to accommodate this new group that occupied, in the words of one undergraduate observer who wrote for the *Cambridge Magazine* in 1912, a position of "strange divinity."[30]

Contending with the female undergraduate thus entailed adjustments in behavior, institutional changes, and specifically crafted rhetorical flourishes that served to mark the women of Girton, Newnham, Somerville, and Lady Margaret Hall as fundamentally different and, in the process, highlighted their inability to effectively challenge the Oxbridge man's hold over the university, his masculinity, and his claims to power in Britain's professional society. In labeling women students outsiders, male undergraduates focused most frequently on their inability to comprehend fully what the essence of college and university life should be—a balanced mix of work and pleasure.[31] In an article that appeared in an 1872 issue of the *Tatler in Cambridge,* very early in the movement for the university education of women, Vincent Henry Stanton (a Trinity undergraduate from 1866 to 1870 and a young college fellow when he wrote this piece) observed that "[f]or a long while, though men may come here to play, women will only come to work." While Stanton was clearly aware that these women had to work extra hard to prove themselves, he also sought to underscore their incompatibility with the university and their inability to understand what, to him, was clearly a masculine form of education. He did so by assuming the position of knowledgeable host and instructing them, in one paragraph, to take advantage of "the attractions of that knowledge of the world and of character which residence in a university can alone give."[32] Couched in helpful terms, this passage highlighted the distinctions that existed between the worlds of the "sweet girl graduate" and the Cambridge man who best knew how to live life at the 'varsity.

Oxbridge men intended these views of female undergraduates as unknowing and wholly incompatible outsiders to function as further barriers to their entry into university culture. In constructing them, they drew quite distinctly on prevailing ideas about women's roles and traditional notions of femininity. The differences between male and female undergraduate life were also elaborated, however, when junior members of the men's colleges assiduously constructed definitions of these women that challenged their femininity, underscored the unnaturalness of their pursuit of an intellectual life, and pointed to the ways in which they upset more generally the masculine worldview of university students. Men at Oxford and Cambridge, in responding to the dramatic changes of the later nineteenth century, attempted to assert control over their environment by recasting gender ideologies to both accommodate change and assert the superiority and resiliency of the masculine in this context. Sometimes this was accomplished rather simply with quips that denigrated the intellectual attainments of female students and pointed to their anomalous, strange, and wholly ambiguous status as a new and entirely inferior category of womanhood. In one brief example, a contributor to the *Cantab* in 1872 found that the female college instructor defied labeling and could not be fitted into the gender order. Was she to be a tutor or a "tutoress," he wondered.[33]

More poignant still were those images of female students that positioned them outside the matrix of heterosexual relations and heterosociability that had come to figure so prominently in undergraduate culture. Many male undergraduates considered female students ugly, excessively brainy, and sexually neutered or ambiguous, precisely because they had decided to pursue a degree course and might eschew marriage for an academic career. This characterization was tellingly conveyed in an 1894 book of Cambridge sketches that juxtaposed two images of the Girton girl, one "as she is" and one "as she might be" (fig. 6.1). Such women had little or no value for Oxbridge men, who increasingly began to draw explicit connections between normative masculine socialization and romantic attachments with idealized women who were accommodating, physically attractive, charming, and ultimately compliant and unthreatening.

Female students thus challenged the gender divide and represented, for many undergraduates, a reversal of the ordinary: a world turned upside down in which women dominated emasculated men academically, socially, and sexually and threatened the integrity of not only the universities but also British society more generally. A poem that appeared in the Cambridge paper *May Bee* in June of 1884 warned readers, for example, about the dangerous implications of reversing gender roles. In the piece, entitled "The Higher Education of Women," an equally well educated couple is described, in an evocative final stanza, as having an untraditional relationship in which the mathematically inclined wife has clearly gained the upper hand and the male partner has been relegated to the kitchen:

And thus I win my lovely bride,
With $\tan_2 x$ I woo and win her,
Now, while she calculates the tide
In Sirius, *I* cook the dinner.[34]

The fears and anxieties associated with the masculinity of the female undergraduate, her unwelcome presence, and her anomalous sexual and social status became, in some instances, almost too much for Oxbridge men to handle. While they generally confined their comments to some of the issues discussed in this section or to silly references to womanly pettiness and fashion-consciousness, occasionally their worries boiled over and manifested in outright and vituperative misogyny.[35] In a poem entitled "Villanette" that appeared in the Oxford paper *'Varsity* in 1901, for ex-

A GIRTON GIRL.

AS SHE IS

A GIRTON GIRL.

AS SHE MIGHT BE

Fig. 6.1. Contrasting images of the female student. *Types* (Cambridge: Redin, 1894), pp. 6–7.
By permission of the Syndics of the Cambridge University Library, shelf mark Cam.d.894.9.

ample, the disruptive, intrusive, and painstakingly conscientious female student is depicted as driving male undergraduates "insane." While the word may have been partially intended to acknowledge the woman's ability to catch the man's attention and rile his romantic imagination, the final stanza conveyed some of the difficulties men had in adjusting to the situation at hand and betrayed just how disgusted at least some of them had become:

These words may seem immoderate,
Yet sick at heart we cry again:

"She is the sum of all I hate,
The 'sweet girl-undergraduate.'"[36]

Episodes of Gender Conflict

Between 1880 and 1920, demands that women be allowed to attend lectures with men and even take degrees prompted a set of responses that
functioned, in highly elaborate ways, as ritualized enactments of masculine
privilege and camaraderie and occasionally as violent displays of male solidarity; performances that were intended to preserve and even bolster foundering gender identities as Oxford and Cambridge students forestalled,
confronted, and even, in some cases, adapted to the tumultuous changes of
the late nineteenth and early twentieth centuries. This general climate of
hostility meant that nearly every area of educational provision for women
at the ancient universities elicited comments, sometimes extremely caustic, from male undergraduates and dons alike.

The presence of women in undergraduate lectures prompted numerous
responses from Oxbridge students and functioned as one important site of
conflict in this period. Beginning in the 1870s, women attended lectures
in classics, history, mathematics, and a wide array of other subjects, usually
on the sufferance of individual dons and on an ad hoc basis, in the various
male colleges of both universities.[37] While some men at Oxford, including
A. G. Vernon of Christ Church and J. Franck Bright of University College,
opened their lectures to women, the atmosphere within the university and
among students more generally was not always welcoming.[38] Indeed the
vehement comments of John Ruskin, who, as a professor of art, refused in
1871 to admit women to his public lectures, reflect one strain of the sentiment of opposition that was fairly pervasive in Oxford: "I cannot let the
bonnets in, on any conditions this term. The three public lectures will be
chiefly on angles, degrees of colour-prisms . . . and other such things, of no
use to the female mind and they would occupy the seats in mere disappointed puzzlement."[39] While Ruskin and other opponents would eventually relent and admit "the bonnets," it is important to bear in mind that
protests of this sort established a precedent for how undergraduates themselves might react to women once they began to set foot in the hallowed
spaces of university and college lecture halls.[40]

The obstreperous editors of and contributors to the *Undergraduate*, an
Oxford weekly that ran for nearly a full year in 1888, adopted some of
Ruskin's ideas (along with a number of others) when they addressed the
increasingly visible and troubling presence of women at college lectures.

This subject had, by the 1880s, become a common topic of discussion among Oxford journalists and the men they wrote for. As in most matters, male students disagreed about the integration of women into undergraduate society, a disagreement that revealed just how unevenly the women of Somerville, Lady Margaret Hall, St. Hugh's, and St. Hilda's were assimilated and accommodated. While some contributors to the *Undergraduate* looked positively on the presence of women—one even lauded their tenacity and diligence in attending a lecture on a snowy February day—it is safe to say that most were firmly opposed. The strength of their opposition was expressed in a telling episode of conflict that exploded in the paper's pages in November.[41]

In a brief notice published on the eighth day of that month, the editors of the *Undergraduate* described the mixed environment of the lecture hall as too much to handle, and they lashed out. Here, the presence of women precipitated a genuine crisis that threw into question traditional gender and sexual roles and forced undergraduates, once again, to reconfigure the categories of both the masculine and the feminine. The passage quoted here reveals concerns about the meaning and implications of female encroachment into a male preserve and into male pleasures:

> It is quite a pleasure among the wilderness of sterile and useless lectures to come across a real good one. One that is not only amusing but also instructive. Sidgwick's lectures on Sophocles at Corpus are a vast exception to the general rule. But what or wherefore women should attend is somewhat perplexing. The play this term is the *Oedipus Rex,* which is distinctly spicy in parts, as for instance where the hero marries his mother after unkindly sending his papa to kingdom come. It is a most comical sight to watch the face of the lecturer, who at all events is a gentleman, as he describes the working out of these chaste complications. Needless to say the only place where a blush is not is on the face of these creatures, miscalled women, who not only grin, but apparently enjoy all the "stronger" bits. This is what we have come to, a lecturer cannot lecture in peace, nor undergrads listen, without being put to blush by a pack of shameless females.[42]

This represented quite a dramatic departure indeed from that wintry February day when men and women were one in "storm and Schools."[43] Generally, lectures, especially at Oxford, were seen as dispensable components of an undergraduate education and certainly not integral to one's preparation for examinations.[44] The relative ease with which women were accepted at some lectures seemed to depend on the quality of the material and the personality of the lecturer. The popularity of this particular lecture among men and its decidedly "spicy" content led the *Undergraduate* to declare it inappropriate for college women; this author attempted to preserve male control over the educational process and exercise a kind of perverse chivalry that allowed men to police the sensual reactions of women.

By responding to the racy bits in uncharacteristic ways, these women challenged the male undergraduates' and the lecturer's power over the material and consequently over the women themselves. As they subverted stereotypes, these female undergraduates also threatened the oppositional definition of the feminine that was so central to the male undergraduate's conception of himself and the work he conducted within the university. The author of this piece tried to mitigate the dangers of this episode by denying the "pack of shameless females" their femininity in one word, saying they were "miscalled women." The disruption experienced in this instance and the extreme nature of the *Undergraduate*'s response must not, however, be viewed as isolated incidents. Rather, the episode needs to be read very explicitly as a broadly symbolic reaction that allowed students to express displeasure not only about this particular lecture but also about the state of gender relations more generally within the university.

Disciplinary officials did not consider the caustic comments in the *Undergraduate* entirely unproblematic, and the differing views of dons and undergraduates reveal just how significant and extensive intergenerational conflict between these two groups was. The disagreements over this simple, if highly offensive, statement reflect not only disparate opinions about how men should behave but also the ways in which masculine identities could fracture, even in the face of the potent threat that women students were thought to represent. While dons often accepted women into their lectures only grudgingly, they could not countenance such blatant ungentlemanly conduct from their undergraduate charges. For them, the sting of these editorial comments was not warranted even when the women in question conducted themselves like a "pack of shameless females." This episode became something of a *cause célèbre* as undergraduates and dons battled in the weeks following the appearance of this piece, and the conflict received extensive press coverage in national newspapers.[45]

These printed accounts fill in much of the detail of a case that has yielded surprisingly little archival material.[46] Lancelot Julian Bathurst, an undergraduate member of New College, was summoned before the dean of that college after he had been identified as one of the *Undergraduate*'s editors. Bathurst was held accountable and was forced to bear full responsibility for the piece, even though the article could not be attributed to him directly. In fact, its authorship remains something of a mystery.[47] The reasons for and the precise nature of the disciplinary proceedings were identified in the report on the incident in the *Times*'s university intelligence column on December 6: "Some particular passages were pointed out to Mr. Bathurst as offensive on various grounds, and one paragraph was especially commented on as involving a grave and criminal libel on some ladies who could easily be identified. Mr. Bathurst was then informed that the sentence of the College was that he should be sent down from the University until October, 1889, since he had admitted his full editorial responsibility."[48]

A similar report in the *Pall Mall Gazette* on the third of December also recounted the events leading up to and following the incident. This account differed from the piece in the *Times* in its speculation that the strong reaction of the New College officials could not be attributed solely to the impropriety of the *Undergraduate*'s editorial comments. The harshness of the sentence imposed, the author of the *Gazette* piece argued, was due more to the displeasure of self-interested fellows who had taken offense to "certain personal skits upon themselves" that had appeared periodically in the paper. This author saw the offending paragraph as a "pretext to hide the real grievance."[49] If this is true, Bathurst was the victim of his association with a paper that had a history of publishing outspoken critiques and penetrating barbs directed at dons, a hypothesis on which undergraduate supporters of Bathurst readily capitalized.[50] Its plausibility reflects just how seriously some college fellows took these periodic challenges to their own masculine identities.

The dons of New College imposed a fairly harsh sentence in sending Bathurst down for nearly a full year. Condemned for his impudence and injurious actions against "respectable women in the notorious booklet,"[51] Bathurst found himself exiled from the community of men for this infraction—a sentence which fellow undergraduates, including his friend and associate Theodore Wilfrid Fry (a New College undergraduate himself from 1886 to 1889) declared unjust.[52] His father, Allen Alexander, the sixth Earl Bathurst, who quite naturally resented the brusque treatment of his son and worried (as Samuel Downing did about Reginald when the latter was accused of cheating in 1882) about the implications of this punishment for his son's future, protested what he saw as a rush to judgment. The sentence, he opined, was particularly harsh considering that Lancelot had honorably admitted full editorial responsibility even though he was just "one of a committee of nine or ten who discharged the duties" of the position.[53]

Undergraduates reacted to news of the don's disciplinary response in ways that both challenged the authority of university and college officials and celebrated manly courage, social accomplishments, and Bathurst's elevated position in undergraduate society, of which he was, according to the report in the *Pall Mall Gazette,* a "leading and popular member."[54] To his colleagues, Bathurst epitomized integrity, a loosely defined professionalism, masculine courage, and outspokenness. To at least some dons, he was a rogue who failed to exercise caution, behaved in an ungentlemanly manner, and neglected his responsibilities as a young man on the cusp of adulthood.

Undergraduates of New College, in choosing to support Bathurst, forcefully protested the decisions of dons and tried to assert the supremacy of their vision of youthful manhood. In so doing, they displayed a disregard for gentlemanly ethics (at least as they were defined by the dons) that was, in their minds, warranted by the actions of the brash women who threatened their position within the university and did not themselves conform to prescribed gender norms. Such disregard would resurface in another context when the suffragettes of the Women's Social and Political Union, at their most militant stage early in the twentieth century, encountered thoroughly ungentlemanly responses and physical attacks from police and politicians alike who struggled to retain power and maintain control in the face of change.[55] In interpreting the reactions of undergraduates to the Bathurst case, it is important to bear this point in mind. These New College students were not only supporting a colleague or challenging the authority of dons, they were in fact asserting a particular view about the position of women in the university and taking a stand on what they thought were dangerous shifts in a precariously ordered system of gender relations and roles, a system in which bold assertions of masculine power were required to bolster male authority.

The first organized response was a petition signed by nearly the entire undergraduate population of New College (about 170 or 180 students) that opposed the harshness of the punishment imposed on the popular Bathurst.[56] His supporters were unsuccessful in their plea to have his sentence remitted, but their protests and their attempts to express solidarity did not end with this gesture. Undergraduates used the day of his expulsion as an opportunity to articulate their position even more forcefully. On Thursday, November 22, "shortly before two o'clock," the front quadrangle of New College became "crowded with expectant undergraduates." The appearance of Mr. Bathurst prompted, according to the *Pall Mall Gazette,* "loud and prolonged cheering." The "body of enthusiastic admirers" chose this point in the proceedings to further display their support for him by taking "the horse . . . from the shafts" of the cab and drawing it *en masse* "up the Broad and even to the station." Before his final departure by train, Bathurst gave a speech denouncing the "excessive, unprecedented, and unjust" nature of his punishment, which was loudly cheered and incited the crowd to even further action later that evening in college, where "the feeling ran very high" and where a sense of outrage about the treatment of students generally was palpable.[57]

Violators of college statutes and codes of behavior might, then, be exalted by an undergraduate's peers even as college deans and other officials castigated them. For his compatriots, Bathurst's irreverence represented the ultimate expression of defiance and youthful virility: an assertion of independence that both openly challenged the power of the dons and made Bathurst a paragon worthy of admiration. The parade that marked Bathurst's departure from Oxford and celebrated his character was part of an established tradition of mock funerals and processions, common at both institutions and routinely enacted for students sent down for disciplinary infractions.[58] At Cambridge this practice, which endured over the seventy-year period examined in this book, consisted of collecting the "body" of the vanquished undergraduate "from the man's college" and placing it "into a hansom cab." "A procession" then "went through town to the railway station, with mourners in appropriate attire and a choir singing hymns." At the station, the "body" was "put into the guard's van," whence the "victim" was removed from Cambridge to his place of permanent residence (usually his parents' home). Expressions of solidarity with the admonished undergraduate exaggerated the severity of the punishment, and consequently the harshness of those who sat in judgment of him, while providing an opportunity to display the cohesiveness of the male undergraduate community, especially as it defied authority.[59]

Students also protested the Bathurst expulsion in several other ways. Many, for example, removed their names from the list for dinner in hall on the day he was sent down. This "boycott" continued on subsequent evenings[60] and was accompanied by further expressions of outrage and solidarity including fireworks, bonfires, and, on one occasion, undergraduates rising in hall to sing "Bathurst's a Jolly Good Fellow."[61] These gestures of support for the banished student functioned as explicitly ritualized celebrations of camaraderie. They also constituted public assertions of a vision of masculinity increasingly under threat, a point underscored in an amusing "manifesto," published by the so-called Oxford Undergraduate Revolutionary League in December of 1888, that protested the attacks on the freedom of an "expatriated brother." This call to action explicitly referred to Bathurst's heroism and stoic manhood: "Take example from the hero who has been torn from our midst: no unmanly sobs betrayed the anguish of his patriot heart as he marched boldly and calmly to meet his exile: tearless and unmoved he bade farewell to the weeping comrades, for well he knew that groans and cries can profit nothing, if there be no deeds to follow."[62] The hyperbolic celebrations of masculine virtue contained in these different responses to the Bathurst crisis employed discourses of masculinity as weapons against women and dons alike; barbed spears and plates of armor were intended to establish the primacy of youthfulness and protect fragile identities.

As women came closer to being granted full membership in these ancient foundations, they continued to struggle against masculine definitions of university life that relied on the notion that women, the female, and the feminine were things distinct from these peculiar institutional environments. The 1890s, in particular, were another moment of gender conflict during which relations between male undergraduates and female students were strained. As the universities debated the issue of degrees for women (debates that also took place at Cambridge in 1887 and the early 1920s and at Oxford in 1920–1921), male and female students engaged in a struggle of words (and actions) that resulted in further reconfigurations of gender identities, feverish and sometimes nasty debates, and hostile assertions of an aggressive and ultimately unpleasant version of British masculinity.

Occasionally, increasingly feminist women students, in advocating female degrees, directly challenged the masculine culture of the university, openly transgressed the boundaries of the gender divide, and tried to reformulate definitions that relied on the unrelenting maleness of the universities.[63] The author of an article entitled "The Question of Degrees" that appeared in the June 1895 issue of the *Fritillary*, for example, openly addressed the inferior status of women within the university while explicitly challenging the notion that Oxford was an exclusively male training school:

> The older and more conservative of the Oxford Dons on the one hand still cling to the monastic theory of the University. They like to think of the grey town by the Isis as a place where the youth who are to take the lead in the work of the country may pass a few years in (more or less) learned seclusion—where what women there are dwell in "high walled courts" and keep themselves decently out of sight. They forget that . . .

the Women's Halls, and the presence of women in lecture-rooms and examination-rooms . . . have destroyed for ever the University of their ideal. They may keep if they choose the empty form, but the substance is gone.[64]

Though this author's assumption that only "the older and more conservative" segment of the university population felt this way was optimistic (as we have seen, most younger men did so as well), such an analysis of the environment in which women struggled to gain recognition indicates how the language of gender and sexual difference permeated and informed discussions of educational change. Also, by engaging in debate at this level, some advocates for women's education alerted their supporters to the idea that their struggle consisted of something more than merely altering statutes. Rather, it entailed both redefining university culture and rethinking masculine and feminine spheres, activities, and spaces. This author thus sought to both point to the peculiarities and deficiencies of a dominant ethos and expose the armor of masculinity that surrounded the universities as mere artifice, an empty and ultimately vulnerable shell that served no one's interest, least of all that of the women who were seeking admission to degrees.

Despite these open challenges, the unrelentingly masculine atmosphere of the universities never really dissipated. In fact, cultural and rhetorical battles of this sort, coupled with proposals at Oxford in 1895–1896 and at Cambridge in 1897 to admit women formally to degrees, resulted in even more forceful, and occasionally ugly, articulations of masculine privilege. Undergraduates who saw themselves as guarding the citadel and protecting it from "nasty forward minxes" (as Adam Sedgwick, a Cambridge professor of geology, called them in 1865) and "harpies" (as one contributor to the *Granta* labeled them in 1897) functioned not as gallant knights but rather as unscrupulous fighters capable of anything.[65] The word "harpies" appeared during the tumultuous spring of 1897, when the question of degrees for women was put to a formal vote before Cambridge University's largest governing body, the Senate.[66] Rita McWilliams Tullberg has admirably narrated the administration's perspective on the events leading up to and immediately following this vote in her book *Women at Cambridge*.[67] The episode revealed the tense nature of this gendered "war of words," as it was described by one contributor to the *Cambridge Review* (the official newspaper of the university, written mostly for dons and described by the editors of the *Granta* as "our dear great aunt").[68]

For two months prior to the vote, the question of women's degrees was debated in several different venues. As well as official university publications and student newspapers and magazines, this issue was hotly contested in the popular press, in published position papers, and in pro and anti posters intended to sway undecided members of the Senate. Undergraduates themselves weighed in very heavily against women's degrees. The *Granta* contributor who called women students "harpies" did not rest there, but went on to use foreboding words of danger that functioned, in part, as a rhetorical call to arms. "No longer can we regard the question of Women's Degrees from a calm and philosophic point of view," he warned. "The time has passed for expressing pious opinions, and indulging in threadbare jests." He exhorted his readers to think about the implications of a university in which men and women were on equal footing. In addition to reminding his audience that "five out of every six junior men are opposed to the scheme," he also sought, through a variety of techniques, to address questions of masculine privilege and the links that existed between a segregated system of education, quality instruction for men and women alike, and the broader exercise of male power. He asserted, "the present scheme threatens the prosperity not only of our University—and thank heaven, it *is* still our University—but of women's education." Rather than attempting to argue that women should be denied degrees outright, he maintained that a system of separate degrees and indeed a separate university for the female students of Girton and Newnham was what was required if men were to keep Cambridge theirs and theirs alone.[69]

Other events leading up to the vote in the Senate House served to strengthen masculine defenses against an insidious threat and aggressively and unambiguously asserted a version of manliness that promoted outright misogyny and violence (justified in the *Granta* with explicit references to the "Women's War")[70] while forcefully articulating the sanctity of the homosocial in ways that bordered on the pathological. For example, although undergraduate opinion was generally not solicited by the governing bodies of either university in the period under consideration here, more than two thousand male students signed a petition against women's degrees that was submitted to the Senate in early May. This public assertion of student opinion was characterized by a *Granta* contributor as a "splendid response" to the dangers afoot.[71] Efforts of this sort operated as calls for male solidarity, a call that was also evident in a request by editors of the *Granta,* in the days leading up to the vote, that undergraduates "whose fathers are Masters of Arts of this University" cross the generational divide and "persuade" them "to come up to vote in the Senate against the present proposals. The issue is vital to the interests of the University, and no steps ought to be omitted whereby the *resident feeling* may be supported from without."[72]

The proposal to award women degrees produced the sharpest responses from male undergraduates on two occasions in the spring of 1897: during a debate in the Cambridge Union on May 11 and on the day of the Senate vote. These events were exclusively male affairs in which the privileges associated with university membership and elite masculine status were displayed and enacted in several unique settings. The Union debate, held in the society's rooms in central Cambridge during the traditional Tuesday evening meeting, was a highly publicized affair. Both the *Granta* and the *Cambridge Review*, each of which was strongly opposed to women's degrees, anticipated its impact and commented on the peculiarities of its organization in the days immediately preceding the event. The *Granta* author, for example, commented explicitly on the special arrangements that had to be made to discuss the issue of women's degrees: "The Debate . . . at the Union, is to be thrown open to the University. No ladies are to be admitted, and, therefore, both floor and gallery will be at the service of the Undergraduate. An enormous attendance is expected, and the main importance of the gathering will be that at least the grounds on which Undergraduate opinion is based will be clearly set forth and defended." This "occasion," "in every sense historic," at which all undergraduates, not just members of the Union, were expected to discuss the future of the university, necessitated the complete exclusion of women. As a result, they were not even allowed to assume their usual marginal status in the proceedings as spectators in isolated galleries.[73] Contributors to the *Cambridge Review*, in discussing the Union Society meeting, saw this exclusion as justified precisely because it "allow[ed] both sides to speak their minds without prejudice."[74]

On the day of the debate, throngs of students crowded through the doors of the Union Society to participate in this momentous event and hundreds more were turned away.[75] The May 15 issue of the *Granta,* published the Saturday afterward, commented not only on the general demeanor of those in attendance but also on what was said and by whom. As a general summary, the author of an article entitled "To the Senate" provided readers with the following assessment: "There was perfect order, both sides enjoyed an unbroken hearing, and at the end the voting proved once again that the balance against the present proposals is becoming more marked every day." What struck this undergraduate journalist the most was the "overwhelming sense of the gravity of the situation" that permeated the room. The sincerity and seriousness with which undergraduates conducted themselves on the day of the debate was not, according to the author, "actuated by prejudice" or a "hostility to the higher education of women"; it was, rather, motivated by a desire to see the "unique position of . . . Cambridge—the Cambridge of the English gentleman" preserved intact. In this instance, undergraduates cleverly tried to couch hostility and vehement opposition in chivalric terms. Coeducation, in their estimation, would only lead to disaster: a blurring of gender roles that would ultimately prove to be a disadvantage to women, whose education concerned and gentlemanly Cambridge students wanted to remain "untrammeled by ideas essentially masculine."[76]

The reports on the debate reveal a broad range of opinions and a climate marked by high levels of emotion and physical acts of aggression: fevered performances in which men tried to assert their presence by stomping their feet rhythmically and yelling out words of condemnation. Speeches for and against the proposal under consideration went on for several hours. Arguments varied in quality and content but almost all discussed, not the specifics of the recommendations per se, but the broader implications for men and women alike. Philip Whitwell Wilson, a Clare College undergraduate from 1894 to 1897 (as well as president of the Union Society in 1896 and editor of the *Granta* during the Lent and May Terms of 1897)[77] argued against the proposal because it threatened "the integrity of the university" and would, if passed, invariably result in "a long course of agitation, warfare and strife." On the other side of the divide, Thomas Francis Robert MacDonnell, a St. John's College undergraduate from 1895 to 1898, argued on behalf of the proposal on the basis of rather pragmatic considerations. He asserted that his own "thoughts were all for the women" and their professional prospects: "When a girl tries to get a post at a local school, what do those yokels—the parson, the lawyer, doctor, etc.—know of Tripos Certificates, and such technicalities?" His ultimately positive view of coeducation was a minority opinion in the room that evening. In addition to eschewing the language of gender conflict, he also saw fit to articulate in his speech the benefits of a mixed educational environment by stating rather simply, "women's education needs men's influence, and men's women's."[78]

The views of people like Henry Martineau Fletcher finally won out at the end of the day, however. Fletcher, a Trinity College undergraduate from 1889 to 1892, was, at the time of the Union Society debate, a recent graduate with a compelling interest in the question at hand. As a member of the audience, he elected to speak on the side condemning the proposal and began his remarks with an incendiary comment that revealed just how much this debate was, indeed, about gender roles and the socialization of men: "We want no HERMAPHRODITE COMPOUND that lacks the good parts of both its elements." Fletcher, as something of a gender purist, took the view that the only thing that mattered to his opponents was the plight of women, not the concerns, fears, and needs of men. This led the inconsiderate advocates for women's degrees to forget, according to Fletcher, that "Cambridge exists not for mere erudition, but for the education of the male youth of England—education of body, mind, feelings; and its object is to make a man a finished gentleman." He concluded with a simple, and undoubtedly poignant and persuasive, statement that must have appealed to a large segment of the audience: "We have come to the dividing of the ways. It is best that men and women (educationally) should part here." In the end, views like those expressed by Fletcher remained dominant and the resolution "That this meeting strongly condemns the recommendation of the Women's Degree Syndicate," was overwhelmingly carried with 1,083 aye votes and 138 nos.[79]

The debate in the union was not, of course, the last word on the issue. Indeed, the climax to this episode of gender conflict was reached on the day of the vote itself, May 21, 1897, when great crowds gathered outside the Senate House as voting M.A.s arrived from around the country to participate in the proceedings. The streets surrounding the Senate House were, according to most accounts, a sight to behold for all who flooded into Cambridge on that day. Banners with messages like "Frustrate Feminine Fanatics" appeared on Trinity Street (a main thoroughfare near the Senate House) and a "canvas" that read "Cambridge expects every M.A.n to do his duty" was stretched across the same road. Large groups of students, with some outside observers and a small number of women (presumably sympathetic to the men's cause) interspersed, greeted the M.A.s as they entered the Senate House that afternoon to vote. Men who entered through the Placet (in favor) door were booed and called names like "traitor" and "goat," while those who went in to place a Non-Placet (opposed) vote were praised with phrases like "well voted." The atmosphere outside the Senate House took on the character of a festival as tiny bits of brilliantly colored confetti, fireworks (including Roman candles and "dozens of crackers"), and flour flew through the air.[80]

This was, however, a festival with a definite edge. Actions that scholars like Rita McWilliams Tullberg have interpreted as mere larks were, in fact, loaded with tremendous symbolism.[81] Undergraduates, for example, hung "[a]bove Messrs Macmillan and Bowes' shop," across the street from Great St. Mary's Church, an effigy of a "liberated" woman dressed in bloomers and riding a bicycle, described in one account of the day's events as a "thing in 'rational' blue and pink upon a bicycle."[82] As a symbolic representation of the female undergraduate, this figure became a focal point on the day of the vote and figured prominently in observers' descriptions of this important event. Other effigies, like a "she-dummy in cap and gown with a golden pigtail" that appeared on Trinity Street, caricatured the "sweet girl graduate" and allowed undergraduates to express physical aggression toward women by torturing dummies, without actually harming any of the students of Girton and Newnham.[83] Placards reminding women of their place conveyed the sense of threat felt by these men and the connections they made between the protection of homosocial spaces, the preservation of power and authority, and the maintenance of elite status. "Get Thee to Girton, Beatrice, Get Thee to Newnham, This is No Place for You Maids" and "No Woman Shall Come Within a Mile of My Courts" were slogans unambiguous in their meaning.[84]

Other posters contained catchphrases implying that a man's worthiness, and consequently his right to claim manhood status, was measured by his ability to protect the university and preserve its masculine character. Among these, according to the *Cambridge Review*, was "The 'Varsity for men and men for the 'Varsity.'"[85] Women's colleges on the outskirts of town, women even in lectures and examinations could be begrudgingly countenanced, but women as full members represented too much of a challenge to the gender order. They destabilized masculine identities in a setting where they should have been at their most secure, a point which was clearly not lost on those voting in the Senate House, where the proposal was defeated by a vote of 1,707 to 661. Undergraduate members, in a separate, non-binding ballot, also made their opinion known by voting against the extension of privileges to Cambridge women by 2,137 to 298, indicating just how widespread opposition to these measures was and would continue to be for many years to come.[86]

"Bonfires were the order of the evening" following the announcement of these results and were generally accompanied by the continued detonation of fireworks and some wanton acts of destruction. These public assertions of strength as well as frivolity allowed Cambridge men to mark the spaces surrounding the university as their exclusive preserve.[87] Some of these public celebrations, in certain instances directed against the women who were waging "war" on the university, contained within them great potential for violence and physical harm. Indeed, threats of physical injury extended beyond the figurative or the symbolic when about two hundred undergraduates, armed with an effigy of the "New Woman," stormed the closed gates of Newnham College. While this potentially explosive protest concluded peacefully with the undergraduates loudly giving "three cheers for Newnham" and dispersing, as both the *Cambridge Review* and the *Granta* reported, it reflects just how high feelings ran over this issue and, once again, the extent to which behavior normally considered to be most inappropriate for these young men might be deemed reasonable when it was directed against the ambiguously positioned female student who challenged the male prerogatives of degrees, full university membership, and voting privileges.[88]

The vehemence of these reactions and the effectiveness of strategies intended to further marginalize women meant that they were excluded from degrees and full privileges at Oxford until 1920 and at Cambridge until 1948. It would take the dislocating experiences of the two World Wars, broader social changes in the interwar period (including the introduction of women's suffrage), and government pressure in the form of a Royal Commission, established in 1919, to force the universities to clarify women's status. Cambridge held on for nearly three more decades and generally seemed more intransigent and steadfast than Oxford in its refusal to award women degrees (although it did agree to grant them "titles of degrees" in 1921). Still, ambivalence, and in some instances open hostility (such as when Cambridge professor William Ridgeway labeled women students "feminist tyrants" organized into "battalions" in a 1920 letter to Falconer Madan),[89] continued to characterize reactions at both institutions as members struggled to make sense of what these changes would mean for their particular vision of the gender order.

The Reaction to Foreign Students

The presence of women was not the only new thing in the late nineteenth and early twentieth centuries that worried traditional Oxbridge undergraduates and undermined their feelings of both security and superiority. Oxford and Cambridge men also fretted excessively, after the 1850s, about the presence of non-Anglican and non-Christian students and of undergraduates from other parts of the world, a change made possible by the reforms of the 1850s, 1860s, and 1870s. The latter group, which consisted primarily of students (white and non-white) who traveled to Britain, by steamship, from the far reaches of the empire,[90] were, for many, the very embodiment of modern reforming impulses: dangerous signs of a race, nation, empire, and established way of life under siege. Indian students, by the final decades of the nineteenth century, constituted the majority of these foreigners and were the group most targeted in discussions of the issue by white undergraduates: Student enrollment grew at each university from around 2,000 in 1870 to roughly 4,500 in 1920 (with sharp decreases during the war years), but Indian students never constituted more than about 2–3 percent of the total student population.[91] Undergraduates from Africa made up an even smaller minority, and students from Canada, Australia, and New Zealand could also be found throughout these years. The number and percentage of foreign students generally increased throughout this period. By 1920, in fact, a full 30 percent of matriculants at Oxford were from the Commonwealth, Europe, the United States, and other foreign countries.[92]

The presence of students from non-Christian and foreign backgrounds, especially after 1870, presented challenges to the prevailing conceptions of the undergraduate and the university described in chapter 1 and seemed to expose, for many, the precariousness of Britain's imperial position, the resiliency of British institutions in an age of dramatic change, and the artificial and constructed nature of national and racial identities.[93] Colonial, foreign, and Indian students personified change, and their contributions were either ignored or undermined by undergraduates struggling to reinforce their own Britishness. At the same time, then, that Oxbridge men were reconfiguring their views of the gender order to cope with the presence of female students, they also had to redraw the boundaries that separated insiders from outsiders, Britons from foreigners, colonizers from colonized, white from black, home from abroad, superior from inferior, and acceptable from unacceptable in order to contain "the foreign element." As the boundaries of physical separation and statutory exclusion disappeared, undergraduates manipulated the rhetoric of race, nation, and empire to create new distinctions and social boundaries that helped them ensure that recently arrived foreigners also remained outsiders, even as they grew in number and in strength.

As they attempted to cope with the changes that marked the years after 1850, undergraduates often resorted to prognostications about the dangers of outside interference and "foreign" infiltration: forces that, for many, represented potentially devastating modern influences. The intrusion of outside peoples and of alien customs and ways of doing things, and the intervention of meddlesome government officials, were viewed not as simple attempts at reform but, rather, as attacks on a peculiar form of life that epitomized British uniqueness and ascendancy, and as threats to the autonomy of the universities. The author of an article on university life that appeared in an 1861 issue of the Oxford publication *Great Tom* dis-

cussed, among other matters, the particulars of the university reforms initiated by the Royal Commissions of 1850–1852 and implemented in the
subsequent Oxford Act of 1854 and Cambridge Act of 1856. He boldly
asserted, "They tell us unmistakably that University Life as a thing distinct from other life, is gradually approaching its end. Reforms, singularly
free from any improving effect, inexorable Courts of Law, Transatlantic
freshmen, and an unsympathizing public are uniting against it."[94] In his
view, the distinctive features of university life and their essential British
"goodness" were challenged not only by the general reforming impulse but
also by transatlantic foreigners hailing most likely, in this instance, from
the United States or Canada. The use of an image of the invading outsider
was an important precedent for representing change as a threatening, foreign, and ultimately predatory other, a frightening bogeyman who needed
to be carefully monitored and, when necessary, attacked.

Oxford and Cambridge men alike commented with some frequency
upon the climate of reform that marked the years after 1850. While some
wrote letters protesting, for example, the removal of religious tests and the
decline of the Anglican monopoly, others saw fit to note rather simply, as
one anonymous fellow of an Oxford college did in an 1876 pamphlet entitled *Spiritual Destitution at Oxford*, "We are living in the midst of great
changes."[95] Verse, a common form of expression in undergraduate newspapers, magazines, and reviews, often enabled Oxbridge men to express their
views on reform in ways that were both humorous and instructive. In so
doing, they continued to rely on images of different religious and racial
groups as dangerous invaders. *Great Tom* reprinted one response to the
Commission of the early 1850s in an 1861 issue. Its author addressed an
audience of junior and senior members at a Brasenose College celebration
called an Ale:

> Enough of this: the warmth of either side
> Let us cool down and in the tankard hide;
> And drink to Alma Mater—drink to all
> Who would not see her Institutions fall.
> May she keep safe, when danger near her lurks,
> From Jews, John Russell, Infidels and Turks.[96]

Aside from casting blame on the interfering Lord John Russell, who was
prime minister in 1850 when the first university commission was convened, the author chose to focus on the dangers posed by non-Christian
religious groups whom, in their essentialized difference from British Chris-

tians, he saw as a considerable threat to the established institutions of the university. This threat was underscored for many by the 1858 Jewish Relief Act, which allowed Jews to sit as members in the House of Commons.[97] Certainly, proposals to eliminate religious tests for matriculation and degrees meant that such groups might indeed establish a presence at the universities. This shift away from strict Anglican control did eventually necessitate significant administrative changes that enabled, for example, Jewish students to be admitted to degrees at Cambridge "in such a form as not to offend . . . religious convictions."[98] This meant that, in these cases, specifically Christian references were excluded from the standard Latin forms of admission.

Despite these limited attempts to accommodate religious difference, Jews and other groups were frequently portrayed as un-English during this period.[99] In fact, the very familiarity and proximity of religious others may have rendered them as frightening and threatening to a Protestant institution and nation as racial others were. Catholics occupied a similar position as symbols of foreign influence in the midst of the university,[100] especially after John Henry Newman, a brilliant Oxford scholar and one of the leading figures of the Anglican Church, "defected" to Rome in 1845 and the Catholic hierarchy in England was restored by Pope Pius IX in 1850. In 1883, for instance, sixty-one of seventy undergraduates at Pembroke College, Oxford submitted a petition to the master protesting the visit of Mr. Hartwell de la Garde Grissell, an alumnus of the university and chamberlain to Pope Leo XIII, in which he was described as "notorious in Oxford as a proselytising schismatic" whose presence in an Anglican institution was anomalous and "most distasteful."[101] Indeed, Linda Colley's insistence on the centrality of the continental Catholic other to the formation of British national identities in the eighteenth century can be extended at least to the end of the nineteenth and perhaps into the twentieth.[102] The fact that these groups were seen to pose a formidable challenge reflects the extent to which the Jew, the infidel, the Turk, and, perhaps most significantly, the Catholic functioned as effective signposts in conveying images of an institution under siege.

Exaggerated depictions of the various dangers posed by other outside groups, most notably foreigners, within the university were used routinely to spread fear of and concern about racial and imperial others, to highlight the potentially cataclysmic consequences of reform, and to underline contemporary ideas about racial and national difference.[103] A particularly glaring example of this practice appeared at Cambridge in 1870. In an attempt at humor, the founders of the *Moslem in Cambridge* prophetically depicted the university as it might be in 1890, with its white, Christian, and male—and, consequently, British—character erased. The publication itself was a student response to the debate over the further abolition of Anglican religious tests (in this case for fellowships and other university emoluments) that marked the years 1869–1871 and culminated in the passage of the Universities Tests Act of 1871, which did away with virtually all barriers to non-Anglicans and indeed non-Christians. In general terms, the publication functioned in two ways: it expressed collective anxiety about change while illustrating the potentially dangerous effects of transforming impulses by depicting the university as completely and humorously altered by the proposed reforms. Visual and verbal renderings of imperial, racial, and religious others were used to illustrate the potential impact of a cosmopolitanism that threatened the cultural identity and integrity of not just the university but Great Britain itself.

In an illustration entitled "The Return from the University Sermon" that appeared in the November 1870 issue of the *Moslem in Cambridge,* the vice-chancellor and his entourage, all of whom are represented as foreigners of some sort, parade past the familiar Cambridge architectural landmarks of the Senate House and King's College Chapel, but there is one incongruity in the landscape: the appearance of a pagoda-like structure in the center background that serves both to remind readers of the dire consequences of change and to highlight the symbolic importance of these stately buildings (fig. 6.2). By depicting the university in a state of absurd and untenable diversity and associating that diversity with an almost circus-like lack of seriousness and purpose, the artist underscored the unified British character of Cambridge as a Christian, white, and fundamentally national institution. These sentiments were reinforced by a simple and straightforward rhyme, most likely written by Gerald S. Davies of Christ's College, which also appeared in the *Moslem in Cambridge* and highlighted for readers the dangers inherent in this altered state of affairs:

> In an ancient and grave University,
> All at once there appeared a diversity
> Of Turks, Greeks, and Jews,
> Hottentots and Hindoos,
> Which altered that grave University.[104]

Renderings of this predicted cataclysmic transformation appeared repeatedly in this publication during its brief run. One editorial warning described a Cambridge twenty years in the future with the following words:

Fig. 6.2. An artistic vision of the future that transforms a normally solemn university procession into a multiracial and multiethnic spectacle. "The Return from the University Sermon, 1890," *Moslem in Cambridge . . . 1890,* no. 2 (November 1870), illustration between pp. 2 and 3. By permission of the Syndics of the Cambridge University Library, shelf mark Cam.b.31.44.1(2).

The day has come when the professors of an effete and obsolete faith have dwindled to a mere handful, and the time may not be far distant when even these shall pass away from among us—when every man shall be to himself his own measure, his own guide, and his own faith. We need only point, to show that we do not boast immeasuredly, to the grand Mussulman foundation that has taken the place of the worn-out Christian Asylum of Trinity College—to the settlement of Red Indians who occupy Downing College,—to the Aborigines of Queens—the Cossacks of Magdalen—the Fire-eaters of Sidney, and similar foundations, in proof of the Cosmopolitan character that we have now assumed. Hand in Hand with this advance has gone the Sister scheme of FEMALE EDU-CATION. . . . we need only point to the fact of the Senior Classic of this year being a lady.[105]

This passage presents some of the more extreme dangers of reform in its depiction of a transformed Cambridge. Although wildly inflated, it does reflect, quite clearly, the extent to which fear of change could take on a very specific and highly prejudicial form. Illustrated in this short article is the eradication of Cambridge's Christian foundation, its cultural integrity and homogeneity as a white British institution, and its position as a training ground for young male elites. Similar prophecies appeared on several other occasions throughout the Victorian and Edwardian periods. The popular and successful Oxford weekly paper *'Varsity,* for example, reiterated in 1907 exaggerated concerns about the fate of the British-born

gentleman in an institution under siege by predicting that by 1920 "the inclusion of a British-born competitor" on the Oxford athletics team would alone be "sufficient to excite comment."[106]

Specific crises (prompted by the reformist impulses at work in late-nineteenth-century Britain) that threatened the institutional sanctity of the universities were not, however, needed for undergraduates to implement coping strategies of this sort. Comparisons with other cultures were, as we have already seen, staple fare in the student press and a common feature of an undergraduate world preoccupied with not only proving the superiority of the British (and, one could easily argue, English) perspective but also setting up the university as an oppositional bulwark, an institution that could function as a substitute for the nation at large and resist those things which most threatened national integrity. In this way, contrasts between the Oxbridge undergraduate and his French counterpart served to remind readers of the *Tatler in Cambridge* of those traits that differentiated the British student from his continental inferior.[107] Similarly, the invocation of religious difference in undergraduate attempts at humor could also establish some essential distinctions between Christian tradition and "oriental" practices, represented in one note in the Oxford *Shotover Papers* by sun worship: "An Oriental member of the University writes to us to deny the report that he was seen in his nightshirt, on the roof of his College Chapel, sacrificing fuzees to the rising sun."[108] And, finally, even when the outsider was a fellow Briton, an "inferior" heritage could serve to distinguish him from the true undergraduate; thus the ideal student's "unaccented" English provided a marked contrast to the brogue of a recently arrived Scots freshman "from very far beyond the Tweed."[109]

Accommodating Foreign Students

Dire predictions about the consequences of diversity or simplistic comparisons between the British and some alien other do not constitute the entire picture in this examination of reactions to foreign students and the various ways in which the rhetoric of race, empire, and nation operated in undergraduate culture. As the real presence of foreigners began to increase after 1880, depictions of imperial, racial, and national others became something more than rhetorical exercises and definitional strategies. With these changes, discussions of these issues in the student press came to represent not mere verbal wrangles but genuine, if unequal, struggles for power in which those in the majority attempted to maintain control while newcomers began to seek and receive some recognition.

Institutional provisions were certainly made to accommodate these new students, but the general climate of hostility that they encountered was not, as we shall see, altered substantially by administrative measures that were intended to control them, rather than encourage their acceptance. Students of other races who were also non-Christian, of course, were exempted from religious tests after the reforms of the 1850s and 1871. Aside from this rather simple measure, Oxford and Cambridge were assisted in accommodating these new undergraduates, especially those from the Indian subcontinent, by such organizations as the National Indian Association, founded in 1871 to promote the dissemination of knowledge about India, and, after 1909, by a students' department administered by the India Office and responsible for overseeing educational matters related to Indians studying in the United Kingdom.[110] Oxford in the 1870s also created an Indian Institute which, like the National Indian Association, had among its many objectives the teaching of subjects related to India, the promotion of Indian research, and the formation of a scholarly community premised on the principles of "personal intercourse" and the "interchange of ideas." It also drew together candidates for the Indian Civil Service and was seen to be instrumental in the "befriending and aiding [of the] native students from India who occasionally matriculate at Oxford."[111]

In considering the special circumstances of foreign students, authorities thought largely of Indians, which can be attributed, as we have already seen, primarily to sheer numbers. Certain requirements were altered, for example, to accommodate the different educational backgrounds of these undergraduates. At Oxford, in the first public examinations for degrees (Mods. or Prelims.), "candidates born in India of parents born in India" were allowed to substitute either Sanskrit or Arabic for either Greek or Latin.[112] Exceptions were also made at Cambridge, where officials were more lenient, resulting in a larger number of Indian undergraduates than at Oxford.[113]

The presence of Indian students, like that of other non-white and foreign undergraduates at Oxford and Cambridge after 1870, often precipitated remarks in student publications. In that year, for example, a Christ's College, Cambridge magazine titled *Fleur-de-Lys* noted the presence of two "Hindoo" gentlemen in college during the May term.[114] Such students were still a small minority in the undergraduate population, which near the end of the nineteenth century approached 3,500 at Cambridge, but the comments elicited from undergraduates by these new circumstances represented racial and national difference as a curiosity to be highlighted. The arrival of a prominent Egyptian student, for example, inspired Edward Jupp to write in a letter to his mother in October of 1869, "Prince H[assan], the Viceroy's son, has arrived at Oxford, but has not yet shewn himself at Christ Church. . . . So we now have Jew, Turk, Infidel and Heretic all together."[115] Similarly, visitors such as Anna Florence Ward commented explicitly on the presence of non-white foreigners in their observations of university life. In her diary entry for June 18, 1876, for example, Ward wrote the following about Christian Frederick Cole, a native of Sierra Leone and an undergraduate at University College: "Saw Cole (Coal?) also (the nigger)."[116] Images of Cole, who was something of a novelty at Oxford in the 1870s, also emphasized for British undergraduates the incongruity of a university-educated man in a traditional African setting, portraying him, in one instance, wearing academic dress in a "primitive" West African village and surrounded by sexualized semi-nude women.[117] Other representations of non-white students relied on the power of racial caricature to further establish notions of difference. One image from the Cambridge book *Types,* entitled "From Afric's Coral Strand," portrayed an African unhappily and uncomfortably attired in western dress and academic cap and gown to emphasize the distinction between real students and interlopers.[118]

The success of foreign students might also elicit commentary from observers. In particular, the British-born undergraduate might react badly to threats to his intellectual or social ascendancy. In one case in March of 1874, the recipient of the Boden scholarship at Oxford "for proficiency in Sanskrit Language and Literature," an Indian student of St. Mary Hall by the name of Brajendranath De, found himself the subject of a humorous undergraduate "ode" in the *Shotover Papers*.[119] Rather than celebrating De's accomplishment, the author chose to focus on the foreignness of the scholar's name and the difficulties encountered in trying to pronounce or, for that matter, even spell it correctly.[120] Certainly, undergraduates of British descent were also ridiculed, sometimes relentlessly, in student publications. Something, however, remains unique in the focus of this ode. The emphasis on strangeness and incomprehensibility highlighted the peculiar nature of a situation made possible only by recent changes. By reinforcing and caricaturing De's foreign status, this contributor ensured, however unwittingly, that barriers to acceptance continued to be erected within the university even after students from a range of backgrounds began to appear in college quads.

Depictions of possible and mostly improbable scenarios, caricatures, and stereotypes also highlighted the reluctance of British-born undergraduates to take these new students seriously or fully accept difference. In a fictional account of an undergraduate prank at Balliol College, Oxford the butt of the joke, an Indian student by the name of Rumsetjee Dumsetjee whose rooms were flooded by the college fire brigade, was described in terms which emphasized his "Oriental swarthiness" and the general inability of foreigners to adjust to the "English climate," which Dumsetjee found to be "particularly uncongenial." The "Oriental's" penchant for heat and the difficulties he encountered in acclimatizing to an environment characterized as specifically "English" served to accentuate the incongruities of the situation created by the recent influx of foreigners. Dumsetjee's persistence in "keeping up a bright fire at most hours in the day," even in the "almost tropical heat of June," "procured him the honour" of the pranksters' visit and reprobation and functioned as a telling indicator of this outsider's foreignness.[121] These contrasts, and the absurdity of such behavior in British institutions, were similarly illustrated by discussions of, for example, a "swarthy" Maori football team at Balliol,[122] a lecture at Christ's College, Cambridge populated exclusively by "primitive" non-white students dressed incongruously in academic gowns (Christ's College, like Oxford's Balliol, was popular with foreign students, especially those preparing for the Indian Civil Service examinations),[123] and, once again, an undergraduate student body that included, as one headline in the Oxford *Ephemeral* noted in 1893, a substantial "foreign element."[124]

The twentieth century witnessed further increases in the number of Indian and other foreign matriculants at both universities. This growth precipitated additional initiatives on the part of the government and these institutions in an attempt to cope with these changes. The Students' Department at the India Office, for example, took on the role of official guardian of some Indian students, especially with respect to financial matters, while the universities formed separate committees to address issues related to foreign, colonial, and Indian undergraduates. At Cambridge, for example, the Intercollegiate Indian Students' Committee was formed in 1916 while, in that same year, Oxford created an Oriental Students Delegacy to oversee the activities and progress of these undergraduates, many of whom did not belong to a college but rather matriculated as unattached or non-collegiate students.[125] With somewhat similar intentions, the government convened two committees, one in 1907 and one in 1922, to inquire into the situation of Indian students in Britain generally.[126]

Other considerations were also factored into administrative decisions about the increasingly diverse student bodies of Oxford and Cambridge. The senior proctor at Cambridge, F. J. Dykes, observed in his annual report for 1913–1914 that an "excessive proportion" of immorality cases (i.e., liaisons with prostitutes) involved "coloured students" and, in his opinion, they required a degree of scrutiny generally not applied to British-born undergraduates.[127]

Furthermore, by this time the need to offer some special form of guidance to these students had become quite apparent to officials. Undergraduates could generally acquire all the information they needed to prepare themselves for a university career from calendars, student handbooks, and guidebooks, but foreign students in 1902 were provided with an additional source in a pamphlet titled *Colonial and Indian Students at Oxford.* In 1906, a general *Guide for the Use of Colonial, Indian and Foreign Students,* which contained information specific to their special circumstances, was published. Undoubtedly intended to assist, such gestures also served to create additional distinctions and underscore the peculiarity of their situation as foreigners.

Cambridge, Racial Discord, and the *Granta* Episode

Discussions of the changing racial composition of the university continued apace in the twentieth century. One important difference, however, emerged as the numbers of foreigners grew. As students of different races and national origins took up the usual undergraduate pursuit of forming societies and clubs—such as the Indian Majlis, founded at both Cambridge and Oxford in the late nineteenth century—they gave themselves a voice with which they could engage in debate and challenge prevailing racial constructs.[128] On occasion, these debates and rhetorical flourishes about the universities' changing racial character developed into outright acrimony.

A notable example of this kind of struggle occurred in 1901 in the pages of the prominent Cambridge publication *Granta.* In an article written under the pseudonym of Jehu Pryde, one undergraduate addressed the problems created by what he called the "Black Peril," describing the presence of foreign students (particularly those from Asia) at the Cambridge Union and their participation more generally in undergraduate life in wholly unflattering terms. The author began his invective by drawing on imperial imagery and vocabulary to characterize changes in the racial composition of Union membership: "It is not only a black peril which threatens the University, but a yellow peril and a brown peril to boot. The University is in the peril of submersion. The vital principles of our existence are at stake. Shall Cambridge be a Colony of Bombay, shall she be affiliated to Pekin, shall her streets grow darker and darker until she sinks at last into a seething vortex of unmitigated melanthropy?"[129] By employing ideas of colonization that reinforced the sense of threat to the assumed, but precarious, British character and integrity of Cambridge, the author reversed the process of imperialism and applied it to the university context to highlight the potentially catastrophic consequences of the situation. Furthermore, and perhaps more importantly for the argument presented here, he connected racial integrity and supremacy and the "vital principles of our existence." The presence of darker faces in this piece symbolized a general threat to not only the university, then, but also the very identity (racial, social, cultural, and national) that membership in that university underscored and fostered for the majority.

The author sounded the alarm when he predicted an uncertain future for the British in Cambridge. In the hyperbole used so liberally by undergraduate contributors to student publications, he asked, "is not Sanskrit rapidly displacing the King's English as a medium of Union conversation?" emphasizing a perceived increase in inarticulate presentations and speeches. The Oxford and Cambridge Unions, rather than acting as training grounds for future statesmen and politicians, were both, he warned, in danger of becoming centers of ineptitude. In one instance, he contrasted the superiority of British rhetorical skills with the outsiders' inability to perform up to expected standards, characterizing an unspecified foreigner as pouring forth "an unbroken stream of broken patter, word follows word, words too crowded to be intelligible, too disconnected to be humorous, words merely, unmeaning, tedious, voluble. One by one the few poor whites remaining slip away in disgust. More Asiatics enter and sit in compact masses drinking in the turgid stream of verbose inanity with apparent avidity." The gradual erosion of the Union as a center of national excellence became a metaphor for the damaging effects of increased foreign enrollments, a danger that was reinforced by comments such as "the number of Orientals is increasing with alarming rapidity."[130] In this passage, the author highlighted one factor necessary for success in the Oxbridge environment—the ability to converse in an erudite and skillful manner, which he assumed to be quintessentially and peculiarly British and the hallmark of famous parliamentarians and intellectuals alike.

Descriptions of Cambridge as a British institution continued to rely on rigid conceptions of what the racial and religious composition of the university should be. Britishness, as it was embodied in Cambridge and "her" sons, remained, in Pryde's view, largely oppositional. These concerns were revealed in an invidious comparison of Oxford and Cambridge: "Oxford is still a white university; Cambridge is rapidly becoming the property of the blackman." General worries about the predominance of "black" men were not, however, the only fears Pryde expressed. He also chose to focus on religious difference, noting that a "black" majority was antithetical to an institution intended to be not only white and British but also Christian. Issuing warnings about the distinct possibility of a "Black vote" in Union elections, Pryde cautioned his readers, "Already the degrading spectacle may be witnessed of candidates for office practising heathen rites, attending Oriental mysteries in the lower parts of Cambridge, in order to curry favour with the Indians."[131] Such fears were not, of course, well founded. British-born students predominated among elected officials throughout the period surveyed by this study, indicating further the extent to which such exaggerated statements were utilized more as rhetorical devices in articulating anxieties about change and in constructing definitions of Britishness than as genuine warnings about an impending peril.[132]

The offensive nature of this piece did not go unnoticed. Most important, perhaps, was the response it elicited from the president of the Indian Majlis Society in Cambridge. The author, a Punjabi undergraduate by the name of Fazl-I-Husain who matriculated at Christ's College in 1899 (after receiving a B.A. from Punjab University in 1897), relied on conceptions of British propriety and courtesy as he began his critique of the offending article. In his letter to the *Granta* editor, he attacked Pryde's criticism of non-white students as a cheap measure to win notoriety "by vilifying those who happen to be in a minority, differing in creed, or colour, or race." In moving on to a discussion of empire, Husain attempted to articulate a more inclusive conception of imperial rule. His strongest statement contended that the publication of Pryde's invective had outraged many members of the university, who shared a "sense of shame that you, Sir, have allowed your pages so to transgress against that Imperial courtesy which surely must bind together the most varied elements of His Majesty's subjects."[133] By appealing to imperial values and British propriety, Husain accomplished two things in this struggle. In rigorously scrutinizing the actions of those responsible for the *Granta,* he underscored the significance of empire in the discourse of undergraduates while subverting the usual depiction of the other as the transgressor of imperial values and courtesy. Also, by challenging prevailing conceptions of differences in behavior between British undergraduates and their foreign counterparts, he questioned and destabilized the dichotomy between British superiority and foreign inferiority.

While allowing the publication of this letter of protest, the editor of the *Granta* attempted to mitigate, somewhat, its moral force with a brief paragraph in the "Motley Notes" section of the magazine. In addition to characterizing Jehu Pryde's comments as "friendly strictures" and lamenting the hostility which they generated, the editor described the performance of one Union speaker, a student from Ceylon (Sri Lanka) by the name of Obeyesekere,[134] who had objected to Pryde's article in an address to the Union the day after it appeared: "I was inclined to think that one of the points where our mysterious correspondent was certainly in error was in describing the native of Ceylon as 'refined and intelligent.' The language employed by this honorable Cingalese can only be described as unmitigated Billingsgate."[135] Obeyesekere's inability to speak fittingly and formally, a skill admired among Union orators, effectively negated in this description any moral force his objections might have possessed. Again, this depiction drew on a perceived dichotomy between the refined and intelligent language usually employed in Union debates and the vulgarities of Billingsgate. Class and linguistic, as well as racial, differences were used, then, to distinguish not only those external to Cambridge from those within it, but also various factions within the university from one another.

Pryde's reaction to the response of the Indian Majlis, while fleetingly apologetic, reiterated his initial point about the position of Indians within the Union, which he considered "out of proportion to their powers of speaking."[136] He emphasized that articulateness and proficiency in English were integral criteria for participation in Union activities. Rather than concentrating on racial difference in this passage, he attempted to illustrate the Britishness of Cambridge undergraduate life and define those who were included within it by establishing boundaries that relied on random assessments of competency in English. Foreign undergraduates themselves may have indeed felt that the ability to speak "properly" was essential to success in the university, if a 1913 Oxford advertisement announcing English lessons for foreign students is any indication.[137]

This exchange makes clear that there was no hegemonic perspective on the desirability of the presence of foreign students, and it reflects some of the tensions that the changes of the twentieth century produced. As Oxford and Cambridge and their members struggled with the growth of these institutions as international and increasingly cosmopolitan universities, those who were most obviously outsiders quickly became the targets of attack and ostracism.[138] By denigrating the potential contribution of these newcomers to Oxford and Cambridge society, British undergraduates struggled to retain their position of superiority and assert their prominence in the face of increasing anxiety and ambiguity. Certainly some foreign students, especially those of British parentage from the "white" dominions, assimilated quite easily and, on occasion, an Indian student was able to gain respect. It is, however, intended to indicate that the rhetoric of race, empire, and nation employed by the majority of undergraduates could and often did forget these exceptions, descending rather quickly into unmitigated racial, religious, and ethnic prejudice and snobbery.

The tensions that arose between this rhetoric of race, empire, and nation that was predominant in the universities and the occasional nonwhite student who was able to infiltrate the mainstream are illustrated in a brief discussion of the famous undergraduate cricketer Prince Ranjitsinjhi (a Trinity College student who matriculated in 1889) in a popular book on Cambridge by F. A. Reeve. Reeve described Ranjitsinjhi as an outstanding player and a "most attractive personality." The unattributed comments of a contemporary, however, reveal the persistence of the "orientalist" perspective even when the "oriental" other was engaged in the most British of sporting activities. This person attributed Ranji's prowess not to his ability as a sportsman but rather to mystical powers: "He's no cricketer. He's a conjurer, an Eastern juggler."[139] While undoubtedly intended to compliment his abilities as a batsman, the recourse to a vocabulary of racial, imperial, and religious "otherness" indicated, in this peculiar way, just how persistent these attitudes remained well into the twentieth century and how crucial contrasting categories continued to be in definitions of Britishness.

This assessment is confirmed by the comments of Indian students themselves, who noted the hostile environment of the ancient universities throughout the period covered by this study. Undergraduate organizations like the Indian Majlis Society protested this state of affairs during the first decade of the century, and in 1916 the Indian Students' Friends' Society presented a list of grievances it had compiled on behalf of Indian students in the United Kingdom to the department of the India Office responsible for these undergraduates as evidence of racial inequity. This list confirmed much of what was revealed in the *Granta* exchange about the state of race relations with a succinct observation: "unfortunate manifestation[s] of race and colour prejudice against Indian students" existed "even at the seats of learning."[140]

Oxford and the Rhodes Scholars

Contact with and exposure to foreign students was also expedited through several other means at the beginning of the twentieth century. The most notable of these remains an important feature of Oxford University to this day. The bequest made by the arch-imperialist Cecil Rhodes created, in 1902, a system of lucrative scholarships that enabled students from the "white" colonies (Canada, Australia, New Zealand, and South Africa), Jamaica, Bermuda, the United States, and Germany (until 1916 and again, briefly, in the 1930s) to attend Oxford, enjoy its privileges, add "breadth to their views for their instruction in life and manners and . . . [instill] into their minds the advantages to the Colonies as well as to the United Kingdom of the retention of the unity of the Empire."[141] Again, the mere suggestion of this scheme produced a range of responses from senior members and undergraduates.[142] Their reactions relied on images of not only racial but national difference to both articulate anxiety about Rhodes's proposals and contrast British heritage and Oxbridge traditions with the inferior traits and potentially harmful effects of foreign cultures. The Rhodes bequest, like the presence of Indian students, produced several distinct responses that derived force from the familiar devices of stereotyping and caricature. On the whole, these white colonial and former colonial foreigners, through a shared language, religious traditions, and family connections, remained more familiar than "black" colonials. Still, the competitive nature of the relationship between the United States, Germany, and Great Britain, particularly as these countries struggled to achieve industrial, military, and naval supremacy early in the twentieth century, meant that Britons were forever conscious of those differences that, in their minds, rendered them superior. These might be made especially apparent in institutions like Oxford and Cambridge where British men so obviously retained the upper hand.

Occasionally these discussions assumed a positive tone. One commentator emphasized the unalterable character of Oxford as an institution:

"while it is certain that Oxford will change the Rhodesians, it is unlikely that the Rhodesians will do much to change the University in the course of their residence here."[143] Furthermore, in enumerating the advantages of Oxford to foreigners in his will, Cecil Rhodes provided undergraduates with a brief opportunity to navel-gaze and contemplate their unique position, leading one contributor to the *Oxford Point of View* in 1902 to observe, "the charm and influence of Oxford are not only things to gush about in moments of conversational dullness: they exist." These are things, he concludes, "which have left their mark for life."[144]

Generally, however, undergraduate journalists resorted to the usual negative characterizations of foreign influence. Depictions of the various changes these new groups would bring also relied on humor to punctuate and highlight national and cultural differences. In discussions of this most recent change, undergraduates drew on earlier conceptions of different nationalities. Americans, even before they infiltrated Oxford as Rhodes scholars, were often the butt of jokes that alluded to their amusing accents, pretensions to greatness, and ignorance of British ways.[145] "Nasal-voiced Americans" who were unable to comprehend the significance of prominent Oxford landmarks, for example, provided another useful contrast to the knowledgeable British undergraduate.[146] The appearance of this group of former colonials as Rhodes scholars, even when viewed favorably, still provided opportunities to highlight national differences and the unassailable character of the British and their institutions: "We welcome them heartily. . . . During the first week of term we can make no mistake, and a careful survey of the 'High' or the 'Corn' [prominent Oxford streets] during the busy time of the day will save the expense of a journey to New York. But let our American friends take as kindly to us as we intend to do towards them. Let them in Rome do as the Romans do, without, however, forgetting that they are *not* Romans, though of this there is little chance."[147]

Authors and cartoonists portrayed university traditions such as the boat races as fundamentally altered, once again, by the presence of these Americans, colonials, and Germans. The Eights Week magazine *Bump* published an introductory article on May 3, 1902, that emphasized, in a humorous vein, the altering character of the university and its athletic traditions in another prophetic vision, this time in 1950. The author of "Oxford in Transformation" portrayed the scene by the river during race week with a number of foreign characteristics:

> The tow-path nuisance has not abated and there was a regrettable incident. One of the "cowboys," who have recently gone up to John's, shot

the Wadham cox in the back during a moment of excitement. An attempt at lynching failed, and the corps of Wadham, whose boat was bumped in consequence of the catastrophe, sent a challenge to every man in John's. The duels took place with sabres in the Parks last night. Several of the combatants will bear honorable scars for life; Dowell of Wadham, who lost his nose and got three severe cuts on the face was feted afterwards and elected a member of the "blood" Laager-beer Club.[148]

References to foreign forms of violence such as shooting in the back, American lynching, and the saber dueling of German university students provided useful, albeit stereotyped, reminders to the reader of national difference.[149] Poor sportsmanship, amusingly described in this passage and applied to the context of a British athletic event, served to distinguish the unruliness of foreign athletes from the better behaved British. The implied distinctions in this article between British and foreign, disciplined and unruly, and sportsmanlike and ungentlemanly behavior were especially effective devices when employed, as we have seen, at those moments when anxieties about British performance and position in the world were more pronounced.[150]

Artistic depictions were also vitally important in this capacity. The 1906 book *Cap and Gown* reprinted cartoons from the immensely popular *'Varsity* that further illustrate this point. In particular, "The American Invasion" and "The Teutonic Invasion," raised several significant issues (fig. 6.3).[151] As we have seen elsewhere, concern about recent changes, in this case the addition of Rhodes scholars to the undergraduate population of Oxford, was expressed through images that highlighted national and cultural differences. Often, cartoons used in this manner relied on a common conception and knowledge of established university traditions and undergraduate pursuits. In these examples, aspects of undergraduate culture such as athletic contests, shared leisurely meals, familiar architectural landmarks, dress, and unhindered masculine companionship were supplanted by the invading Rhodes scholars and their foreign cultures and customs.

* * *

By exploring these various challenges to unified undergraduate identities and the perception that university reform in the years after 1850 represented an assault on the British nation and its institutions and traditions, it is possible to expose, in this very specific context, the precarious and constructed nature of all class, racial, ethnic, national, and gender identi-

THE AMERICAN INVASION.

What the Rhodes' Scholars might have brought about.

Fig. 6.3. Graham Hoggarth's vision of an Americanized Oxford. *Cap and Gown: Varsity Humours by G. Hoggarth and Others* (Oxford: Holywell, 1906), p. 17. By permission of the Bodleian Library, University of Oxford, shelf mark G.A. Oxon. 4° 219(16).

ties. In reacting to changes, Oxford and Cambridge undergraduates sought first and foremost to preserve intact what they thought was most essential to their own sense of place and self. The growing presence of women at the ancient universities after 1870 and several specific episodes of gender conflict threw into question, as we have seen, assumptions about the masculine nature of these environments, the idea of male culture, and ultimately these young men's understanding of patriarchal order and power.

Similarly, the presence of foreign students, both white and non-white, prompted certain crises, like the *Granta* episode, which required undergraduates to think a bit more self-consciously about what it meant to be both British and white (categories often assumed to be absolute givens). When the certainties of imperial and racial relations were challenged, as they were when newcomers asserted themselves in the Union, mobilized as a clique or "set," or, in the case of religious outsiders, forced changes to Anglican traditions, those undergraduates who were in the majority responded in ways that enabled them to both accommodate change and minimize its impact on their own terms. In so doing, they ensured that potentially damaging "colonial encounters," interactions with foreign others, and contact with women undergraduates on turf designated white, British, and male did not subvert the dichotomy of insider and outsider that was so central to the Oxbridge undergraduate's racial, national, and gender identities.

The full admission of women, the advent of a genuine form of coeducation during the 1970s, and a greater level of tolerance for cultural and racial diversity have made these institutions more hospitable places for the children and grandchildren of these newcomers and a whole wave of postwar immigrants from the Commonwealth. Still, casual observations by Eric Williams, prime minister of Trinidad in the 1960s and an Oxford student in the 1930s, that "no native, however detribalised, could fit socially into All Souls"; by a Canadian Rhodes scholar who harshly contended that "bigotry, racism and sexism . . . characterized Oxford and all English society [in the 1950s]"; and by an Oxford English tutor that "exams [in the 1990s] are designed and set by a male-structured course and a male-structured concept of education," make one wonder just how successful the strategies adopted in coping with change in the late nineteenth and early twentieth centuries were in the years after 1920 and what their legacy is for these institutions in the twenty-first century.[152]

Conclusion

Oxford and Cambridge, like most institutions of higher learning, entered the twenty-first century with their fair share of problems, financial and otherwise. In May of 2000 many of the issues discussed in this book, especially the construction of elite identities and the perpetuation of elite status and masculine privilege, came to a head in a public debate about admissions policies and standards at Magdalen College, Oxford. The case involved an accomplished sixth-form student at the state-funded Monkseaton Community High School, a young woman from North Tyneside by the name of Laura Spence, who was rejected by the college but accepted at Harvard University with a substantial financial aid package. As the issue emerged as a *cause célèbre* in the national papers, a debate was sparked between Gordon Brown, publicity-hungry chancellor of the exchequer under Tony Blair, and a variety of other figures, including Magdalen's president Anthony Smith, who sought to defend the college and the university more generally against what he called ill-founded and spurious charges of elitism.

Indeed, the entire nation seemed to weigh in on the issue in the days and months following the news of Spence's rejection. Gordon Brown, in the opening salvos of a controversy that persists even now, pulled few punches in attacking Oxford for passing Laura over in filling the eight spots that Magdalen had that year for undergraduates interested in studying medicine. In a speech he delivered at a Trades Union Congress conference on May 25, 2000, Brown attacked inequalities in the education system: "David Blunkett and I both take the same view that it is scandalous that someone from North Tyneside, Laura Spence, with the best qualifications and who wants to be a doctor, should be turned down by Oxford University using an interview system more reminiscent of the old school network and the old school tie than justice. It is about time for an end to that old Britain where what matters more are the privileges you are born with, rather than the potential you actually have."[1] Brown tweaked, in this speech, some rather sensitive issues for Britain's ancient universities, where, according to John O'Leary in an article that was published in the *Times* the day after the chancellor's speech, "students from the independent sector [i.e., independent schools, not publicly funded ones] remain in the majority."[2] By leveling charges of old boy-ism and class bias, Brown struggled to expose not only an elitist but a masculinist worldview that was, as we have seen, carefully formulated in the years between 1850 and 1920 and that still persists, at least in the minds of some, in the new millennium.

Naturally, the university and its supporters did not allow these challenges to go unanswered. In the days and weeks that followed, Oxford students who attended state-sponsored schools before matriculating at the university were interviewed in the press to refute charges of gender, class, educational, and regional bias and the notion that they were, in some way or another, disadvantaged. The *Times* reported that Ed Fitzgerald, a Magdalen undergraduate educated at a comprehensive school (that is, one that does not require applicants to pass an entrance exam) and president of the college's Sherington Society for medical students, was most unhappy about Brown's comments, openly worrying that they would discourage applications to Magdalen from other state-school students. In an attempt to refute notions of stuffy and snobby elitism, he contrasted the interview process at Oxford to that at other institutions. "When I went for interview at medical school here [at Oxford] we actually received a letter saying 'please dress informally,'" whereas at "Leeds, Leicester and Liverpool, everyone turned up in suits and ties." "Here," he concluded, "was the one place where people turned up in jeans and a jumper."

Other students interviewed by the *Times* were at pains to counter popular perceptions of a masculine Oxford dominated by public school boys in the mold of Sebastian Flyte and Charles Ryder, the central characters in Evelyn Waugh's *Brideshead Revisited*. Another state school–educated student, a woman named Helen Comford who was the newly elected president of the Magdalen Junior Common Room, challenged this perception directly when she observed, "the JCR committee is two-thirds female which completely destroys the whole idea of colleges being run by public schoolboys." Offering further evidence that Magdalen eschewed elitism, she enumerated her efforts to reach out to students from inner cities and attract more state-educated freshmen. Students also attempted to refute notions that Oxford students revere, unthinkingly, the established traditions of the university and cling to a crusty, elitist worldview. Discussing the tradition of formal club dining, for instance, Ed Fitzgerald noted that "very occasionally you come across somebody in the evening walking round in a white tie outfit but the other students just think they are silly."[3]

Undergraduates were not, of course, the only ones to respond to Brown's charges, particularly those that indicted the university for not accepting enough students from working-class, northern, and industrial backgrounds, or enough non-white students. In an interview with journalist Valerie Grove, for instance, Anthony Smith discussed his disappointment with what he characterized as the government's unfair attack on Oxford privilege and defended the track record of his college in recruiting and matriculating students from state schools, who made up 48 percent of the undergraduate population in 2000. Smith openly lamented the effects of the Spence controversy. "What I care about the most," he observed, "is the kids who come to this college. We now have to reassure them that they deserve to be here." "The most damnable aspect of all this," he continued, "is the suggestion that comprehensive students have been spatchcocked into the college because of their social background, while public schools will feel they have to apologise for their existence. For a senior politician to cause these assumptions is disgraceful. They will inhibit the very people we are hoping will apply."[4]

The emotions generated on both sides of the debate clearly ran very high indeed, emerging out of a context of worries about a "brain-drain" to America, Labour Party fears about the perpetuation of elitism and slippery and sometimes disingenuous guarantees of equal opportunity, and the ever-present machinations of politicians keen to score points with constituents. At the core of these debates are many key questions about the nature of the ancient universities and their traditional association with elite status, and a persistent notion that they remain hostile to outsiders of a variety of different stripes, including women. One contributor to the *World Socialist Web Site* asked, "who is likely to be more comfortable, and therefore confident, in an Oxbridge interview situation? A working-class girl from the heavily-industrial Northeast with no family background of university acceptance, or a Southern public-school boy unfazed by received-pronunciation accents, crusty dons, or ancient buildings?"[5] For several different observers, alarming statistics betraying links between Britain's wealthy establishment and Oxbridge privilege compounded these more general concerns about the inequities inherent at these institutions. The editors of an education journal, for example, noted in August 2000 that the "bottom 50 per cent of the population in terms of affluence (measured by social class) are greatly underrepresented in the 'top five' universities. These students gain only 10 per cent of places compared with an expected 14 per cent based on school performance."[6] Similarly, the correspondent to the *World Socialist Web Site* noted, somewhat more caustically, that "[s]tatistically neither university can defend its policy of discrimination against working-class state-school applicants. They currently make up less than 50 percent of Oxford's intake (despite accounting for almost three quarters of all university applicants)."[7]

What can this contemporary episode, somewhat inappropriately called a "scandal" by Gordon Brown, tell us about the masculine elite worldviews constructed by Oxford and Cambridge students during the Victorian and Edwardian eras, a period of tremendous growth and increased international prestige for the ancient universities? Clearly, the institution at the center of this recent controversy has been transformed by twentieth-century changes that have broadened the population base from which Oxford students are drawn and largely eliminated formal policies of gender segregation. It would be inappropriate, then, to conclude here that the elite worldviews attacked by Gordon Brown and the contributor to the *World Socialist Web Site* were exactly the same as those embraced by the undergraduates who matriculated between 1850 and 1920. It would, however, be equally inappropriate not to recognize, as most involved in the debate have, the continuum on which these charges operate. Government officials and university administrators, college tutors and undergraduates alike need, in their consideration of questions of access, to seriously contemplate the history of masculine exclusivity and elitism if they hope to effectively broaden the reach and impact of these ancient foundations. Understanding how elites are created and perpetuated, not just through material privileges and financial success, but through the acquisition of a cultural capital placed beyond the reach of most, allows for a more nuanced and ultimately more detailed understanding of why the debates about Laura Spence have sparked so much interest.[8]

The attacks on the university in May 2000 were, in fact, as much attacks on a historically constructed elitism as they were indictments of Oxford's inability to democratize. Understanding that an Oxbridge degree has historically granted access to the levers of government, the most coveted posts in the civil service, and top positions in City law firms and merchant banks, critics were responding to statistics such as the overwhelming predominance of Oxbridge-educated prime ministers. In Britain, there have been 53 prime ministers since Robert Walpole first assumed the position in 1721. Of these 53, 40 (including the current Labour Party leader) have been educated at either Oxford or Cambridge (14 at the latter and 26 at the former). In some ways then, what was being debated in the Spence affair was not the efficacy of the Oxford Access Scheme and other efforts (governmental or institutional) to broaden the student base but rather the legacies of the Victorian and Edwardian period, when the modern and highly masculinized elite sensibilities associated with both universities emerged as salient features of the peculiar worldviews fostered at these institutions.[9]

Contemporary government officials and university administrators are not, however, the only ones to have underplayed this important history in considering the structures of elitism. Historians of Britain have generally addressed the importance of Oxford and Cambridge to the nation, the role of these institutions in elite production, and their significance as national symbols in frustratingly passing and brief ways, when they have done so at all. The important work of historians like William Lubenow, J. A. Mangan, Sheldon Rothblatt, and Reba Soffer aside, the ways in which those who attended these institutions lived their lives, made sense of what it meant to be an undergraduate, and assigned specific meanings to the experience have all too often been ignored or subsumed in accounts that have tended to privilege administrative and curricular matters, highlight official perspectives, or chronicle the activities of one specific group. The central objective of this study has been to dissect not the attitudes of administrators and dons but, rather, what Frank Aydelotte, an American Rhodes scholar who matriculated at Brasenose College in 1905, identified as the deep "impression" made by the university "upon her sons"; the "ways in which . . . life at Oxford stamps upon the men who live it this distinctive character."[10] In so doing, it has sought to locate the history of undergraduate life within broader nineteenth- and early-twentieth-century narratives of masculine socialization, professionalization, and imperial expansion, to mention but a few of the themes addressed in the preceding pages.

This book has problematized and, I hope, rendered more understandable the worldviews of Oxford and Cambridge undergraduates by taking as a serious subject of study the ways in which these views were articulated and expressed through a variety of distinctive cultural forms between the years 1850 and 1920, a period of intense reform that transformed these institutions into thoroughly modern universities. While undergraduates, as they prepared for their futures, may have been taught the values of public service, intelligent citizenship, and civic responsibility through the study of disciplines like history, the manner in which they assigned meaning to both the academic and non-academic sides of life played an equally important role in fostering a national, university-trained, and culturally privileged professional elite.[11] Students' definitions of the university as a unique little world or of undergraduates as the best Britain had to offer were attempts to solidify and express confidently an elite status that this era of profound social change and cultural dislocation had rendered precarious, even when the students' material advantages were glaringly apparent. Attempts to "construct superiority" coincided with the development of a more explicit and clearly articulated sense that the universities were engaged in a national and imperial mission. Percy Ewing Matheson, secretary of the Oxford and Cambridge Schools Examination Board and a New College fellow, alluded to this point when he observed in 1895, "It is clearly desirable that the great public services [the home and colonial civil services] should, as far as may be, be accessible through the ordinary avenues of higher education and that their personnel should consist of those who have enjoyed the contact with men and studies which university life affords."[12]

The elite position of the Oxbridge undergraduate was not, however, predicated solely on notions of his superiority or ability to assume a position of power. Notions of exclusivity also remained important and were reinforced through multiple strategies that routinely identified insiders and outsiders within these milieus and demarcated the universities as social spaces in which cultural knowledge clearly translated into power. Undergraduates, and many of their peers outside the universities, thus highlighted difference as they struggled to assert their dominance over women, members of the working classes, other races, and other nations.

In exploring student magazines, newspapers, pamphlets, and reviews, this study has privileged the undergraduate perspective often neglected or downplayed in larger institutional histories. In so doing, it has revealed some of the primary concerns of junior members and illustrated what figured most prominently in their representations of university life. Undergraduates were preoccupied not only with their status in British society, but with how their involvement in specific activities within the universities set them apart from others. Furthermore, as young men who were struggling to traverse the rocky road from boyhood to manhood, they were consumed—whether discussing college rooms, struggles with dons, the structures of discipline, examinations, or athletics—by a desire to find and define what were often elusive and slippery identities.

The biggest part of young undergraduates' search for identity entailed defining what it meant to be a British man. They were transformed at the university as much by assuming the mantle of manhood as by preparing for a life of leadership and public service, revealing the extent to which gender and class (as well as racial and national) identities intersected, over-lapped, and often blurred in Oxbridge contexts. While class permeated the language employed by undergraduates in this period, it was often sub-sumed by more explicit discussions of masculinity and anxieties about gender identity. This was partly because these young men's class position was so assured and assumed that it hardly needed to be constantly reiter-ated. It was also, however, due to the fact that the vocabulary of profes-sional masculinity (even in its most fragmented form) became, within this period, the primary means through which Oxford and Cambridge men both articulated and understood their elite position in British society. Within a university setting, ruminations on the undergraduate's future status as a professional man were, of course, about his position within British socio-economic structures. They were also, however, articulate ex-pressions of the increasingly important relationship in the later nineteenth century between the symbiotically linked search for meaningful and remu-nerative work and upper-middle-class male identities.

Every activity within the university, then, was significant in the for-mation of undergraduate masculine identities. The wrangles that occurred between undergraduates and college and university officials represented not just struggles over authority and discipline but, rather, broader gen-erational disputes over definitions of manhood, contests often fought over access to the public spaces of these university communities. Similarly, ex-aminations functioned, within such a context, not just as academic exer-cises that undergraduates were required to submit to for a degree. They were, in fact, trials of manhood and tests of character that steeled privi-leged adolescents, as they competed for honors and for professional futures. They were also, however, one of the many arenas in which it was possible for British undergraduates, assumed to epitomize the stiff upper lip, to articulate fears and anxieties about their role as imperial leaders and their status as unimpeachably masculine men. Additionally, the intercollegiate boat races were not just further manifestations of this penchant for com-petition but important social rituals that allowed undergraduates to cele-brate the ideal of the male athlete, the athletic body, and male knowledge of university traditions, while reinforcing and occasionally challenging a gender and sexual order that was predicated on marked distinctions between the admittedly blurred categories of male and female, masculine and feminine, and normative and deviant. When the intensely masculine culture of Oxbridge seemed threatened, as it was when women began to enter these institutions in the 1870s, most undergraduates intensified their efforts to define the university as a male space, preserve their autonomy, and assert their power and presence through both physical and rhetorical acts, as they did in 1888 at Oxford and in 1897 at Cambridge. In this way, the crises pinpointed in this study not only highlight the fragility of the identities that were forged within these institutions but illustrate just how central ideas about gender difference were in conceptions of these little worlds.

While I have linked the history of undergraduate culture to concepts of Britishness, whiteness, and imperial authority (and illustrated important points of intersection), my central preoccupation has been with the psychic, physical, and spatial dimensions of masculine identity formation for one very particular, and ultimately very powerful, group of young men. In undertaking this work, I have explored how ideas about gender difference, particularly undergraduate attempts to distinguish between frequently overlapping and uneasily segregated male and female spaces, figured prominently in middle- and upper-middle-class worldviews and became, within this period, central components of the elite perspectives that circulated in imperial Britain. By situating Oxbridge men within the gender conflicts of the nineteenth and early twentieth centuries, I have illustrated not only how they negotiated the transition from boyhood to manhood but also how they endeavored, often in the most caustic of ways, to preserve male power and privilege in the face of mounting social change.

The significance of this study, I hope, extends somewhat beyond these observations; contained within this material are partial explanations of why the products of these institutions governed the nation and their families, administered the empire, and created policy in the ways that they did. Indeed, government reports, literary representations of Oxford and Cambridge, and personal memoirs all reveal the extent to which the cultural forms described in the preceding pages profoundly affected those who attended these institutions. When the British government wanted to examine secondary education in 1895, for example, it matter-of-factly turned to the universities for evidence about the state of affairs. As men who had naturally assumed their position at the fore of the intellectual and educational elite, Oxbridge tutors and fellows like Cambridge historian Oscar Browning and Knightsbridge Professor of Moral Philosophy Henry Sidgwick offered, in the memoranda they submitted to the Royal Commission on Secondary Education, perspectives on the educational system that betrayed how successfully the masculine and elite worldviews of the universities had been formulated and imparted. Thomas Raleigh, a fellow at All Souls College, Oxford observed that "[c]lose connexion with the universities has done much to maintain the high character of our Civil Service." He concluded his discussion of the undergraduate's unique ability to perform well by characterizing the Oxford student as an exemplar of British manhood, revealing in the process just how pervasive belief in inherent superiority was: "As with teachers, so with officials; any good Oxford man will make a civil servant, diplomatist, & c., if he has character, and if he falls into the hands of superiors who know how to train him."[13]

Men of letters like Siegfried Sassoon, a Cambridge undergraduate in the first decade of the twentieth century, also embraced a number of the attitudes dissected in this book, even as they occasionally criticized the deleterious consequences of university socialization. In his *Memoirs of a Fox-Hunting Man,* the first novel in his semi-autobiographical trilogy, Sassoon commented on the importance of university education in preparing one for life. Percival G. Pennett, trustee for young George Sherston, the novel's protagonist, observes to his charge, "[o]ne of the objects of an University career is to equip the student for the battle of life, and as you grow older you will find that people are estimated in the world by the results they have obtained at the Varsity. It is a kind of stamp upon a man and is supposed to indicate the stuff of which he is made." In enumerating the advantages of completing a degree, Pennett delineates the attributes of professional manhood: "G. Sherston, M.A., will rank higher than plain G. Sherston, and the mere fact of your being able to attach the magic letters to your name will show that whatever may be your capabilities you have at any rate grit and perseverance." While the appeal fails to convince George not to leave Cambridge, he, and by extrapolation Sassoon himself, readily admits the veracity of these words: "[e]verything the letter said was so true."[14]

While a systematic analysis of the influences of the university experience on Oxbridge men later in life is beyond the purview of this study, it must be recognized that the worldviews, values, and attitudes that they had regularly imbibed in college rooms (along with beer, claret, and port) had a profound impact on the perspectives of graduates as they assumed the mantle of imperial leadership and real manhood. The preservation of male hegemony in the political sphere, gendered and racial rhetoric in speeches and policy papers, notions of nationality predicated on assumptions of difference, and repeated invocations of the masculine and the feminine as explanatory concepts, all undoubtedly had their genesis in educational cultures that routinely constructed meaning, organized their rituals, and preserved traditions to privilege the masculine over the feminine, the male over the female, the British over the foreign, and the superior over the inferior.

Notes

Preface

1. Forster wrote *Maurice* in 1914, but it was only published after his death in 1970. See E. M. Forster, *Maurice: A Novel* (New York: W. W. Norton, 1971).

2. On this point, see Ian Carter's study of the postwar university novel, *Ancient Cultures of Conceit: British University Fiction in the Post-war Years* (London: Routledge, 1990).

3. The best portrayals of Oxford and Cambridge in the Merchant-Ivory corpus are their adaptations of two E. M. Forster novels, *Maurice* (1987) and *Howards End* (1992).

4. For one critique and attempt at correction or clarification, see Rachel Johnson, ed., *The Oxford Myth* (London: Weidenfeld and Nicolson, 1988).

5. For eclectic discussions of some of the myths associated with the English, see Roy Porter, ed., *Myths of the English* (Cambridge: Polity, 1992).

6. Joseph A. Soares, *The Decline of Privilege: The Modernization of Oxford University* (Stanford: Stanford University Press, 1999).

7. For one reaction to these criticisms, see Alan Ryan, "Getting In," *Oxford Today: The University Magazine* 13, no. 1 (Michaelmas issue, 2000): 5–6.

8. Toby Young, "Class," in *The Oxford Myth*, ed. Rachel Johnson, p. 6.

9. Jan Morris, ed., *The Oxford Book of Oxford* (Oxford: Oxford University Press, 1978), p. 239.

10. The volume of work on the colleges and universities is too extensive to cite here. For some good examples, see Christopher Brooke, *A History of Gonville and Caius College* (Woodbridge, U.K.: Boydell, 1985); John Jones, *Balliol College: A History, 1263–1939* (Oxford: Oxford University Press, 1988); and John Twigg, *A History of Queen's College, Cambridge, 1448–1986* (Woodbridge, U.K.: Boydell, 1987). The multi-volume histories of the universities, which have been published over the past twenty years, represent the best work on these institutions to date. See T. H. Aston, ed., *The History of the University of Oxford*, vols. 1–8 (Oxford: Oxford University Press, 1984–2000); and Christopher N. L. Brooke, ed., *A History of the University of Cambridge*, vols. 1–4 (Cambridge: Cambridge University Press, 1988–1997).

Introduction

1. "Oxford in the Victorian Age," *Blackwood's Edinburgh Magazine* 169, no. 1025 (March 1901): 336–337.

2. Ibid., pp. 337, 339.

3. Charles Bowen, *At the Opening of Balliol New Hall*, excerpted in Thomas Seccombe and H. Spencer Scott, eds., *In Praise of Oxford: An Anthology in Prose and Verse* (London: Constable, 1912), 2:760.

4. R. D. Anderson, *Universities and Elites in Britain since 1800* (London: Macmillan, 1992), pp. 14–17.

5. The scholarship on the public schools is extensive. See, for example, Jonathan

Gathorne-Hardy, *The Old School Tie: The Phenomenon of the English Public School* (New York: Viking, 1977); J. R. de S. Honey, *Tom Brown's Universe: The Development of the Victorian Public School* (London: Millington, 1977); E. C. Mack, *The Public Schools and British Public Opinion since 1860: The Relationship between Contemporary Ideas and the Evolution of an English Institution* (New York: Columbia University Press, 1941); David Newsome, *Godliness and Good Learning: Four Studies on a Victorian Ideal* (London: Cassell, 1961); and P. J. Rich, *Chains of Empire: English Public Schools, Masonic Cabalism, Historical Causality, and Imperial Clubdom* (London: Regency, 1991). On the study of classics at the public schools, see Christopher Stray, *Classics Transformed: Schools, Universities, and Society in England, 1830–1960* (Oxford: Clarendon, 1998).

6. Reba Soffer, *Discipline and Power: The University, History, and the Making of an English Elite, 1870–1930* (Stanford: Stanford University Press, 1994), p. 3.

7. T. W. Heyck, *The Transformation of Intellectual Life in Victorian England* (London: Croom Helm, 1982), p. 9. For two perspectives on the ways in which some dons clung to older perspectives, see Stefan Collini, *Public Moralists: Political Thought and Intellectual Life in Britain, 1850–1930* (Oxford: Clarendon, 1991); and Martin J. Wiener, *English Culture and the Decline of the Industrial Spirit, 1850–1980* (Cambridge: Cambridge University Press, 1981).

8. On aspects of the reform process, see Peter Searby, *A History of the University of Cambridge: 1750–1870,* vol. 3 of *A History of the University of Cambridge,* ed. Christopher N. L. Brooke (Cambridge: Cambridge University Press, 1997), pp. 472–544.

9. A. J. Engel, *From Clergyman to Don: The Rise of the Academic Profession in Nineteenth-Century Oxford* (Oxford: Oxford University Press, 1983). Sheldon Rothblatt also covers aspects of this in his *The Revolution of the Dons: Cambridge and Society in Victorian England* (New York: Basic Books, 1968).

10. On religious changes, see V. H. H. Green, *Religion at Oxford and Cambridge* (London: SCM Press, 1964), pp. 297–337.

11. On the development of these various disciplines, see Norman Chester, *Economics, Politics, and Social Studies in Oxford, 1900–1985* (London: Macmillan, 1986); and Soffer, *Discipline and Power.*

12. On the social origins of the Oxbridge student body, see Harold Perkin, *The Rise of Professional Society: England since 1800* (London: Routledge, 1989), pp. 370–372; Rothblatt, *Revolution of the Dons,* pp. 86–93; and Lawrence Stone, "The Size and Composition of the Oxford Student Body, 1580–1910," in *The University in Society,* ed. Lawrence Stone (Princeton: Princeton University Press, 1974), 1:74. See also C. Arnold Anderson and Miriam Schnaper, *School and Society in England: Social Backgrounds of Oxford and Cambridge Students* (Westport, Conn.: Greenwood, 1952); and H. Jenkins and D. C. Jones, "Social Class of Cambridge University Alumni of the 18th and 19th Centuries," *British Journal of Sociology* 1, no. 2 (June 1950): 93–116. On the connection between university education and the assumption of power, see R. Anderson, *Universities and Elites in Britain since 1800,* p. 49; Reba Soffer, "The Modern University and National Values, 1850–1930," *Historical Research* 60, no. 142 (June 1987): 166; and Ray Jones, *The Nineteenth-Century Foreign Office: An Administrative History* (London: Weidenfeld and Nicolson, 1971), pp. 165–188.

13. Richard Symonds, *Oxford and Empire: The Last Lost Cause?* (New York: St. Martin's, 1986), pp. 257–283. On the presence of Indian students in Britain, see Shompa Lahiri, *Indians in Britain: Anglo-Indian Encounters, Race, and Identity, 1880–1930* (London: Frank Cass, 2000).

14. See Vera Brittain, *The Women at Oxford: A Fragment of History* (London: Harrap, 1960); Janet Howarth, "'In Oxford but . . . not of Oxford': The Women's Colleges," in *Nineteenth-Century Oxford, Part 2,* ed. M. G. Brock and M. C. Curthoys, vol. 7 of *The History of the University of Oxford,* ed. T. H. Aston (Oxford: Oxford University

Press, 2000); Janet Howarth, "Women," in *The Twentieth Century,* ed. Brian Harrison, vol. 8 of *The History of the University of Oxford,* ed. T. H. Aston (Oxford: Clarendon, 1994); Susan J. Leonardi, *Dangerous by Degrees: Women at Oxford and the Somerville College Novelists* (New Brunswick: Rutgers University Press, 1989), pp. 1–45; and Rita McWilliams Tullberg, *Women at Cambridge,* rev. ed. (Cambridge: Cambridge University Press, 1998).

15. Sheldon Rothblatt asserts that the modern undergraduate emerges in the early nineteenth century. While components of the modern student identity are certainly present then, it took the reforms of the mid-nineteenth century and the growth of certain traditions after 1850 to create the undergraduate "type," who dominated well into the twentieth century. See Sheldon Rothblatt, *The Modern University and Its Discontents: The Fate of Newman's Legacies in Britain and America* (Cambridge: Cambridge University Press, 1997), pp. 106–178.

16. On the early-nineteenth-century vision of middle-class masculinity, see Leonore Davidoff and Catherine Hall, *Family Fortunes: Men and Women of the English Middle Class, 1780–1850* (Chicago: University of Chicago Press, 1987).

17. Newsome, *Godliness and Good Learning,* pp. 195–239. On other aspects of this ideal, see Norman Vance, *The Sinews of the Spirit: The Ideal of Christian Manliness in Victorian Literature and Religious Thought* (Cambridge: Cambridge University Press, 1985). On some of these features of nineteenth- and twentieth-century masculinity, see Michael Roper and John Tosh, eds., *Manful Assertions: Masculinities in Britain since 1800* (London: Routledge, 1991). For an overview of some of these developments and recent historiography, see Martin Francis, "The Domestication of the British Male? Recent Research on Nineteenth- and Twentieth-Century British Masculinity," *Historical Journal* 45, no. 3 (September 2002), pp. 637–652.

18. Davidoff and Hall, *Family Fortunes,* pp. 149–192; and M. Jeanne Peterson, *Family, Love, and Work in the Lives of Victorian Gentlewomen* (Bloomington: Indiana University Press, 1989).

19. John Tosh, *A Man's Place: Masculinity and the Middle-Class Home in Victorian England* (New Haven: Yale University Press, 1999).

20. Ibid., pp. 170–194.

21. On masculinity and empire, see Mrinalini Sinha, *Colonial Masculinity: The "Manly Englishman" and the "Effeminate Bengali" in the Late Nineteenth Century* (Manchester: Manchester University Press, 1995). On militarism and athleticism, see Graham Dawson, *Soldier Heroes: British Adventure, Empire, and the Imagining of Masculinities* (London: Routledge, 1994); and J. A. Mangan, *Athleticism in the Victorian and Edwardian Public School: The Emergence and Consolidation of an Educational Ideology* (Cambridge: Cambridge University Press, 1981). On boys' magazines, see Kelly Boyd, *Manliness and the Boys' Story Paper, 1855–1940* (Basingstoke, U.K.: Palgrave, 2002).

22. On the idea of crisis in masculine identity formation, see R. W. Connell, *Masculinities* (Berkeley: University of California Press, 1995), pp. 84–86.

23. Angus McLaren, *The Trials of Masculinity: Policing Sexual Boundaries, 1870–1930* (Chicago: University of Chicago Press, 1997). For a general overview of these crises, see Susan Kingsley Kent, *Gender and Power in Britain, 1640–1990* (London: Routledge, 1999), pp. 152–310. On various concerns relating to sexuality, see Frank Mort, *Dangerous Sexualities: Medico-moral Politics in England since 1830,* 2nd ed. (London: Routledge, 2000).

24. On the consequences of the First World War, see Joanna Bourke, *Dismembering the Male: Men's Bodies, Britain, and the Great War* (Chicago: University of Chicago Press, 1996).

25. Sinha, *Colonial Masculinity,* p. 131.

26. Eric Hobsbawm, "Introduction: Inventing Traditions," in *The Invention of*

Tradition, ed. Eric Hobsbawm and Terence Ranger (Cambridge: Cambridge University Press, 1983), pp. 1–14.

27. Contemporary observers of Oxford and Cambridge tend to assume that all traditions within these institutions are time-honored and long established, not relatively recent inventions. See Bill Bryson, "The Style and Substance of Oxford," *National Geographic* 188, no. 5 (November 1995): 114–137.

28. Soffer, *Discipline and Power,* p. 5.

29. On the importance of social rituals and cultural performances, see John J. MacAloon, *Rite, Drama, Festival, Spectacle: Rehearsals toward a Theory of Cultural Performance* (Philadelphia: Institute for the Study of Human Issues, 1984). One attempt to dissect the meaning of undergraduate rituals, at Canadian universities, appears in Keith Walden, "Hazes, Hustles, Scraps, and Stunts: Initiations at the University of Toronto, 1880–1925," in *Youth, University, and Canadian Society: Essays in the Social History of Higher Education,* ed. Paul Axelrod and John G. Reid (Montreal: McGill–Queen's University Press, 1989), pp. 94–96, 112, 116.

30. The classic interpretation of the political impact of these changes is George Dangerfield, *The Strange Death of Liberal England* (New York: Capricorn Books, 1961). For a different take on some of the reactions to these changes, see Judith R. Walkowitz, *City of Dreadful Delight: Narratives of Sexual Danger in Late-Victorian London* (Chicago: University of Chicago Press, 1992), p. 19. On the challenges of and reactions to feminism, see Susan Kingsley Kent, *Sex and Suffrage in Britain, 1860–1914* (Princeton: Princeton University Press, 1987), pp. 184–219. On colonial encounters in the metropole, see Antoinette Burton, *At the Heart of the Empire: Indians and the Colonial Encounter in Late-Victorian Britain* (Berkeley: University of California Press, 1998).

31. Elaine Showalter has characterized this period as a time of "sexual anarchy." See her *Sexual Anarchy: Gender and Culture at the Fin de Siècle* (New York: Viking, 1990).

32. Joan W. Scott, "Gender: A Useful Category of Historical Analysis," in *Gender and the Politics of History* (New York: Columbia University Press, 1988), p. 50.

33. On athleticism in the universities, see J. A. Mangan, "'Oars and the Man': Pleasure and Purpose in Victorian and Edwardian Cambridge," *British Journal of Sports History* 1, no. 3 (December 1984): 245–271; and J. A. Mangan, "Lamentable Barbarians and Pitiful Sheep: Rhetoric of Protest and Pleasure in Late Victorian and Edwardian 'Oxbridge,'" *Victorian Studies* 34, no. 4 (summer 1991): 473–489. On the Apostles, see W. C. Lubenow, *The Cambridge Apostles, 1820–1914: Liberalism, Imagination, and Friendship in British Intellectual and Professional Life* (Cambridge: Cambridge University Press, 1998), pp. 27–89. There are some gendered analyses of other elite institutions of higher learning. See Kim Townsend, *Manhood at Harvard: William James and Others* (New York: W. W. Norton, 1996).

34. Scott, "Gender: A Useful Category of Historical Analysis," pp. 44, 46, 50. For more social scientific approaches, see Barbara Rogers, *Men Only: An Investigation into Men's Organizations* (London: Pandora, 1988); and Lynne Segal, *Slow Motion: Changing Masculinities, Changing Men* (London: Virago, 1990).

35. My understanding of discourse is derived, in part, from Michel Foucault, who sees discourse as types or systems of knowledge (in this case, about gender and sexuality). See his *The Archaeology of Knowledge,* trans. A. M. Sheridan Smith (New York: Pantheon Books, 1972).

36. R. W. Connell sees the concept of hegemony as a process whereby "one form of masculinity rather than others is culturally exalted." *Masculinities,* p. 77.

37. On masculine styles in the Victorian era, see James Eli Adams, *Dandies and Desert Saints: Styles of Victorian Masculinity* (Ithaca, N.Y.: Cornell University Press, 1995).

38. The idea of a continuum of behavior and desire is covered most effectively in George Chauncey, *Gay New York: Gender, Urban Culture, and the Making of the Gay Male World, 1890–1940* (New York: Basic Books, 1994), pp. 1–29, 47–97. For a British discussion, see Matt Houlbrook, "Soldier Heroes and Rent Boys: Homosex, Masculinities, and Britishness in the Brigade of Guards, circa 1900–1960," *Journal of British Studies* 43, no. 3 (July 2003): 351–388.

39. Natalie Zemon Davis, the cultural historian of early modern France, promoted this idea in the 1980s. See Robb Harding and Judy Coffin, "Interview with Natalie Zemon Davis," in *Visions of History*, by MARHO, the Radical Historians Organization, ed. Henry Abelove et al. (New York: Pantheon Books, 1983), p. 112. See also Natalie Z. Davis, "Anthropology and History in the 1980s: The Possibilities of the Past," *Journal of Interdisciplinary History* 12, no. 2 (autumn 1981): 227–252.

40. Raymond Williams, *Keywords: A Vocabulary of Culture and Society* (London: Croom Helm, 1976), p. 76.

41. See Lynn Hunt, "Introduction: History, Culture, and Text," in *The New Cultural History*, ed. Lynn Hunt (Berkeley: University of California Press, 1989), p. 22. This point is also made by Richard Johnson in his "What is Cultural Studies Anyway?" *Social Text* 16 (winter 1986–1987): 48. For recent perspectives on cultural history, see Victoria E. Bonnell and Lynn Hunt, eds., *Beyond the Cultural Turn: New Directions in the Study of Society and Culture* (Berkeley: University of California Press, 1999).

42. Clifford Geertz, *The Interpretation of Cultures* (New York: Basic Books, 1973), p. 5. Geertz's lead has been followed by a number of scholars working in the disciplines of history and cultural studies. See, for example, Patrick Brantlinger, *Crusoe's Footprints: Cultural Studies in Britain and America* (London: Routledge, 1990); Robert Darnton, "The Symbolic Element in History," *Journal of Modern History* 58, no. 1 (March 1986): 218–233; Natalie Z. Davis, *Fiction in the Archives: Pardon Tales and Their Tellers in Sixteenth-Century France* (Stanford: Stanford University Press, 1987); and Erika Diane Rappaport, *Shopping for Pleasure: Women in the Making of London's West End* (Princeton: Princeton University Press, 2000).

43. Pierre Bourdieu, *The State Nobility: Elite Schools in the Field of Power*, trans. Lauretta C. Clough (Stanford: Stanford University Press, 1996), p. 180.

44. My thinking on the various meanings of social spaces is informed by the work of Michel de Certeau, *The Practice of Everyday Life*, trans. Steven F. Rendall (Berkeley: University of California Press, 1984); and Doreen Massey, *Space, Place, and Gender* (Minneapolis: University of Minnesota Press, 1994).

45. Andrew Kirkendall also embraces this approach to the study of education in a recent book on Brazil. See his *Class Mates: Male Student Culture and the Making of a Political Class in Nineteenth-Century Brazil* (Lincoln: University of Nebraska Press, 2002). Again, the work of Bourdieu is instrumental here. See Pierre Bourdieu, *Language and Symbolic Power*, ed. John B. Thompson, trans. Gino Raymond and Matthew Adamson (Cambridge, Mass.: Harvard University Press, 1999), pp. 117–126; and Pierre Bourdieu, *Distinction: A Social Critique of the Judgement of Taste*, trans. Richard Nice (Cambridge, Mass.: Harvard University Press, 1984).

46. For one approach that looks at cultural reproduction among elites, see Sara Delamont, *Knowledgeable Women: Structuralism and the Reproduction of Elites* (London: Routledge, 1989).

47. "Editorial Notes," *Undergraduate* 1, no. 1 (January 24, 1888): 1.

48. E. P. Thompson, *The Making of the English Working Class* (New York: Vintage Books, 1966), p. 12.

49. For a recent example of this type of scholarship, see Alan Kidd and David Nicholls, eds. *Gender, Civic Culture, and Consumerism: Middle-Class Identity in Britain,*

1800–1940 (Manchester: Manchester University Press, 1999). For another application of Thompson's ideas to the study of elites, see David Kuchta, "The Making of the Self-Made Man: Class, Clothing, and English Masculinity, 1688–1832" in *The Sex of Things: Gender and Consumption in Historical Perspective,* ed. Victoria de Grazia and Ellen Furlough (Berkeley: University of California Press, 1996), p. 64. Although some cultural studies scholars have utilized these ideas in examining British elites, Stefan Collini has rightly pointed to a general deficiency in their work, which has tended to focus more on those who were dominated than on those doing the dominating. See his "The Passionate Intensity of Cultural Studies," *Victorian Studies* 36, no. 4 (summer 1993): 455–460.

50. See, for example, Charles Edward Mallet, *A History of the University of Oxford* (London: Methuen, 1927), 3:487. J. A. Mangan has also noted the utility of these sources. See his "'Oars and the Man'" and "Lamentable Barbarians and Pitiful Sheep."

51. In January 1888, when the student population of Oxford hovered around 2,800, the *Undergraduate* noted in its second issue that its first had sold in excess of a thousand copies. "Editorial Notes," *Undergraduate* 1, no. 2 (January 31, 1888): 17. This seems to be corroborated by a report by a Cambridge contemporary who noted, with envy, that circulation figures for the *Undergraduate* were at 1,100. "Notes," *Cambridge Fortnightly,* no. 2 (February 7, 1888): 5. On the frequency of pass-on readership in British culture more generally during this period, see Alan J. Lee, *The Origins of the Popular Press in England, 1855–1914* (London: Croom Helm, 1976), pp. 35–36.

52. In offering her critique of autobiographies as sources, Helen Lefkowitz Horowitz also observes that they are, paradoxically, both "tainted" and "indispensable." See her *Campus Life: Undergraduate Cultures from the End of the Eighteenth Century to the Present* (Chicago: University of Chicago Press, 1987), p. xiii.

53. T. C. Sandars, "Undergraduate Literature," *Saturday Review of Politics, Literature, Science, and Art* 3, no. 70 (February 28, 1857): 196; and Harry Currie Marillier, *University Magazines and their Makers. By Harry Currie Marillier, Knyght Erraunt to ye Set of Odd Volumes* (London: Bedford, 1899), p. 10. Other groups in British society produced publications that were equally revealing. On lower-middle-class clerks in London, see Susan Pennybacker, *A Vision for London, 1889–1914: Labour, Everyday Life, and the LCC Experiment* (London: Routledge, 1995); and, on teachers in London, see Dina M. Copelman, *London's Women Teachers: Gender, Class, and Feminism, 1870–1930* (London: Routledge, 1996).

54. [William Lucas Collins], "Light and Dark Blue," *Blackwood's Edinburgh Magazine* 100, no. 612 (October 1866): 449–450. The author was a Jesus College, Oxford man who matriculated in 1833 and finally took a B.A. in 1838.

55. Joan Scott, "The Evidence of Experience," *Critical Inquiry* 17, no. 4 (summer 1991): 793. On this language-centered approach, see Dominick LaCapra, *History and Criticism* (Ithaca, N.Y.: Cornell University Press, 1985); and Hayden White, *The Content of the Form: Narrative, Discourse, and Historical Representation* (Baltimore: Johns Hopkins University Press, 1987).

56. Joseph Kelly and Timothy Kelly, "Searching the Dark Alley: New Historicism and Social History," *Journal of Social History* 25, no. 3 (spring 1992): 688.

57. For one discussion of this process, see Regenia Gagnier, *Subjectivities: A History of Self-Representation in Britain, 1832–1920* (Oxford: Oxford University Press, 1991), p. 8.

58. For a brief and interesting attempt at understanding this dynamic in Oxford culture, see Kali Israel, *Names and Stories: Emilia Dilke and Victorian Culture* (New York: Oxford University Press, 1999), pp. 92–97. Edward Said's work on how western cultures interpreted the east has been especially influential in defining the concept of "otherness" for historians. See his *Orientalism* (New York: Pantheon Books, 1978).

These ideas are still present in his more recent work, but in a modified form; see his *Culture and Imperialism* (New York: Knopf, 1993). For one recent criticism of the idea, see David Cannadine, *Ornamentalism: How the British Saw Their Empire* (Oxford: Oxford University Press, 2001).

59. "Apologia pro vita nostra," *Bulldog* 1, no. 1 (February 28, 1896): 1.

60. On the study of humor, see Jerry Palmer, *Taking Humour Seriously* (London: Routledge, 1994). A conceptual framework for the sociology of humor is contained in Chris Powell and George E. C. Paton, introduction to *Humour in Society: Resistance and Control,* ed. Chris Powell and George E. C. Paton (London: Macmillan, 1988), pp. xiii–xxii.

61. On the broader institutional identity, see John Willis Clark, *Old Friends at Cambridge and Elsewhere* (London: Macmillan, 1900); and Charles Oman, *Memories of Victorian Oxford and Some Early Years* (London: Methuen, 1941).

62. For one contemporary discussion of a typical day, see Frank Aydelotte, *The Oxford Stamp and Other Essays* (New York: Oxford University Press, 1917), pp. 5–9. See also Harold George, "Oxford at Home," *Strand Magazine* 9 (January 1895): 109–115; Brian Harrison, "College Life, 1918–1939," in *The Twentieth Century,* ed. Harrison, pp. 103–104; and Helen Fowler and Laurence Fowler, eds., *Cambridge Commemorated: An Anthology of University Life* (Cambridge: Cambridge University Press, 1984), pp. 219–232, 252–281.

1. Constructing Superiority

1. "University Life," *Great Tom: A University Magazine,* no. 1 (May 1861): 6.

2. "Our Fourth Year," *Granta* 5, no. 75 (January 16, 1892): 130.

3. Pierre Bourdieu, *The State Nobility: Elite Schools in the Field of Power,* trans. Lauretta C. Clough (Stanford: Stanford University Press, 1996), p. 73.

4. Scholars working in a number of different areas have noted this tendency in the formation of national, racial, and gender identities. See, for example, Linda Colley, *Britons: Forging the Nation, 1707–1837* (New Haven: Yale University Press, 1992), p. 6; Cynthia Herrup, "Introduction," *Journal of British Studies* 31, no. 4 (October 1992): 307–308; and Catherine Hall, *Civilising Subjects: Colony and Metropole in the English Imagination, 1830–1867* (Chicago: University of Chicago Press, 2002). For one sociological perspective on this process, see Barbara Rogers, *Men Only: An Investigation into Men's Organisations* (London: Pandora, 1988).

5. Bourdieu, *The State Nobility,* p. 102.

6. On aspects of this process in India, see Mrinalini Sinha, *Colonial Masculinity: The "Manly Englishman" and the "Effeminate Bengali" in the Late Nineteenth Century* (Manchester: Manchester University Press, 1995). On British social life in Africa, see Dane Kennedy, *Islands of White: Settler Society and Culture in Kenya and Southern Rhodesia, 1890–1939* (Durham: Duke University Press, 1987). For an interesting discussion of public schools, secret societies, and the "Masonic" ideal, see P. J. Rich, *Chains of Empire: English Public Schools, Masonic Cabalism, Historical Causality, and Imperial Clubdom* (London: Regency, 1991).

7. Sheldon Rothblatt, "The Student Sub-culture and the Examination System in Early 19th Century Oxbridge," in *The University in Society,* ed. Lawrence Stone (Princeton: Princeton University Press, 1974), 1:252–261; and Sheldon Rothblatt, *The Modern University and Its Discontents: The Fate of Newman's Legacies in Britain and America* (Cambridge: Cambridge University Press, 1997), pp. 112–123.

8. Reba Soffer, *Discipline and Power: The University, History, and the Making of an English Elite, 1870–1930* (Stanford: Stanford University Press, 1994).

9. Rothblatt, *The Modern University and Its Discontents,* p. 62.

10. Jan Morris, ed., *The Oxford Book of Oxford* (Oxford: Oxford University Press, 1978), pp. 331–332.

11. Joseph Wells, *The Charm of Oxford,* illus. W. G. Blackall (London: Simpkin, Marshall, Hamilton and Kent, 1920), p. 8.

12. [R. W. Livingstone], "Alma Mater," *Oxford and Cambridge Review,* no. 1 (June 1907): 15–16. Examples abound of the tendency to view architecture in this way. The spires of Oxford have served as an inspiration for literary work on more than one occasion. See Matthew Arnold, "The Scholar-Gipsy" (1853) and "Thyrsis" (1867), quoted in *The Oxford Book of Oxford,* ed. Morris, pp. 256–259; and Winifred M. Letts, "The Spires of Oxford," in *The Spires of Oxford and Other Poems* (New York: E. P. Dutton, 1918), p. 34.

13. For a perspective on the moral lessons history and other disciplines provided at a non-elite level, see Stephen Heathorn, *For Home, Country, and Race: Constructing Gender, Class, and Englishness in the Elementary School, 1880–1914* (Toronto: University of Toronto Press, 2000).

14. Robert Willis, *The Architectural History of the University of Cambridge and of the Colleges of Cambridge and Eton, Edited with Large Additions and Brought Up to the Present Time by John Willis Clark* (Cambridge: Cambridge University Press, 1886), 1:iii.

15. Edward K. Jupp to a very young brother, November 3, 1868, *Correspondence of a Junior Student of Christchurch Oxford, in the Years 1868–1870* (Blackheath: privately published, 1871), p. 21.

16. George Nugent Bankes, *Cambridge Trifles; or, Splutterings from an Undergraduate Pen* (London: Sampson Low, Marston, Searle and Rivington, 1881), pp. 83–84.

17. Ralph Durand, *Oxford: Its Buildings and Gardens,* illus. William Wildman (London: Grant Richards, 1909), pp. 2–3.

18. On general developments and the growth of university education since 1800, see R. D. Anderson, *Universities and Elites in Britain since 1800* (London: Macmillan, 1992). On the University of London, see F. M. L. Thompson, ed., *The University of London and the World of Learning, 1836–1986* (London: Hambledon, 1990); and Sheldon Rothblatt, "London: A Metropolitan University?" in *The University and the City: From Medieval Origins to the Present,* ed. Thomas Bender (Oxford: Oxford University Press, 1988), pp. 119–149. On the development of the red brick or civic universities, see W. H. G. Armytage, *Civic Universities: Aspects of a British Tradition* (London: Benn, 1955). On the ways in which undergraduates established connections between architecture and the traditions of student life, see Helen Lefkowitz Horowitz, *Alma Mater: Design and Experience in the Women's Colleges from their Nineteenth-Century Beginnings to the 1930s* (New York: Alfred A. Knopf, 1984).

19. In her study of American undergraduate cultures, Helen Lefkowitz Horowitz has also noted the particular features of this process. See her *Campus Life: Undergraduate Cultures from the End of the Eighteenth Century to the Present* (Chicago: University of Chicago Press, 1987), pp. 12–13.

20. "Carfax," "Words and Their Derivations," *Shotover Papers* 1, no. 4 (May 2, 1874): 58.

21. These phrases appeared with great frequency throughout this period. See, for example, [Godfrey Lushington], "Oxford," *Oxford and Cambridge Magazine,* no. 1 (April 1856): 245; "Jottings from the Journal of a Japanese," *Cambridge Tatler,* no. 2 (March 13, 1877): 9; [Alfred Douglas], "Editorial," *Ephemeral,* no. 1 (May 18, 1893): 2; "Freshmen," *Isis,* no. 153 (October 22, 1898): 3; "The Onlooker," "Letters to the Unimportant. No. 1, To A. Toady, Esq.," *Screed* 1, no. 1 (November 11, 1899): 6; and "Thoughts That Occur. 'I See That All Things Come to an End,'" *'Varsity* 8, no. 24 (June 17, 1909): 604.

22. On this, see Christopher N. L. Brooke, *A History of the University of Cambridge:*

1870–1990, vol. 4 of *A History of the University of Cambridge,* ed. Christopher N. L. Brooke (Cambridge: Cambridge University Press, 1993), 247, 249.

23. See John Tosh, *A Man's Place: Masculinity and the Middle-Class Home in Victorian England* (New Haven: Yale University Press, 1999), pp. 170–194. While Tosh maintains that this tendency intensified in the 1880s, the evidence from Oxbridge indicates it was present from at least 1850 in the ancient universities. On the importance of associational life generally, see John Tosh, "What Should Historians Do with Masculinity? Reflections on Nineteenth-Century Britain," *History Workshop Journal,* no. 38 (autumn 1994): 179–202.

24. See, for example, "Editorial Notes," *Undergraduate* 1, no. 10 (May 16, 1888): 145–147.

25. For a partial history of this ideal, see A. J. Engel, *From Clergyman to Don: The Rise of the Academic Profession in Nineteenth-Century Oxford* (Oxford: Oxford University Press, 1983).

26. Charles Dickens, "A Dictionary of the University of Oxford," in *Dickens's Dictionary of Oxford and Cambridge* (London: Macmillan, 1884), p. 78.

27. "Editorial Notes," *Undergraduate* 1, no. 1 (January 24, 1888): 1.

28. Desmond F. T. Cooke, "Oxford in the Long Vacation," *Oxford Point of View* 2, no. 7 (August 1903): 156–157.

29. During these years, female undergraduates were moved to vacant men's colleges while the women's colleges, which were relatively new buildings, functioned as hospitals and hostels. See J. M. Winter, "Oxford and the First World War," in *The Twentieth Century,* ed. Brian Harrison, vol. 8 of *The History of the University of Oxford,* ed. T. H. Aston (Oxford: Clarendon, 1994), 11–15.

30. Brooke, *A History of the University of Cambridge: 1870–1990,* p. 331.

31. "The Death and Resurrection of Oxford," *'Varsity* 14, no. 330 (October 20, 1914): 4. On disruptions and changes at Oxford during the war, see Robert Graves, *Goodbye to All That* (London: The Folio Society, 1981), pp. 214–217.

32. Robert Pearce-Edgcumbe, "Biographical Sketch," in Arthur Clement Hilton, *The Works of Arthur Clement Hilton, Together with His Life and Letters,* ed. Robert Pearce-Edgcumbe (Cambridge: Macmillan and Bowes, 1904), p. 68.

33. Rogers, *Men Only,* p. 129.

34. Dickens, "A Dictionary of the University of Oxford," p. 117. For an earlier expression of these same sentiments, see Pembroke, "Good-Bye," *College Rhymes,* no. 3 (1862): 50–51.

35. "Thoughts That Occur," *'Varsity* 6, no. 23 (June 13, 1907): 337.

36. "Thoughts That Occur. 'I See That All Things Come to an End,'" 604.

37. On chivalry and its resurgence in the nineteenth century, see Mark Girouard, *The Return to Camelot: Chivalry and the English Gentleman* (New Haven: Yale University Press, 1981).

38. E. H. Knatchbull-Hugessen, "My Oxford Days," in *Reminiscences of Oxford by Oxford Men, 1559–1850,* ed. L. M. Quiller-Couch (Oxford: Clarendon, 1892), pp. 400–401.

39. "On Coming Back to School," *Cambridge Tatler,* no. 4 (April 17, 1877): 1.

40. Tosh, *A Man's Place,* pp. 102–122, 170–194.

41. Mrs. Jupp to Edward Jupp, October 16, 1896, *Correspondence of a Junior Student of Christchurch Oxford,* p. 70.

42. For a skeptical view of the efficacy of these reading parties as working holidays, see Edward C. Lefroy, "The Long Vacation," in *Undergraduate Oxford: Articles Re-printed from "The Oxford and Cambridge Undergraduates' Journal,"* 1876, 7 (Oxford: privately printed, 1878), pp. 1–6.

43. Four examples from one publication illustrate this: "Au Revoir," *Isis,* no. 160

(December 10, 1898): 113–114; "Of Next Term," *Isis,* no. 264 (March 14, 1903): 243–244; "On Coming Up," *Isis,* no. 265 (May 2, 1903): 259–260; "Here We Are Again!" *Isis,* no. 377 (January 25, 1908): 151–152.

44. Scholars in other disciplines have noted that socially conditioned gender roles influence the ways that men and women perceive time. See, for an earlier example, Thomas J. Cottle, *The Present of Things Future: Explorations of Time in Human Experience* (New York: Free Press, 1974), pp. 102–123.

45. [R. S. Copleston], *Oxford Spectator,* no. 8 (December 12, 1867): 3.

46. Martin Francis, "The Domestication of the Male? Recent Research on Nineteenth- and Twentieth-Century British Masculinity," *Historical Journal* 45, no. 3 (September 2002): 637. On the symbiotic relationship between the public and the private, see Leonore Davidoff and Catherine Hall, *Family Fortunes: Men and Women of the English Middle Class, 1780–1850* (Chicago: University of Chicago Press, 1987).

47. Peter M. Lewis attempts to use this type of analysis in his "Mummy, Matron, and the Maids: Feminine Presence and Absence in Male Institutions, 1934–63," in *Manful Assertions: Masculinities in Britain since 1800,* ed. Michael Roper and John Tosh (London: Routledge, 1991), pp. 168–189.

48. [Copleston], *Oxford Spectator,* no. 8, pp. 3–4. Other discussions of vacations also highlight this complementarity. See, for example, "Au Revoir," p. 114; and "Dorothea," *Squib,* May 1908, pp. 1–2.

49. Increasing professionalism and the triumph of a professional ideal in British society are admirably detailed in Harold Perkin's *The Rise of Professional Society: England since 1880* (London: Routledge, 1989).

50. "Oxford," *Cambridge Observer* 1, no. 10 (November 8, 1892): 10.

51. "Foreword," *Pageant Post,* June 1907, p. 1.

52. The best expression of the sense of exclusion that women felt is to be found in Virginia Woolf's *A Room of One's Own* (New York: Harcourt Brace, 1929).

53. On the symbolic meanings attached to different social spaces, see Doreen Massey, "Places and Their Pasts," *History Workshop Journal,* no. 39 (spring 1995): 188; and John A. Agnew and James S. Duncan, eds., *The Power of Place: Bringing Together Geographical and Sociological Imaginations* (Boston: Unwin Hyman, 1989).

54. "Thoughts That Occur," *'Varsity* 14, no. 329 (October 13, 1914): 3–4.

55. For one example, see Edward Jupp to his aunt, June 7, 1869, *Correspondence of a Junior Student of Christchurch Oxford,* p. 56.

56. "On Oxford Novels," *Isis,* no. 266 (May 9, 1903): 275.

57. [W. H. Devenish?], "Introduction," *"Fors Togigera." Letters to Our Mothers and Sisters from Oxford. No. 1. May-Day on Magdalen Tower* (Oxford: J. Vincent, 1874), p. 3.

58. "Oxford in the Vac," *Vacuum* 1, no. 1 (May 1, 1900): 2–3.

59. "Little John and the Union," *Shotover Papers* 1, no. 3 (April 18, 1874): 33.

60. "S.," "Review of 'Martin Legrand's *The Cambridge Freshman; or Memoirs of Mr. Golightly,*" *Tatler in Cambridge,* no. 29 (November 3, 1871): 33. For other examples of this tendency, see "Tittle-Tattle," *Oxford Tatler,* no. 3 (May 15, 1886): 35; and "The Cambridge Point of View," *Oxford Point of View* 2, no. 6 (May 1903): 99.

61. George Saintsbury, "Novels of University Life," *Macmillan's Magazine,* no. 77 (March 1898): 340.

62. "Local Colour," *'Varsity* 1, no. 20 (November 5, 1901): 310.

63. J. R. Seeley, *The Student's Guide to the University of Cambridge* (Cambridge: Deighton, Bell, 1863), p. 9.

64. See Thomas De Quincey, "An 'Oxford Man,'" excerpted in Thomas Seccombe and H. Spencer Scott, eds., *In Praise of Oxford: An Anthology in Prose and Verse* (London: Constable, 1912), 2:413.

65. "O. C." [A. H. Lawrence], *Reminiscences of Cambridge Life* (London: privately printed, 1889), p. 46.

66. John Roget, *Cambridge Customs and Costumes: Containing Upwards of One Hundred and Fifty Vignettes by the Author of "Familiar Illustrations of the Language of Mathematics"* (Cambridge: Macmillan, 1851), p. 1; and "Reynold Greenleaf" [Gordon Campbell], "To My Gown," *Shotover Papers* 1, no. 10 (November 14, 1874): 155.

67. Charles Dickens, "A Dictionary of the University of Cambridge," in *Dickens's Dictionary of Oxford and Cambridge,* p. 47.

68. "Those Things Which We Ought NOT to Have Done," *Freshman,* October 1909, p. 7.

69. On clubs, see Tosh, *A Man's Place,* pp. 127–132; and Simon Gunn, *The Public Culture of the Victorian Middle Class: Ritual and Authority and the English Industrial City, 1840–1914* (Manchester: Manchester University Press, 2000), pp. 84–105.

70. C. Arnold Anderson and Miriam Schnaper, *School and Society in England: Social Backgrounds of Oxford and Cambridge Students* (Westport, Conn.: Greenwood, 1952). Reba Soffer addresses the issue of class background throughout her *Discipline and Power,* especially pp. 10–12, 179–180.

71. "Oxford Manners," *Oxford Critic and University Magazine,* no. 1 (June 1857): 21.

72. While these generalizations hold true, Lawrence Stone did note a slight widening of the social origins from which students at Oxford were drawn in this period. See his "The Size and Composition of the Oxford Student Body, 1580–1910," in *The University in Society,* ed. Stone, 1:60–67. On professional backgrounds and income levels, see Perkin, *The Rise of Professional Society,* pp. 369–372, 28–31, 78–79; and W. C. Lubenow, *The Cambridge Apostles, 1820–1914: Liberalism, Imagination, and Friendship in British Intellectual and Professional Life* (Cambridge: Cambridge University Press, 1998), pp. 90–105.

73. Pierre Bourdieu, *Distinction: A Social Critique of the Judgement of Taste,* trans. Richard Nice (Cambridge, Mass.: Harvard University Press, 1984), p. 102. To a certain extent, I am trying to refine the economic perspective on elites offered, for example, in the work of W. D. Rubinstein. See his *Wealth and Inequality in Britain* (London: Faber and Faber, 1986).

74. Patrick Joyce, *Visions of the People: Industrial England and the Question of Class, 1848–1914* (Cambridge: Cambridge University Press, 1991); and Dror Wahrman, *Imagining the Middle Class: The Political Representation of Class in Britain, c. 1780–1840* (Cambridge: Cambridge University Press, 1995).

75. David Cannadine has noted the persistence of an aristocratic hold on power, prestige, and wealth until at least the 1880s, when the arrival of new non-landed elites was symbolized by the appearance of such publications as the *Directory of Directors* and *Who Was Who.* See David Cannadine, *Aspects of Aristocracy: Grandeur and Decline in Modern Britain* (New Haven: Yale University Press, 1994), p. 36.

76. Lubenow, *The Cambridge Apostles,* p. 3. On the embrace of aristocratic values, see Martin Wiener, *English Culture and the Decline of the Industrial Spirit, 1850–1980* (Cambridge: Cambridge University Press, 1981).

77. [Lushington], "Oxford," p. 245.

78. "Editorial," *Momus: A Semi-occasional University Periodical,* no. 3 (March 15, 1869): 20.

79. The middle class had tended to highlight its moral superiority at least since the beginning of the nineteenth century. See Susan Kingsley Kent, *Gender and Power in Britain, 1640–1990* (London: Routledge, 1999), pp. 155–178; and Davidoff and Hall, *Family Fortunes,* pp. 103, 150–155, 275.

80. Edward Thomas, *Oxford: Painted by John Fulleylove, R.I. Described by Edward Thomas* (London: A. and C. Black, 1903), p. 107.

81. On the gentlemanly capitalist, see P. J. Cain and A. G. Hopkins, *British Imperialism: Innovation and Expansion, 1688–1914* (London: Longman, 1993).

82. "A Word about Fathers," *Granta* 1, no. 5 (February 15, 1889): 3.

83. "On Oxford Novels," p. 276.

84. These figures are drawn from Daniel I. Greenstein, "The Junior Members, 1900–1990: A Profile," in *The Twentieth Century,* ed. Harrison, pp. 68–69.

85. "Modern Oxford Reformers," *Pageant Post,* June 1907, p. 8.

86. George Nugent Bankes, *A Cambridge Staircase: By the Author of "A Day of My Life at Eton," "About Some Fellows," Etc.* (London: Sampson Low, Marston, Searle and Rivington, 1883), p. 7.

87. On medical training, see Peter Searby, *A History of the University of Cambridge: 1750–1870,* vol. 3 of *A History of the University of Cambridge,* ed. Christopher N. L. Brooke (Cambridge: Cambridge University Press, 1997), 193–202.

88. "Cambridge Chit-Chat: Miscellaneous," *Cantab,* no. 1 (April 1873): 92. On the gentlemanly ideal in medical education, see Terrie M. Romano, "Gentlemanly versus Scientific Ideals: John Burdon Sanderson, Medical Education, and the Failure of the Oxford School of Physiology," *Bulletin of the History of Medicine* 71, no. 2 (summer 1997): 224–248.

89. [Hugh Reginald Haweis], "Editor's Address," *Lion University Magazine,* no. 1 (May 1858): 5.

90. "Cambridge and Democracy," *Cambridge Observer* 1, no. 13 (November 29, 1892): 9. On the growth of business careers, see Brooke, *A History of the University of Cambridge: 1870–1990,* 603.

91. The importance of imperial culture in the formation of domestic identities is also emphasized in Antoinette Burton, *Burdens of History: British Feminists, Indian Women, and Imperial Culture, 1865–1915* (Chapel Hill: University of North Carolina Press, 1994); and Jonathan Schneer, *London 1900: The Imperial Metropolis* (New Haven: Yale University Press, 1999).

92. For a straightforward narrative of Oxford's role in the development of the empire, see Richard Symonds, *Oxford and Empire: The Last Lost Cause?* (New York: St. Martin's, 1986).

93. "Editorial," *Pageant Post,* June 1907, pp. 2–3.

94. Brooke, *A History of the University of Cambridge: 1870–1990,* 78. Up until the 1850s poorer students paid their way by working as servants (called "servitors" in Oxford and "sizars" in Cambridge) for more fortunate and socially superior undergraduates. The abolition of these positions minimized class divisions within the universities but also limited further the routes to higher education open to less wealthy students. See Anderson and Schnaper, *School and Society,* pp. 4–5.

95. "F. Anstey" [Thomas Anstey Guthrie], *A Long Retrospect* (Oxford: Oxford University Press, 1936), p. 84.

96. On the distinction between town and gown, see Nick Mansfield, "Grads and Snobs: John Brown, Town, and Gown in Early Nineteenth-Century Cambridge," *History Workshop Journal,* no. 35 (spring 1993): 184–198.

97. [Edward Nolan], *Oxford Spectator,* no. 18 (May 5, 1868): 1. A similar description, emphasizing this division, can be found over thirty years later in "Things Seen," *'Varsity* 2, no. 39 (June 10, 1902): 575.

98. The classic interpretation of some of the concerns that this rise generated is found in George Dangerfield, *The Strange Death of Liberal England* (New York: Capricorn Books, 1961). For a recent interpretation of the years between 1870 and 1914,

see José Harris, *Private Lives, Public Spirit: A Social History of Britain, 1870–1914* (Oxford: Oxford University Press, 1993), pp. 191–196.

99. For several examples that illustrate these themes and others, see "Our Own Penny-a-Liner" [Arthur Clement Hilton], "Cambridge Chit-Chat," *Light Green: A Superior and High Class Periodical,* no. 1 (May 1872): 16; "On Bedmakers," *Cambridge Meteor,* no. 7 (June 14, 1882): 125–127; "Scouts," *Undergraduate* 1, no. 16 (November 1, 1888): 243–244; "Book," "On College Servants," *Blue: A 'Varsity Journal* 2, no. 12 (November 14, 1893): 4; and "My Laundress. A Frenzy," *Octopus,* no. 1 (May 23, 1895): 3.

100. For one example of this, see "Advice to My Laundress," *Squeaker,* no. 1 (May 1893), p. 4.

101. See "On Bedmakers"; "My Laundress. A Frenzy"; and "Sharks," *Squib,* May 1908, pp. 13–14.

102. Frank Rutter, "The Bedder," *'Varsity Types: Scenes and Characters from Undergraduate Life,* illus. Stephen Haweis (London: R. A. Everett, 1903), p. 145.

103. On this, see Burton, *Burdens of History,* pp. 5–6; and Stephen Heathorn, "'Let Us Remember That We, Too, Are English': Constructions of Citizenship and National Identity in English Elementary School Reading Books, 1880–1914," *Victorian Studies* 38, no. 3 (spring 1995): 399–401.

104. The most thorough exploration of this theme has been undertaken by Linda Colley in her *Britons,* pp. 17, 24–25, 33–35, 86, 88–90, 251–252, 312, 368.

105. "Y" [G. L. Reves], "French Novels," *Tatler in Cambridge,* no. 25 (October 25, 1871): 20.

106. "The Ordinary Undergraduate," *Rattle* 1, no. 3 (February 27, 1886): 3.

107. "The Corpse in the Cargo (Borrowed from Ibsen)," *Snarl,* no. 2 (November 14, 1899): 14.

108. On the impact of the Indian Mutiny on notions of racial difference, see Thomas Metcalf, *The Aftermath of Revolt: India, 1857–1870* (Princeton: Princeton University Press, 1964), pp. 289–327; and Thomas Metcalf, *Ideologies of the Raj* (Cambridge: Cambridge University Press, 1994). On the consequences of the Morant Bay Rebellion, see Hall, *Civilising Subjects,* pp. 23–65, 243–264.

109. On the Rifle Corps, see John Gillis, *Youth and History: Tradition and Change in European Age Relations, 1770–Present* (New York: Academic, 1981), p. 96.

110. "The True Volunteer," *College Rhymes,* no. 2 (1861): 32.

111. This construction is nicely addressed in Sinha, *Colonial Masculinity.*

112. "Manners Maketh Man," *Screed* 1, no. 1 (November 11, 1899): 5.

113. On crises of confidence precipitated by the Boer War, see Perkin, *The Rise of Professional Society,* pp. 56–61, 158; and Anna Davin, "Imperialism and Motherhood," *History Workshop Journal,* no. 5 (spring 1978): 9–65.

114. "As Others See Us. I. By a Belgian," *'Varsity* 1, no. 9 (April 23, 1901): 133.

2. The Transition from Boyhood to Manhood

1. William Wordsworth, "Oxford, May 30, 1820," in *The Poems,* ed. John O. Hayden (New Haven: Yale University Press, 1977), 2:406.

2. "A Greeting," *Granta* 5, no. 67 (October 17, 1891): 1.

3. Rev. H. G. Woods, "University Sermon. Oxford. March 1st," *Oxford Review: The Undergraduates' Journal,* o.s. no. 432, n.s. no. 7 (March 4, 1885): 161. On the age of undergraduates, see Lawrence Stone, "The Size and Composition of the Oxford Student Body, 1580–1910," in *The University in Society,* ed. Lawrence Stone (Princeton: Princeton University Press, 1974), 1:69–71, 74. On Hall's influence, see Paula Fass,

The Damned and the Beautiful: American Youth in the 1920s (New York: Oxford University Press, 1977), p. 14.

4. On this, see John Gillis, *Youth and History: Tradition and Change in European Age Relations, 1770–Present* (New York: Academic, 1981); E. Anthony Rotundo, *American Manhood: Transformations in Masculinity from the Revolution to the Modern Era* (New York: Basic Books, 1993), pp. 56–74; and John Springhall, *Coming of Age: Adolescence in Britain, 1860–1960* (Dublin: Gill and Macmillan, 1986), pp. 46–55.

5. Charles Dickens, "Dictionary of the University of Oxford," in *Dickens's Dictionary of Oxford and Cambridge* (London: Macmillan, 1884), p. 63.

6. Victor Turner, *The Ritual Process: Structure and Anti-structure* (Chicago: Aldine, 1969), p. 167.

7. John Darwin, "The Growth of an International University," in *The Illustrated History of Oxford University*, ed. John Prest (Oxford: Oxford University Press, 1993), p. 336.

8. On this, see John Tosh, *A Man's Place: Masculinity and the Middle-Class Home in Victorian England* (New Haven: Yale University Press, 1999), p. 103. On working-class rites of passage, see Keith McClelland, "Masculinity and the 'Representative Artisan' in Britain, 1850–1880," in *Manful Assertions: Masculinities in Britain since 1800*, ed. Michael Roper and John Tosh (London: Routledge, 1991), p. 81.

9. While Mangan generally avoids explicit discussions of masculinity, he does come to similar conclusions about the extent of the conflict between dons and students. See his "Lamentable Barbarians and Pitiful Sheep: Rhetoric of Protest and Pleasure in Late Victorian and Edward 'Oxbridge,'" *Victorian Studies* 34, no. 4 (summer 1991): 477, 481–484. For several discussions of the ways in which intergenerational conflict figured into constructions of masculinity in African cultures, see Lisa A. Lindsay and Stephan F. Miescher, eds., *Men and Masculinities in Modern Africa* (Portsmouth, N.H.: Heinemann, 2003).

10. Sheldon Rothblatt has explored some of the features of the don/student divide at mid-century in his *The Revolution of the Dons: Cambridge and Society in Victorian England* (New York: Basic Books, 1968), pp. 190–197. On the early nineteenth century, see his "The Student Sub-culture and the Examination System in Early 19th Century Oxbridge," in *The University in Society*, ed. Stone, 1:263–265, 301–303. I am partly refuting here one of William Lubenow's arguments about don/student relations. See his *The Cambridge Apostles, 1820–1914: Liberalism, Imagination, and Friendship in British Intellectual and Professional Life* (Cambridge: Cambridge University Press, 1998), pp. 301–304.

11. For a discussion of this, see John Tosh, "What Should Historians Do with Masculinity? Reflections on Nineteenth-Century Britain," *History Workshop Journal*, no. 38 (autumn 1994): 189.

12. Graham Dawson, *Soldier Heroes: British Adventure, Empire, and the Imagining of Masculinities* (London: Routledge, 1994), p. 1. On gender as performance or pose, see Judith Butler, *Gender Trouble: Feminism and the Subversion of Identity* (New York: Routledge, 1990); and Mark Simpson, *Male Impersonators: Men Performing Masculinity* (London: Cassell, 1994).

13. On this, see Christopher N. L. Brooke, *A History of the University of Cambridge: 1870–1990*, vol. 4 of *A History of the University of Cambridge*, ed. Christopher N. L. Brooke (Cambridge: Cambridge University Press, 1993), 247, 249; and Daniel I. Greenstein, "The Junior Members, 1900–1990: A Profile," in *The Twentieth Century*, ed. Brian Harrison, vol. 8 of *The History of the University of Oxford*, ed. T. H. Aston (Oxford: Clarendon, 1994), 52–53.

14. On the importance of classics to the education of future leaders, see Linda Dowling, *Hellenism and Homosexuality in Victorian Oxford* (Ithaca, N.Y.: Cornell Univer-

sity Press, 1994), pp. 106–120; and Christopher Stray, *Classics Transformed: Schools, Universities, and Society in England, 1830–1960* (Oxford: Clarendon, 1998). On the development of these ideas at the public school, see J. R. de S. Honey, *Tom Brown's Universe: The Development of the Victorian Public School* (London: Millington, 1977), pp. 209–229. On shifting concepts of manliness in the public school, see David Newsome, *Godliness and Good Learning: Four Studies on a Victorian Ideal* (London: Cassell, 1961).

15. See J. A. Mangan, *Athleticism in the Victorian and Edwardian Public School: The Emergence and Consolidation of an Educational Ideology* (Cambridge: Cambridge University Press, 1981), pp. 122–127; and Mangan, "Lamentable Barbarians and Pitiful Sheep," p. 476.

16. "O. C." [A. H. Lawrence], *Reminiscences of Cambridge Life* (London: privately printed, 1889), p. 55.

17. While compulsory games became a standard feature of school life by the final few decades of the nineteenth century, Oxbridge students could never be coerced in the same way. See Honey, *Tom Brown's Universe*, p. 114. This is not, as we shall see, meant to imply that athleticism did not play an important role in the universities.

18. "O. C." [A. H. Lawrence], *Reminiscences of Cambridge Life*, p. 47. For an earlier example, see "Public Schools and Private Tutors," *Cambridge Terminal Magazine*, no. 2 (February 1859): 65.

19. George Nugent Bankes, *A Cambridge Staircase: By the Author of "A Day of My Life at Eton," "About Some Fellows," Etc.* (London: Sampson Low, Marston, Searle and Rivington, 1883), p. 6.

20. [Hugh Reginald Haweis], "Confessions of a Welsh Rabbit Eater," *Lion University Magazine*, no. 2 (November 1858): 110.

21. "A Pembroke Graduate," "The Disturbances at Pembroke College, Oxford, March 8, 1883," in *Oxford University Miscellaneous Papers*, vol. 4, Bodleian Library, Oxford, G.A. Oxon b. 140.

22. "Open Letter. I. To Any Freshman," *'Varsity* 6, no. 1 (October 18, 1906): 9.

23. [George Otto Trevelyan], "A Satire," *Bear University Magazine*, no. 1 (October 1858): 7.

24. See E. Anthony Rotundo, "Boy Culture: Middle-Class Boyhood in Nineteenth-Century America," in *Meanings for Manhood: Constructions of Masculinity in Victorian America*, ed. Mark C. Carnes and Clyde Griffen (Chicago: University of Chicago Press, 1990), pp. 15–36. For one contemporary discussion of this tendency, see Dickens, "A Dictionary of the University of Oxford," p. 47.

25. "The Encaenia," *Oxford Undergraduate's Journal*, no. 65 (June 1, 1870): 775. See also "Alfred Pennysong" [Arthur Clement Hilton], "The May Exam," *Light Green: A Superior and High Class Periodical*, no. 2 (November 1872): 4.

26. "Editorial Notes," *Undergraduate* 1, no. 5 (February 21, 1888): 65. On the influence of the Union, see V. H. H. Green, "The University and the Nation," in *The Illustrated History of Oxford University*, ed. Prest, p. 69; and Brian Harrison, "Politics," in *The Twentieth Century*, ed. Harrison, pp. 381–385.

27. On the aesthetes in the twentieth century, see Brian Harrison, "College Life, 1918–1939," in *The Twentieth Century*, ed. Harrison, p. 99. One early plea for toleration with respect to this group appeared in *Aestheticism and Intolerance: A Protest* (Oxford: B. H. Blackwell, 1882).

28. This fashion, in both the example cited here and in Waugh's description of 1920s Oxford, functioned as a clear marker of the aesthetic man, which Flyte so flamboyantly embodied. See Evelyn Waugh, *Brideshead Revisited* (London: Longmans, Green, 1968), p. 9.

29. "Visions of Childhood," *Why Not?* no. 1 (1911): 7.

30. "Our Freshman's Term," *Cambridge Terminal Magazine,* no. 3 (April 1859): 111.

31. [Edward Nolan], *Oxford Spectator,* no. 20 (May 19, 1868): 3.

32. "Some More Platitudes," *'Varsity* 1, no. 17 (October 15, 1901): 257.

33. [Edward Nolan], *Oxford Spectator,* no. 20, p. 3.

34. "The Passing Hour," *'Varsity* 8, no. 1 (October 15, 1908): 307. On the evolutionary metaphor, see "Evolution," *'Varsity* 2, no. 31 (March 4, 1902): 473.

35. See [Edward Nolan], *Oxford Spectator,* no. 20, p. 4; and "Evolution," p. 472.

36. "Evolution," p. 473.

37. "The Parting of the Ways," *Isis,* no. 392 (June 20, 1908): 436. On the breadwinner ethic, see Michael Kimmel, *Manhood in America: A Cultural History* (New York: Free Press, 1996), p. 20; Peter Stearns, *Be a Man! Males in Modern Society,* 2nd ed. (New York: Holmes and Meier, 1990), pp. 69–73, 104–118; and Tosh, "What Should Historians Do with Masculinity?" pp. 184–186.

38. Charles Dickens, "A Dictionary of the University of Cambridge," in *Dickens's Dictionary of Oxford and Cambridge,* p. 48.

39. For one example of this see "N." [V. H. Stanton], "The *Tatler's* 'Paternal' to the Freshman," *Tatler in Cambridge,* no. 21 (October 16, 1871): 1.

40. "Heard in 'The High,'" *Isis,* no. 249 (October 25, 1902): 10; John Roget, *A Cambridge Scrap-Book* (Cambridge: Macmillan, 1859), pp. 2–3; and "A Parable," *'Varsity* 3, no. 44 (November 11, 1902): 53.

41. "A Parable," p. 53; "Of Shop," *Cantab,* no. 2 (March 1873): 161–164; "Good Words, or the Thursday at Home," *Undergraduate* 1, no. 15 (October 25, 1888): 229–230; and "Ye Ballade of Ye Holie Freshman," *Isis,* no. 153 (October 22, 1898): 7.

42. "A Word of Welcome," *Granta* 19, no. 404 (October 14, 1905): 1–2.

43. "An Idyll," *May Bee,* no. 2 (June 5, 1884): 28.

44. "A Word to the Wise," *Granta* 7, no. 117 (October 14, 1892): 1.

45. Dons are called "old fools" in [T. H. White], *Oxford Spectator,* no. 22 (June 2, 1868): 2; and "relics" in "Oxford Types. (By a Type-Writer—Not Mr. Punch's) No. III —The Ancient Don," *Isis,* no. 16 (February 4, 1893): 40. Browning is often held up as the ideal of the affectionate don. For one discussion of his career, see Lubenow, *The Cambridge Apostles,* pp. 301–304. I am challenging, somewhat, Sheldon Rothblatt's recent assertion that greater harmony existed between these two groups in the Victorian era. See his *The Modern University and Its Discontents: The Fate of Newman's Legacies in Britain and America* (Cambridge: Cambridge University Press, 1997), p. 128.

46. Stephan Miescher and Lisa A. Lindsay, introduction to *Men and Masculinities in Modern Africa,* ed. Lindsay and Miescher, p. 9.

47. See Gillis, *Youth and History,* pp. 100–105. For one contemporary perspective on the sometimes tortured relationship between fathers and sons, see Simpson, *Male Impersonators,* pp. 12–13, 36–37, 75–77, 121–123.

48. On the age of dons, see A. J. Engel, *From Clergyman to Don: The Rise of the Academic Profession in Nineteenth-Century Oxford* (Oxford: Oxford University Press, 1983), p. 294.

49. Alfred Douglas, "An Undergraduate on Oxford Dons," *Spirit Lamp* 2, no. 3 (November 18, 1892): 71; "Our Freshman's Term," *Cambridge Terminal Magazine,* no. 2 (February 1859): 58; "Operatic Fragment, No. 5. The Master's Chorus," *Cambridge Tatler,* no. 5 (April 24, 1877): 4; "Open Letter. I. To Any Freshman," p. 9; "A Don," "Undergraduates," *'Varsity* 6, no. 13 (February 21, 1907): 226.

50. "University Life," *Great Tom: A University Magazine,* no. 1 (May 1861): 9.

51. [T. H. White], *Oxford Spectator,* no. 22, p. 2.

52. "Blues and Firsts," *Isis,* no. 8 (October 29, 1892): 25–26; "Dons and Men," *'Varsity* 3, no. 41 (October 21, 1902): 1–3.

53. "The Lay Pulpit. No. II.—Unrequited Love," *Shotover Papers* 1, no. 2 (March 9, 1874): 24.

54. Douglas, "An Undergraduate on Oxford Dons," p. 73.

55. On the emergence of this obsession with healthy bodies in the nineteenth century, see Bruce Haley, *The Healthy Body and Victorian Culture* (Cambridge, Mass.: Harvard University Press, 1978). For an overview, covering the crises around the Boer War among other things, see Michael Anton Budd, *The Sculpture Machine: Physical Culture and Body Politics in the Age of Empire* (New York: New York University Press, 1997).

56. See Graham Hoggarth, ed., *Cap and Gown: Varsity Humours by G. Hoggarth and Others* (Oxford: Holywell, 1906), p. 41.

57. Paul Fussell, *The Great War and Modern Memory* (Oxford: Oxford University Press, 1975), pp. 25–29.

58. "Peck," "An Open Letter to My Tutor—Charlie Angler," *Meteor,* no. 1 (May 1911): 4–5; and "What the Moon Saw at Cambridge," *Cambridge Tatler,* no. 5 (April 24, 1877): 2–3.

59. "To My Tutor," *Shotover Papers* 1, no. 10 (November 14, 1874): 159.

60. "A One-Sided Friendship," *Magnum,* no. 1 (October 1908): 12. Another example of this is contained in "The Don and the Undergraduate," *Bump,* no. 3 (May 16, 1901): 4.

61. For an example of this see "Louis Noel Songe," "Sallies in Blunderland," *Blue, A 'Varsity Journal* 1, no. 1 (April 25, 1893): 8.

62. Douglas, "An Undergraduate on Oxford Dons," p. 72.

63. On aspects of the homosocial nature of clubs, see Matthew Hilton, *Smoking in British Popular Culture, 1800–2000: Perfect Pleasures* (Manchester: Manchester University Press, 2000), pp. 34–35; and P. J. Rich, *Chains of Empire: English Public Schools, Masonic Cabalism, Historical Causality, and Imperial Clubdom* (London: Regency, 1991), especially pp. 145–185. For an examination of the importance of the concept of "clubbability" to imperial rule and the demarcation of social space, see Mrinalini Sinha, "Britishness, Clubbability, and the Colonial Public Sphere: The Genealogy of an Imperial Institution in Colonial India," *Journal of British Studies* 40, no. 4 (October 2001): 489–556.

64. "Aleph," "The Oxford Union," *Great Tom: A University Magazine,* no. 2 (June 1861): 67.

65. "Union Reform," *Cambridge Terminal Magazine,* no. 1 (December 1858): 30. For another discussion of the Union as an important student society, see Edward C. Lefroy, "The Union," in *Undergraduate Oxford: Articles Re-printed from the "Oxford and Cambridge Undergraduates' Journal," 1876, 7* (Oxford: privately printed, 1878), pp. 118–125. On the importance of the concept of the "freeborn Englishmen" in British nationalist discourses, see Hugh Cunningham, "The Language of Patriotism," in *Patriotism: The Making and Unmaking of British National Identity,* ed. Raphael Samuel (London: Routledge, 1989), 1:59.

66. See Keith Thomas, "College Life, 1945–1970," in *The Twentieth Century,* ed. Harrison, pp. 190–191; and Brooke, *A History of the University of Cambridge: 1870–1990,* p. 328.

67. William Everett, *On the Cam: Lectures on the University of Cambridge in England* (London: S. O. Beeton, 1868), p. 112.

68. Diary of Anna Florence Ward, Magdalen College Archives, Oxford, MS 618, p. 83.

69. Bankes, *A Cambridge Staircase,* pp. 3–4.

70. Edward Jupp to his father, January 16, 1869, *Correspondence of a Junior Student of Christchurch Oxford, in the Years 1868–1870* (Blackheath: privately printed, 1871), pp. 40–41.

71. "O. C." [A. H. Lawrence], *Reminiscences of Cambridge Life,* p. 41.

72. On the delegacies at Oxford, see Oxford University Lodging House Delegacy,

Statements {Concerning Defects Alleged to Exist in the Lodging House}, Bodleian Library, Oxford, G.A. c. 84 (496); and *Lodging Houses Licensed (1868–1916),* Bodleian Library, Oxford, G.A. Oxon 4 (245).

73. See, for example, "Digs," *'Varsity* 1, no. 1 (January 22, 1901): 6; and "New Digs," *'Varsity* 13, no. 309 (November 11, 1913): 15, 18.

74. "Digs," p. 6.

75. On variations in collegiate wealth and incomes, see J. P. Dunbabin, "Finance since 1914," in *The Twentieth Century,* ed. Harrison, pp. 656–659; and Brooke, *A History of the University of Cambridge: 1870–1990,* pp. 73–81, 598 (a summary of early-twentieth-century college incomes).

76. For two examples of how college rooms were furnished, see Raymond Blathwayt, "Young Oxford of To-day. A Talk With Professor Max Muller," *Quiver: An Illustrated Magazine for Sunday and General Reading* 27 (September 1894): 553–554; and "Our Special Commissioner," "Young Cambridge of To-Day," *Quiver: An Illustrated Magazine for Sunday and General Reading* 28 (October 1895): 32.

77. Erika Diane Rappaport, *Shopping for Pleasure: Women in the Making of London's West End* (Princeton: Princeton University Press, 2000). For an assessment of the ways in which consumption, during the eighteenth-century consumer revolution, was dominated by not just possessive women but acquisitive men, see Margot Finn, "Men's Things: Masculine Possession in the Consumer Revolution," *Social History* 25, no. 2 (May 2000): 133–155. On aspects of masculine consumption in the period covered by this study, see Christopher Breward, *The Hidden Consumer: Masculinities, Fashion, and City Life, 1860–1914* (Manchester: Manchester University Press, 1999).

78. George Nugent Bankes, *Cambridge Trifles; or, Splutterings from an Undergraduate Pen* (London: Sampson Low, Marston, Searle and Rivington, 1881), pp. 18–19.

79. Ibid., pp. 13–14.

80. "O. C." [A. H. Lawrence], *Reminiscences of Cambridge Life,* p. 43.

81. On income levels, see Harold Perkin, *The Rise of Professional Society: England since 1880* (London: Routledge, 1989), pp. 90–95. On university costs, see Rothblatt, *Revolution of the Dons,* pp. 65–75. Rothblatt's figures are drawn from *The Student's Guide to the University of Cambridge* and *The Student's Handbook to the University and Colleges of Cambridge.* My own reading of these guidebooks confirms his assessment. See J. R. Seeley, *The Student's Guide to the University of Cambridge* (Cambridge: Deighton, Bell, 1863), pp. 63–64; and Cambridge University, *The Student's Handbook to the University and Colleges of Cambridge* (Cambridge: Cambridge University Press, 1907), pp. 53–54. One early Oxford paper observed that £200 per annum was not an unreasonable allowance. See "Reviews," *Great Tom: A University Magazine,* no. 1 (May 1861): 48.

82. Compton Mackenzie, "Undergraduates at the Beginning of the Century," *Oxford* 5, no. 2 (winter 1938): 74.

83. Seeley, *The Student's Guide to the University of Cambridge,* p. 50.

84. T. F. C. Huddleston, *University Expenses and Collegiate Students,* with an introduction by Rev. Canon Browne (Cambridge: Deighton and Bell, 1892), p. 76.

85. "Bow-Wow," *Squeaker,* no. 1 (May 1893): 2.

86. "The Tipped," *Spirit Lamp* 1, no. 2 (May 13, 1892): 23–24.

87. Huddleston, *University Expenses and Collegiate Students,* p. 94.

88. On credit arrangements in general, see Rappaport, *Shopping for Pleasure,* pp. 53–55.

89. *Correspondence on the "Bread and Butter" Issue at Oxford* (1865), p. 4, Bodleian Library, Oxford, G.A. Oxon 8° 92 (3).

90. "Editorial Notes," *Undergraduate* 1, no. 16 (November 1, 1888): 243.

91. "Advertisement for *The Rubaiyat of Some-of-us. A Parody by J. G. Brandon Thomas, Pictures by Segar*" (Oxford, October 1913), in *Miscellaneous Parodies and Satirical*

Pamphlets on Oxford University, Seeley Mudd Library, Yale, Lmd 73 1. Edward Fitzgerald's translation of the quatrain verses of the eleventh- and twelfth-century Persian poet Omar Khayyam, which went through multiple editions, was enormously popular in Britain in the late nineteenth and early twentieth centuries. On aspects of this popularity, see Christopher Decker, ed., *Edward Fitzgerald's* Rubaiyat of Omar Khayyam: *A Critical Edition* (Charlottesville: University Press of Virginia, 1997).

92. [Edward Nolan], *Oxford Spectator,* no. 20, p. 4.

93. See [T. H. White], *Oxford Spectator,* no. 18 (May 5, 1868): 4; "Bills," *Undergraduate* 1, no. 15 (October 25, 1888): 232; and James Grant Brandon Thomas, *The Rubaiyat of Some-of-us: Being Certain Undergraduate Parodies of the Illustrious Persian,* illus. "Segar" (Oxford: Holywell, 1913), p. 12. On aspects of the town/gown relationship in early-nineteenth-century Cambridge, see Nick Mansfield, "Grads and Snobs: John Brown, Town, and Gown in Early Nineteenth-Century Cambridge," *History Workshop Journal,* no. 35 (spring 1993), pp. 184–198.

94. "The Late Edgar Allan Toe" [Arthur Clement Hilton], "The Bills," *Light Green: A Superior and High Class Periodical,* no. 1 (May 1872): 9.

95. Register of the Chancellor's Court, 1865–1905, Oxford University Archives, Hyp/A/71b.

96. Chancellor's Court Papers, 1915–21, Oxford University Archives, no shelf mark.

97. The classic interpretation of this phenomenon is Thorstein Veblen's study of American consumer culture, *The Theory of the Leisure Class* (New York: Penguin Books, 1994).

98. Bankes, *A Cambridge Staircase,* p. 4.

99. See Leonore Davidoff and Catherine Hall, *Family Fortunes: Men and Women of the English Middle Class, 1780–1850* (Chicago: University of Chicago Press, 1987); and Tosh, *A Man's Place.*

100. On aspects of dens and hunting lodges, see Tina Loo, "Of Moose and Men: Hunting for Masculinities in British Columbia, 1880–1939," *Western Historical Quarterly* 32, no. 3 (autumn 2001): 296–319.

101. "The Vision of Mirtha," *Shotover Papers* 1, no. 9 (October 31, 1874): 141.

102. Thomas, *The Rubaiyat of Some-of-Us,* p. 19. The pleasures and symbolic importance of an easy chair in college rooms were highlighted in two other accounts. See "A.," "Postprandial," *Boomerang: An Oxford and Cambridge Miscellany,* no. 1 (October 23, 1875), p. 11; and "A Friend Indeed," *Vacuum* 1, no. 1 (May 1, 1900), pp. 8–9.

103. "Rooms," *Undergraduate* 1, no. 17 (November 8, 1888): 265. For another commentary on furnishings as a marker of status and, in this instance, "mental calibre," see "How to Furnish Artistically Our College Rooms," *Light Blue Incorporated with the Light Green,* no. 1 (May 1873): 27.

104. On "sets" as a defining feature of college life, see "Oxford Clubs and Societies," *Undergraduate* 1, no. 15 (October 25, 1888): 230–231. On specific types, see "Campaigners," *New Rattle* 2, no. 1 (May 14, 1891): 3; "Dagonet" [A. W. Dollard], "The Enthusiastic Man," *Ye Rounde Table: An Oxford and Cambridge Magazine* 1, no. 1 (February 2, 1878): 3–4; and "The Bore," *'Varsity* 1, no. 6 (February 26, 1901): 81–82.

105. See [H. M. Naidley], *Oxford Commemoration by a Fellow of Experientia* (London, 1888), p. 3.

106. See Asa Briggs, *Victorian Things* (London: Batsford, 1988). For a gendered (if heavily female) approach to consumption, see Victoria de Grazia and Ellen Furlough, eds., *The Sex of Things: Gender and Consumption in Historical Perspective* (Berkeley: University of California Press, 1996).

107. "How to Furnish Artistically Our College Rooms," p. 27.

108. Bankes, *A Cambridge Staircase,* p. 16.

109. Bankes, *A Cambridge Staircase*, p. 87. On the formation of boundaries in defining hegemonic masculinities, see Angus McLaren, *The Trials of Masculinity: Policing Sexual Boundaries, 1870–1930* (Chicago: University of Chicago Press, 1997). On hegemony generally, see R. W. Connell, *Masculinities* (Berkeley: University of California Press, 1995), pp. 76–81.

110. "Rooms," p. 265.

111. Montague Compton, "The Undergraduate's Garden," *Oxford Point of View* 2, no. 8 (November 1903): 244.

112. "University Portrait Gallery," *Momus: A Semi-occasional University Periodical*, no. 3 (March 15, 1869): 24; "Algernon Languish," *Cambridge Tatler*, no. 5 (April 24, 1877): 11; "Critical Studies II—Bombastes Furioso," *'Varsity* 1, no. 4 (February 12, 1901): 51.

113. "Critical Studies. II.—Bombastes Furioso," p. 51; [R. S. Copleston], *Oxford Spectator*, no. 10 (February 11, 1868): 3; "Heard in 'The High,'" *Isis*, no. 267 (May 16, 1903): 300.

114. On the gendered and sexualized fears associated with aestheticism, see Mary Warner Blanchard, *Oscar Wilde's America: Counterculture in the Gilded Age* (New Haven: Yale University Press, 1998), pp. 19–27, 38–42.

115. Dickens, "A Dictionary of the University of Oxford," p. 120. On these cleavages, see "Cliques," *Cambridge Tatler*, no. 2 (March 13, 1877): 2–3; "Clubs and Societies," *Blue: A 'Varsity Journal* 2, no. 11 (November 7, 1893): 4; and "Concerning Unpopularity," *Alma Mater*, no. 1 (November 29, 1899): 6–7.

116. Bankes, *A Cambridge Staircase*, p. 13.

117. Ibid., p. 26.

118. "University Types. No. 1. Green-Tea Grindley," *Cambridge Tatler*, no. 4 (April 17, 1877): 7–8.

119. Bankes, *A Cambridge Staircase*, p. 16.

120. "Rooms," p. 266. On mountain climbing, see Peter H. Hansen, "Albert Smith, the Alpine Club, and the Invention of Mountaineering in Mid-Victorian Britain," *Journal of British Studies* 34, no. 3 (July 1995), pp. 300–324. On smoking, see Hilton, *Smoking in British Popular Culture*, pp. 17–37.

121. *Types* (Cambridge: Redin, 1894), p. 2.

122. "Rooms," p. 265.

123. Frank Rutter, "The Blood," in *'Varsity Types: Scenes and Characters from Undergraduate Life*, illus. Stephen Haweis (London: R. A. Everett, 1903), p. 115.

124. McLaren, *The Trials of Masculinity*, p. 7. On sexology in British culture, see Lucy Bland and Laura Doan, eds., *Sexology in Culture: Labelling Bodies and Desires* (Chicago: University of Chicago Press, 1998).

125. On the early twentieth century, see Brian Harrison, "College Life, 1918–1939," in *The Twentieth Century*, ed. Harrison, p. 104.

126. For a brief discussion of London clubs and their role in fostering a sense of exclusivity among men, see Leonore Davidoff, *The Best Circles: Society, Etiquette, and the Season* (London: Croom Helm, 1973), p. 24.

127. Dickens, "A Dictionary of the University of Oxford," p. 128.

128. Mackenzie, "Undergraduates at the Beginning of the Century," pp. 68–74.

129. "O. C." [A. H. Lawrence], *Reminiscences of Cambridge Life*, p. 130.

130. "On Breakfasts," *Isis*, no. 155 (November 5, 1898): 34.

131. "Little Dinners," *Cambridge Tatler*, no. 8 (May 15, 1877): 2.

3. "Your Name and College, Sir?"

1. E. M. Forster, *Maurice: A Novel* (New York: W. W. Norton, 1971), pp. 75, 79.

2. T. F. C. Huddleston, *University Expenses and Collegiate Students*, with an introduction by Rev. Canon Browne (Cambridge: Deighton and Bell, 1892), p. 63.

3. On medieval origins, see "Statement of Mr. Goldwin Smith on the Colleges and Halls of Oxford," in *The Recommendations of the Oxford University Commissioners, with Selections from Their Report; and A History of the University Subscription Tests, Including Notices of the University and Collegiate Visitations,* ed. James Heywood (London: Longman, Brown, Green, and Longmans, 1853), p. 395. On the impact of the war, see V. H. H. Green, *A History of Oxford University* (London: B. T. Batsford, 1974), pp. 188–189. On discipline in the early nineteenth century, see Sheldon Rothblatt, "The Student Subculture and the Examination System in Early 19th Century Oxbridge," in *The University in Society,* ed. Lawrence Stone (Princeton: Princeton University Press, 1974), 1:276; and Sheldon Rothblatt, *The Modern University and Its Discontents: The Fate of Newman's Legacies in Britain and America* (Cambridge: Cambridge University Press, 1997), pp. 125–148.

4. J. R. Seeley, *The Student's Guide to the University of Cambridge* (Cambridge: Deighton, Bell, 1863), p. 44.

5. On collegiate regulations relating to the behavior of fellows, see Cambridge University, *Statutes for the University of Cambridge and for the Colleges within It, Made, Published, and Approved (1878–1882) under the Universities of Oxford and Cambridge Act, 1877. With an Appendix of Acts and Orders* (Cambridge: Cambridge University Press, 1883) pp. 99, 138, 418; and Oxford University, *Statutes Made for the Colleges and St. Edmund Hall in the University of Oxford in Pursuance of the Universities of Oxford and Cambridge Act, 1923, and Approved by the King in Council* (Oxford: Clarendon, 1927), pp. 17, 14, 16.

6. Michel Foucault, *Discipline and Punish: The Birth of the Prison,* trans. Alan Sheridan (New York: Pantheon Books, 1977), p. 149.

7. For one humorous employment of the rhetoric of rebellion, see "Down with the Dons! Second Series. Manifesto of the Oxford Undergraduate Revolutionary League (Oxford, December 1888)," in *New College Scrapbook,* Bodleian Library, Oxford, G.A. Oxon c. 282.

8. This term applied to matriculated undergraduates.

9. Lynda Nead, "Mapping the Self: Gender, Space, and Modernity in Mid-Victorian London," *Environment and Planning A* 29 (1997): 659–672.

10. Two important studies that pay careful attention to the connections between gender and modern urban subjectivities are Judith R. Walkowitz, *City of Dreadful Delight: Narratives of Sexual Danger in Late-Victorian London* (Chicago: University of Chicago Press, 1992); and Erika Diane Rappaport, *Shopping for Pleasure: Women in the Making of London's West End* (Princeton: Princeton University Press, 2000).

11. For other perspectives on the relationship between urban spaces and modern sexual and gender identities, see Matt Houlbrook, "Towards a Historical Geography of Sexuality," *Journal of Urban History* 27, no. 4 (May 2001): 497–504; and Philip Hubbard, "Desire/Disgust: Mapping the Moral Contours of Heterosexuality," *Progress in Human Geography* 24, no. 2 (2000): 191–217.

12. Cambridge University, *Ordinances of the University of Cambridge* (Cambridge: Cambridge University Press, 1888), title page. On these developments generally, see John Prest, "City and University," in *The Illustrated History of Oxford University,* ed. John Prest (Oxford: Oxford University Press, 1993), pp. 1–38.

13. On this, see J. R. Tanner, ed., *The Historical Register of the University of Cambridge, Being a Supplement to the "Calendar" with a Record of University Offices, Honours and Distinctions to the Year 1910* (Cambridge: Cambridge University Press, 1917), p. 206; and Prest, "City and University," pp. 16–17.

14. Christopher N. L. Brooke and Roger Highfield, *Oxford and Cambridge,* photographs by Wim Swaan (Cambridge: Cambridge University Press, 1988), p. 163.

15. For discussions of these and other offices, see H. P. Stokes, *Ceremonies of the University of Cambridge* (Cambridge: Cambridge University Press, 1927), p. 1; and

L. H. Dudley Buxton and Strickland Gibson, *Oxford University Ceremonies* (Oxford: Clarendon, 1935), pp. 129–136.

16. Graduate members of both universities were B.A.s who, after the elapse of seven years since matriculation and the payment of a small fee, were elevated to M.A. status and the rights and privileges that accompanied this degree.

17. Oxford University, *The Historical Register of the University of Oxford. Being a Supplement to the Oxford University Calendar with an Alphabetical Record of University Honours and Distinctions, Completed to the End of Trinity Term, 1888.* (Oxford: Clarendon, 1888), p. 13. On Cambridge, see Tanner, ed., *The Historical Register of the University of Cambridge . . . to the Year 1910,* p. 6. On governance generally, see A. J. Engel, *From Clergyman to Don: The Rise of the Academic Profession in Nineteenth-Century Oxford* (Oxford: Oxford University Press, 1983), pp. 59–65.

18. For a concise, interesting discussion of the importance of these political issues at Cambridge, see Gordon Johnson, *University Politics: F. M. Cornford's Cambridge and His Advice to the Young Academic Politician* (Cambridge: Cambridge University Press, 1994), pp. 9–84.

19. Oxford University, *The Historical Register of the University of Oxford . . . 1888,* p. 40.

20. Charles Dickens, "A Dictionary of the University of Cambridge," in *Dickens's Dictionary of Oxford and Cambridge* (London: Macmillan, 1884), p. 35.

21. Buxton and Gibson, *Oxford University Ceremonies,* p. 11; and Dickens, "A Dictionary of the University of Cambridge," pp. 69–70.

22. Buxton and Gibson, *Oxford University Ceremonies,* p. 11. In registering, the undergraduate was also required to provide the university with background information about himself and his family. See, for example, "Matriculation Form for 1900," in *Oxford University Miscellaneous Papers,* vol. 1, Bodleian Library, Oxford, G.A. Oxon b. 137.

23. "Memorandum to Undergraduates on Matriculation, 1904," in *Oxon Miscellaneous,* Bodleian Library, Oxford, G.A. Oxon c. 107.

24. On this metaphor in the United States, see Mark Carnes, *Secret Ritual and Manhood in Victorian America* (New Haven: Yale University Press, 1989), pp. 93–127.

25. Dickens, "A Dictionary of the University of Cambridge," p. 34. For another discussion of the praelector, see Tanner, ed., *The Historical Register of the University of Cambridge . . . to the Year 1910,* pp. 183–184, 352. On the ceremony, see Stokes, *Ceremonies of the University of Cambridge,* pp. 28–35.

26. Buxton and Gibson, *Oxford University Ceremonies,* p. 78.

27. On attempts to regulate these activities at the Encaenia, see "Circular Regarding Commemoration for April 30, 1875," in *Letters and Papers Received by C. L. Shadwell, Esq. during His Term of Office as Proctor,* Bodleian Library, Oxford, G.A. Oxon c. 33.

28. On female guests, see Curators of the Theatre, "Regulations for Accommodation of Company Resorting to the Theatre at the Commemoration on the Morning of Wednesday the 12th of June, 1872," and Curators of the Theatre, "Commemoration, 1907," in *Oxford University Miscellaneous Papers,* vol. 2, Bodleian Library, Oxford, G.A. Oxon b. 138. On the "pit," see Charles Dickens, "A Dictionary of the University of Oxford," in *Dickens's Dictionary of Oxford and Cambridge,* p. 37.

29. Curators of the Theatre, "Commemoration, 1876," in *Oxford University Miscellaneous Papers,* vol. 2.

30. Dickens, "A Dictionary of the University of Cambridge," p. 34.

31. Throughout the period examined here this practice remained common, particularly on Commencement Day at Cambridge and during the Encaenia or Commemoration at Oxford. One episode is included in Jan Morris, ed., *The Oxford Book of Oxford* (Oxford: Oxford University Press, 1978), p. 176.

32. Dickens, "A Dictionary of the University of Oxford," p. 36.

33. Robert Pearce-Edgcumbe, "Biographical Sketch," in Arthur Clement Hilton, *The Works of Arthur Clement Hilton, Together with His Life and Letters,* ed. Robert Pearce-Edgcumbe (Cambridge: Macmillan and Bowes, 1904), pp. 53–54.

34. "June 2, 1865," Vice-Chancellor's Papers, Cambridge University Archives, C.U.R. 44.1(215).

35. A Tutor, "To the Undergraduate Members of the University," circa 1876, in *Oxford University Miscellaneous Papers,* vol. 4, Bodleian Library, Oxford, G.A. Oxon b. 140.

36. See Keith Thomas, "College Life, 1945–1970," in *The Twentieth Century,* ed. Brian Harrison, vol. 8 of *The History of the University of Oxford,* ed. T. H. Aston (Oxford: Clarendon, 1994), 201–202.

37. Oxford University, *The Student's Handbook to the University and Colleges of Oxford* (Oxford: Clarendon, 1873), p. 23.

38. Cambridge University, *Statutes for the University of Cambridge,* p. 139.

39. "Meeting, November 27, 1877," Diaries of Falconer Madan, vol. 1: Private Account No. 1, p. 14, Brasenose College Archives, Oxford.

40. Undergraduates were generally held to be accountable for anything that went on in their rooms. See *City and Borough of Oxford, 1885. Before the Revising Barrister, September 8th, 9th, 10th, 12th, 19th and 26th, Alfred Chichele Plowden, Esq. Copy of Short-hand Writers' Notes of the Evidence Relating to Occupation of College Rooms, to Which is Appended the Decision of the Revising Barrister* (Oxford, 1885).

41. See Thomas, "College Life, 1945–1970," pp. 201–202.

42. See Oxford University, *The Student's Handbook to the University and Colleges of Oxford,* p. 23; and Cambridge University, *The Student's Handbook to the University and Colleges of Cambridge* (Cambridge: Cambridge University Press, 1910), p. 55.

43. "College Meeting, October 19, 1877," and "College Meeting, February 1, 1878," Diaries of Falconer Madan, vol. 1, pp. 9, 21.

44. "College Meeting (Special) 1 p.m. Thursday, November 20, 1879," Diaries of Falconer Madan, vol. 2: Private Account No. 2, pp. 175–176.

45. Brasenose authorities also imposed similar punishments after an incident in 1892. See "Disciplinary Meeting: Monday, November 7, 1892," Diaries of Falconer Madan, vol. 3: Brasenose College Meetings.

46. "At the Breakfast Table," *Blue, A 'Varsity Journal* 1, no. 1 (April 25, 1893): 3. Attendance at chapel or roll call (an option instituted to accommodate those who were not members of the Anglican Church) remained compulsory until the twentieth century. See Christopher N. L. Brooke, *A History of the University of Cambridge: 1870–1990,* vol. 4 of *A History of the University of Cambridge,* ed. Christopher N. L. Brooke (Cambridge: Cambridge University Press, 1993), pp. 111–121. The complete demise of compulsory chapel at Oxford after 1945 is detailed in Thomas, "College Life, 1945–1970," p. 201.

47. "Revelry by Night," *Isis,* no. 111 (November 28, 1896): 85. For another Oxford example of this theme of don as nocturnal obstacle, see Alfred Douglas, "Sir Thomas Jones. A Ballad of Magdalen," *Spirit Lamp* 2, no. 4 (December 6, 1892): 103–105.

48. Frith is identified as the author of this piece in "F. Anstey" [Thomas Anstey Guthrie], *A Long Retrospect* (Oxford: Oxford University Press, 1936), p. 92.

49. [Walter Frith], "Programme of the Recent Jesus Festivities," *Cambridge Tatler,* no. 10 (May 29, 1877): 4–5.

50. John Willis Clark, handwritten comment on a copy of the reprint of *Cambridge Tatler,* no. 10 (May 29, 1877; reprint, July 1877), in the collection of the Cambridge University Library, Cam.b.31.42.1.

51. "Anstey" [Thomas Anstey Guthrie], *A Long Retrospect,* p. 92.

52. See J. A. Mangan, *Athleticism in the Victorian and Edwardian Public School: The*

Emergence and Consolidation of an Educational Ideology (Cambridge: Cambridge University Press, 1981), p. 187.

53. Foucault, *Discipline and Punish,* p. 215.

54. On aspects of this, see Julie S. Gibert, "Women Students and Student Life at England's Civic Universities before the First World War," *History of Education* 23, no. 4 (December 1994): 409–410.

55. See, for example, "Whereas Students of the University . . . February 28, 1866," Vice-Chancellor's Papers, Cambridge University Archives, C.U.R. 44.1(217); and "Notice To Junior Members of the University . . . May 13, 1901," in *Oxford University Miscellaneous Papers,* vol. 1.

56. William Everett, *On the Cam: Lectures on the University of Cambridge in England* (London: S. O. Beeton, 1868), p. 113. On this dynamic, see Foucault, *Discipline and Punish,* pp. 195–228.

57. "The Proctors find it necessary . . . May Term 1890," Proctors' Notebooks, p. 31, Cambridge University Archives, O.V.78.

58. A proctor recorded this observation in 1912. See "Beaver," Proctors' Manuals (1897), p. 99, Oxford University Archives, WPγ7/5. While this manual is dated 1897, it contains notes from proctors who served in later years. Ongoing discussions of disciplinary issues were common in these notebooks and provide interesting glimpses into how this system of rules and regulations was modified over time.

59. See "Memorandum to Undergraduates on Matriculation, 1904," in *Oxon Miscellaneous;* and Proctors' Manuals (1902–1903), p. 144, Oxford University Archives, WPγ7/6.

60. [R. S. Copleston], *Oxford Spectator,* no. 9 (February 4, 1868): 3.

61. *Letters and Papers Received by C. L. Shadwell, Esq.*

62. "A Fine Tale," *Undergraduate* 1, no. 18 (November 15, 1888): 283.

63. "Edict Sanctioned by the Senate, March 3, 1870," Vice-Chancellor's Papers, Cambridge University Archives, C.U.R. 44.1(222).

64. "Memorandum to Undergraduates on Matriculation, 1904," *Oxon Miscellaneous.*

65. "Dining in Hotels &c.," Proctors' Manuals (1897), p. 94. The occasional leniency displayed by subsequent proctors can be seen in the notes contained in "Dining," Proctors' Manuals (1897), p. 134.

66. Proctors' Book, Names, Oxford University Archives, PR 1/23/4/1.

67. W. W. Jackson to C. L. Shadwell, item 35, *Letters and Papers Received by C. L. Shadwell, Esq.*

68. "Dinners," Proctors' Manuals (1887), p. 30, Oxford University Archives, WPγ7/4.

69. "May 5," Proctors' Notebooks, p. 45.

70. Procuratorial Experiences and Observations in the Year 1852, 3, p. 24, Oxford University Archives, WPγ8 (21). For examples of minor infractions, see "December 6, 1893," Proctors' Notebooks, p. 48; "January 21, 1901," Proctors' Notebooks, p. 58; and J. Maude and A. Butler, "The Proctors desire respectfully . . . June 4, 1892," in *Oxford University Miscellaneous Papers,* vol. 1.

71. "Memorandum to Undergraduates on Matriculation, 1904," in *Oxon Miscellaneous.*

72. See Charles Edward Mallet, *A History of the University of Oxford* (London: Methuen, 1927), 3:185–196. These prohibitions remained in place throughout the period examined here. See, for example, "WHEREAS many students have of late been . . . February 12, 1850," Vice-Chancellor's Papers, Cambridge University Archives, C.U.R. 44.1(205); and "Memorandum to Undergraduates on Matriculation, July 1907," in *Oxford University Miscellaneous Papers,* vol. 1.

73. "The Empire Music Hall: (Cowley Road)," Proctors' Manuals (1897), pp. 129–130.

74. Ibid.

75. "1905, April 30," Proctors' Notebooks, p. 65.

76. For discussions of these powers at Oxford, see "Cinematograph Theatres," Proctors' Manuals (1902–1903), p. 148.

77. "Cinematograph Theatres," entry dated 1912–1913, Proctors' Manuals (1897), pp. 159–161.

78. Tracy C. Davis, *Actresses as Working Women: Their Social Identity in Victorian Culture* (London: Routledge, 1991), p. 147.

79. "Miss Kitty Gordon," *Oxford and Cambridge Illustrated* 2, no. 7 (May 10, 1907): cover illustration; and "Miss Camille Clifford," *Oxford and Cambridge Illustrated* 2, no. 12 (June 15, 1907): cover illustration. On other emblems of modernity in both the nineteenth and the twentieth centuries, see Marshall Berman, *All That Is Solid Melts into Air: The Experience of Modernity* (New York: Simon and Schuster, 1982).

80. Proctors' Book, Names.

81. Tracy Davis, *Actresses as Working Women,* pp. 78–86. The history of prostitution in both Oxford and Cambridge has been explored in the work of, respectively, A. J. Engel and Philip Howell. Engel's concerns are largely those of the 1970s social historian. He sought, in his article on the subject (published in 1979), to accurately describe the presence and experiences of prostitutes in Oxford while exploring official attitudes and the gradual erosion of the university's jurisdiction over prostitution. Howell, as a historical geographer, uses Cambridge in a recent piece as a case study to chart the emergence of the regulationist impulse prior to the passage of the first Contagious Diseases Act in 1864. Howell's work, informed by more recent scholarship on geographical contact zones in urban spaces, also pays attention to the problems associated with the publicly exposed sexuality of prostitutes and their clients and proctorial attempts to regulate social space. Neither of these scholars really addresses the issues of masculine and generational conflict, the invention of heterosexuality, and the contested nature of public space. See Arthur J. Engel, "'Immoral Intentions': The University of Oxford and the Problem of Prostitution, 1827–1914," *Victorian Studies* 23, no. 1 (autumn 1979), pp. 79–107; and Philip Howell, "A Private Contagious Diseases Act: Prostitution and Public Space in Victorian Cambridge," *Journal of Historical Geography* 26, no. 3 (July 2000): 376–402.

82. On "new women" as threatening and destabilizing exemplars of modernity, see Rappaport, *Shopping for Pleasure;* and Angela Woollacott, *To Try Her Fortune in London: Australian Women, Colonialism, and Modernity* (New York: Oxford University Press, 2001).

83. Jonathan Ned Katz, *The Invention of Heterosexuality* (New York: Dutton, 1995).

84. Hubbard, "Desire/Disgust," pp. 191–217.

85. "The City Band," entry dated 1905–1906, Proctors' Manuals (1897), p. 131.

86. Judith Walkowitz, "Going Public: Shopping, Street Harassment, and Streetwalking in Late Victorian London," *Representations,* no. 62 (spring 1998): 1–30.

87. "Whereas Students of the University . . . February 28, 1866," Vice-Chancellor's Papers; and "The Vice-Chancellor and Proctors desire . . . May 28, 1885," in *Oxford University Miscellaneous Papers,* vol. 1.

88. "Memorandum to Undergraduates on Matriculation, July 1907," in *Oxford University Miscellaneous Papers,* vol. 1. On automobile culture, see Sean O'Connell, *The Car in British Society: Class, Gender, and Motoring, 1896–1939* (Manchester: Manchester University Press, 1998).

89. "Bad Women," entry dated 1905–1906, Proctors' Manuals (1897), p. 105.

90. "1913–1914," Proctors' Notebooks, p. 103.

91. These figures are drawn from Spinning House Committals: Files of Mandates, Graces and Committals, 1823–94, Cambridge University Archives, T.VIII.1–3.

92. See, for Cambridge, "To Members of the Senate of the University of Cam-

bridge, February 9 and February 10, 1892," Flysheets re: Proctorial Jurisdiction, Cambridge University Archives, U.P. 60 (28–29); and "Report of the Council of the Senate, 29 May 1893," Files Relating to Proctors in General, Cambridge University Archives, C.U.R. 41.3. On these changes, see D. A. Winstanley, *Later Victorian Cambridge* (Cambridge: Cambridge University Press, 1947), pp. 91–119.

93. See Engel, "'Immoral Intentions,'" pp. 99–104; and Howell, "A Private Contagious Diseases Act," p. 386.

94. "To Members of the Senate of the University of Cambridge, February 9 and February 10, 1892."

95. See "Bad Women," Proctors' Manuals (1897), p. 103; and "Bad Women," Proctors' Manuals (1887), p. 120.

96. On brothels, see "Houses of Ill Fame," Proctors' Manuals (1887), p. 119; and "Notorious Houses of Ill-Fame, 1919–1920," Proctors' Notebooks. On immorality, especially in the years leading up to the First World War, see "1912–1913," Proctors' Notebooks, p. 84; and "1913–1914," Proctors' Notebooks, p. 103.

97. J. R. de S. Honey, *Tom Brown's Universe: The Development of the Victorian Public School* (London: Millington, 1977), pp. 192–195. On aspects of medicalization and criminalization, see Ivan Dalley Crozier, "The Medical Construction of Homosexuality and Its Relation to the Law in Nineteenth-Century England," *Medical History* 45, no. 1 (January 2001): 61–82; and Frank Mort, *Dangerous Sexualities: Medico-moral Politics in England since 1830,* 2nd ed. (London: Routledge, 2000).

98. "N" [Edward Nolan], *Oxford Spectator,* no. 20 (May 19, 1868; reprinted edition): 80.

99. See Jeffrey Weeks, *Sex, Politics, and Society: The Regulation of Sexuality since 1800,* 2nd ed. (London: Longmans, 1989), pp. 99–109.

100. "Cinematograph Theatres," entry dated 1912–1913, Proctors' Manuals (1897), p. 159.

101. The case is discussed in "June 8, 1905" and "June 14, 1905," Proctors' Notebooks, pp. 68–69; the quotations in this paragraph and the next are taken from there.

102. "Masseurs, February 5, 1914," Proctors' Manuals (1902–1903), p. 155.

103. This case appears in "11 February 1911," University of Oxford: Proctors' Book, Names.

104. For a very general discussion, see Peter N. Stearns, *Be A Man! Males in Modern Society,* 2nd ed. (New York: Holmes and Meier, 1990), pp. 124–126. Between 1910 and 1920, undergraduates were "caught with girls" (an ambiguous term that generally meant they had been found with prostitutes, in "suspect houses," or with actresses) 138 times by proctors. While this is not a huge number, it does reflect a level of activity that is not to be discounted. See Proctors' Book, Names.

105. Case of Daisy Hopkins, 1891–92, Cambridge University Archives, T.VIII.4. Philip Howell has also noted these practices. See Howell, "A Private Contagious Diseases Act," p. 382.

106. Spinning House Committals: Files of Mandates, Graces and Committals, entries 128, 175, and 525.

107. See "Joseph Storer Clouston—Ug of Magd College," and "1 December 1897—Ernest Brocklehurst," University Justice Court Books (1871–1926), Oxford University Archives, no shelf mark.

108. "Meeting, March 2, 1885," Proctors' Notebooks, p. 3.

109. "Serious Case," Proctors',Manuals (1902–1903), p. 111.

110. This was indeed a common reaction to being discovered by the proctors. See, for example, "February 1, 1893," Proctors' Notebooks, p. 44; and "January 31, 1894," Proctors' Notebooks, p. 49.

111. "C. E. Haselfoot to Controller of Lodging House Delegacy, December 8, 1903," Miscellaneous Correspondence of the Lodging House Delegacy (1903), Oxford University Archives, LHD/C/1/21.

112. "November 11, 1891, Special Meeting," Proctors' Notebooks, pp. 38–39.

113. "Perverted Proverbs," *Bump,* Eights Week Number (May 1909): 7.

114. H. A. M., "Love Is Blind: Varsity Sketches No. 4," and "My Cousin, Sir: Varsity Sketches No. 5," *Ten Satirical Postcards* (1906), Cambridge University Library, Cam.d.906.19.

115. On the ways in which certain of these cultural forms contributed to the construction of the heterosexual ideal, see Peter Bailey, "Parasexuality and Glamour: The Victorian Barmaid as Cultural Prototype," *Gender and History* 2, no. 2 (summer 1990), pp. 148–172; Tracy Davis, "Indecency and Vigilance in the Music Halls," in *British Theatre in the 1890s: Essays on Drama and the Stage,* ed. Richard Foulkes (Cambridge: Cambridge University Press, 1992), pp. 11–131; and Rappaport, *Shopping for Pleasure,* pp. 192–203.

116. On this increasing gulf, see John Gillis, *Youth and History: Tradition and Change in European Age Relations, 1770–Present* (New York: Academic, 1981), pp. 99–105; and John Springhall, *Coming of Age: Adolescence in Britain, 1860–1960* (Dublin: Gill and Macmillan, 1986), pp. 8–9, 45–64.

117. Friar Tuck [Francis G. Stokes], "The Lay Pulpit: No. 1.—Social Sacrifices," *Shotover Papers* 1, no. 1 (February 23, 1874): 10.

118. "Sir Bors," "A Nocturne," *Ye Rounde Table: An Oxford and Cambridge Magazine* 1, no. 2 (February 23, 1878): 29–32.

119. "Maid Marion" [F. S. Pulling], "Simple Truths for Freshmen," *Shotover Papers* 1, no. 10 (November 14, 1874), p. 150. Similar sentiments are also expressed in an earlier Oxford publication: see [T. H. White], *Oxford Spectator,* no. 18 (May 5, 1868): 4.

120. "Ode to a Bull-Dog," *Clown* 1, no. 3 (June 2, 1891): 6; and "Lines to a Bulldog: A Frank Warning," *Oxford Tatler,* no. 1 (May 1, 1886): 7.

121. "Dedicated to the Shades of Past Five Shillings," *New Rattle* 2, no. 2 (May 15, 1891): 4.

122. "Editorial Notes," *Undergraduate* 1, no. 15 (October 25, 1888): 225.

123. Proctors' Book, Names. Numerous discussions of proctors' ability to fine appeared in the undergraduate press. See "The Dream of the Junior Proctor," *Harlequin,* no. 3 (May 5, 1866): 4; "Tittle-Tattle," *Oxford Tatler,* no. 1 (May 1, 1886): 4; and "Song," *Bump,* no. 2 (May 20, 1899): 5–6.

124. Procuratorial Experiences and Observations in the Year 1852, 3, pp. 1, 24.

125. "Editorial Notes," *Undergraduate* 1, no. 8 (May 2, 1888): 114; and "Editorial Notes," *Undergraduate* 1, no. 19 (November 22, 1888): 290.

126. "Bob Sawyer," "Lays of the Proctor," *Undergraduate* 1, no. 4 (February 14, 1888): 61; and "Aeschylus Warneth ye Undergraduate," *Isis,* no. 1 (April 27, 1892): 5.

127. "Two Little Rubber Shoes," *Isis,* no. 19 (February 25, 1893): 72; and "H. F. B. B-S.," "The Nightly Pestilence," in *Cap and Gown: Varsity Humours by G. Hoggarth and Others,* ed. Graham Hoggarth (Oxford: Holywell, 1906), p. 14.

4. Those "Horrid," "Holy" Schools

Part of this chapter appeared as "Competitive Examinations and the Culture of Masculinity in Oxbridge Undergraduate Life, 1850-1920," *History of Education Quarterly* 42, no. 4 (winter 2002): 544-578. Copyright by History of Education Society. Reprinted by permission.

1. On smoking and masculinity, see Matthew Hilton, *Smoking in British Popular Culture, 1800–2000: Perfect Pleasures* (Manchester: Manchester University Press, 2000), pp. 17–40, 116–137.

2. J. R. Seeley, *The Student's Guide to the University of Cambridge* (Cambridge: Deighton, Bell, 1863), p. 15.

3. [W. Hopkins], "I. Remarks on Competitive Examinations, Particularly on the Examination for Appointments in the Indian Civil Service," *Occasional Papers on University Matters and Middle Class Education,* no. 3 (December 1859): 101.

4. Reba Soffer, *Discipline and Power: The University, History, and the Making of an English Elite, 1870–1930* (Stanford: Stanford University Press, 1994), p. 136. For an example of press coverage, see "University Intelligence," *Times,* June 27, 1900, p. 11.

5. For two classic accounts, see R. J. Montgomery, *Examinations: An Account of Their Evolution as Administrative Devices in England* (London: Longmans, Green, 1965), p. xii; and John Roach, *Public Examinations in England, 1850–1900* (Cambridge: Cambridge University Press, 1971).

6. Harold Perkin, *The Rise of Professional Society: England since 1880* (London: Routledge, 1989); and Soffer, *Discipline and Power.* See also Gillian Sutherland, "Examinations and the Construction of Professional Identity: A Case Study of England, 1800–1950," *Assessment in Education* 8, no. 1 (March 2001): 51–64.

7. Andrew Warwick, in a book that was published as this study was being prepared for the press, has noted the cultural and social significance that students at Cambridge attached to the Mathematical Tripos examinations. His analysis does not, however, adequately address gender issues. See Andrew Warwick, *Masters of Theory: Cambridge and the Rise of Mathematical Physics* (Chicago: University of Chicago Press, 2003), pp. 114–226.

8. Sheldon Rothblatt, "The Student Sub-culture and the Examination System in Early 19th Century Oxbridge," in *The University in Society,* ed. Lawrence Stone (Princeton: Princeton University Press, 1974), 1:247–303; and Sheldon Rothblatt, "Failure in Early Nineteenth-Century Oxford and Cambridge," *History of Education* 11, no. 1 (March 1982): 1–21. While Rothblatt focuses almost exclusively on the pre-1850 period, in a recent revision of some of his earlier work he does refer to the growth of the competitive ideal in the 1860s. See his *The Modern University and Its Discontents: The Fate of Newman's Legacies in Britain and America* (Cambridge: Cambridge University Press, 1997), pp. 190–200.

9. Pierre Bourdieu, *The State Nobility: Elite Schools in the Field of Power,* trans. Lauretta C. Clough (Stanford: Stanford University Press, 1996), p. 104.

10. Henry Latham, *On the Action of Examinations Considered as a Means of Selection* (Cambridge: Deighton, Bell, 1877), p. 153.

11. On aspects of this broad transformation, see David Newsome, *Godliness and Good Learning: Four Studies on a Victorian Ideal* (London: Cassell, 1961).

12. On masculine anxieties, see Michael Kimmel, "The Contemporary 'Crisis' of Masculinity in Historical Perspective," in *The Making of Masculinities: The New Men's Studies,* ed. Harry Brod (Boston: Unwin Hyman, 1987), pp. 103–119, 122.

13. G. V. Cox, *Recollections of Oxford,* 2nd ed. (London: Macmillan, 1870), pp. 39–40.

14. Quoted in Charles Edward Mallet, *A History of the University of Oxford* (London: Methuen, 1927), 3:165. This passage has been frequently cited as an example of the deficiencies of the system as it existed in the eighteenth century. See Montgomery, *Examinations,* p. 6.

15. James Heywood, ed., *The Recommendations of the Oxford University Commissioners, with Selections from Their Report; and A History of the University Subscription Tests, Including Notices of the University and Collegiate Visitations* (London: Longman, Brown, Green, and Longmans, 1853), pp. 254–269.

16. See Montgomery, *Examinations,* pp. 6–7; and Christopher Stray, "The Shift from Oral to Written Examination: Cambridge and Oxford, 1700–1900," *Assessment in Education* 8, no. 1 (March 2001): 33–50.

17. On this development and some of the differences between Oxford and Cambridge, see Peter Searby, *A History of the University of Cambridge: 1750–1870,* vol. 3 of *A History of the University of Cambridge,* ed. Christopher N. L. Brooke (Cambridge: Cambridge University Press, 1997), p. 159; and M. C. Curthoys, "The Examination System," in *Nineteenth-Century Oxford, Part 1,* ed. M. G. Brock and M. C. Curthoys, vol. 6 of *The History of the University of Oxford,* ed. T. H. Aston (Oxford: Oxford University Press, 1997), pp. 344–346.

18. Montgomery, *Examinations,* p. 7; and H. D. Jocelyn, "The University's Contribution to Classical Studies," in *The Illustrated History of Oxford University,* ed. John Prest (Oxford: Oxford University Press, 1993), pp. 170–171.

19. Jocelyn, "The University's Contribution to Classical Studies," pp. 169–171.

20. For discussions of these broader trends, see T. W. Heyck, *The Transformation of Intellectual Life in Victorian England* (London: Croom Helm, 1982), pp. 155–189; and Sheldon Rothblatt, "The Diversification of Higher Education in England," in *The Transformation of Higher Learning, 1860–1930: Expansion, Diversification, Social Opening, and Professionalization in England, Germany, Russia, and the United States,* ed. Konrad H. Jarausch (Chicago: University of Chicago Press, 1983), pp. 131–148.

21. See Soffer, *Discipline and Power;* and Reba Soffer, *Ethics and Society in England: The Revolution in the Social Sciences, 1870–1914* (Berkeley: University of California Press, 1978).

22. On Cambridge, see Christopher N. L. Brooke, *A History of the University of Cambridge: 1870–1990,* vol. 4 of *A History of the University of Cambridge,* ed. Christopher N. L. Brooke (Cambridge: Cambridge University Press, 1993), 294. Mark Curthoys has also observed this trend in Oxford, where in the 1850s over half the B.A.s granted were pass degrees, while in 1909–1910 only 16 percent were. Curthoys, "The Examination System," p. 360.

23. William Everett, *On the Cam: Lectures on the University of Cambridge in England* (London: S. O. Beeton, 1868), p. xxv.

24. Heywood, ed., *The Recommendations of the Oxford University Commissioners,* p. 5.

25. George Nugent Bankes, *Cambridge Trifles; or, Splutterings from an Undergraduate Pen* (London: Sampson Lowe, Marston, Searle and Rivington, 1881), pp. 84–85.

26. See Benjamin Jowett, "Examinations during the Year 1886, February 22, 1886," in *Oxford University Miscellaneous Papers,* vol.1, Bodleian Library, Oxford, G.A. Oxon b. 137. Prior to 1882 at Cambridge, the Triposes generally occurred in January. See Brooke, *A History of the University of Cambridge: 1870–1990,* p. 298.

27. "May," *Ye Rounde Table: An Oxford and Cambridge Magazine* 1, no. 4 (May 11, 1878): 50.

28. Everett, *On the Cam,* p. 54; and *'Varsity* 13, no. 327 (June 9, 1914): 21.

29. The "Marble Palace" remark is in Jocelyn, "The University's Contribution to Classical Studies," p. 174. On the building of the New Schools, see "The New Schools at Oxford," *Times,* June 2, 1882, p. 4; and Geoffrey Tyack, "The Architecture of the University and the Colleges," in *The Illustrated History of Oxford University,* ed. Prest, pp. 112–113.

30. Alfred Denis Godley, "A Song of the Schools," in *Verses to Order* (London: Methuen, 1892), pp. 40–41.

31. These concepts are employed, in varying ways, in *'Varsity* 13, no. 327 (June 9, 1914): 21; [R. S. Copleston], *Oxford Spectator* no. 29 (November 24, 1868): 3; "Carfax," "Words and their Derivations," *Shotover Papers* 1, no. 4 (May 2, 1874): 58; and "F. Anstey" [Thomas Anstey Guthrie], *A Long Retrospect* (Oxford: Oxford University Press, 1936), p. 99.

32. Arthur Clement Hilton to his mother, November 25, 1870, in *The Works of Arthur Clement Hilton, Together with His Life and Letters,* ed. Robert Pearce-Edgcumbe

(Cambridge: Macmillan and Bowes, 1904), p. 59. Hilton was reflecting on the experiences of his friends. He would have completed the Previous examination himself during the 1869–1870 academic year.

33. This changed in the 1880s, when the additional subjects became mechanics, French, and German. See Cambridge University, *The Cambridge University Calendar* (Cambridge: Deighton, Bell, 1886), p. 13.

34. Everett, *On the Cam,* p. 55.

35. "Ye Gentle Art of Cribbing," *Isis,* no. 20 (March 4, 1893): 85.

36. Cambridge University, *The Cambridge University Calendar,* 1857, p. 13; 1878, p. 25; and 1896, pp. 46–47.

37. "O. C." [A. H. Lawrence], *Reminiscences of Cambridge Life* (London: privately printed, 1889), p. 57.

38. "Editorial Notes," *Undergraduate* 1, no. 8 (May 2, 1888): 115.

39. On tutorials, which figured much more prominently at Oxford than at Cambridge, see A. J. Engel, *From Clergyman to Don: The Rise of the Academic Profession in Nineteenth-Century Oxford* (Oxford: Oxford University Press, 1983); and Soffer, *Discipline and Power,* pp. 23, 133. On the importance of reading parties during vacations, see Charles Dickens, "A Dictionary of the University of Oxford," *Dickens's Dictionary of Oxford and Cambridge* (London: Macmillan, 1884), pp. 100–106. On the significance of hiring private tutors, see "How to Get Through the Pass Schools," *Oxford Examiner,* no. 3 (Trinity term, 1890): 19–20.

40. Everett, *On the Cam,* p. 65. On aspects of this in the first half of the century, see Rothblatt, *The Modern University and Its Discontents,* pp. 190–211.

41. "Kalendar," *Oxford Tatler,* no. 2 (May 8, 1886): 17. For another example, see "Calendar," *Cambridge Magazine* 1, no. 13 (May 18, 1912): 334.

42. "Hints to Examiners," *Momus: A Semi-occasional University Periodical,* no. 2 (April 1, 1868): 10.

43. "Sir Kay" [A. P. Poley]. "Notes," *Ye Rounde Table: An Oxford and Cambridge Magazine* 1, no. 5 (June 1, 1878) 80.

44. "X. A." [Christopher Wordsworth], "Tripos Fever," *Tatler in Cambridge,* no. 28 (November 1, 1871): 31.

45. "On Examination Papers," *Oxford Examiner,* no. 1 (October 1889): 19.

46. *'Varsity* 13, no. 327 (June 9, 1914), p. 21.

47. "Motley Notes," *Granta* 5, no. 91 (June 16, 1892): 395; and "O. C." [A. H. Lawrence], *Reminiscences of Cambridge Life,* p. 56.

48. Everett, *On the Cam,* pp. 55–56.

49. For a discussion of some of these issues, see Daphne Spain, "The Spatial Foundations of Men's Friendships and Men's Power," in *Men's Friendships,* ed. Peter Nardi (Newbury Park, Calif.: Sage Publications, 1992), pp. 69–72.

50. Everett, *On the Cam,* p. 96.

51. "O. C." [A. H. Lawrence], *Reminiscences of Cambridge Life,* p. 144.

52. Hilton, *The Works of Arthur Clement Hilton,* pp. 59–60; and "Thoughts That Occur," *'Varsity* 6, no. 23 (June 13, 1907): 347.

53. "The Vision of Mirtha," *Shotover Papers* 1, no. 9 (October 31, 1874): 139–140.

54. "Songs for the 'Little' & 'Great' Go," *Oxford Wit,* no. 1 (1855): 18–19.

55. For specific examples of how undergraduates viewed these preparations, see "Epitaph on a Departed Long Vacation," *College Rhymes,* no. 5 (1864): 125–126; and "P. M. W.," "The Song of the Shirk," *Light Blue Incorporated with the Light Green,* no. 1 (May 1873): 25–26.

56. Judith Butler, *Gender Trouble: Feminism and the Subversion of Identity* (London: Routledge, 1990), pp. 24–25, 134–149.

57. Everett, *On the Cam,* p. 66; John Tosh, *A Man's Place: Masculinity and the*

Middle-Class Home in Victorian England (New Haven: Yale University Press, 1999), pp. 4–5, 115–116.

58. For examples of this, see "C. H. C.," "Simple Simon in for His Little-Go," *College Rhymes,* no. 7 (1866): 154; and "Society Notes," *Jokelet,* no. 1 (January 1886): 2. Reba Soffer also points to this view of examinations in *Discipline and Power,* p. 137.

59. On this ideal, see Peter Gay, *The Cultivation of Hatred* (New York: W. W. Norton, 1993), pp. 112–116; and Rothblatt, *The Modern University and Its Discontents,* p. 196.

60. "Society Notes," p. 2.

61. "Human Sacrifices at Oxford," *Shotover Papers* 1, no. 6 (May 30, 1874): 83.

62. "Voices from 'The Schools.' No. I," *Great Tom: A University Magazine,* no. 2 (June 1861): 17–19. The language of affliction, trial, and ordeal also appears in [R. S. Copleston], *Oxford Spectator,* no. 31 (December 8, 1868; reprinted edition): 181; and *'Varsity* 13, no. 327 (June 9, 1914): 22.

63. "Carfax," "Words and Their Derivations," p. 58.

64. [R. S. Copleston], *Oxford Spectator,* no. 30 (December 1, 1868; reprinted edition): 173; and "X. A." [Christopher Wordsworth], "Tripos Fever," 30–31. For a later example, see "Tripos Fever," *Granta* 2, no. 12 (May 17, 1889): 1.

65. "Oxford and Public Schools Intelligence," *Cambridge Tatler,* no. 3 (March 20, 1877), pp. 9–10.

66. Victor Turner, *The Ritual Process: Structure and Anti-structure* (Chicago: Aldine, 1969), p. 167.

67. "By Way of Introduction," *Bump,* no. 2 (May 20, 1899): 2; and John Aston, "The Imp of Schools," *Bump,* no. 4 (May 23, 1902): 11.

68. "The Cambridge Sphinx," *Cambridge Observer* 1, no. 16 (January 31, 1893): 5.

69. "Editorial Notes," *Undergraduate* 1, no. 13 (June 6, 1888): 193.

70. "X. A." [Christopher Wordsworth], "Tripos Fever," p. 29. For another description of a nightmare, see "Dream before the Coming General Examination," *Momus: A Semi-occasional University Periodical,* no. 2 (April 1, 1868): 13.

71. "Oxford and Public Schools Intelligence," p. 9.

72. *'Varsity* 13, no. 327 (June 9, 1914): 22.

73. On this cultural tendency, see John M. MacKenzie, "The Imperial Pioneer and Hunter and the British Masculine Stereotype in Late Victorian and Edwardian Times," in *Manliness and Morality: Middle-Class Masculinity in Britain and America, 1800–1940,* ed. J. A. Mangan and James Walvin (New York: St. Martin's, 1987), pp. 176–198; and Kelly Boyd, "Exemplars and Ingrates: Imperialism and the Boys' Story Paper, 1880–1930," *Historical Research* 67, no. 163 (June 1994): 143–155.

74. On different manifestations of this soldier ideal in the Victorian and Edwardian eras, see Graham Dawson, *Soldier Heroes: British Adventure, Empire, and the Imagining of Masculinities* (London: Routledge, 1994); and Joseph Kestner, *Masculinities in Victorian Painting* (Aldershot, U.K.: Scolar, 1995), pp. 48–79.

75. "Thoughts That Occur. 'The Schools,'" *'Varsity* 8, no. 17 (April 29, 1909): 501–502; and "E. R. W." (Exeter College), "Sequel to 'Parva Licet Componere Magnis'; or, the LARKY Gownsman in for 'Greats,'" *College Rhymes,* no. 3 (1862): 123. On children's literature, see Kathryn Castle, *Britannia's Children: Reading Colonialism through Children's Books and Magazines* (Manchester: Manchester University Press, 1996).

76. "Elegy on an Undergraduate Graveyard," *Snarl,* no. 2 (November 14, 1899): 15.

77. [Hugh Reginald Haweis], "Editor's Address," *Lion University Magazine,* no. 1 (May 1858): 5; "Editorial," *Pageant Post,* June 1907, pp. 2–3; and "The Ordinary Undergraduate," *Rattle* 1, no. 3 (February 27, 1886), p. 3.

78. "The Ordinary Undergraduate"; and "Manners Maketh Man," *Screed* 1, no. 1 (November 11, 1899): 5.

79. Mrinalini Sinha, *Colonial Masculinity: The "Manly Englishman" and the "Effeminate Bengali" in the Late Nineteenth Century* (Manchester: Manchester University Press, 1995), p. 112.

80. Everett, *On the Cam,* p. 92.

81. "Thoughts on the Christmas Vacation," *College Rhymes,* no. 6 (1865): 32; and " . . . Qui honore non ambiunt," *New Cut,* May 1914, p. 39.

82. "To My Pen. (Picked Up in the New Schools)," *Isis,* no. 4 (June 8, 1892): 28.

83. On these events, see Brooke, *A History of the University of Cambridge: 1870–1900,* pp. 324–325.

84. "Nemo," "Voices from 'The Schools,' No. II," *Great Tom: A University Magazine,* no. 2 (June 1861): 85.

85. "Thoughts That Occur," *'Varsity* 6, no. 23 (June 13, 1907): 347.

86. Everett, *On the Cam,* p. 66.

87. "Tripos Fever," *Granta,* p. 1; and "Lights of a Moderator," *Momus: A Semi-occasional University Periodical,* no. 1 (March 3, 1866): 5.

88. For other examples of the war metaphor, see "Epitaph on a Departed Long Vacation"; and "X. Y. B.," "Objectless," *College Rhymes,* no. 8 (1867): 72.

89. "A Schools Ditty. AIR—'Three little maids from schools.'" *Rattle* 2, no. 7 (February 23, 1887): 4.

90. "Ballade of the Mods. Man," *Bulldog* 1, no. 2 (March 13, 1896): 38.

91. [H. T. Sheringham], "The Classical Tripos," *Bubble: A May Week Magazine,* June 10, 1898, p. 14.

92. "A Causerie," *Pink for the May Week,* no. 1 (June 5, 1899): 2. For another Cambridge example of this contrast, see Rotundus, "Oxford Letter," *Cambridge Tatler,* no. 10 (May 29, 1877): 12.

93. See, for example, an excerpt from G. W. E. Russell's *Social Silhouettes* that appeared in *In Praise of Oxford: An Anthology in Prose and Verse,* ed. Thomas Seccombe and H. Spencer Scott (London: Constable, 1912), 2:445.

94. Dickens, "A Dictionary of the University of Oxford," p. 119.

95. Everett, *On the Cam,* p. 92.

96. W. J. Reader, *Professional Men: The Rise of the Professional Class in Nineteenth-Century England* (New York: Basic Books, 1966), pp. 100–115.

97. Dickens, "A Dictionary of the University of Oxford," p. 119.

98. "Thoughts That Occur. 'The Schools,'" p. 501.

99. "Advice to Scholars," *Playmates: The Oxford "Chums,"* May 1909, p. 19.

100. "Tripos Fever," *Granta* 2, no. 12, p. 1.

101. "Thoughts That Occur. 'The Schools,'" p. 501. For other examples, see "Cambridge and Competition," *Granta* 1, no. 3 (February 1, 1889): 3; and "The Futility of Examinations," *Granta* 5, no. 89 (June 4, 1892): 357–358.

102. Arthur Clement Hilton to his mother, November 25, 1870, in *The Works of Arthur Clement Hilton,* p. 59; and Edward Jupp to a sister, November 1868, *Correspondence of a Junior Student of Christchurch Oxford, in the Years 1868–1870* (Blackheath: privately printed, 1871), p. 29.

103. "The Questionist's Vision," *Cambridge Terminal Magazine,* no. 3 (April 1859): 107.

104. "A Letter," *Isis,* no. 2 (May 11, 1892): 15.

105. These roles are discussed in John Tosh, "Domesticity and Manliness in the Victorian Middle Class: The Family of Edward White Benson," in *Manful Assertions: Masculinities in Britain since 1800,* ed. Michael Roper and John Tosh (London: Routledge, 1991), pp. 59–65.

106. "P. M. W.," "The Song of the Shirk," p. 26; and "Apologetically Dedicated to the Memory of the Late Charles Wolfe," *College Rhymes,* no. 6 (1865): 49.

107. "F. Anstey" [Thomas Anstey Guthrie], *A Long Retrospect*, p. 100.

108. John Williams, *"Is My Son Likely to Pass?" Or, A Few Words to Parents upon the Most Prevalent Intellectual Diseases Incident to School and College Life: With Suggestions as to Their Treatment and Cure: Also, An Appendix Containing Letters on the Subject of Classical Education* (London: Rivingtons, 1864), p. 15.

109. Herbert Newman Mozley, "The Speech Delivered on June 13th, 1883, before the Referees (Appointed by Grace of the Senate, May 31st) in the Case of Mr. R. P. N. Downing of Emmanuel College," p. 11, in *The Downing Translation Papers*, Cambridge University Library, Cam.c.882.44.

110. S. P. Downing to W. Chawner, June 1, 1880, Emmanuel College Archives, Cambridge.

111. T. Hyde Hills, "Certificate of Health for R. Downing, February 26, 1881," Emmanuel College Archives, Cambridge.

112. See George S. R. Kitson Clark, *The Making of Victorian England* (Cambridge, Mass.: Harvard University Press, 1962), pp. 255–260; and Soffer, *Discipline and Power*, pp. 22, 157.

113. Samuel Penrose Downing, *The Late Classical Tripos. Irresponsibility of Examiners in Accusing Candidates of Unfair Practices. An Appeal to the Chancellor, the Vice-Chancellor, the Council and the Masters and Fellows of the University of Cambridge* (Sutton Waldron Rectory, Shaftesbury: privately printed, April 1882), p. 4; and Reginald P. N. Downing, *The Late Classical Tripos Examination* (Sutton Waldron Rectory, Shaftesbury: privately printed: April 1882).

114. S. Downing, *The Late Classical Tripos*, p. 8.

115. Ibid., p. 3.

116. Samuel Penrose Downing, *The Classical Tripos Enquiry. Irresponsibility of Examiners in Accusing Candidates of Unfair Practices: A Second Appeal* (Sutton Waldron Rectory, Shaftesbury: privately printed, October 1882), pp. 27–29.

117. S. P. Downing to W. Chawner, March 6, 1882, Emmanuel College Archives, Cambridge.

118. Quoted by Herbert Newman Mozley in his "The Speech Delivered on June 13th, 1883," p. 12.

119. S. P. Downing to W. Chawner, April 20, 1882, Emmanuel College Archives, Cambridge; and S. Downing, *The Classical Tripos Enquiry*, p. 5. On the importance of the concept of English liberty to definitions of the British nation, see Stephen Heathorn, *For Home, Country, and Race: Constructing Gender, Class, and Englishness in the Elementary School, 1880–1914* (Toronto: University of Toronto Press, 2000), pp. 56–84.

120. S. Downing, *The Late Classical Tripos*, p. 19.

121. S. Downing, *The Classical Tripos Enquiry*, p. 5.

122. S. Downing, *The Late Classical Tripos*, p. 9.

123. Ibid., p. 13.

124. Mozley, "The Speech Delivered on June 13th, 1883," pp. 4, 12.

125. Herbert Norman Mozley, "A Supplementary Statement of the Facts Relating to Mr. Downing's Case, November 1883," p. 6, in *The Downing Translation Papers*.

126. R. P. N. Downing to W. Chawner, November 20, 1883, Emmanuel College Archives, Cambridge.

127. R. P. N. Downing to the reverend, the vice-chancellor of the University of Cambridge, November 15, 1883, in *The Downing Translation Papers*.

128. "Editorial," *Pageant Post*, June 1907, p. 3.

5. "Impervious to the Gentler Sex?"

1. Max Beerbohm, *Zuleika Dobson* (New York: Random House, 1926), p. 111.

2. On the psychological and sexual dimensions of gender identity formation,

see John Tosh, "What Should Historians Do with Masculinity? Reflections on Nine-teenth-Century Britain," *History Workshop Journal,* no. 38 (autumn 1994): 179–202. J. A. Mangan's work on sport has focused more on the spread of the athletic ideal than on the gendered rituals or psychological implications of university athleticism. See J. A. Mangan, "Lamentable Barbarians and Pitiful Sheep: Rhetoric of Protest and Pleas-ure in Late Victorian and Edwardian 'Oxbridge,'" *Victorian Studies* 34, no. 4 (summer 1991): 473–489; and J. A. Mangan, "'Oars and the Man': Pleasure and Purpose in Victorian and Edwardian Cambridge," *British Journal of Sports History* 1, no. 3 (Decem-ber 1984): 245–271.

3. Sociologists and anthropologists of sport have helped to define the parameters of the field. See Michael Messner, "Boyhood, Organized Sports, and the Construc-tion of Masculinities," *Journal of Contemporary Ethnography* 18, no. 4 (January 1990): 416–444.

4. J. A. Mangan's *Athleticism in the Victorian and Edwardian Public School: The Emergence and Consolidation of an Educational Ideology* (Cambridge: Cambridge Univer-sity Press, 1981) remains the best study of the topic. On the obsession with bodily health, see Michael Anton Budd, *The Sculpture Machine: Physical Culture and Body Poli-tics in the Age of Empire* (New York: New York University Press, 1997); and Bruce Haley, *The Healthy Body and Victorian Culture* (Cambridge, Mass.: Harvard University Press, 1978).

5. Richard Holt, *Sport and the British: A Modern History* (Oxford: Oxford Univer-sity Press, 1990), pp. 83–86.

6. Patrick McDevitt, "Muscular Catholicism: Nationalism, Masculinity, and Gaelic Team Sports, 1884–1916," *Gender and History* 9, no. 2 (August 1997): 262–284.

7. See "Modern Oxford Reformers," *Pageant Post,* June 1907, p. 8; and "The Corpse in the Cargo (Borrowed from Ibsen)," *Snarl,* no. 2 (November 14, 1899): 14.

8. One Oxford report from the early twentieth century reflects the predomi-nance of these fields in the career paths of scholarship students. See *Return of Entrance Scholarships and Exhibitions Awarded to Students Beginning in the University in October 1911* (Oxford: n.p., n.d.).

9. On the relationship between sport and empire, see J. A. Mangan, ed., *The Cultural Bond: Sport, Empire, and Society* (London: Frank Cass, 1992); and J. A. Mangan, *The Games Ethic and Imperialism: Aspects of the Diffusion of an Ideal* (Harmondsworth, U.K.: Viking, 1986). On the use of gender in delineating differences between colo-nizers and colonized, see Mrinalini Sinha, *Colonial Masculinity: The "Manly Englishman" and the "Effeminate Bengali" in the Late Nineteenth Century* (Manchester: Manchester Uni-versity Press, 1995).

10. "As Others See Us. I. By a Belgian," *'Varsity* 1, no. 9 (April 23, 1901): 133.

11. Judith Butler's discussion of gender as "always a doing" seems to have par-ticular explanatory value in considering the phenomenon of the boat races. See her *Gender Trouble: Feminism and the Subversion of Identity* (New York: Routledge, 1990), pp. 25, 33, 136, 140–141.

12. See Jonathan Ned Katz, "The Invention of Heterosexuality," *Socialist Review* 20, no. 1 (January–March 1990): 7–34; and Jonathan Ned Katz, *The Invention of Heterosexuality* (New York: Dutton, 1995). See also Michel Foucault, *The History of Sexuality, Volume 1: An Introduction,* trans. Robert Hurley (New York: Vintage Books, 1990).

13. On the ambivalent response to the demands of domesticity, see John Tosh, *A Man's Place: Masculinity and the Middle-Class Home in Victorian England* (New Haven: Yale University Press, 1999), pp. 170–194. For an American example, see Randy D. McBee, "'He Likes Women More Than He Likes Drink and That Is Quite Unusual': Working-Class Social Clubs, Male Culture, and Heterosocial Relations in the United States, 1920s–1930s," *Gender and History* 11, no. 1 (April 1999): 84–112.

14. On ways in which the curriculum at Victorian Oxford could provide similar opportunities, see Linda Dowling, *Hellenism and Homosexuality in Victorian Oxford* (Ithaca, N.Y.: Cornell University Press, 1994).

15. For a discussion of some of these ideas, see Roberta J. Park, "Biological Thought, Athletics, and the Formation of a 'Man of Character,' 1830–1900," in *Manliness and Morality: Middle-Class Masculinity in Britain and America, 1800–1940,* ed. J. A. Mangan and James Walvin (New York: St. Martin's, 1987), p. 11.

16. Holt, *Sport and the British,* p. 3.

17. Christopher N. L. Brooke and Roger Highfield, *Oxford and Cambridge,* photographs by Wim Swaan (Cambridge: Cambridge University Press, 1988), p. 276.

18. W. E. Sherwood, *Oxford Rowing: A History of Boat-Racing at Oxford from the Earliest Times with a Record of the Races* (Oxford: Henry Frowde, 1900), p. 5.

19. Ibid., p. 7.

20. While the origins of the term "May Week" are apparent, "Eights" requires some explanation. It refers to the number of rowers in each boat. This figure does not, of course, include the coxswain who called strokes.

21. *Boating Life at Oxford. With Notes on Oxford Training and Rowing at the Universities* (London: James Hogg and Son, 1868), p. 24.

22. John Venn, *Early Collegiate Life* (Cambridge: W. Heffer and Sons, 1913), pp. 266–267.

23. See Christopher N. L. Brooke, *A History of the University of Cambridge: 1870–1990,* vol. 4 of *A History of the University of Cambridge,* ed. Christopher N. L. Brooke (Cambridge: Cambridge University Press, 1993), p. 298. H. C. Porter has detailed some of these developments in his "May Week," *Cambridge,* no. 20 (1987): 45–52.

24. "Commemoration," *Oxford Undergraduate's Journal,* no. 9 (June 13, 1866): 65.

25. "Commemoration," *Oxford Undergraduate's Journal,* no. 34 (June 10, 1868): 297. On some of the problems posed to men by women in public, see Erika Diane Rappaport, *Shopping for Pleasure: Women in the Making of London's West End* (Princeton: Princeton University Press, 2000).

26. Diary of Anna Florence Ward, Magdalen College Archives, Oxford, MS 618, pp. 85, 90–100.

27. *Isis,* no. 5 (June 20, 1892), cover.

28. "Editorial Notes," *Undergraduate* 1, no. 10 (May 16, 1888): 145.

29. "Events of the Week," *Beldragon: The May Week Magazine,* no. 1 (June 7, 1895): 14–15. For an Oxford example, see "Engagements," *Barge,* no. 2 (May 19, 1904): 2.

30. H. C. Porter, "May Week," p. 51.

31. *May Term Festivities,* nos. 1–4 (Cambridge: John P. Gray, 1891–1894).

32. "To All Sorts and Conditions of Men," *Beldragon: The May Week Magazine,* no. 1 (June 7, 1895): 1.

33. Harry C. Marillier, *University Magazines and Their Makers. By Harry Currie Marillier, Knyght Erraunt to Ye Sette of Odd Volumes* (London: Bedford, 1899), p. 49.

34. "By Way of Introduction," *Bump,* no. 1 (May 21, 1898): 4.

35. "The Summer Eights. Charts for Marking the Changes of Position Daily," *Bump,* no. 3 (May 16, 1901): 11; and "Chart of the Summer Eights, 1912," *Buller,* Eights Week Number (May 1913), n.p., page labeled "Helen."

36. "Rowing. The Eights," *Undergraduate* 1, no. 10 (May 16, 1888): 151. For other examples of this, see "Boating," *Blue 'Un: A Journal of University Life,* no. 1 (May 31, 1884): 4; and "On the River. The Coming Bumps," *Bump,* no. 3 (May 16, 1901): 10.

37. Descriptions of undergraduate pluck were especially prominent. One contributor to an Oxford publication, for example, congratulated the Cambridge University boat for a "very plucky fight" in 1893. See "The Boat Races and Sports," *Blue: A 'Varsity Journal* 3, no. 1 (April 25, 1893): 6.

38. "Boating," p. 4.

39. "On and about 'The Cam,'" *Cam: A "May Week" Magazine,* no. 1 (June 9, 1894): 1; and "Pausanias at the Togger," *'Varsity* 1, no. 7 (March 5, 1901): 97.

40. "Rowing. The 'Varsity Eight. Frere Joins His Confreres," *Undergraduate* 1, no. 7 (March 6, 1888): 99.

41. "Editorial," *Barge,* no. 2 (May 19, 1904): 1.

42. "Haddon Hall," "Opening Verse," *Mushroom: A May Week Magazine* 1, no. 1 (June 8, 1894): 1.

43. See Butler, *Gender Trouble,* p. 25.

44. Charles Dickens, "The Dictionary of the University of Cambridge," in *Dickens's Dictionary of Oxford and Cambridge* (London: Macmillan, 1884), p. 12.

45. "On and about 'The Cam,'" p. 1. For other descriptions of these divisions, see "O. C." [A. H. Lawrence], *Reminiscences of Cambridge Life* (London: privately printed, 1889), p. 33; and "Ideals, Some Pessimism, and a Toast," *Isis,* no. 268 (May 23, 1903): 307–308.

46. George Nugent Bankes, *A Cambridge Staircase: By the Author of "A Day of My Life at Eton," "About Some Fellows," Etc.* (London: Sampson Low, Marston, Searle and Rivington, 1883), p. 39.

47. On this active/passive dichotomy in defining normative heterosexuality, see Philip Hubbard, "Desire/Disgust: Mapping the Moral Contours of Heterosexuality," *Progress in Human Geography* 24, no. 2 (2000): 197.

48. "On and about 'The Cam,'" p. 1. For an earlier example that similarly attempts to define gendered roles, see "Cam-bridge," *May Bee,* no. 7 (June 11, 1884): 102–104.

49. "The Aquatic Derby," *Light Blue Incorporated with the Light Green,* no. 1 (May 1873): 21.

50. "Robert Southey," "The Battle of the Bumping," *New Rattle,* supplement, May 19, 1891, p. 2.

51. "The Oxford and Cambridge Boat Race, 1875," in *"Squibs and Crackers": Miscellaneous Cambridge Papers, 1799–1904, Collected and Compiled by J. W. Clark,* item 124b, Cambridge University Library, Cam. a. 500.9.

52. [George Otto Trevelyan], "Trinity Boat Song," *Bear University Magazine,* no. 1 (October 1858): 26.

53. See Sinha, *Colonial Masculinity.* On exceptions to this general rule (especially as it relates to the martial attributes that the British admired in Punjabi Sikhs and Nepalese Gurkhas), see Heather Streets, "'The Right Stamp of Man': Military Imperatives and Popular Imperialism in Late Victorian Britain" (Ph.D. diss., Duke University, 1998).

54. "On the River. The Torpids," *'Varsity* 1, no. 4 (February 12, 1901): 58.

55. "University Types: No. II—The Rowing Man," *New Rattle* 2, no. 3 (May 16, 1891): 2.

56. On militarism in the scouting movement, see John Springhall, "The Boy Scouts, Class, and Militarism in Relation to British Youth Movements, 1908–1930," *International Review of Social History* 16, part 2 (1971): 125–158.

57. On public schools, see Mangan, *Athleticism in the Victorian and Edwardian Public School,* pp. 191–196; and J. A. Mangan, "Games Field and Battlefield: A Romantic Alliance in Verse and the Creation of Militaristic Masculinity," in *Making Men: Rugby and Masculine Identity,* ed. John Nauright and Timothy J. L. Chandler (London: Frank Cass, 1996), pp. 140–157.

58. "On the River," *'Varsity* 1, no. 2 (January 29, 1901): 27.

59. "A Speech in Season: *After Thucydides,*" *Rattle* 1, no. 3 (February 27, 1886): 2–3.

60. "A Famous Victory. —(*A Fragment of Ancient History*)," *Rattle* 2, no. 1 (February 16, 1887): 2–3.

61. See "A Tub-Foursman," "A Triumphal Ode," *Undergraduate* 1, no. 18 (November 15, 1888): 282–283; and "A Lately Discovered Fragment of Thucydides," *New Rattle* 1, no. 3 (May 24, 1890): 3.

62. Graham Dawson, *Soldier Heroes: British Adventure, Empire, and the Imagining of Masculinities* (London: Routledge, 1994).

63. "Little John" [Wilson W. E. Morrison], "Show Sunday," *Shotover Papers* 1, no. 6 (May 30, 1874): 81.

64. See, for example, "Advice to Our Visitors," *Wasp,* no. 1 (June 12, 1891): 3.

65. On chivalry, see "Sketches of the Ordinary and the Extraordinary. The Ordinary Girl," *Rattle* 1, no. 1 (February 25, 1886): 2. For an infrequent critique of this sort of chivalry, see "Oxford," *Cambridge Observer* 1, no. 5 (May 31, 1892): 10.

66. George Nugent Bankes, *Cambridge Trifles; or, Splutterings from an Undergraduate Pen* (London: Sampson Low, Marston, Searle and Rivington, 1881), p. 68.

67. "A Guide to Oxford," *Ye Rounde Table: An Oxford and Cambridge Magazine* 1, no. 3 (March 16, 1878): 46.

68. "Editorial," *Meteor,* no. 1 (May 1911): 1.

69. "Five Bumps," *Bump,* no. 5 (May 23, 1903): 4.

70. For another example of this kind of contrast, see "Editorial," *Barge,* no. 2.

71. On improvements to rooms and securing accommodations, see "Our Visitors," *Cambridge Tatler,* no. 9 (May 22, 1877): 1; and "Notice on Advertising," *Spirit Lamp* 1, no. 1 (May 6, 1892), back cover. On displaying Oxford, see "Guy Thorne," "Editorial," *Barge,* May 1905, p. 1.

72. T. S., "People Up," *Undergraduate* 1, no. 15 (October 25, 1888): 237–238.

73. Tosh, *A Man's Place,* pp. 170–194. On settlement houses, see Seth Koven, "From Rough Lads to Hooligans: Boy Life, National Culture, and Social Reform," in *Nationalisms and Sexualities,* ed. Andrew Parker et al. (New York: Routledge, 1992), pp. 369–371.

74. C. B. Gull, "Family Correspondence," *Eights Week Opinions,* May 20, 1909, pp. 20–23.

75. "Alphabet Antics in Oxenford," *Bump,* Eights Week Number (May 1909): 12.

76. "H. R. Playfair," "What Can We Do with Mamma?" *Octopus,* no. 5 (May 28, 1895): 1–2. The problems posed by these demands and students' desire to impress are also discussed in "Growler," *May Term and Maidens* (Cambridge, 1901), pp. 11–17.

77. "The Only Boat Left," *Cam: A "May Week" Magazine,* no. 1 (June 9, 1894): 22; and George Nugent Bankes, *Cambridge Trifles,* p. 67.

78. "Are We Really Fond of Our People?" *Granta* 5, no. 87 (May 21, 1892): 325–326.

79. "A. R." "'He Jests at Scars That ——,'" *Cam: A "May Week" Magazine,* no. 1 (June 9, 1894): 12. On this image in British culture, see Susan P. Casteras, *Images of Victorian Womanhood in English Art* (Rutherford, N.J.: Associated University Presses, 1987), p. 166; David Holbrook, *Images of Women in Literature* (New York: New York University Press, 1989), pp. 155–190, 267–268; and, on the range of ideals and deviations in the Victorian period, Lynda Nead, *Myths of Sexuality: Representations of Women in Victorian Britain* (Oxford: Basil Blackwell, 1988).

80. "Are We Really Fond of Our People?" p. 325; and "A Romance of the May Term. Chapter 1," *Momus: A Semi-occasional University Periodical,* no. 2 (April 1, 1868): 15.

81. "Welcome," *Granta* 12, no. 264 (June 10, 1899): 369–370.

82. Bankes, *Cambridge Trifles,* p. 67.

83. "Notes from Cambridge," *Souvenir,* June 19, 1893, p. 7.

84. "At the Breakfast Table," *Blue: A 'Varsity Journal* 1, no. 6 (May 30, 1893): 43.

85. This shift in outlook with respect to women, as a component of the youthful

male experience, is discussed in E. Anthony Rotundo, *American Manhood: Transformations in Masculinity from the Revolution to the Modern Era* (New York: Basic Books, 1993), pp. 104–108.

86. "A. R." "He Jests at Scars That ———," p. 12.

87. "Faites vos jeux, messieurs," *Bubble: A May Week Magazine,* June 10, 1898, p. 5. On the development of the ideal, see Leonore Davidoff and Catherine Hall, *Family Fortunes: Men and Women of the English Middle Class, 1780–1850* (Chicago: University of Chicago Press, 1987).

88. See John Tosh, "Imperial Masculinity and the Flight from Domesticity in Britain, 1880–1914," in *Gender and Colonialism,* ed. Timothy P. Foley et al. (Galway: Galway University Press, 1995, pp. 72–85); and Tosh, *A Man's Place,* pp. 179–194. For a feminist perspective on how "compulsory heterosexuality" has functioned as an oppressive force, especially in the lives of lesbians, see Adrienne Rich, "Compulsory Heterosexuality and Lesbian Existence," *Signs: Journal of Women in Culture and Society* 5, no. 4 (summer 1980): 631–660.

89. "The Athletics," *Momus: A Semi-occasional University Periodical,* no. 3 (March 15, 1869): 18. The masculine character of these athletic events was also contrasted, on occasion, with feminine interest in fashion. See [P. Comyns-Carr], "The Ladies Letter," *Octopus,* no. 2 (May 24, 1895): 10; and "The Inevitable Ladies Letter," *Bump,* no. 1 (May 21, 1898): 9–10.

90. "Campaigners," *New Rattle* 2, no. 1 (May 14, 1891): 3.

91. "Warning to Visitors," *Undergraduate* 1, no. 11 (May 23, 1888): 174–175.

92. "Advice to Our Visitors"; and "Guide to Cambridge," *Half Blue,* May Term, 1896, pp. 1–3.

93. "Peggy," "What I Think of Undergraduates. [By an Eights Week Girl]," *'Varsity* 6, no. 21 (May 30, 1907): 324. For another example, see "Robert Southey," "The Battle of the Bumping."

94. "Our Freshman's Term," *Cambridge Terminal Magazine,* no. 3 (April 1859): 108–111. See also [T. H. White], *Oxford Spectator,* no. 4 (December 3, 1867): 2.

95. "N." [V. H. Stanton], "The *Tatler's* 'Paternal' to the Freshman," *Tatler in Cambridge,* no. 21 (October 16, 1871): 3.

96. "Cliques," *Cambridge Tatler,* no. 2 (March 13, 1877): 3; and "University Types, No. 3—Beefsteak Rowley," *Cambridge Tatler,* no. 6 (May 1, 1877): 7.

97. For another example, see "Alligators on the Banks of the Isis," *New Rattle* 1, no. 3 (May 24, 1890): 2–3.

98. "The Galley Slave," *Spirit Lamp* 1, no. 1 (May 6, 1892): 3.

99. "Of Skulls and Numskulls," *Spirit Lamp* 1, no. 3 (May 20, 1892): 43.

100. The importance of hierarchies in definitions of masculinity is noted in Tosh, "What Should Historians Do with Masculinity?" pp. 190–191.

101. For one discussion of this development, see Jeffrey Weeks, *Coming Out: Homosexual Politics in Britain, from the Nineteenth Century to the Present* (London: Quartet, 1977). George Chauncey discusses the consequences of this pathologizing in his examination of gay culture in New York City: *Gay New York: Gender, Urban Culture, and the Making of the Gay Male World, 1890–1940* (New York: Basic Books, 1994). Rictor Norton has attempted to shift the focus of the "queer" historical agenda away from the "invention of the modern homosexual" by assuming the position of "queer cultural essentialist" in his book *The Myth of the Modern Homosexual: Queer History and the Search for Cultural Unity* (London: Cassell, 1997).

102. Other authors have noted features of this dynamic. See, for example, Eve K. Sedgwick, *Between Men: English Literature and Male Homosocial Desire* (New York: Columbia University Press, 1985).

103. "The Ordinary Undergraduate," *Rattle* 1, no. 3 (February 27, 1886): 3.

104. For one example, see "P. L. O.," "Meleager," *Spirit Lamp* 1, no. 5 (June 3, 1892): 65.

105. On this process, see Katz, *The Invention of Heterosexuality,* pp. 18–32, 83–112.

106. "Isis Idols. No. CCCL. Mr. Albert Mason Stevens, Rhodes Scholar, Balliol College; O.U.A.C.," *Isis,* no. 374 (November 23, 1907): 107.

107. "The Brand of Isis," *Oxford Point of View* 1, no. 3 (October 1902): 168.

108. On the multiplicity of subversive meanings in a range of cultural images, see Martin Duberman, ed. *Queer Representations: Reading Lives, Reading Cultures* (New York: New York University Press, 1997); and Eve K. Sedgwick, *Tendencies* (Durham, N.C.: Duke University Press, 1993), p. 3. On the various ways in which desire between men could be expressed and portrayed, see Richard Dellamora, *Masculine Desire: The Sexual Politics of Victorian Aestheticism* (Chapel Hill: University of North Carolina Press, 1990).

109. "Things That Go Bump on the River," *Word,* no. 24 (May 27–June 9, 1992): 18; and Ramachandra Guha, "Cricket and Politics in Colonial India," *Past and Present* 161 (November 1998): 157.

6. Girl Graduates and Colonial Students

A portion of the latter section of this chapter appeared as "'The Foreign Element': Newcomers and the Rhetoric of Race, Nation, and Empire in 'Oxbridge' Undergraduate Culture, 1850-1920," *Journal of British Studies* 37, no. 1 (January 1998): 54-90. University of Chicago Press. © 1998 by the North American Conference on British Studies. All rights reserved.

1. In addition to the work on the history of women's higher education cited in the introduction, see Gillian Sutherland, "The Movement for the Higher Education of Women: Its Social and Intellectual Context in England c. 1840–80," in *Politics and Social Change in Modern Britain: Essays Presented to A. F. Thompson,* ed. P. J. Waller (New York: St. Martin's, 1987), pp. 91–116; and Martha Vicinus, *Independent Women: Work and Community for Single Women, 1850–1920* (Chicago: University of Chicago Press, 1985), pp. 121–162.

2. Antoinette Burton notes the importance of exploring this dynamic in "Colonial Encounters in Late-Victorian England: Pandita Ramabai at Cheltenham and Wantage, 1883–6," *Feminist Review,* no. 49 (spring 1995): 29–49. For discussions of reversed colonial encounters, see Antoinette Burton, *At the Heart of the Empire: Indians and the Colonial Encounter in Late-Victorian Britain* (Berkeley: University of California Press, 1998); and Angela Woollacott, *To Try Her Fortune in London: Australian Women, Colonialism, and Modernity* (New York: Oxford University Press, 2001).

3. On whiteness as a social construct, see Woollacott, *To Try Her Fortune in London,* pp. 12–15, 142–143, 187–188. For an important American interpretation, see David E. Roediger, *The Wages of Whiteness: Race and the Making of the American Working Class,* rev. ed. (London: Verso, 1999), pp. 5–11, 21, 66–71.

4. Vera Brittain used the word "unofficial" to indicate the ambiguous status of women at Oxford prior to 1920. See her *The Women at Oxford: A Fragment of History* (London: Harrap, 1960), p. 70.

5. On the numbers relating to female students, see Janet Howarth, "Women," in *The Twentieth Century,* ed. Brian Harrison, vol. 8 of *The History of the University of Oxford,* ed. T. H. Aston (Oxford: Clarendon, 1994), p. 350; and Christopher N. L. Brooke, *A History of the University of Cambridge: 1870–1990,* vol. 4 of *A History of the University of Cambridge,* ed. Christopher N. L. Brooke (Cambridge: Cambridge University Press, 1993), pp. 302, 331. For figures on the total undergraduate populations, see A. J. Engel, *From Clergyman to Don: The Rise of the Academic Profession in Nineteenth-*

Century Oxford (Oxford: Oxford University Press, 1983), p. 291; and H. C. Porter, "May Week," *Cambridge,* no. 20 (1987): 49.

6. Kali Israel, *Names and Stories: Emilia Dilke and Victorian Culture* (New York: Oxford University Press, 1999), p. 94.

7. See Sara Delamont, *Knowledgeable Women: Structuralism and the Reproduction of Elites* (London: Routledge, 1989), pp. 65–160; Sutherland, "The Movement for the Higher Education of Women," pp. 91–116; and Vicinus, *Independent Women,* pp. 123–135. For a discussion of this process at other universities, see Carol Dyhouse, *No Distinction of Sex? Women in British Universities, 1870–1939* (London: UCL Press, 1995).

8. On these predictions, see Susan Kingsley Kent, *Sex and Suffrage in Britain, 1860–1914* (Princeton: Princeton University Press, 1987), pp. 43–49; and Joan N. Burstyn, *Victorian Education and the Ideal of Womanhood* (London: Croom Helm, 1980), pp. 85–98.

9. Carol Dyhouse notes this general omission in her *No Distinction of Sex?* p. 5. Her recent work on London medical schools in the interwar period looks more closely at one type of masculine culture. See Dyhouse, "Women Students and the London Medical Schools, 1914–39: The Anatomy of a Masculine Culture," *Gender and History* 10, no. 1 (April 1998): 110–132.

10. Vicinus, *Independent Women,* pp. 121–162; and Howarth, "Women," pp. 345–375.

11. On the problems of space, see "Review of the Term," *Girton Review,* no. 3 (December 1882): 2; and "Review of the Term," *Girton Review,* no. 4 (March 1883): 2. On insufficient library resources, see "Correspondence," *Girton Review,* no. 1 (March 1882): 15.

12. On this, see Deborah Gorham, "A Woman at Oxford: Vera Brittain's Somerville Experience," *Historical Studies in Education* 3, no.1 (spring 1991): 1–2.

13. See, for example, "Correspondence," *Girton Review,* no. 16 (March 1887): 16; and "Intercollegiate Letters," *Girton Review,* no. 11 (July 1885): 7–8.

14. "A Plea for Societies," *Girton Review,* no. 11 (July 1885): 5–6.

15. See, for example, the reports of clubs in *Girton Review,* no. 9 (December 1884).

16. See "A Tripos Candidate," "Correspondence," *Girton Review,* no. 3 (December 1882): 15; and "Three Victims out of Seventy," "Correspondence," *Girton Review,* no. 9 (December 1884): 16.

17. "Newnham," *Cambridge Observer* 1, no. 5 (May 31, 1892): 9.

18. Edith Terry, "Social Customs," in *A Newnham Anthology,* ed. Ann Phillips (Cambridge: Cambridge University Press, 1979), p. 54.

19. "Review of the Term," *Girton Review,* no. 2 (July 1882): 2.

20. Emily Elizabeth Constance Jones, *As I Remember: An Autobiographical Ramble* (London: A. and C. Black, 1922), p. 55.

21. J. G. Fitch, "Women and the Universities," *Contemporary Review* 58 (August 1890): 248.

22. "A Song of Degrees," *Girton Review,* no. 7 (March 1884): 20.

23. Jane E. Wilson, "Prize Song," *Girton Review,* no. 16 (March 1887): 8.

24. "Senior Soph," "Women's Degrees," *Cambridge Fortnightly,* no. 3 (February 21, 1888): 43–46.

25. "Editorial Notes," *Undergraduate* 1, no. 8 (May 2, 1888): 115.

26. "Women's Degrees at the Union," *Bulldog* 1, no. 2 (March 6, 1896): 22.

27. On this process, see Angus McLaren, *The Trials of Masculinity: Policing Sexual Boundaries, 1870–1930* (Chicago: University of Chicago Press, 1997).

28. On the impact of the "New Woman," see Elaine Showalter, *Sexual Anarchy: Gender and Culture at the Fin de Siècle* (New York: Viking, 1990), pp. 38–58; Judith Walkowitz, *City of Dreadful Delight: Narratives of Sexual Danger in Late-Victorian London*

(Chicago: University of Chicago Press, 1992), pp. 41–80; and Woollacott, *To Try Her Fortune in London.*

29. Some of the distinctions between the masculine and the feminine were delineated in [Hilaire Belloc], "Genders," *Octopus,* no. 3 (May 25, 1895): 5.

30. "The Sufferance Problem," *Cambridge Magazine* 1, no. 1 (January 20, 1912): 25.

31. For one good example, see "A Day of Her Life," *Undergraduate* 1, no. 9 (May 9, 1888): 131–132.

32. "N" [V. H. Stanton], "On University Women," *Tatler in Cambridge,* no. 76 (May 27, 1872): 61–64.

33. "Cambridge Chit-Chat: Miscellaneous," *Cantab,* no. 1 (April 1873): 92.

34. "The Higher Education of Women," *May Bee,* no. 4 (June 7, 1884): 54.

35. See "From Keble to the House: Somerville," *'Varsity* 1, no. 1 (January 22, 1901): 15; and "From Keble to the House: Lady Margaret Hall," *'Varsity* 1, no. 4 (February 12, 1901): 63.

36. "Villanette," *'Varsity* 1, no. 13 (May 21, 1901): 194.

37. Laurence Fowler and Helen Fowler, eds. *Cambridge Commemorated: An Anthology of University Life* (Cambridge: Cambridge University Press, 1984), p. 235.

38. On this process, see Janet Howarth, "'In Oxford but . . . not of Oxford': The Women's Colleges," in *Nineteenth-Century Oxford, Part 2,* ed. M. G. Brock and M. C. Curthoys, vol. 7 of *The History of the University of Oxford,* ed. T. H. Aston (Oxford: Oxford University Press, 2000), pp. 248–249.

39. Quoted in Jan Morris, ed., *The Oxford Book of Oxford* (Oxford: Oxford University Press, 1978), p. 286.

40. For a discussion of this episode, see Brittain, *The Women at Oxford,* pp. 39–40.

41. "Editorial Notes," *Undergraduate* 1, no. 5 (February 21, 1888): 68. For an expression of support for women at Cambridge, see "Q," "The Women's First Step," *Cambridge Fortnightly,* no. 1 (January 24, 1888): 4–5.

42. "Editorial Notes," *Undergraduate* 1, no. 17 (November 8, 1888): 259–260.

43. "Editorial Notes," *Undergraduate* 1, no. 5, p. 68.

44. Robert Currie, "The Arts and Social Studies, 1914–1939," in *The Twentieth Century,* ed. Harrison, p. 131.

45. The editors of the *Undergraduate* commented on various misrepresentations of the case in the popular press in "What the Papers Say," *Undergraduate* 1, no. 21 (December 6, 1888): 332–333.

46. There is no information on the incident in the archives of New College. Author's correspondence with Caroline Dalton, New College Archivist, September 20, 2000.

47. "Bathurst did not write the paragraph but was the responsible editor of The Undergraduate. He was 'Shank's Mare.'" Falconer Madan, handwritten comments on a copy of *Undergraduate* 1, no. 17 (November 8, 1888): 259, in the collection of the Seeley Mudd Library, Yale University, Lmd 78 +Un25.

48. "University Intelligence," *Times,* December 6, 1888, in *New College Scrapbook,* Bodleian Library, Oxford, G.A. Oxon c. 282.

49. "The 'Row' at Oxford: Strained Relations between the Dons and Undergraduates," *Pall Mall Gazette,* December 3, 1888, in *New College Scrapbook.*

50. "Editorial Notes," *Undergraduate* 1, no. 20 (November 29, 1888): 306.

51. "Notes and News," *Oxford Magazine,* December 5, 1888, in *New College Scrapbook.*

52. "J. F." [Theodore Wilfrid Fry], "Sent Down," *Undergraduate* 1, no. 21 (December 6, 1888): 331.

53. Earl Bathurst, "New College and Mr. Bathurst. To the Editor of the Times," *Times,* December 8, 1888, in *New College Scrapbook.*

54. "The 'Row' at Oxford."

55. See Kent, *Sex and Suffrage in Britain,* pp. 200–203.

56. "Editorial Notes," *Undergraduate* 1, no. 20, gives the figure of 170, while "The 'Row' at Oxford" gives 180.

57. "The 'Row' at Oxford."

58. On this practice, see G. C. Richards, *An Oxonian Looks Back: 1885–1945,* ed. J. F. C. Richards (New York, 1960), p. 51, typescript at the Homer Babbidge Library, University of Connecticut; and "Confidential Printed Letter from V-C to Various Members of Colleges (to Be Addressed in Pen) Relating to "Mock Funerals," March 6, 1908, Oxford University Archives, PR 1/23/8.

59. F. A. Reeve, *Varsity Rags and Hoaxes* (Cambridge: Oleander, 1977), pp. 30–33.

60. See "The 'Row' at Oxford" and "Notes and News." Madan uses the word "boycott" in his marginalia. See Madan, handwritten comments on a copy of *Undergraduate* 1, no. 20, p. 306.

61. See Madan, handwritten comments on a copy of *Undergraduate* 1, no. 20, p. 306; "What the Papers Say," p. 332; and "Notes and News," p. 2.

62. "Down with the Dons! Second Series. Manifesto of the Oxford Undergraduate Revolutionary League, December 1888," in *New College Scrapbook.*

63. Janet Howarth, "'In Oxford but . . . not of Oxford,'" pp. 247, 290–294.

64. "The Question of Degrees," *Fritillary,* no. 5 (June 1895): 78–79.

65. Sedley Taylor Papers, Cambridge University Library, MSS 6093.210, quoted in Rita McWilliams Tullberg, *Women at Cambridge,* rev. ed. (Cambridge: Cambridge University Press, 1998), p. 23; and "Women's Degrees," *Granta* 10, no. 208 (April 24, 1897): 263.

66. On March 3, 1896, Oxford's Congregation had rejected a resolution to admit women to the B. A. by a vote of 215 to 140. Undergraduate opposition was reflected in the Oxford Union, which rejected a motion on the admission of women by a vote of 165 to 55. See Brittain, *The Women at Oxford,* pp. 106–110.

67. McWilliams Tullberg, *Women at Cambridge,* pp. 90–118.

68. *Cambridge Review* 18, no. 456 (May 6, 1897): 322; and "Notes," *Granta* 10, no. 210 (May 8, 1897): 284.

69. "Women's Degrees," p. 264.

70. The editors of the *Granta* chose to introduce their reports on the events leading up to the vote with this particular title. See "The Women's War," *Granta* 10, no. 211 (May 15, 1897): 322–324.

71. "The Two Memorials," *Granta* 10, no. 210 (May 8, 1897): 295–296.

72. "Notes," p. 300.

73. "The Two Memorials," p. 296.

74. *Cambridge Review* 18, no. 456 (May 6, 1897): 322.

75. "The Women's War," p. 322.

76. "To the Senate," *Granta* 10, no. 211 (May 15, 1897): 312.

77. On Wilson's editorship of the *Granta,* see F. A. Rice, *The "Granta" and Its Contributors, 1889–1914* (London: Constable, 1924), p. 26.

78. "The Women's War," p. 322.

79. Ibid., pp. 322–324.

80. These descriptions are drawn from two sources. See "The Women's War," *Granta* 10, no. 212 (May 22, 1897): 334–335; and *Cambridge Review* 18, no. 459 (May 27, 1897): 374–375.

81. McWilliams Tullberg, *Women at Cambridge,* pp. 115, 117–118.

82. *Cambridge Review* 18, no. 459 (May 27, 1897), p. 374.

83. Ibid.

84. Reeve, *Varsity Rags and Hoaxes,* pp. 15–18.

85. *Cambridge Review* 18, no. 459 (May 27, 1897), p. 374.

86. See Brooke, *A History of the University of Cambridge: 1870–1990,* p. 325.

87. *Cambridge Review* 18, no. 459 (May 27, 1897), p. 375.

88. Ibid., p. 376. In the *Granta,* see "The Women's War," *Granta* 10, no. 212, p. 335.

89. William Ridgeway to Falconer Madan, 10 December 1920, in *Material on Women Students.* Bodleian Library, Oxford, G.A. Oxon c. 34.

90. On the experience of travel to Britain from Australia, see Woollacott, *To Try Her Fortune in London,* pp. 20–46.

91. One recent study has tackled the subject of Indian students in Great Britain. See Shompa Lahiri, *Indians in Britain: Anglo-Indian Encounters, Race, and Identity, 1880–1930* (London: Frank Cass, 2000). While Lahiri notes the extent to which Indians encountered cultural arrogance, racial discrimination, and social derision in Britain, she neither dissects the institutional cultures that these students encountered nor addresses how racism operated both as a real force and as a discursive construction.

92. On the full student population, see Brooke, *A History of the University of Cambridge: 1870–1990,* p. 594; Engel, *From Clergyman to Don,* p. 291; and H. C. Porter, "May Week," p. 49. Between 1871 and 1893, 49 Indian students matriculated at Oxford. A government committee inquiring into the status of Indian students in 1907 reported that 32 were enrolled at Oxford and 87 at Cambridge. See Richard Symonds, *Oxford and Empire: The Last Lost Cause?* (New York: St. Martin's, 1986), p. 257. Numbers at Oxford, not surprisingly, declined during the war. In the Trinity term of 1920, however, the delegates for "Oriental" students reported that the number of students from the "Orient," most of whom were from India, stood at 74. By the following autumn, that number had risen to 123. See Delegates for Oriental Students, Minutes of Meetings, 1916–44, Minutes of the University Delegates Committees, Oxford University Archives, UDC/M/20/1. In 1919–1920, the Intercollegiate Indian Students' Committee reported that there were 97 Indian students in residence at Cambridge. See Bernard Manning, "Secretary's Report for 1919–1920," Intercollegiate Indian Students' Committee, Minutes, 1916–43, Cambridge University Archives, Min. VII.12.

93. This is a point raised in the oft-cited work of Benedict Anderson. See his *Imagined Communities: Reflections on the Origin and Spread of Nationalism,* rev. ed. (London: Verso, 1991).

94. "University Life," *Great Tom: A University Magazine,* no. 1 (May 1861): 6.

95. A Fellow of a College, *Spiritual Destitution at Oxford: A Letter to the Right Reverend the Lord Bishop of Oxford; Being an Appeal to his Lordship to Provide Facilities for Divine Worship and Instruction in the Faith for 2,500 Undergraduates Residing for a Considerable Portion of Each Year within the Limits of His Jurisdiction* (Oxford: G. Shrimpton, 1876), p. 3. For a discussion of the question of religious tests, see "Letter to His Grace, the Archbishop of Canterbury, 1867," Vice-Chancellor's Correspondence, Cambridge University Archives, V.C. Corr.III.1(3); and "Letter to His Grace, the Archbishop of Canterbury, 1871," Vice-Chancellor's Correspondence, Cambridge University Archives, V.C. Corr. III.1(38). In one case, an undergraduate view of reform was cautiously optimistic: [Godfrey Lushington], "Oxford," *Oxford and Cambridge Magazine,* no. 1 (April 1856): 242–243.

96. "G. J. W.," "Brasenose Ale," *Great Tom: A University Magazine,* no. 2 (June 1861): 91.

97. On British Jews and broader questions of national identity, see David Feldman, *Englishmen and Jews: Social Relations and Political Culture, 1840–1914* (New Haven: Yale University Press, 1994), pp. 10–15, 45–47.

98. File on the Admission of a Jew. Cambridge University Archives, C.U.R. 28.1.1 (40.1–5).

99. On the prominence of this phenomenon in political culture, see Anthony Wohl, "'Dizzi-Ben-Dizzi': Disraeli as Alien," *Journal of British Studies* 34, no. 3 (July 1995): 377–381.

100. "Tristram" [A. E. Housman], "Varsity Ballads.—No. 2 Over to Rome," *Ye Rounde Table: An Oxford and Cambridge Magazine* 1, no. 5 (June 1, 1878): 68–69.

101. "Petition to the Master and Fellows of Pembroke College, Oxford," June 8, 1883, in *Oxford University Miscellaneous Papers,* vol. 4, Bodleian Library, Oxford, G.A. Oxon b. 140.

102. See Linda Colley, "Britishness and Otherness: An Argument," *Journal of British Studies* 31, no. 4 (October 1992): 316–323. This argument is also developed more fully in her *Britons: Forging the Nation, 1707–1837* (New Haven: Yale University Press, 1992). On anti-Catholicism, see D. G. Paz, *Popular Anti-Catholicism in Mid-Victorian England* (Stanford: Stanford University Press, 1992).

103. For a discussion of another manifestation of this, see H. L. Malchow, "Frankenstein's Monster and Images of Race in Nineteenth-Century Britain," *Past and Present* 139 (May 1993): 90–130.

104. [Gerald S. Davies?], "Nursery Rhymes," *Moslem in Cambridge . . . 1890,* no. 3 (April 1871): 3.

105. [Gerald S. Davies?], "The Editor's Address," *Moslem in Cambridge . . . 1890,* no. 1 (November 1870): 1.

106. "The Varsity Sports of 1920," *'Varsity* 6, no. 17 (May 2, 1907): 276.

107. "Y" [G. L. Reves], "French Novels," *Tatler in Cambridge,* no. 25 (October 25, 1871): 20.

108. "Arrowlets," *Shotover Papers* 1, no. 6 (May 30, 1874): 96.

109. Graham Hoggarth, "Rugger Captain (To Freshman from Very Far beyond the Tweed)," in *Cap and Gown: 'Varsity Humours by G. Hoggarth and Others,* ed. Graham Hoggarth (Oxford: Holywell, 1906), p. 37.

110. For a brief history, see India Office, *Memorandum on the Position of Indian Students in the United Kingdom* (London, 1916), pp. 1–10. For a more recent discussion, see Lahiri, *Indians in Britain,* pp. 10–15.

111. Monier Williams, *The Indian Institute in the University of Oxford: The Circumstances Which Have Led to Its Establishment, and the Objects It Is Intended to Effect, with a List of Its Supporters, a Statement of Receipts and Expenditure, and an Appeal for Further Aid,* 3rd ed. (Oxford, 1883), pp. 4–6.

112. The requirement of Greek (but not Latin) was finally abolished for all students at Oxford and Cambridge after 1920.

113. See Symonds, *Oxford and Empire,* p. 258. On the preference for Cambridge, see also Hira Lal Kumar, "Oxford University and the Indian Students," *Indian Appeal: A Monthly Magazine on Religious, Social, Educational, and Political Questions of India* 4, no. 24 (April 1892): 299–300.

114. "Occasional Notes," *Fleur-de-Lys* 1, no. 2 (May 21, 1870): 12.

115. Edward Jupp to his mother, October 25, 1869, *Correspondence of a Junior Student of Christchurch Oxford, in the Years 1868–70* (Blackheath: privately printed, 1871), p. 72. Prince Hassan was the son of Ismael Pasha, khedive of Egypt. He matriculated at Christ Church in October of 1869 and was created a D.C.L. in June of 1872. See Oxford University, *Alumni Oxonienses: The Members of the University of Oxford, 1715–1886: Their Parentage, Birthplace and Year of Birth, with a Record of Their Degrees. Being the Matriculation Register of the University, Alphabetically Arranged, Revised and Annotated by Joseph Foster* (Oxford: Parker, 1888), 2:624.

116. Diary of Anna Florence Ward, Magdalen College Archives, Oxford, MS 618.

117. "King Cole's Return. Home Sweet Home," *Shrimpton's Caricatures,* 3:555, Bodleian Library, Oxford University. G.A. Oxon 40 (396).

118. *Types* (Cambridge: Redin, 1894), p. 10.
119. On the scholarship itself, see "Boden Scholarships," Oxford University, *The Oxford University Calendar for the Year 1882* (Oxford: Clarendon, 1882), pp. 52–53.
120. "Shoddy," "Ode to the Boden Scholars," *Shotover Papers* 1, no. 2 (March 9, 1874): 24. In the ode the name is spelled "Brahajerandath De."
121. [H. M. Naidley], *Oxford Commemoration by a Fellow of Experientia* (London, 1888), p. 7–15.
122. "Editorial Notes," *Undergraduate* 1, no. 15 (October 25, 1888): 226.
123. "A Lecture at Christ's," *Cam: A "May Week" Magazine,* no. 1 (June 9, 1894): 19.
124. "The Foreign Element," *Ephemeral,* no. 5 (May 23, 1893): 34–35.
125. See "Memorandum: The Position of Indian Students in the United Kingdom; Reports of the Intercollegiate Indian Students' Committee," Cambridge University Archives, Min. VII.12; "Register of Colonial and Indian Students from June 1902," Registers of Privileged Students: Colonial and Indian Students, Oxford University Archives, UR/L/12/1; Papers Relating to Indian and Other Oriental Students c. 1920, Oxford University Archives, LMD/SF/1/5; and Accounts of the Oriental Students Delegacy, Oxford University Archives, UDC/A/2, UDC/M/20/1.
126. See Symonds, *Oxford and Empire,* p. 259.
127. F. J. Dykes, "Proctor's Report for 1913–14," Proctors' Notebooks, Cambridge University Archives, O.V.78., p. 104. On uninhibited sexual license as a familiar trope in colonial discourse, see Nancy Paxton, "Mobilizing Chivalry: Rape in British Novels about the Indian Uprising of 1857," *Victorian Studies* 36, no. 1 (fall 1992): 5–30; and Vron Ware, *Beyond the Pale: White Women, Racism, and History* (London: Verso, 1992). On the presumed childlike nature of Indians and the need for vigilance in the metropole, see Allen Greenberger, *The British Image of India: A Study in the Literature of Imperialism, 1850–1966* (London: Oxford University Press, 1969), pp. 42–43.
128. On the Oxford Majlis, see *Oxford University Miscellaneous Papers,* vol. 12, Bodleian Library, Oxford, G.A. Oxon b. 148. A colonial club whose members included Australians, Canadians, Rhodesians, South Africans, and, oddly enough, Americans was also formed in the early 1900s. See "Notice of the Oxford Colonial Club," in *Oxford University Miscellaneous Papers,* vol. 11, Bodleian Library, Oxford, G.A. Oxon b. 147.
129. "Jehu Pryde," "The Black Peril," *Granta* 14, no. 300 (February 4, 1901): 174.
130. Ibid., pp. 174–175.
131. Ibid., p. 175.
132. See Percy Craddock et al., *Recollections of the Cambridge Union, 1815–1939* (Cambridge: Bowes and Bowes, 1953), pp. 169–192.
133. Fazl-I-Husain, letter to the editor, *Granta* 14, no. 301 (February 9, 1901): 201. The editor protested that Husain should not confuse his opinions with those expressed by Pryde: "I absolutely refuse to submit to having his [Pryde's] possibly spiteful and rather inaccurate accusation fastened onto myself as the President of the Majlis undoubtedly does by his ambiguous use of the pronoun 'you.'" P. 202.
134. Four men with the last name of Obeyesekere were at Cambridge between the years 1898 and 1903. All four were from Ceylon and members of Trinity College. Three—Donald, James Peter, and James Stanley—were brothers. Any one of the four could have been the speaker identified in the Oxford *'Varsity* as the Cingalese Mr. Obeyesekere who was "very angry" with the *Granta.* See "The Other *'Varsity,*" "From Cambridge," *'Varsity* 1, no. 4 (February 12, 1901): 59.
135. "Motley Notes," *Granta* 14, no. 301 (February 9, 1901): 190. "Billingsgate"

is foul or abusive language, after the London fish market of the same name where such invective was common.

136. Pryde, letter to the editor, *Granta* 14, no. 301 (February 9, 1901): 202.

137. "English Language Lessons for Foreign Students," advertisement, *Oxford Manner,* May 1913, p. 21.

138. On Oxford, see John Darwin, "The Growth of an International University," in *The Illustrated History of Oxford University,* ed. John Prest (Oxford: Oxford University Press, 1993), pp. 336–370; and, on Cambridge, Brooke, *A History of the University of Cambridge: 1870–1990,* pp. 511–566. There was, however, some muted support for cosmopolitanism. See "Oxford and the Olympic Games," *'Varsity* 13, no. 305 (October 14, 1913): 3–4.

139. F. A. Reeve, *Cambridge* (London: B. T. Batsford, 1976), pp. 102–103. Rozina Visram has made similar observations about descriptions of Ranjitsinjhi. See her *Ayahs, Lascars, and Princes: Indians in Britain, 1700–1947* (London: Pluto, 1986), p. 673.

140. Quoted in Secretary of State, *Memorandum on the Position of Indian Students,* p. 25.

141. R. F. Scholz and S. K. Hornbeck, *Oxford and the Rhodes Scholarships* (London: Oxford University Press, 1907), p. 11. On the Germans, see J. M. Winter, "Oxford and the First World War," in *The Twentieth Century,* ed. Harrison, p. 5.

142. For some of these reactions, see Symonds, *Oxford and Empire,* p. 115.

143. Montague Compton, "Through Oxford Glasses," *Oxford Point of View* 2, no. 10 (November 1904): 88.

144. Desmond F. T. Cooke, "Through Oxford Glasses," *Oxford Point of View* 1, no. 1 (May 1902): 2.

145. "At the Breakfast Table," *Blue: A 'Varsity Journal* 1, no. 1 (April 15, 1893): 4.

146. "Thoughts That Occur," *'Varsity* 6, no. 23 (June 13, 1907): 347; and "Much" [E. B. Iwan-Muller], "An American in Oxford," *Shotover Papers* 1, no. 5 (May 16, 1874): 71–73.

147. "Thoughts That Occur. 'A Goodly Heritage,'" *'Varsity* 8, no. 1 (October 15, 1908): 303.

148. "Oxford in Transformation," *Bump,* no. 4 (May 23, 1902): 3.

149. On some British reactions to the practice of dueling see Peter Gay, *The Cultivation of Hatred* (New York: W. W. Norton, 1993), pp. 9–11.

150. On these anxieties, see G. R. Searle, *The Quest for National Efficiency: A Study in British Politics and Political Thought, 1899–1914* (Oxford: Basil Blackwell, 1971), pp. 5–15; Anna Davin, "Imperialism and Motherhood," *History Workshop Journal,* no. 5 (spring 1978): 9–65; and Stephen Heathorn, *For Home, Country, and Race: Constructing Gender, Class, and Englishness in the Elementary School, 1880–1914* (Toronto: University of Toronto Press, 2000), p. 27.

151. See *Cap and Gown,* ed. Hoggarth, pp. 17–18.

152. Eric Williams, *Inward Hunger: The Education of a Prime Minister* (London: Deutsch, 1969), p. 45, quoted in Symonds, *Oxford and Empire,* p. 269; David Alexander Mitchell, "One Rhodes Scholar's Unhappy Experience," *Globe and Mail,* February 9, 1991, p. D7; and Dr. Julia Briggs, quoted in Katharine Viner, "In the Finals Analysis," *Guardian,* July 8, 1992, p. 19.

Conclusion

1. Alexandra Frean, John O'Leary, and Philip Webster, "Brown Goes to War over Oxford Elite," *Times,* May 21, 2000, p. 1.

2. John O'Leary, "Defenders Line Up for Renewed Debate," *Times,* May 26, 2000, p. 6.

3. Dominic Kennedy, "Ex-State School Students Angered by Brown Claim," *Times,* May 27, 2000, p. 20.

4. Valerie Grove, "Charges of Betrayal in the Groves of Academe," *Times,* May 27, 2000, p. 21.

5. "Oxbridge—The British Establishment's Essential Club," *World Socialist Web Site,* September 12, 2001, http://www.wsws.org/articles/2001/sep2001/oxb-s12.shtml.

6. "The Case of Laura Spence: Inequalities in Entry to Elite Universities in the UK," *Widening Participation and Lifelong Learning* 2, no. 2 (August 2000): 2, http://www.staffs.ac.uk/journal/Volume2(2)/ed-1.htm.

7. "Oxbridge—the British Establishment's Essential Club."

8. On aspects of cultural capital, see Pierre Bourdieu, *The State Nobility: Elite Schools in the Field of Power,* trans. Lauretta C. Clough (Stanford: Stanford University Press, 1996), pp. 5–6, 215–216; and W. C. Lubenow, *The Cambridge Apostles, 1820–1914: Liberalism, Imagination, and Friendship in British Intellectual and Professional Life* (Cambridge: Cambridge University Press, 1998).

9. For information on the Oxford Access Scheme and a student perspective on the controversy, see "One Spence Piece: The Laura Spence Affair . . . " *Oxford Student,* October 5, 2000, p. 1.

10. Frank Aydelotte, *The Oxford Stamp and Other Essays* (New York: Oxford University Press, 1917), pp. 2–3.

11. On the importance of history in fostering certain values, see Reba Soffer, *Discipline and Power: The University, History, and the Making of an English Elite, 1870–1930* (Stanford: Stanford University Press, 1994).

12. Percy Ewing Matheson, "Memorandum: Royal Commission on Secondary Education, vol. 5, Memoranda and Answers to Questions, 1895," *British Parliamentary Papers* (Shannon: Irish University Press, 1970), 44:201–202.

13. Thomas Raleigh, "Memorandum: Royal Commission on Secondary Education," p. 221.

14. Siegfried Sassoon, *Memoirs of a Fox-Hunting Man* (London: Faber and Faber, 1999), p. 78. For another literary description, see Rupert Brooke, *Letters from America* (London: Sidgwick and Jackson, 1916), pp. 114–115.

Bibliography

Archival Sources

Cambridge University Archives

Cambridge University Register (1852). C.U.R. 97.1 (10).
Case of Daisy Hopkins, 1891–92. T.VIII.4.
File on the Admission of a Jew (1869). C.U.R. 28.1.1 (40.1–5).
Files Relating to Proctors in General. C.U.R. 41.3.
Flysheets re: Proctorial Jurisdiction (1892). U.P. 60 (28–29).
Intercollegiate Indian Students' Committee (1916–1920). Min. VII.12.
Oxford and Cambridge Matriculations Calculated on an Average of 5 Years about Any Given Year from 1544–1930 (compiled by J. A. Venn). Matr.24. (2).
Proctors' Box I (various dates, 1559–1873). O.V.3.21.
Proctors' Notebooks (1884–1920). O.V.78.
Spinning House Committals: Files of Mandates, Graces and Committals (1823–94). T.VIII. 1–3.
Tripos Verses (1816–1894). Exam.M.2.
Vice-Chancellor's Correspondence (1865–67). V. C. Cartmell.
Vice-Chancellor's Correspondence (1867–1871). V.C.Corr.III.1.
Vice-Chancellor's Papers (1850–1871). C.U.R. 44.1.

Cambridge University Library

The Downing Translation Papers. Cam.c.882.44.
Fairbairn Family Album. Cam.a.908.3.
"Squibs and Crackers": Miscellaneous Cambridge Papers, 1799–1904, Collected and Compiled by J. W. Clark. Cam.a.500.9.
Ten Satirical Postcards. Cam.d.906.19.

Cambridge University, Emmanuel College Archives

Papers relating to the case of Reginald P. N. Downing.

Oxford University Archives

Accounts of the Oriental Students Delegacy. UDC/A/A, UDC/M/20/1.
Chancellor's Court Papers, 1915–21. No shelf mark.
"Confidential Printed Letter from V-C to Various Members of Colleges (to Be Addressed in Pen) Relating to 'Mock Funerals'" (March 6, 1908). PR 1/23/8.
Delegates for Oriental Students, Minutes of Meetings (1916–1944). UDC/M/20/1.
Lodging House Delegacy: Papers Relating to Indian and Other Oriental Students, c. 1920. LHD/SF/1/5.
Miscellaneous Correspondence of the Lodging House Delegacy (1903). LHD/C/1/21.
Papers Relating to Indian and Other Oriental Students, c. 1900. LMD/SF/1/5.
Proctors' Book, Names. PR 1/23/4/1.

Proctors' Manuals, 1855, 1887, 1897, 1902–1903. WPγ7/3, WPγ7/4, WPγ7/5, WPγ7/6.
Procuratorial Experiences and Observations in the Year 1852, 3. WPγ8 (21).
Register of the Chancellor's Court, 1865–1905. Hyp/A/71b.
Registers of Privileged Students: Colonial and Indian Students, 1902–1904. UR/L/12/1.
Reports of the Delegacy for Women Students. UDC/A/1, UDC/M/16.
University Justice Court Books (1871–1926). No shelf mark.

Oxford University, Bodleian Library

Association for the Education of Women in Oxford. *Report as to the Rules of Discipline in Force for the Women Students at the University of Oxford* (1909), G.A. Oxon b. 125.
Correspondence on the "Bread and Butter" Issue at Oxford (1865). G.A. Oxon 8° 92 (3).
Letters and Papers Received by C. L. Shadwell, Esq. during His Term of Office as Proctor. G.A. Oxon c. 33.
Lodging House Delegacy. *Statements {Concerning Defects Alleged to Exist in the Lodging House}.* G.A. c. 84 (496).
Lodging Houses Licensed (1868–1916). G.A. Oxon 4 (245)
A Made Up Volume in the Bodleian: Topographical Prints &c., Oxford University Costumes, Arms, Scenes. G.A. Oxon a. 72.
Material on Women Students. G.A. Oxon c. 34.
Miscellaneous Pamphlets: 36 Oxon Pamphlets, 1755–1919. G.A. Oxon 8 (611).
New College Scrapbook. G.A. Oxon c. 282.
Oxford University Miscellaneous Papers, vols. 1–12. G.A. Oxon b. 137–148.
Oxon Miscellaneous. G.A. Oxon c. 107.
Shrimpton's Caricatures. G.A. Oxon 40 (396).

Oxford University, Brasenose College Archives

Diaries of Falconer Madan. In three volumes: Private Account No. 1, Private Account No. 2, and Brasenose College Meetings.

Oxford University, Magdalen College Archives

Diary of Anna Florence Ward, MS 618.

Yale University, Seeley Mudd Library

Burgon, J. W., et al. *Lodging House System: Collection of Pamphlets &c.* Lmd 74 M8 2.
Magdalen College, Oxford Pamphlets (complied by Falconer Madan). Lmd M29 +1.
Miscellaneous Parodies and Satirical Pamphlets on Oxford University. Lmd 73 1.
New College Pamphlets (compiled by Falconer Madan). Lmd 81 N49.

University Periodicals

Cambridge

Academica: An Occasional Journal, 1858.
Agenda, 1907–1909.
Alma Mater, 1899–1900.
Anti-snarl, 1899.
Apocrypha, 1896.
Bear University Magazine, 1858.
Beldragon: The May Week Magazine, 1895.
Blue 'Un: A Journal of University Life, 1884.
Blunderbuss, 1916–1918.
Bubble: A May Week Magazine, 1898.
Buzz, 1916.

Cam: A "May Week" Magazine, 1894.
Cam, 1906.
Cambridge A.B.C., 1894.
Cambridge Annual, 1906.
Cambridge Business Man, 1917–1920.
Cambridge Cataract, 1913.
Cambridge Christian Life: A University Journal, 1913–1914.
Cambridge Essays: Contributed by Members of the University, 1855–1858.
Cambridge Essays, 1888.
Cambridge Examiner, 1881–1884.
Cambridge Fortnightly, 1888.
Cambridge House Magazine, 1901–1912.
Cambridge Magazine, 1899.
Cambridge Magazine, 1912–1920.
Cambridge Meteor, 1882.
Cambridge Musical Notes, 1908.
Cambridge Observer, 1892–1893.
Cambridge Review: A Journal of University Life and Thought, 1879–1920.
Cambridge Tatler, 1877.
Cambridge Terminal Magazine, 1858–1859.
Cambridge Undergraduates' Journal, 1868–1875.
Cambridge University Gazette, A Journal Devoted to University Matters, 1868–1869.
Cambridge University Magazine: A Weekly Journal of General Interest, 1886.
Cambridge Year Book, 1862–1866.
Cantab, 1873.
Cantab, 1892.
Cantab, 1898–1900.
Comment and Criticism, 1913–1914.
Elean, 1907.
Fleur-de-Lys: A Christ's College Magazine, 1870–1871.
Gadfly: The Cambridge Mirror of Morals, Men and Manners, 1888.
Girton Review, 1882–1920.
Gownsman, 1909–1911.
Granta, 1889–1920.
Half Blue, 1896.
Jack-daw, 1900.
K.P., 1893–1894.
Liberal Almanac, 1911.
Liberal Notes, 1913–1914.
Light Blue: A Cambridge University Magazine, 1866–1871.
Light Blue Incorporated with the Light Green: The Cambridge University Magazine, 1873–1875.
Light Green: A Superior and High Class Periodical, 1872.
Lion University Magazine, 1858–1859.
Mandragora, 1913–1914.
May Bee, 1884.
May Bee, 1906.
Middle-Aged Cambridge, 1920.
Momus: A Semi-occasional University Periodical, 1866–1869.
Moslem in Cambridge: A Liberal and Advanced Journal of the Scope, Views, and Tendencies Adapted to the Tastes of All Nations. Conducted by Hadji Seivad and a Talented Heathen Staff, 1890, 1870–1871.

Mushroom: A May Week Magazine, 1894.
New Cambridge, 1919–1920.
New Commentator, 1913.
New Youth, 1915.
*Occasional Papers on University Matters and Middle Class Education; Together with Full
    Information as to the Local Examinations and Recent University Changes*, 1858–1859.
Parrot, 1893.
Pink for the May Week, 1899.
Query, 1907.
Rag, 1896.
Realm, 1855.
Reflector, 1888.
Screed, 1899.
Snarl: An Occasional Journal for Splenetics, 1899.
Spur, 1913–1914.
Tatler in Cambridge, 1871–1872.
True Blue: Occasional Jottings of 'Varsity Vagaries, 1883.
University Extension, 1904–1905.
Wasp, 1891.

Oxford

Anti-teapot Review: A Magazine of Politics, Literature and Art, 1864–1866.
Barge, 1900–1905.
Best Man, 1906.
Blue: A 'Varsity Journal, 1893.
Blue Book, 1912–1913.
Broad: An Illustrated Fortnightly Review of Social and Dramatic Life in Oxford, 1901.
Brown Book: Lady Margaret Hall Chronicle, 1906–1920
Budget: An Eights Week Paper, 1911.
Bulldog, 1896.
Buller, 1913.
Bump, 1898–1903.
Bump, 1909.
Bust: An Eights Week Magazine, 1910.
Chaperon: An Eights Week Magazine, by "Pembie," 1910.
Chaperon, or the Oxford Cher-ivari, 1910.
Cherwell, 1992.
Clown, 1891.
Comet, 1886.
Cornstalker. A Magazine for Eights Week, 1898.
Dark Blue: An University Magazine, 1867.
Dark Blue, 1871–1873.
Eights Illustrated, 1902.
Eights Week Illustrated, 1914.
Eights Week Opinions, 1909.
Eights Week Pie, 1910.
Ephemeral, 1893.
Freshman, 1909.
Fritillary, 1895–1920.
Great Tom: A University Magazine, 1861.
Harlequin. Conducted by Oxford Men, 1866.
Isis, 1892–1920.

J.C.R., 1897–1899.
Jester, 1902.
Jokelet, 1886.
Magnum, 1908.
May Bee, An 8–Day Buzzer, 1900.
Mayonnaise, 1907.
Meteor: Special Gala Eights Week Number, 1911.
New Cut, 1914.
New Rattle, 1890–1892.
Non-collegiate Students' Magazine, 1896–1919.
Octopus, 1895.
Ox: Or the Commemorator's Vade-Mecum, 1907.
Oxford Critic and University Magazine, 1857.
Oxford Essays, 1855.
Oxford Examiner: A Journal for Undergraduates, 1889–1891.
Oxford Examiner Monthly, 1882.
Oxford Fortnightly, 1913.
Oxford Indian, 1914.
Oxford Magazine, 1883–1920.
Oxford Manner, 1913.
Oxford Monthly Programme, 1899.
Oxford Movement, 1908.
Oxford Poetry, 1913–1920.
Oxford Point of View, 1902–1904.
Oxford Rambler, 1882.
Oxford Review: A Weekly Record of University Life and Thought, 1885–1888.
Oxford Review: The Undergraduates' Journal, 1888–1898.
Oxford Review: A Political, Social and Literary Journal for Undergraduates, 1919.
Oxford Socialist, 1908–1909.
Oxford Spectator, 1867–1868.
Oxford Student, 1992.
Oxford Syndicalist, 1912.
Oxford Tatler, 1886.
Oxford Undergraduate's Journal, 1866–1875.
Oxford University Magazine and Review, 1869.
Oxford Wit, 1855.
Pageant Post, 1907.
Pan, 1903–1904.
Pantheon, 1883.
Parasol, 1905.
Parsons' Pleasure, 1913.
Pipe: An Oxford Bi-terminal Magazine, 1900–1901.
Playmates: The Oxford "Chums", 1909.
Proctor, 1896.
Quad: A Terminal Magazine, 1900–1901.
Radcliffe, 1869.
Rattle, 1886–1888.
Replies, 1913.
Right Thing, 1916.
Round Robin, 1908.
Scarlet Runner: A Quarterly, 1899.
Scrap Book, 1866.

Shotover Papers, or, Echoes from Oxford, 1874–1875.
Souvenir: A Paper for Oxford Men and Their Visitors, 1893.
Sphinx: A Varsity Medley, 1907.
Spirit Lamp, 1892–1893.
Squeaker, 1893.
Squib, 1908.
Superman, 1909.
Tuesday Review, 1909.
Umbrella: A Magazine of Silliness, 1905.
Undergraduate, 1888.
Undergraduate Papers, 1857–1858.
Usher: To Ye Pageant, 1907.
Vacuum, 1900.
'Varsity: A Social View of Oxford Life, 1901–1916.
Varsity Characters, 1900.
Varsity Life Illustrated, 1906.
Varsity Vices: The Oxford Truth, 1908.
Waifs and Strays: A Terminal Magazine of Oxford Poetry, 1879–1882.
Why Not? A Post-impressionist Magazine for TOGGERS, 1911.
Word: The Paper for All Oxford Students, 1992.
X: An Unknown Quantity, 1899.
Ye Tea Potte, 1898.
Young Oxford: A Magazine of Constructive Thought Devoted to the Ruskin Hall Movement,
  1899–1903.

Publications Intended for Both Universities

Boomerang: An Oxford and Cambridge Miscellany, 1875.
College Rhymes: Contributed by Members of the Universities of Oxford and Cambridge, 1860–
  1873.
Oxford and Cambridge Illustrated, 1907.
Oxford and Cambridge Magazine: Conducted by Members of the Two Universities, 1856.
Oxford and Cambridge Miscellany, 1920.
*Oxford and Cambridge Reporter; A Journal of University, Bar, and Public School Intelligence,
  and Record of Local Examinations,* 1857–1862.
Oxford and Cambridge Review, 1907–1912.
Oxford and Cambridge Undergraduates' Journal, 1875–1882.
Oxford and Cambridge Undergraduates' Journal with Which is Incorporated the Oxford Review,
  1883–1884.
Oxford and Cambridge Yearbook, 1904.
Oxford Review and Oxford and Cambridge Undergraduates' Journal, 1882–1883.
Ye Rounde Table: An Oxford and Cambridge Magazine, 1878.

Other Published Sources

Adams, James Eli. *Dandies and Desert Saints: Styles of Victorian Masculinity.* Ithaca, N.Y.:
  Cornell University Press, 1995.
Aestheticism and Intolerance: A Protest. Oxford: B. H. Blackwell, 1882.
Agnew, John A., and James S. Duncan, eds. *The Power of Place: Bringing Together Geo-
  graphical and Sociological Imaginations.* Boston: Unwin Hyman, 1989.
Anderson, Benedict. *Imagined Communities: Reflections on the Origin and Spread of Nation-
  alism.* Rev. ed. London: Verso, 1991.

Anderson, C. Arnold, and Miriam Schnaper. *School and Society in England: Social Backgrounds of Oxford and Cambridge Students.* Westport, Conn.: Greenwood, 1952.

Anderson, R. D. *Universities and Elites in Britain since 1800.* London: Macmillan, 1992.

"Anstey, F." [Thomas Anstey Guthrie]. *A Long Retrospect.* Oxford: Oxford University Press, 1936.

Armytage, W. H. G. *Civic Universities: Aspects of a British Tradition.* London: Benn, 1955.

Aston, John. *Varsity Sketches.* Oxford: Holywell, 1902.

Axelrod, Paul, and John G. Reid, eds. *Youth, University, and Canadian Society: Essays in the Social History of Higher Education.* Kingston: McGill–Queen's University Press, 1989.

Aydelotte, Frank. *The Oxford Stamp and Other Essays.* New York: Oxford University Press, 1917.

Bailey, Peter. "Parasexuality and Glamour: The Victorian Barmaid as Cultural Prototype." *Gender and History* 2, no. 2 (summer 1990): 148–172.

Bankes, George Nugent. *A Cambridge Staircase: By the Author of "A Day of My Life at Eton," "About Some Fellows," Etc.* London: Sampson Low, Marston, Searle and Rivington, 1883.

———. *Cambridge Trifles; or, Splutterings from an Undergraduate Pen.* London: Sampson Low, Marston, Searle and Rivington, 1881.

Beerbohm, Max. *Zuleika Dobson.* New York: Random House, 1926.

Bender, Thomas, ed. *The University and the City: From Medieval Origins to the Present.* Oxford: Oxford University Press, 1988.

Berman, Marshall. *All That Is Solid Melts into Air: The Experience of Modernity.* New York: Simon and Schuster, 1982.

Bill, E. G. W. *University Reform in Nineteenth-Century Oxford: A Study of Henry Halford Vaughan, 1811–1885.* Oxford: Clarendon, 1973.

Blanchard, Mary Warner. *Oscar Wilde's America: Counterculture in the Gilded Age.* New Haven: Yale University Press, 1998.

Bland, Lucy, and Laura Doan, eds. *Sexology in Culture: Labelling Bodies and Desires.* Chicago: University of Chicago Press, 1998.

Blathwayt, Raymond. "Young Oxford of To-day. A Talk With Professor Max Muller." *Quiver: An Illustrated Magazine for Sunday and General Reading* 27 (September 1894): 550–554.

Bonnell, Victoria E., and Lynn Hunt, eds. *Beyond the Cultural Turn: New Directions in the Study of Society and Culture.* Berkeley: University of California Press, 1999.

Bourdieu, Pierre. *Distinction: A Social Critique of the Judgement of Taste.* Translated by Richard Nice. Cambridge, Mass.: Harvard University Press, 1984.

———. *Language and Symbolic Power.* Edited by John B. Thompson. Translated by Gino Raymond and Matthew Adamson. Cambridge, Mass.: Harvard University Press, 1999.

———. *The State Nobility: Elite Schools in the Field of Power.* Translated by Lauretta C. Clough. Stanford: Stanford University Press, 1996.

Bourke, Joanna. *Dismembering the Male: Men's Bodies, Britain, and the Great War.* Chicago: University of Chicago Press, 1996.

———. *Working Class Cultures in Britain, 1890–1960: Gender, Class, and Ethnicity.* London: Routledge, 1994.

Boyd, Kelly. "Exemplars and Ingrates: Imperialism and the Boys' Story Paper, 1880–1930." *Historical Research* 67, no. 103 (June 1994): 143–155.

———. *Manliness and the Boys' Story Paper, 1885–1940.* Basingstoke, U.K.: Palgrave, 2002.

Brantlinger, Patrick. *Crusoe's Footprints: Cultural Studies in Britain and America.* London: Routledge, 1990.

Breward, Christopher. *The Hidden Consumer: Masculinities, Fashion, and City Life, 1860–1914.* Manchester: Manchester University Press, 1999.

Briggs, Asa. *Victorian Things.* London: Batsford, 1988.

British Parliamentary Papers. Vol. 44. Shannon: Irish University Press, 1970.

Brittain, Vera. *The Women at Oxford: A Fragment of History.* London: Harrap, 1960.

Brock, M. G., and M. C. Curthoys, eds. *Nineteenth-Century Oxford,* parts 1 and 2. Vols. 6 and 7 of *The History of the University of Oxford,* ed. T. H. Aston. Oxford: Oxford University Press, 1997, 2000.

Brod, Harry, ed. *The Making of Masculinities: The New Men's Studies.* Boston: Unwin Hyman, 1987.

Brooke, Christopher N. L. *A History of Gonville and Caius College.* Woodbridge, U.K.: Boydell, 1985.

———. *A History of the University of Cambridge: 1870–1990.* Vol. 4 of *A History of the University of Cambridge,* ed. Christopher N. L. Brooke. Cambridge: Cambridge University Press, 1993.

Brooke, Christopher N. L., and Roger Highfield. *Oxford and Cambridge.* Photographs by Wim Swaan. Cambridge: Cambridge University Press, 1988.

Brooke, Rupert. *Letters from America.* London: Sidgwick and Jackson, 1916.

Bryson, Bill. "The Style and Substance of Oxford." *National Geographic* 188, no. 5 (November 1995): 114–137.

Budd, Michael Anton. *The Sculpture Machine: Physical Culture and Body Politics in the Age of Empire.* New York: New York University Press, 1997.

Burstyn, Joan N. *Victorian Education and the Ideal of Womanhood.* London: Croom Helm, 1980.

Burton, Antoinette. *At the Heart of the Empire: Indians and the Colonial Encounter in Late-Victorian Britain.* Berkeley: University of California Press, 1998.

———. *Burdens of History: British Feminists, Indian Women, and Imperial Culture, 1865–1915.* Chapel Hill: University of North Carolina Press, 1994.

———. "Colonial Encounters in Late-Victorian England: Pandita Ramabai at Cheltenham and Wantage, 1883–6." *Feminist Review,* no. 49 (spring 1995): 29–49.

Butler, Judith. *Gender Trouble: Feminism and the Subversion of Identity.* New York: Routledge, 1990.

Buxton, L. H. Dudley, and Strickland Gibson. *Oxford University Ceremonies.* Oxford: Clarendon, 1935.

"C., O." [A. H. Lawrence]. *Reminiscences of Cambridge Life.* London: privately printed, 1889.

Cain, P. J., and A. G. Hopkins. *British Imperialism: Innovation and Expansion, 1688–1914.* London: Longman, 1993.

Cambridge University. *The Cambridge University Calendar.* Cambridge: Deighton, Bell, 1857–1909.

———. *The Cambridge University Calendar for the Year 1919–1920.* Cambridge: Cambridge University Press, 1919.

———. *Ordinances of the University of Cambridge.* Cambridge: Cambridge University Press, 1888.

———. *Statutes for the University of Cambridge and for the Colleges within It, Made, Published, and Approved (1878–1882) under the Universities of Oxford and Cambridge Act, 1877. With an Appendix of Acts and Orders.* Cambridge: Cambridge University Press, 1883.

———. *The Student's Guide to the University of Cambridge.* Cambridge: Deighton, Bell, 1893.

———. *The Student's Handbook to the University and Colleges of Cambridge.* Cambridge: Cambridge University Press, 1902, 1907, 1910.

Cannadine, David. *Aspects of Aristocracy: Grandeur and Decline in Modern Britain.* New Haven: Yale University Press, 1994.

———. *Ornamentalism: How the British Saw Their Empire.* Oxford: Oxford University Press, 2001.

Carnes, Mark C. *Secret Ritual and Manhood in Victorian America.* New Haven: Yale University Press, 1989.

Carnes, Mark C., and Clyde Griffen, eds. *Meanings for Manhood: Constructions of Masculinity in Victorian America.* Chicago: University of Chicago Press, 1990.

Carter, Ian. *Ancient Cultures of Conceit: British University Fiction in the Post-war Years.* London: Routledge, 1990.

Casteras, Susan P. *Images of Victorian Womanhood in English Art.* Rutherford, N.J.: Associated Universities Presses, 1987.

Castle, Kathryn. *Britannia's Children: Reading Colonialism through Children's Books and Magazines.* Manchester: Manchester University Press, 1996.

Chauncey, George. *Gay New York: Gender, Urban Culture, and the Making of the Gay Male World, 1890–1940.* New York: Basic Books, 1994.

Chester, Norman. *Economics, Politics, and Social Studies in Oxford, 1900–1985.* London: Macmillan, 1986.

City and Borough of Oxford, 1885. Before the Revising Barrister, September 8th, 9th, 10th, 12th, 19th and 26th, Alfred Chichele Plowden, Esq. Copy of Shorthand Writers' Notes of the Evidence Relating to Occupation of College Rooms, to Which is Appended the Decision of the Revising Barrister. Oxford, 1885.

Clark, George S. R. Kitson. *The Making of Victorian England.* Cambridge, Mass.: Harvard University Press, 1962.

Clark, John Willis. *A Concise Guide to the Town and University of Cambridge in an Introduction and Four Walks.* Cambridge: Bowes and Bowes, 1910.

———. *Old Friends at Cambridge and Elsewhere.* London: Macmillan, 1900.

———, ed. *Ordinances of the University of Cambridge.* Cambridge: Cambridge University Press, 1901, 1908, 1911.

Colley, Linda. "Britishness and Otherness: An Argument." *Journal of British Studies* 31, no. 4 (October 1992): 309–329.

———. *Britons: Forging the Nation, 1707–1837.* New Haven: Yale University Press, 1992.

Collini, Stefan. "The Passionate Intensity of Cultural Studies." *Victorian Studies* 36, no. 4 (summer 1993): 455–460.

———. *Public Moralists: Political Thought and Intellectual Life in Britain, 1850–1930.* Oxford: Clarendon, 1991.

[Collins, William Lucas]. "Light and Dark Blue." *Blackwood's Edinburgh Magazine* 100, no. 612 (October 1866): 446–460.

Colonial and Indian Students at Oxford. London, 1902.

Compulsory Chapel. A Protest. Cambridge, 1892.

Connell, R. W. *Masculinities.* Berkeley: University of California Press, 1995.

Coombes, Annie E. *Reinventing Africa: Museums, Material Culture, and Popular Imagination.* New Haven: Yale University Press, 1994.

Copelman, Dina M. *London's Women Teachers: Gender, Class, and Feminism, 1870–1930.* London: Routledge, 1996.

Cottle, Thomas J. *The Present of Things Future: Explorations of Time in Human Experience.* New York: Free Press, 1974.

Craddock, Percy, et al. *Recollections of the Cambridge Union, 1815–1939.* Cambridge: Bowes and Bowes, 1953.

Crozier, Ivan Dalley. "The Medical Construction of Homosexuality and Its Relation to the Law in Nineteenth-Century England." *Medical History* 45, no. 1 (January 2001): 61–82.

Cunningham, Hugh. "The Language of Patriotism." In *Patriotism,* ed. Samuel, pp. 57–89.

Currie, Robert. "The Arts and Social Studies, 1914–1939." In *The Twentieth Century,* ed. Harrison, pp. 109–138.

Curthoys, M. C. "The Examination System." In *Nineteenth-Century Oxford, Part 1,* ed. Brock and Curthoys, pp. 339–374.

Dangerfield, George. *The Strange Death of Liberal England.* New York: Capricorn Books, 1961.

Darnton, Robert. "The Symbolic Element in History." *Journal of Modern History* 58, no. 1 (March 1986): 218–233.

Darwin, John. "The Growth of an International University." In *The Illustrated History of Oxford University,* ed. Prest, pp. 336–370.

Davidoff, Leonore. *The Best Circles: Society, Etiquette, and the Season.* London: Croom Helm, 1973.

Davidoff, Leonore, and Catherine Hall. *Family Fortunes: Men and Women of the English Middle Class, 1780–1850.* Chicago: University of Chicago Press, 1987.

Davidson, J. *Things Seen in Oxford.* London: Seeley, Service, 1914.

Davin, Anna. "Imperialism and Motherhood." *History Workshop Journal,* no. 5 (spring 1978): 9–65.

Davis, Natalie Z. "Anthropology and History in the 1980s: The Possibilities of the Past." *Journal of Interdisciplinary History* 12, no. 2 (autumn 1981): 227–252.

———. *Fiction in the Archives: Pardon Tales and Their Tellers in Sixteenth-Century France.* Stanford: Stanford University Press, 1987.

Davis, Tracy C. *Actresses as Working Women: Their Social Identity in Victorian Culture.* London: Routledge, 1991.

———. "Indecency and Vigilance in the Music Halls." In *British Theatre in the 1890s,* ed. Foulkes, pp. 111–131.

Dawson, Graham. *Soldier Heroes: British Adventure, Empire, and the Imagining of Masculinities.* London: Routledge, 1994.

de Certeau, Michel. *The Practice of Everyday Life.* Translated by Steven F. Rendall. Berkeley: University of California Press, 1984.

Decker, Christopher, ed. *Edward Fitzgerald's Rubaiyat of Omar Khayyam: A Critical Edition.* Charlottesville: University Press of Virginia, 1997.

de Grazia, Victoria, and Ellen Furlough, eds. *The Sex of Things: Gender and Consumption in Historical Perspective.* Berkeley: University of California Press, 1996.

Delamont, Sara. *Knowledgeable Women: Structuralism and the Reproduction of Elites.* London: Routledge, 1989.

Dellamora, Richard. *Masculine Desire: The Sexual Politics of Victorian Aestheticism.* Chapel Hill: University of North Carolina Press, 1990.

[Devenish, W. H.?]. *"Fors Togigera." Letters to Our Mothers and Sisters from Oxford. No. 1. May-Day on Magdalen Tower.* Oxford: J. Vincent, 1874.

Dickens, Charles. *Dickens's Dictionary of Oxford and Cambridge.* London: Macmillan, 1884.

Dowling, Linda. *Hellenism and Homosexuality in Victorian Oxford.* Ithaca, N.Y.: Cornell University Press, 1994.

Downing, Reginald P. N. *The Late Classical Tripos Examination.* Sutton Waldron Rectory, Shaftesbury: privately printed, April 1882.

Downing, Samuel Penrose. *The Classical Tripos Enquiry. Irresponsibility of Examiners in Accusing Candidates of Unfair Practices: A Second Appeal.* Sutton Waldron Rectory, Shaftesbury: privately printed, October 1882.

——. *The Late Classical Tripos. Irresponsibility of Examiners in Accusing Candidates of Unfair Practices. An Appeal to the Chancellor, the Vice-Chancellor, the Council and the Masters and Fellows of the University of Cambridge.* Sutton Waldron Rectory, Shaftesbury: privately printed, April 1882.

Duberman, Martin, ed. *Queer Representations: Reading Lives, Reading Cultures.* New York: New York University Press, 1997.

Dunbabin, J. P. "Finance since 1914." In *The Twentieth Century,* ed. Harrison, pp. 639–682.

Durand, Ralph. *Oxford: Its Buildings and Gardens.* Illustrated by William Wildman. London: Grant Richards, 1909.

Dyhouse, Carol. *No Distinction of Sex? Women in British Universities, 1870–1939.* London: UCL Press, 1995.

——. "Women Students and the London Medical Schools, 1914–39: The Anatomy of a Masculine Culture." *Gender and History* 10, no. 1 (April 1998): 110–132.

Engel, A. J. *From Clergyman to Don: The Rise of the Academic Profession in Nineteenth-Century Oxford.* Oxford: Oxford University Press, 1983.

——. "'Immoral Intentions': The University of Oxford and the Problem of Prostitution, 1827–1914." *Victorian Studies* 23, no. 1 (autumn 1979): 79–107.

Everett, William. *On the Cam: Lectures on the University of Cambridge in England.* London: S. O. Beeton, 1868.

Fass, Paula. *The Damned and the Beautiful: American Youth in the 1920s.* New York: Oxford University Press, 1977.

Feldman, David. *Englishmen and Jews: Social Relations and Political Culture, 1840–1914.* New Haven: Yale University Press, 1994.

A Fellow of a College. *Spiritual Destitution at Oxford: A Letter to the Right Reverend the Lord Bishop of Oxford; Being an Appeal to His Lordship to Provide Facilities for Divine Worship and Instruction in the Faith for 2,500 Undergraduates Residing for a Considerable Portion of Each Year within the Limits of His Jurisdiction.* Oxford: G. Shrimpton, 1876.

Finn, Margot. "Men's Things: Masculine Possession in the Consumer Revolution." *Social History* 25, no. 2 (May 2000): 133–155.

Fitch, J. G. "Women and the Universities." *Contemporary Review* 58 (August 1890): 240–255.

Foley, Timothy, P., Lionel Pilkington, Sean Ryder, and Elizabeth Tilley, eds. *Gender and Colonialism.* Galway: Galway University Press, 1995.

Forster, E. M. *Maurice: A Novel.* New York: W. W. Norton, 1971.

Foucault, Michel. *The Archaeology of Knowledge.* Translated by A. M. Sheridan Smith. New York: Pantheon Books, 1972.

——. *Discipline and Punish: The Birth of the Prison.* Translated by Alan Sheridan. New York: Pantheon Books, 1977.

——. *The History of Sexuality, Volume 1: An Introduction.* Translated by Robert Hurley. New York: Vintage Books, 1990.

Foulkes, Richard, ed. *British Theatre in the 1890s: Essays on Drama and the Stage.* Cambridge: Cambridge University Press, 1992.

Fowler, Laurence, and Helen Fowler, eds. *Cambridge Commemorated: An Anthology of University Life.* Cambridge: Cambridge University Press, 1984.

Fowler, W. Warde, ed. *An Oxford Correspondence of 1903.* Oxford: B. H. Blackwell, 1904.

Francis, Martin. "The Domestication of the Male? Recent Research on Nineteenth- and Twentieth-Century British Masculinity." *Historical Journal* 45, no. 3 (September 2002): 637–652.

Frean, Alexandra, John O'Leary, and Philip Webster. "Brown Goes to War over Oxford Elite." *Times,* May 21, 2000, p. 1.

Fussell, Paul. *The Great War and Modern Memory*. Oxford: Oxford University Press, 1975.

Gagnier, Regenia. *Subjectivities: A History of Self-Representation in Britain, 1832–1920*. Oxford: Oxford University Press, 1991.

Gathorne-Hardy, Jonathan. *The Old School Tie: The Phenomenon of the English Public School*. New York: Viking, 1977.

Gay, Peter. *The Cultivation of Hatred*. New York: W. W. Norton, 1993.

Geertz, Clifford. *The Interpretation of Cultures*. New York: Basic Books, 1973.

George, Harold. "Oxford at Home." *Strand* 9 (January 1895): 109–115.

Gibert, Julie S. "Women Students and Student Life at England's Civic Universities before the First World War." *History of Education* 23, no. 4 (December 1994): 405–422.

Gillis, John. *Youth and History: Tradition and Change in European Age Relations, 1770–Present*. New York: Academic, 1981.

Girouard, Mark. *The Return to Camelot: Chivalry and the English Gentleman*. New Haven: Yale University Press, 1981.

Godley, Alfred Denis. *Verses to Order*. London: Methuen, 1892.

Gorham, Deborah. "A Woman at Oxford: Vera Brittain's Somerville Experience." *Historical Studies in Education* 3, no. 1 (spring 1991): 1–19.

Gradd, Anunda [pseud.]. *The Quasi-Guide to Eights Week*. Oxford: Holywell, 1907.

Green, V. H. H. *A History of Oxford University*. London: B. T. Batsford, 1974.

———. *Religion at Oxford and Cambridge*. London: SCM Press, 1964.

———. "The University and the Nation." In *The Illustrated History of Oxford University*, ed. Prest, pp. 39–83.

Greenberger, Allen. *The British Image of India: A Study in the Literature of Imperialism, 1850–1966*. London: Oxford University Press, 1969.

Greenstein, Daniel I. "The Junior Members, 1900–1990: A Profile." In *The Twentieth Century*, ed. Harrison, pp. 45–80.

Griffiths, John, ed. *Statutes of the University of Oxford Codified in the Year 1636 under the Authority of Archbishop Laud, Chancellor of the University*. With an introduction by Charles Lancelot Shadwell. Oxford: Clarendon, 1888.

Grove, Valerie. "Charges of Betrayal in the Groves of Academe." *Times*, May 27, 2000, p. 21.

Growler [pseud.]. *May Term and Maidens*. Cambridge, 1901.

Guha, Ramachandra. "Cricket and Politics in Colonial India." *Past and Present* 161 (November 1998): 155–190.

Guide for the Use of Colonial, Indian and Foreign Students. London, 1906.

Gunn, Simon. *The Public Culture of the Victorian Middle Class: Ritual and Authority and the English Industrial City, 1840–1914*. Manchester: Manchester University Press, 2000.

Haley, Bruce. *The Healthy Body and Victorian Culture*. Cambridge, Mass.: Harvard University Press, 1978.

Hall, Catherine. *Civilising Subjects: Colony and Metropole in the English Imagination, 1830–1867*. Chicago: University of Chicago Press, 2002.

Hansen, Peter H. "Albert Smith, the Alpine Club, and the Invention of Mountaineering in Mid-Victorian Britain." *Journal of British Studies* 34, no. 3 (July 1995): 300–324.

Harding, Robb, and Judy Coffin. "Interview with Natalie Zemon Davis." In *Visions of History*, by MARHO, the Radical Historians Organization, ed. Abelove et al., pp. 99–122.

Harris, José. *Private Lives, Public Spirit: A Social History of Britain, 1870–1914*. Oxford: Oxford University Press, 1993.

Harrison, Brian. "College Life, 1918–1939." In *The Twentieth Century,* ed. Harrison, pp. 81–108.

———. "Politics." In *The Twentieth Century,* ed. Harrison, pp. 377–412.

———. *Separate Spheres: The Opposition to Women's Suffrage in Britain.* New York: Holmes and Meier, 1978.

———, ed. *The Twentieth Century.* Vol. 8 of *The History of the University of Oxford,* ed. T. H. Aston. Oxford: Clarendon, 1994.

Heathorn, Stephen. *For Home, Country, and Race: Constructing Gender, Class, and Englishness in the Elementary School, 1880–1914.* Toronto: University of Toronto Press, 2000.

———. "'Let Us Remember That We, Too, Are English': Constructions of Citizenship and National Identity in English Elementary School Reading Books, 1880–1914." *Victorian Studies* 38, no. 3 (spring 1995): 395–427.

Heyck, T. W. *The Transformation of Intellectual Life in Victorian England.* London: Croom Helm, 1982.

Heywood, James, ed. *The Recommendations of the Oxford University Commissioners, with Selections from Their Report; and A History of the University Subscription Tests, Including Notices of the University and Collegiate Visitations.* London: Longman, Brown, Green, and Longmans, 1853.

Hilton, Arthur Clement. *The Works of Arthur Clement Hilton, Together with His Life and Letters.* Edited by Robert Pearce-Edgcumbe. Cambridge: Macmillan and Bowes, 1904.

Hilton, Matthew. *Smoking in British Popular Culture, 1800–2000: Perfect Pleasures.* Manchester: Manchester University Press, 2000.

Hobsbawm, Eric, and Terence Ranger, eds. *The Invention of Tradition.* Cambridge: Cambridge University Press, 1983.

Hoggarth, Graham, ed. *Cap and Gown: Varsity Humours by G. Hoggarth and Others.* Oxford: Holywell, 1906.

Holbrook, David. *Images of Women in Literature.* New York: New York University Press, 1989.

Holt, Richard. *Sport and the British: A Modern History.* Oxford: Oxford University Press, 1990.

Honey, J. R. de S. *Tom Brown's Universe: The Development of the Victorian Public School.* London: Millington, 1977.

Horowitz, Helen Lefkowitz. *Alma Mater: Design and Experience in the Women's Colleges from Their Nineteenth-Century Beginnings to the 1930s.* New York: Alfred A. Knopf, 1984.

———. *Campus Life: Undergraduate Cultures from the End of the Eighteenth Century to the Present.* Chicago: University of Chicago Press, 1987.

Houlbrook, Matt. "Soldier Heroes and Rent Boys: Homosex, Masculinities, and Britishness in the Brigade of Guards, circa 1900–1960." *Journal of British Studies* 43, no. 3 (July 2003): 351–388.

———. "Towards a Historical Geography of Sexuality." *Journal of Urban History* 27, no. 4 (May 2001): 497–504.

Howarth, Janet. "'In Oxford but . . . not of Oxford': The Women's Colleges." In *Nineteenth-Century Oxford, Part 2,* ed. Brock and Curthoys, pp. 237–307.

———. "Women." In *The Twentieth Century,* ed. Harrison, pp. 345–376.

Howarth, Janet, and Mark Curthoys. "The Political Economy of Women's Higher Education in Late Nineteenth- and Early Twentieth-Century Britain." *Historical Research* 60, no. 142 (June 1987): 208–231.

Howell, Philip. "A Private Contagious Diseases Act: Prostitution and Public Space in Victorian Cambridge." *Journal of Historical Geography* 26, no. 3 (July 2000): 376–402.

Hubbard, Philip. "Desire/Disgust: Mapping the Moral Contours of Heterosexuality." *Progress in Human Geography* 24, no. 2 (June 2000): 191–217.

Huddleston, T. F. C. *University Expenses and Collegiate Students.* With an introduction by Reverend Canon Browne. Cambridge: Deighton and Bell, 1892.

Hughes, Thomas. *Tom Brown at Oxford: A Sequel to "School Days at Rugby" by the Author of "School Days at Rugby."* Boston: Ticknor and Fields, 1861.

Hunt, Lynn, ed. *The New Cultural History.* Berkeley: University of California Press, 1989.

India Office. *Memorandum on the Position of Indian Students in the United Kingdom.* London, 1916.

Israel, Kali. *Names and Stories: Emilia Dilke and Victorian Culture.* New York: Oxford University Press, 1999.

Jarausch, Konrad H., ed. *The Transformation of Higher Learning, 1860–1930: Expansion, Diversification, Social Opening, and Professionalization in England, Germany, Russia, and the United States.* Chicago: University of Chicago Press, 1983.

Jary, David, and Liz Thomas. "The Case of Laura Spence: Inequalities in Entry to Elite Universities in the UK." *Widening Participation and Lifelong Learning* 2, no. 2 (August 2000), http://www.staffs.ac.uk/journal/Volume2(2)/ed-1.htm.

Jenkins, H., and D. C. Jones. "Social Class of Cambridge University Alumni of the 18th and 19th Centuries." *British Journal of Sociology* 1, no. 2 (June 1950): 93–116.

Jocelyn, H. D. "The University's Contribution to Classical Studies." In *The Illustrated History of Oxford University,* ed. Prest, pp. 160–195.

Johnson, Gordon. *University Politics: F. M. Cornford's Cambridge and His Advice to the Young Academic Politician.* Cambridge: Cambridge University Press, 1994.

Johnson, Rachel, ed. *The Oxford Myth.* London: Weidenfeld and Nicolson, 1988.

Johnson, Richard. "What Is Cultural Studies Anyway?" *Social Text* 16 (winter 1986–1987): 38–80.

Jones, Emily Elizabeth Constance. *As I Remember: An Autobiographical Ramble.* London: A. and C. Black, 1922.

Jones, John. *Balliol College: A History, 1263–1939.* Oxford: Oxford University Press, 1988.

Jones, Ray. *The Nineteenth-Century Foreign Office: An Administrative History.* London: Weidenfeld and Nicolson, 1971.

Joyce, Patrick. *Visions of the People: Industrial England and the Question of Class, 1848–1914.* Cambridge: Cambridge University Press, 1991.

[Jupp, Edward K.]. *Correspondence of a Junior Student of Christchurch Oxford, in the Years 1868–1870.* Blackheath: privately published, 1871.

Katz, Jonathan Ned. *The Invention of Heterosexuality.* New York: Dutton, 1995.

Kelly, Joseph, and Timothy Kelly. "Searching the Dark Alley: New Historicism and Social History." *Journal of Social History* 25, no. 3 (spring 1992): 677–694.

Kennedy, Dane. *Islands of White: Settler Society and Culture in Kenya and Southern Rhodesia, 1890–1939.* Durham: Duke University Press, 1987.

Kennedy, Dominic. "Ex-State School Students Angered by Brown Claim." *Times,* May 27, 2000, p. 20.

Kent, Susan Kingsley. *Gender and Power in Britain, 1640–1990.* London: Routledge, 1999.

———. *Sex and Suffrage in Britain, 1860–1914.* Princeton: Princeton University Press, 1987.

Kestner, Joseph. *Masculinities in Victorian Painting.* Aldershot, U.K.: Scolar, 1995.

Kidd, Alan, and David Nicholls, eds. *Gender, Civic Culture, and Consumerism: Middle-Class Identity in Britain, 1800–1940.* Manchester: Manchester University Press, 1999.

Kimmel, Michael. "The Contemporary 'Crisis' of Masculinity in Historical Perspective." In *The Making of Masculinities,* ed. Brod, pp. 121–153.

———. *Manhood in America: A Cultural History.* New York: Free Press, 1996.

Kirkendall, Andrew. *Class Mates: Male Student Culture and the Making of a Political Class in Nineteenth-Century Brazil.* Lincoln: University of Nebraska Press, 2002.

"Kit." *Scrawls.* Cambridge, 1881.

Knatchbull-Hugessen, E. H. "My Oxford Days." In *Reminiscences of Oxford,* ed. L. M. Quiller-Couch, pp. 386–401.

Koven, Seth. "From Rough Lads to Hooligans: Boy Life, National Culture, and Social Reform." In *Nationalisms and Sexualities,* ed. Parker et al., pp. 365–391.

Kuchta, David. "The Making of the Self-Made Man: Class, Clothing, and English Masculinity, 1688–1832." In *The Sex of Things,* ed. de Grazia and Furlough, pp. 54–78.

Kumar, Hira Lal. "Oxford University and the Indian Students." *Indian Appeal: A Monthly Magazine on Religious, Social, Educational, and Political Questions of India* 4, no. 24 (April 1892): 299–300.

LaCapra, Dominick. *History and Criticism.* Ithaca, N.Y.: Cornell University Press, 1985.

Lahiri, Shompa. *Indians in Britain: Anglo-Indian Encounters, Race, and Identity, 1880–1930.* London: Frank Cass, 2000.

Latham, Henry. *On the Action of Examinations Considered as a Means of Selection.* Cambridge: Deighton, Bell, 1877.

Lee, Alan J. *The Origins of the Popular Press in England, 1855–1914.* London: Croom Helm, 1976.

Lefroy, Edward C. *Undergraduate Oxford: Articles Re-printed from "The Oxford and Cambridge Undergraduates' Journal," 1876, 7.* Oxford: privately printed, 1878.

Leonardi, Susan J. *Dangerous by Degrees: Women at Oxford and the Somerville College Novelists.* New Brunswick: Rutgers University Press, 1989.

Letts, Winifred M. *The Spires of Oxford and Other Poems.* New York: E. P. Dutton, 1918.

Lewis, Peter M. "Mummy, Matron, and the Maids: Feminine Presence and Absence in Male Institutions, 1934–63." In *Manful Assertions,* ed. Roper and Tosh, pp. 168–189.

Lindsay, Lisa A., and Stephan F. Miescher, eds. *Men and Masculinities in Modern Africa.* Portsmouth, N.H.: Heinemann, 2003.

Loo, Tina. "Of Moose and Men: Hunting for Masculinities in British Columbia, 1880–1939." *Western Historical Quarterly* 32 (autumn 2001): 296–319.

Lubenow, W. C. *The Cambridge Apostles, 1820–1914: Liberalism, Imagination, and Friendship in British Intellectual and Professional Life.* Cambridge: Cambridge University Press, 1998.

MacAloon, John J. *Rite, Drama, Festival, Spectacle: Rehearsals toward a Theory of Cultural Performance.* Philadelphia: Institute for the Study of Human Issues, 1984.

Mack, E. C. *The Public Schools and British Public Opinion since 1860: The Relationship between Contemporary Ideas and the Evolution of an English Institution.* New York: Columbia University Press, 1941.

Mackenzie, Compton. "Undergraduates at the Beginning of the Century." *Oxford* 5, no. 2 (winter 1938): 68–74.

MacKenzie, John M. "The Imperial Pioneer and Hunter and the British Masculine Stereotype in Late Victorian and Edwardian Times." In *Manliness and Morality,* ed. Mangan and Walvin, pp. 176–198.

Malchow, H. L. "Frankenstein's Monster and Images of Race in Nineteenth-Century Britain." *Past and Present* 139 (May 1993): 90–130.

Mallet, Charles Edward. *A History of the University of Oxford.* 3 vols. London: Methuen, 1924–1927.

Mangan, J. A. *Athleticism in the Victorian and Edwardian Public School: The Emergence and*

Consolidation of an Educational Ideology. Cambridge: Cambridge University Press, 1981.

―――. *The Games Ethic and Imperialism: Aspects of the Diffusion of an Ideal.* Harmondsworth, U.K.: Viking, 1986.

―――. "Games Field and Battlefield: A Romantic Alliance in Verse and the Creation of Militaristic Masculinity." In *Making Men,* ed. Nauright and Chandler, pp. 140–157.

―――. "Lamentable Barbarians and Pitiful Sheep: Rhetoric of Protest and Pleasure in Late Victorian and Edwardian 'Oxbridge.'" *Victorian Studies* 34, no. 4 (summer 1991): 473–489.

―――. "'Oars and the Man': Pleasure and Purpose in Victorian and Edwardian Cambridge." *British Journal of Sports History* 1, no. 3 (December 1984): 245–271.

―――, ed. *The Cultural Bond: Sport, Empire, and Society.* London: Frank Cass, 1992.

Mangan, J. A., and James Walvin, eds. *Manliness and Morality: Middle-Class Masculinity in Britain and America, 1800–1940.* New York: St. Martin's, 1987.

Mansfield, Nick. "Grads and Snobs: John Brown, Town, and Gown in Early Nineteenth-Century Cambridge." *History Workshop Journal,* no. 35 (spring 1993): 184–198.

MARHO, the Radical Historians Organization. *Visions of History.* Edited by Henry Abelove et al. New York: Pantheon Books, 1983.

Marillier, Harry Currie. *University Magazines and Their Makers. By Harry Currie Marillier, Knyght Errannt to ye Set of Odd Volumes.* London: Bedford, 1899.

Massey, Doreen. "Places and Their Pasts." *History Workshop Journal,* no. 39 (spring 1995): 182–192.

―――. *Space, Place, and Gender.* Minneapolis: University of Minnesota Press, 1994.

May Term Festivities. Nos. 1–4. Cambridge: John P. Cray, 1891–1894.

McBee, Randy D. "'He Likes Women More Than He Likes Drink and That Is Quite Unusual': Working-Class Social Clubs, Male Culture, and Heterosocial Relations in the United States, 1920s–1930s." *Gender and History* 11, no. 1 (April 1999): 84–112.

McClelland, Keith. "Masculinity and the 'Representative Artisan' in Britain, 1850–1880." In *Manful Assertions,* ed. Roper and Tosh, pp. 74–91.

McDevitt, Patrick. "Muscular Catholicism: Nationalism, Masculinity, and Gaelic Team Sports, 1884–1916." *Gender and History* 9, no. 2 (August 1997): 262–284.

McLaren, Angus. *The Trials of Masculinity: Policing Sexual Boundaries, 1870–1930.* Chicago: University of Chicago Press, 1997.

McWilliams Tullberg, Rita. *Women at Cambridge.* Rev. ed. Cambridge: Cambridge University Press, 1998.

Messner, Michael. "Boyhood, Organized Sports, and the Construction of Masculinities." *Journal of Contemporary Ethnography* 18, no. 4 (January 1990): 416–444.

Metcalf, Thomas. *The Aftermath of Revolt: India, 1857–1870.* Princeton: Princeton University Press, 1964.

―――. *Ideologies of the Raj.* Cambridge: Cambridge University Press, 1994.

Mitchell, David Alexander. "One Rhodes Scholar's Unhappy Experience." *Globe and Mail,* February 9, 1991, p. D7.

Montgomery, R. J. *Examinations: An Account of Their Evolution as Administrative Devices in England.* London: Longmans, Green, 1965.

Morris, Jan, ed. *The Oxford Book of Oxford.* Oxford: Oxford University Press, 1978.

Mort, Frank. *Dangerous Sexualities: Medico-moral Politics in England since 1830.* 2nd ed. London: Routledge, 2000.

[Naidley, H. M.] *Oxford Commemoration by a Fellow of Experientia.* London, 1888.

Nardi, Peter, ed. *Men's Friendships.* Newbury Park, Calif.: Sage Publications, 1992.

Nauright, John, and Timothy J. L. Chandler, eds. *Making Men: Rugby and Masculine Identity.* London: Frank Cass, 1996.

Nead, Lynda. "Mapping the Self: Gender, Space, and Modernity in Mid-Victorian London." *Environment and Planning A* 29 (1997): 659–672.

———. *Myths of Sexuality: Representations of Women in Victorian Britain.* Oxford: Basil Blackwell, 1988.

Newsome, David. *Godliness and Good Learning: Four Studies on a Victorian Ideal.* London: Cassell, 1961.

Norton, Rictor. *The Myth of the Modern Homosexual: Queer History and the Search for Cultural Unity.* London: Cassell, 1997.

O'Connell, Sean. *The Car in British Society: Class, Gender, and Motoring, 1896–1939.* Manchester: Manchester University Press, 1998.

O'Leary, John. "Defenders Line Up for Renewed Debate." *Times,* May 26, 2000, p. 6.

Oman, Charles. *Memories of Victorian Oxford and Some Early Years.* London: Methuen, 1941.

"One Spence Piece: The Laura Spence Affair." *Oxford Student,* October 5, 2000, p. 1.

Our Special Commissioner. "Young Cambridge of To-Day." *Quiver: An Illustrated Magazine for Sunday and General Reading* 28 (October 1895): 28–33.

"Oxbridge—The British Establishment's Essential Club." *World Socialist Web Site,* September 12, 2001, http://www.wsws.org/articles/2001/sep2001.

Oxford Church Tracts, No. 1: "Are You Converted? On the Present Deplorable State of the University, and Why?" Oxford, 1854.

"Oxford in the Victorian Age." *Blackwood's Edinburgh Magazine* 169, no. 1025 (March 1901): 330–339.

Oxford University. *Alumni Oxonienses: The Members of the University of Oxford, 1715–1886: Their Parentage, Birthplace and Year of Birth, with a Record of Their Degrees. Being the Matriculation Register of the University, Alphabetically Arranged, Revised and Annotated by Joseph Foster,* vols. 1–4. Oxford: Parker, 1888.

———. *The Historical Register of the University of Oxford. Being a Supplement to the Oxford University Calendar with an Alphabetical Record of University Honours and Distinctions, Completed to the End of Trinity Term, 1888.* Oxford: Clarendon, 1888.

———. *The Oxford University Calendar, 1868.* Oxford: James Parker, 1868.

———. *The Oxford University Calendar.* Oxford: Clarendon, 1882–1920.

———. *Statutes Made for the Colleges and St. Edmund Hall in the University of Oxford in Pursuance of the Universities of Oxford and Cambridge Act, 1923, and Approved by the King in Council.* Oxford: Clarendon, 1927.

———. *The Student's Handbook to the University and Colleges of Oxford.* Oxford: Clarendon, 1873.

An Oxonian. *Letters Addressed to a Young Gentleman About to Enter the University of Oxford.* Oxford, 1850.

Palmer, Jerry. *Taking Humour Seriously.* London: Routledge, 1994.

Park, Roberta J. "Biological Thought, Athletics, and the Formation of a 'Man of Character,' 1830–1900." In *Manliness and Morality,* ed. Mangan and Walvin, pp. 7–34.

Parker, Andrew, Mary Russo, Doris Sommer, and Patricia Yaeger, eds. *Nationalisms and Sexualities.* New York: Routledge, 1992.

Paxton, Nancy. "Mobilizing Chivalry: Rape in British Novels about the Indian Uprising of 1857." *Victorian Studies* 36, no. 1 (fall 1992): 5–30.

Paz, D. G. *Popular Anti-Catholicism in Mid-Victorian England.* Stanford: Stanford University Press, 1992.

Pennybacker, Susan. *A Vision for London, 1889–1914: Labour, Everyday Life, and the LCC Experiment.* London: Routledge, 1995.

Perkin, Harold. *The Rise of Professional Society: England since 1800.* London: Routledge, 1989.

Peterson, M. Jeanne. *Family, Love, and Work in the Lives of Victorian Gentlewomen.* Bloomington: Indiana University Press, 1989.

Phillips, Ann, ed. *A Newnham Anthology.* Cambridge: Cambridge University Press, 1979.

Porter, H. C. "May Week." *Cambridge,* no. 20 (1987): 45–52.

Porter, Roy, ed. *Myths of the English.* Cambridge: Polity, 1992.

Potts, Robert. *A Brief Account of the Scholarships and Exhibitions Open to Competition in the University of Cambridge, with Specimens of the Examinations Papers.* London: Longmans, Green, 1866.

Powell, Chris, and George E. C. Paton, eds. *Humour in Society: Resistance and Control.* London: Macmillan, 1988.

Prest, John. "City and University." In *The Illustrated History of Oxford University,* ed. Prest, pp. 1–38.

———, ed. *The Illustrated History of Oxford University.* Oxford: Oxford University Press, 1993.

Quiller-Couch, L. M., ed. *Reminiscences of Oxford by Oxford Men, 1559–1850.* Oxford: Clarendon, 1892.

Rappaport, Erika Diane. *Shopping for Pleasure: Women in the Making of London's West End.* Princeton: Princeton University Press, 2000.

Reader, W. J. *Professional Men: The Rise of the Professional Class in Nineteenth-Century England.* New York: Basic Books, 1966.

Reeve, F. A. *Cambridge.* London: B. T. Batsford, 1976.

———. *Varsity Rags and Hoaxes.* Cambridge: Oleander, 1977.

Return of Entrance Scholarships and Exhibitions Awarded to Students Beginning in the University in October 1911. Oxford: n.p., n.d.

Rice, F. A. *The "Granta" and Its Contributors, 1889–1914.* London: Constable, 1924.

Rich, Adrienne. "Compulsory Heterosexuality and Lesbian Existence." *Signs: Journal of Women in Culture and Society* 5, no. 4 (summer 1980): 631–660.

Rich, P. J. *Chains of Empire: English Public Schools, Masonic Cabalism, Historical Causality, and Imperial Clubdom.* London: Regency, 1991.

Richards, G. C. *An Oxonian Looks Back: 1885–1945.* Edited by J. F. C. Richards. New York, 1960. Typescript at the Homer Babbidge Library, University of Connecticut.

Roach, John. *Public Examinations in England, 1850–1900.* Cambridge: Cambridge University Press, 1971.

Roberts, S. C. *The Charm of Cambridge.* Illustrated by W. G. Blackall. London: A. and C. Black, 1929.

Roediger, David E. *The Wages of Whiteness: Race and the Making of the American Working Class.* Rev. ed. London: Verso, 1999.

Rogers, Barbara. *Men Only: An Investigation into Men's Organizations.* London: Pandora, 1988.

Roget, John. *Cambridge Customs and Costumes: Containing Upwards of One Hundred and Fifty Vignettes by the Author of "Familiar Illustrations of the Language of Mathematics."* Cambridge: Macmillan, 1851.

———. *A Cambridge Scrap-Book.* Cambridge: Macmillan, 1859.

Romano, Terrie M. "Gentlemanly versus Scientific Ideals: John Burdon Sanderson, Medical Education, and the Failure of the Oxford School of Physiology." *Bulletin of the History of Medicine* 71, no. 2 (summer 1997): 224–248.

Roper, Michael, and John Tosh, eds. *Manful Assertions: Masculinities in Britain since 1800.* London: Routledge, 1991.

Rothblatt, Sheldon. "The Diversification of Higher Education in England." In *The Transformation of Higher Learning, 1860–1930,* ed. Jarausch, pp. 131–148.

———. "Failure in Early Nineteenth-Century Oxford and Cambridge." *History of Education* 11, no. 1 (March 1982): 1–21.

———. "London: A Metropolitan University?" In *The University and the City,* ed. Bender, pp. 119–149.

———. *The Modern University and Its Discontents: The Fate of Newman's Legacies in Britain and America.* Cambridge: Cambridge University Press, 1997.

———. *The Revolution of the Dons: Cambridge and Society in Victorian England.* New York: Basic Books, 1968.

———. "The Student Sub-culture and the Examination System in Early 19th Century Oxbridge." In *The University in Society,* ed. Stone, pp. 247–303.

Rotundo, E. Anthony. *American Manhood: Transformations in Masculinity from the Revolution to the Modern Era.* New York: Basic Books, 1993.

———. "Boy Culture: Middle-Class Boyhood in Nineteenth-Century America." In *Meanings for Manhood,* ed. Carnes and Griffen, pp. 15–36.

Rubinstein, W. D. *Wealth and Inequality in Britain.* London: Faber and Faber, 1986.

Rutter, Frank. *'Varsity Types: Scenes and Characters from Undergraduate Life.* Illustrated by Stephen Haweis. London: R. A. Everett, 1903.

Ryan, Alan. "Getting In." *Oxford Today: The University Magazine* 13, no. 1 (Michaelmas issue, 2000): 5–6.

Said, Edward. *Culture and Imperialism.* New York: Knopf, 1993.

———. *Orientalism.* New York: Pantheon Books, 1978.

Saintsbury, George. "Novels of University Life." *Macmillan's Magazine,* no. 77 (March 1898): 334–343.

Samuel, Raphael, ed. *Patriotism: The Making and Unmaking of British National Identity.* Vols. 1–2. London: Routledge, 1989.

Sandars, T. C. "Undergraduate Literature." *Saturday Review of Politics, Literature, Science, and Art* 3, no. 70 (February 28, 1857): 196–197.

Sassoon, Siegfried. *Memoirs of a Fox-Hunting Man.* London: Faber and Faber, 1999.

Schneer, Jonathan. *London 1900: The Imperial Metropolis.* New Haven: Yale University Press, 1999.

Scholz, R. F., and S. K. Hornbeck. *Oxford and the Rhodes Scholarships.* London: Oxford University Press, 1907.

Scott, Joan W. "The Evidence of Experience." *Critical Inquiry* 17, no. 4 (summer 1991): 773–797.

———. *Gender and the Politics of History.* New York: Columbia University Press, 1988.

Searby, Peter. *A History of the University of Cambridge: 1750–1870.* Vol. 3 of *A History of the University of Cambridge,* ed. Christopher N. L. Brooke. Cambridge: Cambridge University Press, 1997.

Searle, G. R. *The Quest for National Efficiency: A Study in British Politics and Political Thought, 1899–1914.* Oxford: Basil Blackwell, 1971.

Seccombe, Thomas, and H. Spencer Scott, eds. *In Praise of Oxford: An Anthology in Prose and Verse.* Vol. 2. London: Constable, 1912.

Sedgwick, Eve K. *Between Men: English Literature and Male Homosocial Desire.* New York: Columbia University Press, 1985.

———. *Tendencies.* Durham, N.C.: Duke University Press, 1993.

Seeley, J. R. *The Student's Guide to the University of Cambridge.* Cambridge: Deighton, Bell, 1863.

Segal, Lynne. *Slow Motion: Changing Masculinities, Changing Men.* London: Virago, 1990.

Sherwood, W. E. *Oxford Rowing: A History of Boat-Racing at Oxford from the Earliest Times with a Record of the Races.* Oxford: Henry Frowde, 1900.

Showalter, Elaine. *Sexual Anarchy: Gender and Culture at the Fin de Siècle.* New York: Viking, 1990.

Simpson, Mark. *Male Impersonators: Men Performing Masculinity.* London: Cassell, 1994.

Sinha, Mrinalini. "Britishness, Clubbability, and the Colonial Public Sphere: The Genealogy of an Imperial Institution in Colonial India." *Journal of British Studies* 40, no. 4 (October 2001): 489–556.

———. *Colonial Masculinity: The "Manly Englishman" and the "Effeminate Bengali" in the Late Nineteenth Century.* Manchester: Manchester University Press, 1995.

Soares, Joseph A. *The Decline of Privilege: The Modernization of Oxford University.* Stanford: Stanford University Press, 1999.

Soffer, Reba. "The Development of Disciplines in the Modern English University." *Historical Journal* 31, no. 4 (December 1988): 933–946.

———. *Discipline and Power: The University, History, and the Making of an English Elite, 1870–1930.* Stanford: Stanford University Press, 1994.

———. *Ethics and Society in England: The Revolution in the Social Sciences, 1870–1914.* Berkeley: University of California Press, 1978.

———. "The Modern University and National Values, 1850–1930." *Historical Research* 60, no. 142 (June 1987): 166–187.

———. "Nation, Duty, Character, and Confidence: History at Oxford, 1850–1914." *Historical Journal* 30, no. 1 (March 1987): 77–104.

Spain, Daphne. "The Spatial Foundations of Men's Friendships and Men's Power." In *Men's Friendships,* ed. Nardi, pp. 58–73.

Springhall, John. "The Boy Scouts, Class, and Militarism in Relation to British Youth Movements, 1908–1930." *International Review of Social History* 16, part 2 (1971): 125–158.

———. *Coming of Age: Adolescence in Britain, 1860–1960.* Dublin: Gill and Macmillan, 1986.

Stearns, Peter N. *Be a Man! Males in Modern Society.* 2nd ed. New York: Holmes and Meier, 1990.

Stokes, H. P. *Ceremonies of the University of Cambridge.* Cambridge: Cambridge University Press, 1927.

Stone, Lawrence. "The Size and Composition of the Oxford Student Body, 1580–1910." In *The University in Society,* ed. Stone, pp. 3–110.

———, ed. *The University in Society.* Vol. 1. Princeton: Princeton University Press, 1974.

Stray, Christopher. *Classics Transformed: Schools, Universities, and Society in England, 1830–1960.* Oxford: Clarendon, 1998.

———. "The Shift from Oral to Written Examination: Cambridge and Oxford, 1700–1900." *Assessment in Education* 8, no. 1 (March 2001): 33–50.

Streets, Heather. "'The Right Stamp of Man': Military Imperatives and Popular Imperialism in Late Victorian Britain." Ph.D. diss., Duke University, 1998.

Sutherland, Gillian, "Examinations and the Construction of Professional Identity: A Case Study of England, 1800–1950." *Assessment in Education* 8, no. 1 (March 2001): 51–64.

———. "The Movement for the Higher Education of Women: Its Social and Intellectual Context in England c. 1840–80." In *Politics and Social Change in Modern Britain,* ed. Waller, pp. 91–116.

Symonds, Richard. *Oxford and Empire: The Last Lost Cause?* New York: St. Martin's, 1986.

Tanner, J. R., ed. *The Historical Register of the University of Cambridge, Being a Supplement to the "Calendar" with a Record of University Offices, Honours and Distinctions to the Year 1910.* Cambridge: Cambridge University Press, 1917.

Terry, Edith. "Social Customs." In *A Newnham Anthology,* ed. Phillips, pp. 53–55.

Thomas, Edward. *Oxford: Painted by John Fulleylove, R.I. Described by Edward Thomas.* London: A. and C. Black, 1903.

Thomas, James Grant Brandon. *The Rubaiyat of Some-of-Us: Being Certain Undergraduate Parodies of the Illustrious Persian.* Illustrated by "Segar." Oxford: Holywell, 1913.

Thomas, Keith. "College Life, 1945–1970." In *The Twentieth Century,* ed. Harrison, pp. 189–216.

Thompson, E. P. *The Making of the English Working Class.* New York: Vintage Books, 1966.

Thompson, F. M. L., ed. *The University of London and the World of Learning, 1836–1986.* London: Hambledon, 1990.

Tosh, John. "Domesticity and Manliness in the Victorian Middle Class: The Family of Edward White Benson." In *Manful Assertions,* ed. Roper and Tosh, pp. 44–73.

———. "Imperial Masculinity and the Flight from Domesticity in Britain, 1880–1914." In *Gender and Colonialism,* ed. Foley et al., pp. 72–85

———. *A Man's Place: Masculinity and the Middle-Class Home in Victorian England.* New Haven: Yale University Press, 1999.

———. "What Should Historians Do with Masculinity? Reflections on Nineteenth-Century Britain." *History Workshop Journal,* no. 38 (autumn 1994): 179–202.

Townsend, Kim. *Manhood at Harvard: William James and Others.* New York: W. W. Norton, 1996.

[Trevelyan, George Otto]. *The Cambridge Dionysia, A Classic Dream.* Cambridge, 1858.

Turner, Victor. *The Ritual Process: Structure and Anti-structure.* Chicago: Aldine, 1969.

Twigg, John. *A History of Queen's College, Cambridge, 1448–1986.* Woodbridge, U.K.: Boydell, 1987.

Tyack, Geoffrey. "The Architecture of the University and the Colleges." In *The Illustrated History of Oxford University,* ed. Prest, pp. 84–122.

Types. Cambridge: Redin, 1894.

An Undergraduate. "A Day of His Life at Oxford." *Murray's Magazine* 3 (May 1888): 664–677.

"University Life." *Cornhill Magazine* 11, no. 62 (March 1865): 223–232.

Vance, Norman. *The Sinews of the Spirit: The Ideal of Christian Manliness in Victorian Literature and Religious Thought.* Cambridge: Cambridge University Press, 1985.

Veblen, Thorstein. *The Theory of the Leisure Class.* New York: Penguin Books, 1994.

Venn, J. A., ed. *Alumni Cantabrigienses: A Biographical List of All Known Students, Graduates, and Holders of Office at the University of Cambridge, from the Earliest Times to 1900: Part 2.* Vols. 1–6. Cambridge: Cambridge University Press, 1940–1954.

Venn, John. *Early Collegiate Life.* Cambridge: W. Heffer and Sons, 1913.

Vicinus, Martha. *Independent Women: Work and Community for Single Women, 1850–1920.* Chicago: University of Chicago Press, 1985.

Viner, Katharine. "In the Finals Analysis." *Guardian,* July 8, 1992, p. 19.

Visram, Rozina. *Ayahs, Lascars, and Princes: Indians in Britain, 1700–1947.* London: Pluto, 1986.

Wahrman, Dror. *Imagining the Middle Class: The Political Representation of Class in Britain, c. 1780–1840.* Cambridge: Cambridge University Press, 1995.

Walden, Keith. "Hazes, Hustles, Scraps, and Stunts: Initiations at the University of Toronto, 1880–1925." In *Youth, University, and Canadian Society,* ed. Axelrod and Reid, pp. 94–121.

Walkowitz, Judith. *City of Dreadful Delight: Narratives of Sexual Danger in Late-Victorian London.* Chicago: University of Chicago Press, 1992.

———. "Going Public: Shopping, Street Harassment, and Streetwalking in Late Victorian London." *Representations,* no. 62 (spring 1998): 1–30.

Waller, P. J., ed. *Politics and Social Change in Modern Britain: Essays Presented to A. F. Thompson.* New York: St. Martin's, 1987.

Ware, Vron. *Beyond the Pale: White Women, Racism, and History.* London: Verso, 1992.

Warwick, Andrew. *Masters of Theory: Cambridge and the Rise of Mathematical Physics.* Chicago: University of Chicago Press, 2003.

Waterlow, Sydney, ed. *In Praise of Cambridge: An Anthology in Prose and Verse.* London: Constable, 1912.

Waugh, Evelyn. *Brideshead Revisited.* London: Longmans, Green, 1968.

Weeks, Jeffrey. *Coming Out: Homosexual Politics in Britain, from the Nineteenth Century to the Present.* London: Quartet, 1977.

———. *Sex, Politics, and Society: The Regulation of Sexuality since 1800.* 2nd ed. London: Longmans, 1989.

Wells, J. *Oxford and Its Colleges.* London: Methuen, 1898.

Wells, Joseph. *The Charm of Oxford.* Illustrated by W. G. Blackall. London: Simpkin, Marshall, Hamilton and Kent, 1920.

Whibley, Charles. *In Cap and Gown: Three Centuries of Cambridge Wit.* London: William Heinemann, 1898.

White, Hayden. *The Content of the Form: Narrative, Discourse, and Historical Representation.* Baltimore: Johns Hopkins University Press, 1987.

Wiener, Martin J. *English Culture and the Decline of the Industrial Spirit, 1850–1980.* Cambridge: Cambridge University Press, 1981.

Williams, John. *"Is My Son Likely to Pass?" Or, A Few Words to Parents upon the Most Prevalent Intellectual Diseases Incident to School and College Life: With Suggestions as to Their Treatment and Cure: Also, An Appendix Containing Letters on the Subject of Classical Education.* London: Rivingtons, 1864.

Williams, Monier. *The Indian Institute in the University of Oxford: The Circumstances Which Have Led to Its Establishment, and the Objects It Is Intended to Effect, with a List of Its Supporters, a Statement of Receipts and Expenditure, and an Appeal for Further Aid.* 3rd ed. Oxford, 1883.

Williams, Raymond. *Keywords: A Vocabulary of Culture and Society.* London: Croom Helm, 1976.

Willis, Robert. *The Architectural History of the University of Cambridge and of the Colleges of Cambridge and Eton, Edited with Large Additions and Brought Up to the Present Time by John Willis Clark.* Vol. 1. Cambridge: Cambridge University Press, 1886.

Winstanley, D. A. *Later Victorian Cambridge.* Cambridge: Cambridge University Press, 1947.

Winter, J. M. "Oxford and the First World War." In *The Twentieth Century,* ed. Harrison, pp. 3–26.

Wohl, Anthony. "'Dizzi-Ben-Dizzi': Disraeli as Alien." *Journal of British Studies* 34, no. 3 (July 1995): 375–411.

Woolf, Virginia. *A Room of One's Own.* New York: Harcourt Brace, 1929.

Woollacott, Angela. *To Try Her Fortune in London: Australian Women, Colonialism, and Modernity.* New York: Oxford University Press, 2001.

Wordsworth, William. "Oxford, May 30, 1820." In vol. 2 of *The Poems,* ed. John O. Hayden. New Haven: Yale University Press, 1977.

Young, Toby. "Class." In *The Oxford Myth,* ed. Rachel Johnson, pp. 1–18.

Index

Page numbers in italics indicate illustrations.

Paul R. Deslandes, a specialist in British history,
the history of the British Empire, and the history of gender
and sexuality, is Associate Professor and Chair of the
Department of History at the University of Vermont.